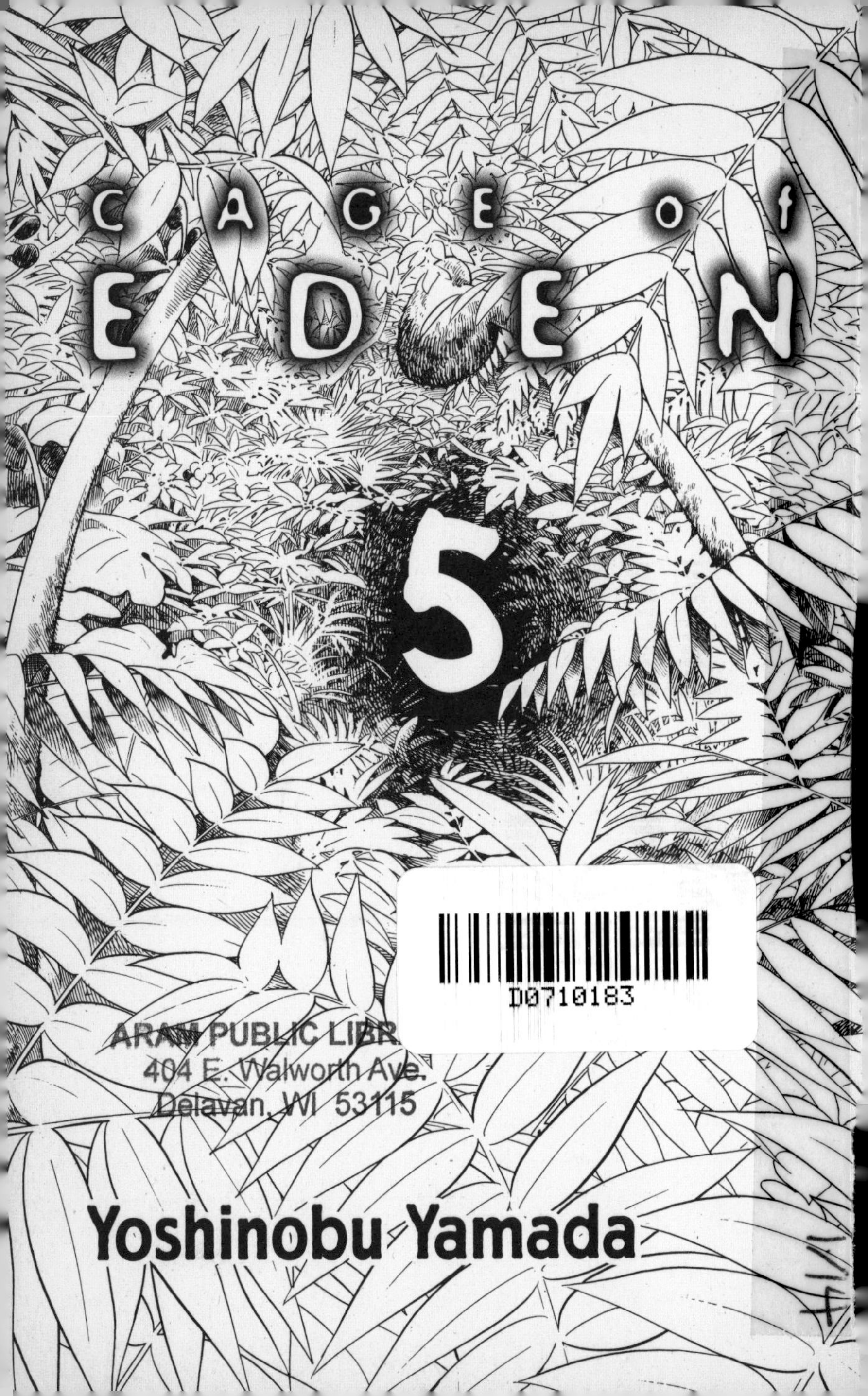
CAGE of
EDEN
5
Yoshinobu Yamada

CAGE of EDEN

Episode 32 The Lost Brain

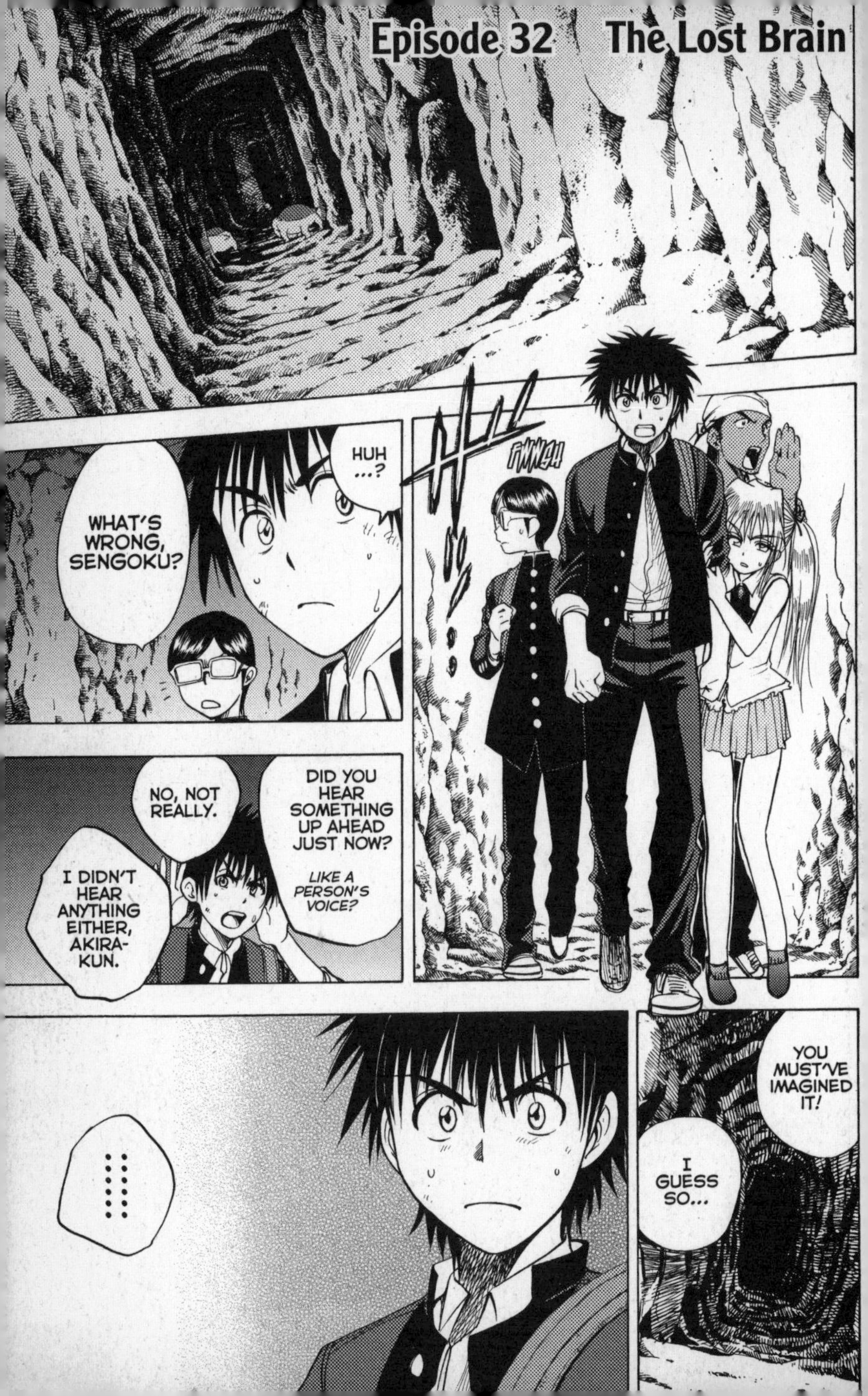
HUH ...?
WHAT'S WRONG, SENGOKU?
DID YOU HEAR SOMETHING UP AHEAD JUST NOW?
LIKE A PERSON'S VOICE?
NO, NOT REALLY.
I DIDN'T HEAR ANYTHING EITHER, AKIRA-KUN.
YOU MUST'VE IMAGINED IT!
I GUESS SO...
......

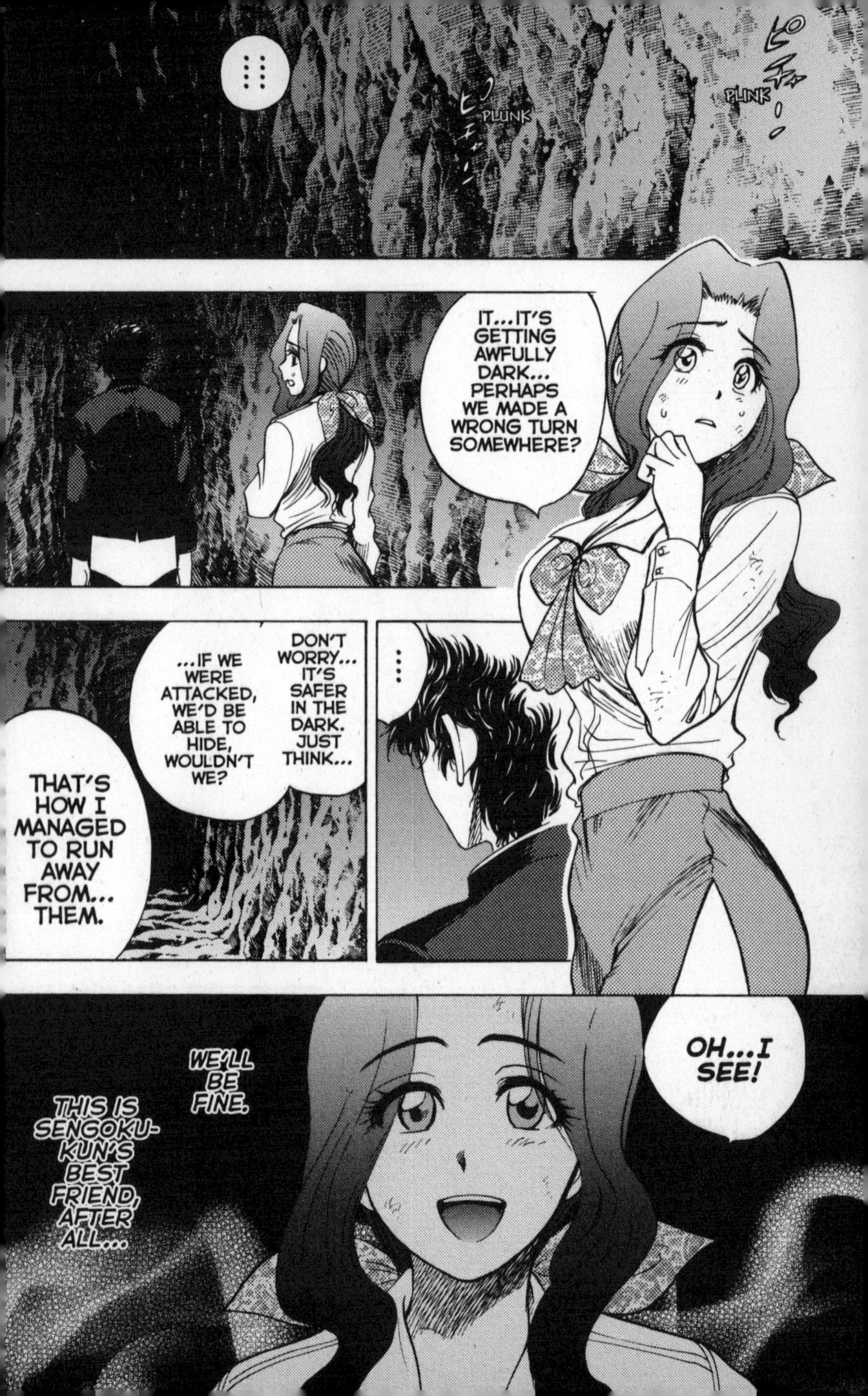
PLUNK
PLUNK
....
IT...IT'S GETTING AWFULLY DARK... PERHAPS WE MADE A WRONG TURN SOMEWHERE?
....
DON'T WORRY... IT'S SAFER IN THE DARK. JUST THINK...
...IF WE WERE ATTACKED, WE'D BE ABLE TO HIDE, WOULDN'T WE?
THAT'S HOW I MANAGED TO RUN AWAY FROM... THEM.
OH...I SEE!
WE'LL BE FINE.
THIS IS SENGOKU-KUN'S BEST FRIEND, AFTER ALL...

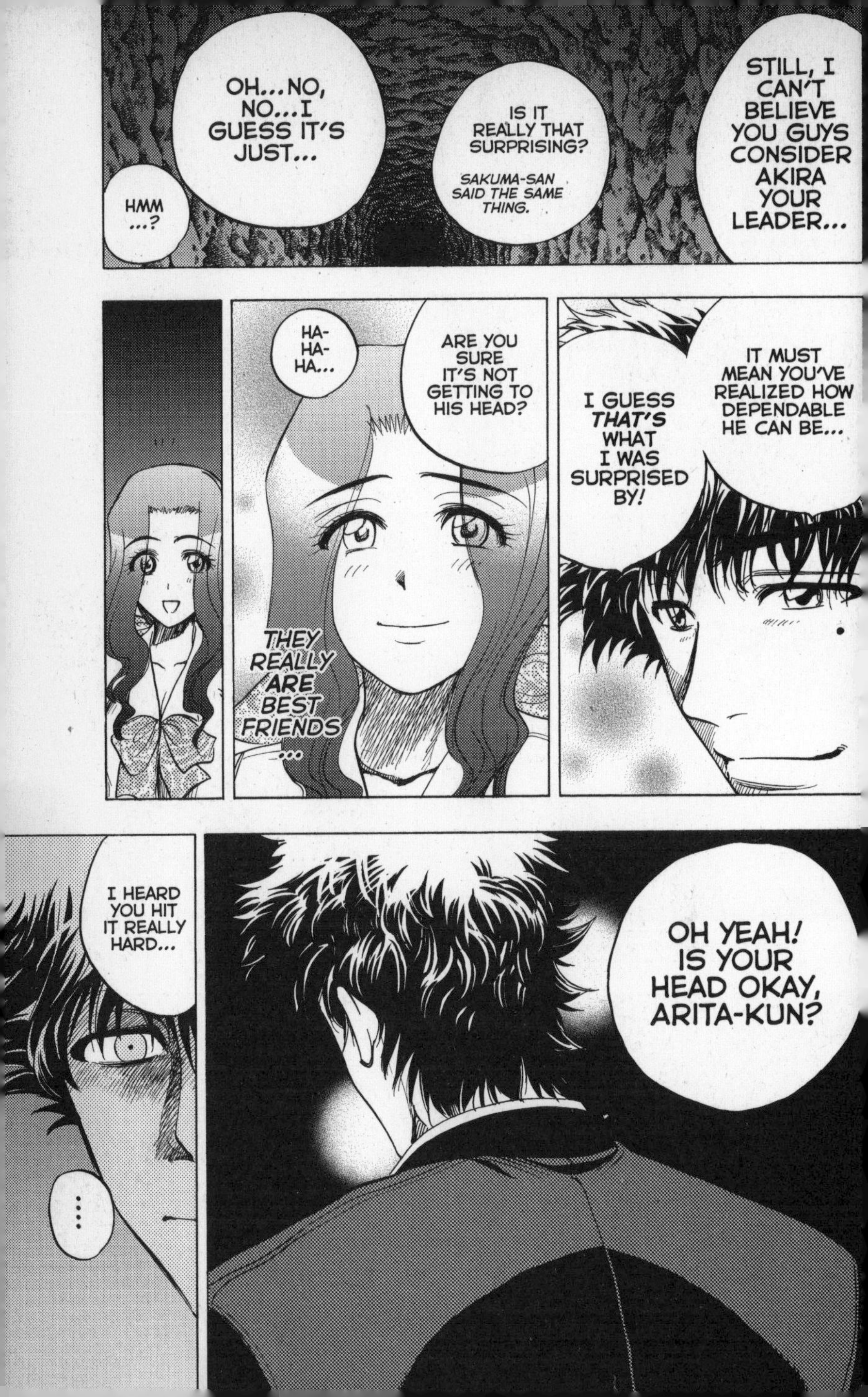
STILL, I CAN'T BELIEVE YOU GUYS CONSIDER AKIRA YOUR LEADER...
IS IT REALLY THAT SURPRISING?
SAKUMA-SAN SAID THE SAME THING.
OH...NO, NO...I GUESS IT'S JUST...
HMM ...?
IT MUST MEAN YOU'VE REALIZED HOW DEPENDABLE HE CAN BE...
I GUESS *THAT'S* WHAT I WAS SURPRISED BY!
ARE YOU SURE IT'S NOT GETTING TO HIS HEAD?
HA-HA-HA...
THEY REALLY ARE BEST FRIENDS...
OH YEAH! IS YOUR HEAD OKAY, ARITA-KUN?
I HEARD YOU HIT IT REALLY HARD...
.....

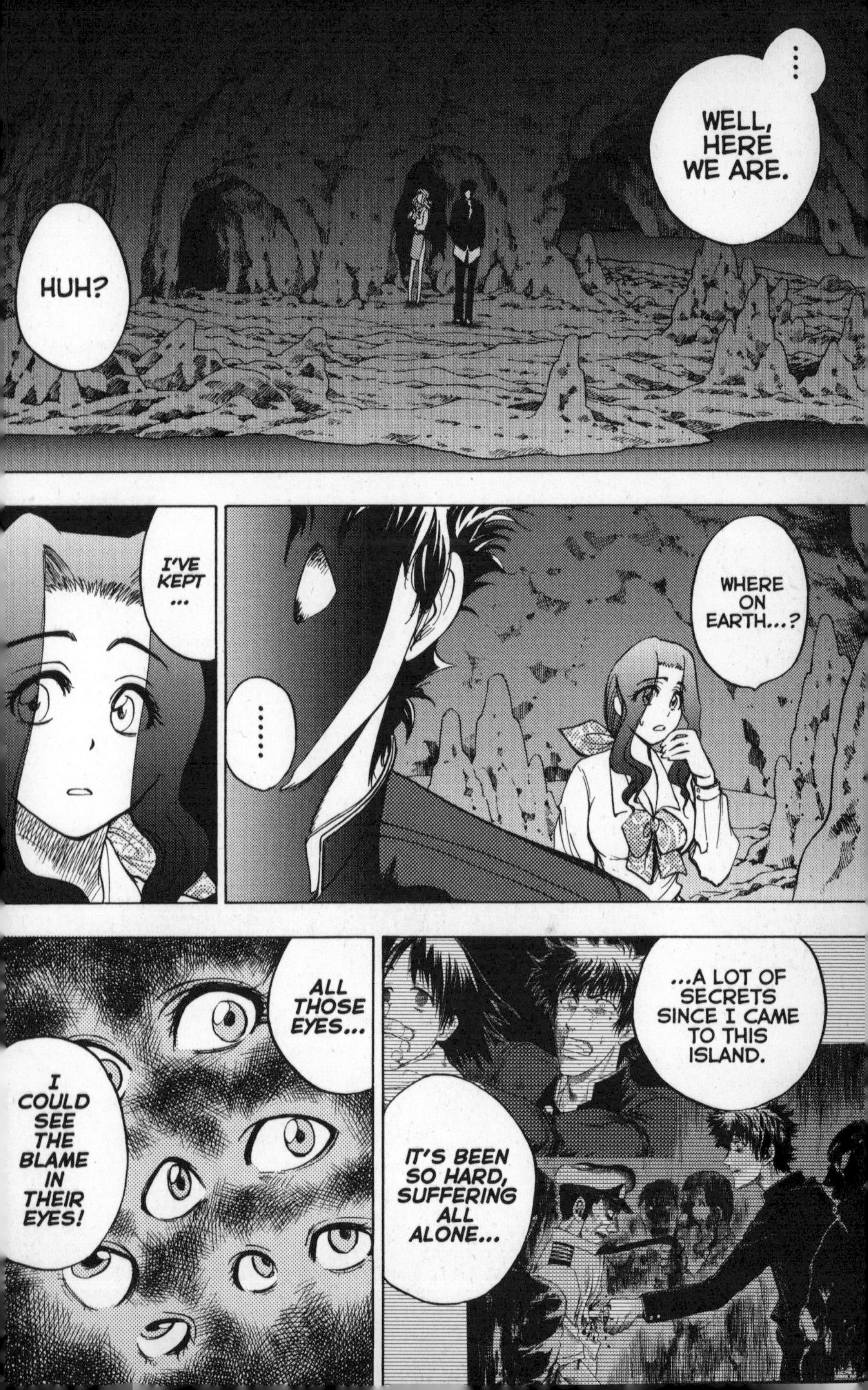
....
WELL, HERE WE ARE.
HUH?
WHERE ON EARTH...?
......
I'VE KEPT ...
...A LOT OF SECRETS SINCE I CAME TO THIS ISLAND.
IT'S BEEN SO HARD, SUFFERING ALL ALONE...
ALL THOSE EYES...
I COULD SEE THE BLAME IN THEIR EYES!

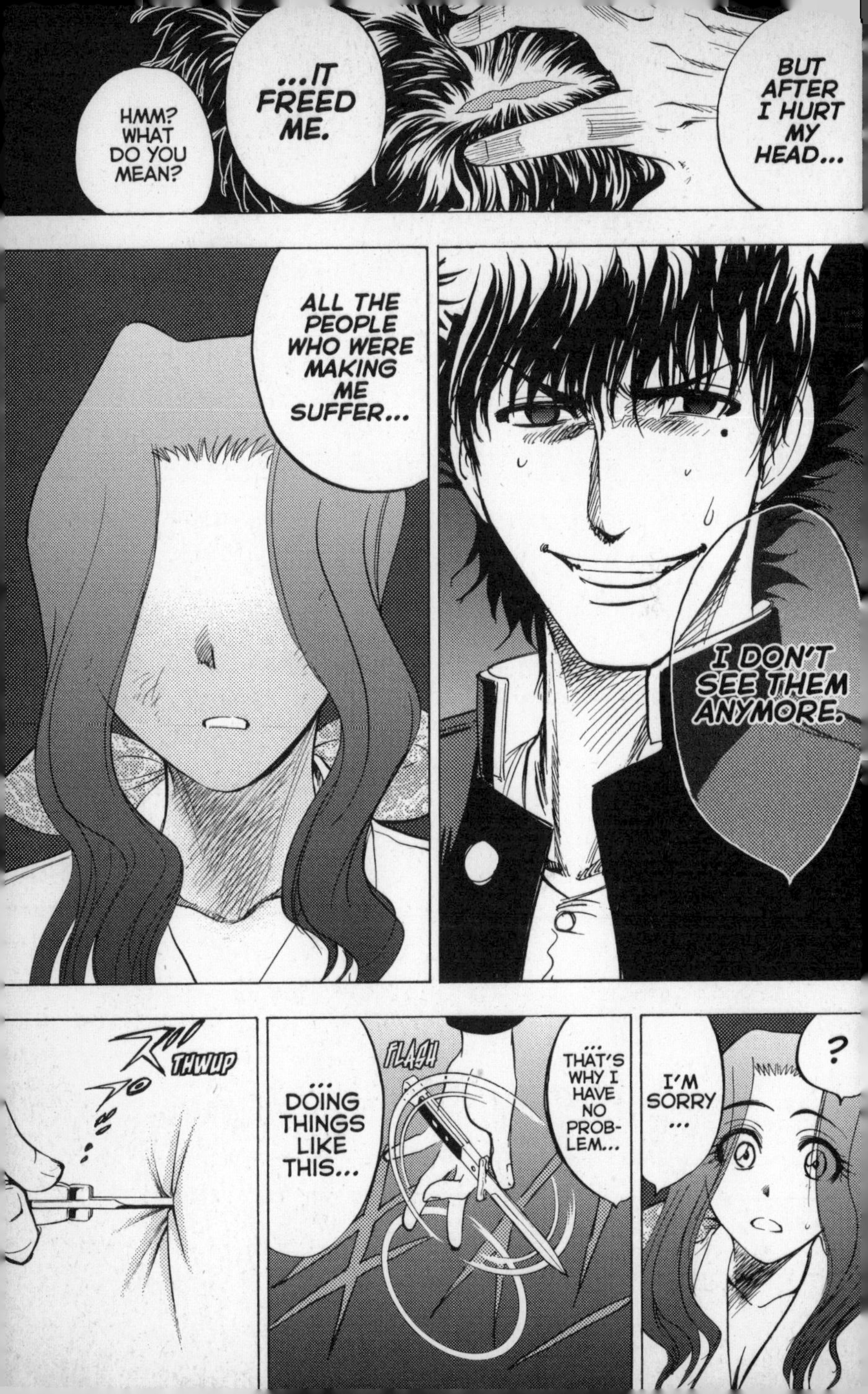
BUT AFTER I HURT MY HEAD...
...IT FREED ME.
HMM? WHAT DO YOU MEAN?
ALL THE PEOPLE WHO WERE MAKING ME SUFFER...
I DON'T SEE THEM ANYMORE.
?
I'M SORRY ...
...THAT'S WHY I HAVE NO PROB-LEM...
FLASH
... DOING THINGS LIKE THIS...
THWUP

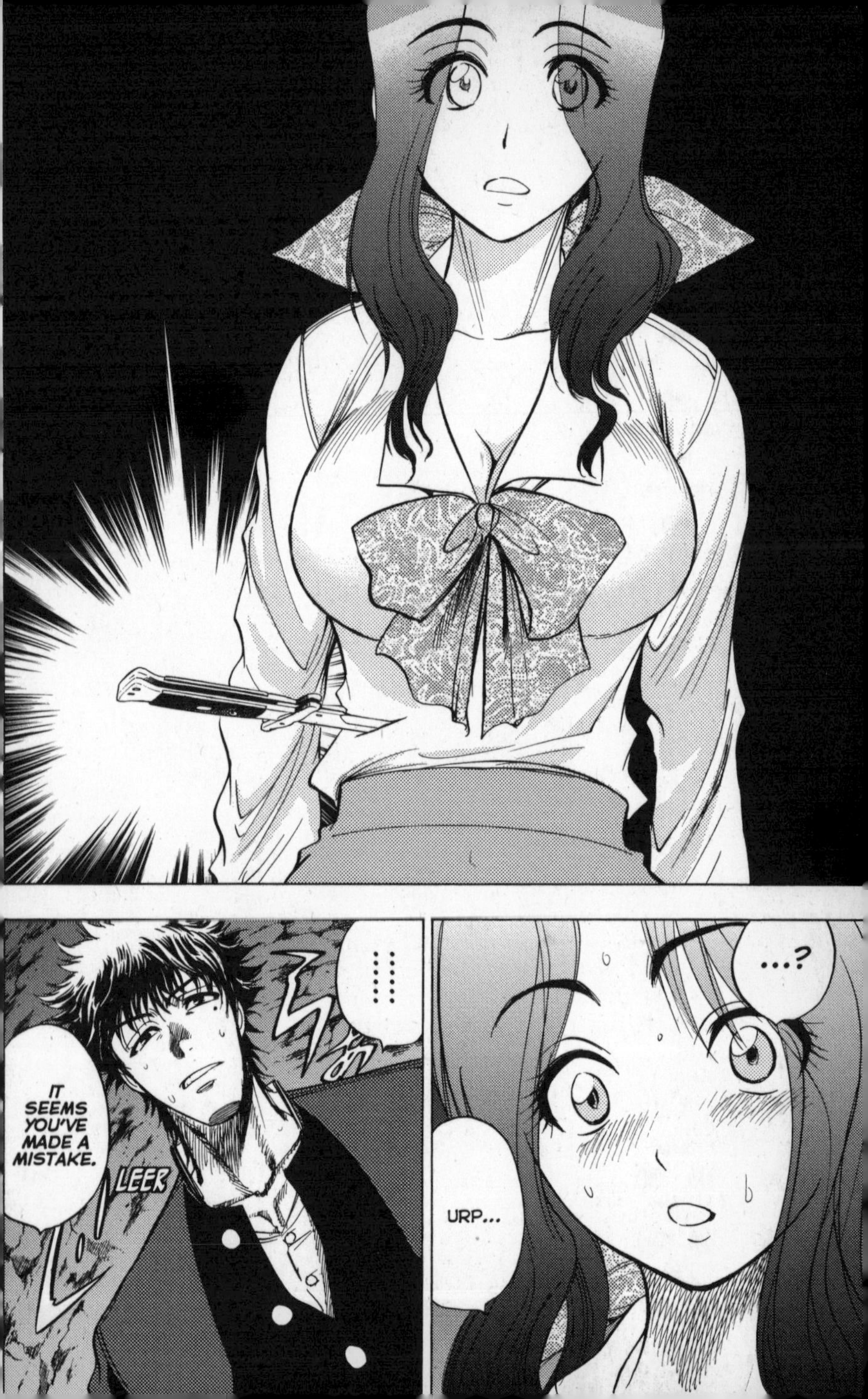
...?
URP...
......
IT SEEMS YOU'VE MADE A MISTAKE.
LEER

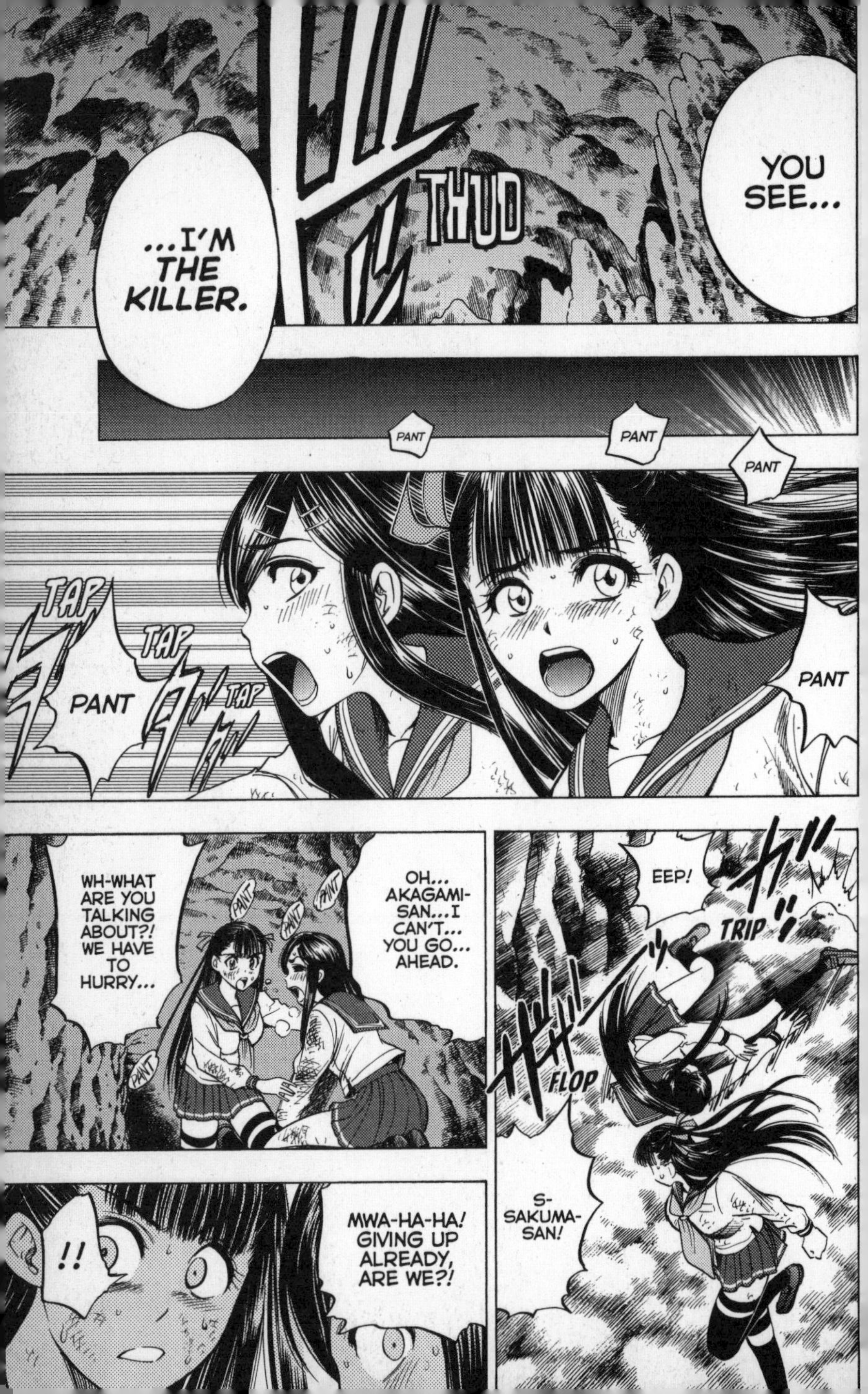
YOU SEE...
THUD
...I'M THE KILLER.
PANT
PANT
PANT
PANT
TAP
TAP
TAP
PANT
EEP!
TRIP
FLOP
S-SAKUMA-SAN!
OH... AKAGAMI-SAN... I CAN'T... YOU GO... AHEAD.
PANT
PANT
WH-WHAT ARE YOU TALKING ABOUT?! WE HAVE TO HURRY...
PANT
PANT
MWA-HA-HA! GIVING UP ALREADY, ARE WE?!
!!

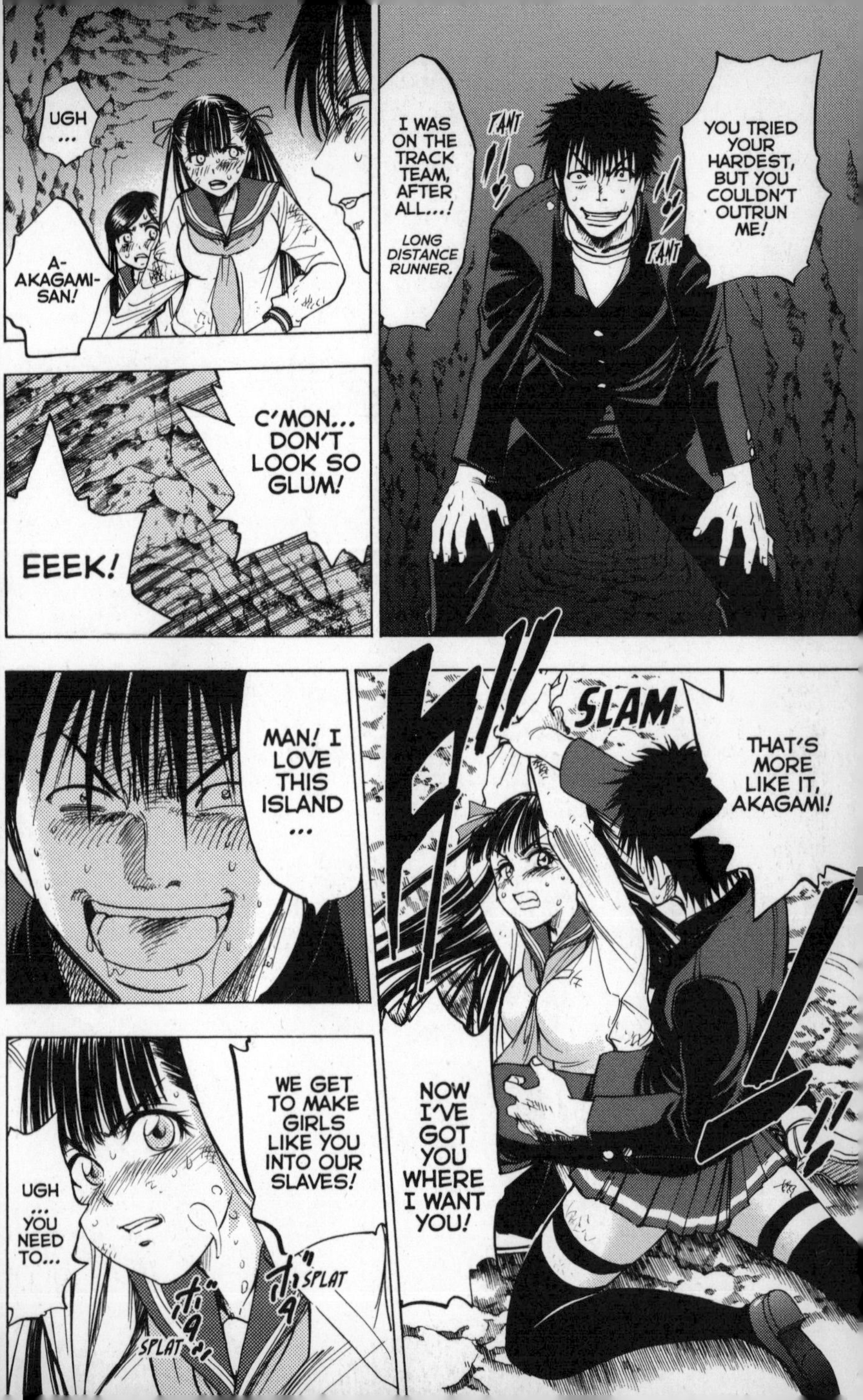
YOU TRIED YOUR HARDEST, BUT YOU COULDN'T OUTRUN ME!
PANT
PANT
I WAS ON THE TRACK TEAM, AFTER ALL...!
LONG DISTANCE RUNNER.
UGH ...
A-AKAGAMI-SAN!
C'MON... DON'T LOOK SO GLUM!
EEEK!
SLAM
THAT'S MORE LIKE IT, AKAGAMI!
NOW I'VE GOT YOU WHERE I WANT YOU!
MAN! I LOVE THIS ISLAND ...
WE GET TO MAKE GIRLS LIKE YOU INTO OUR SLAVES!
UGH ... YOU NEED TO...
SPLAT
SPLAT

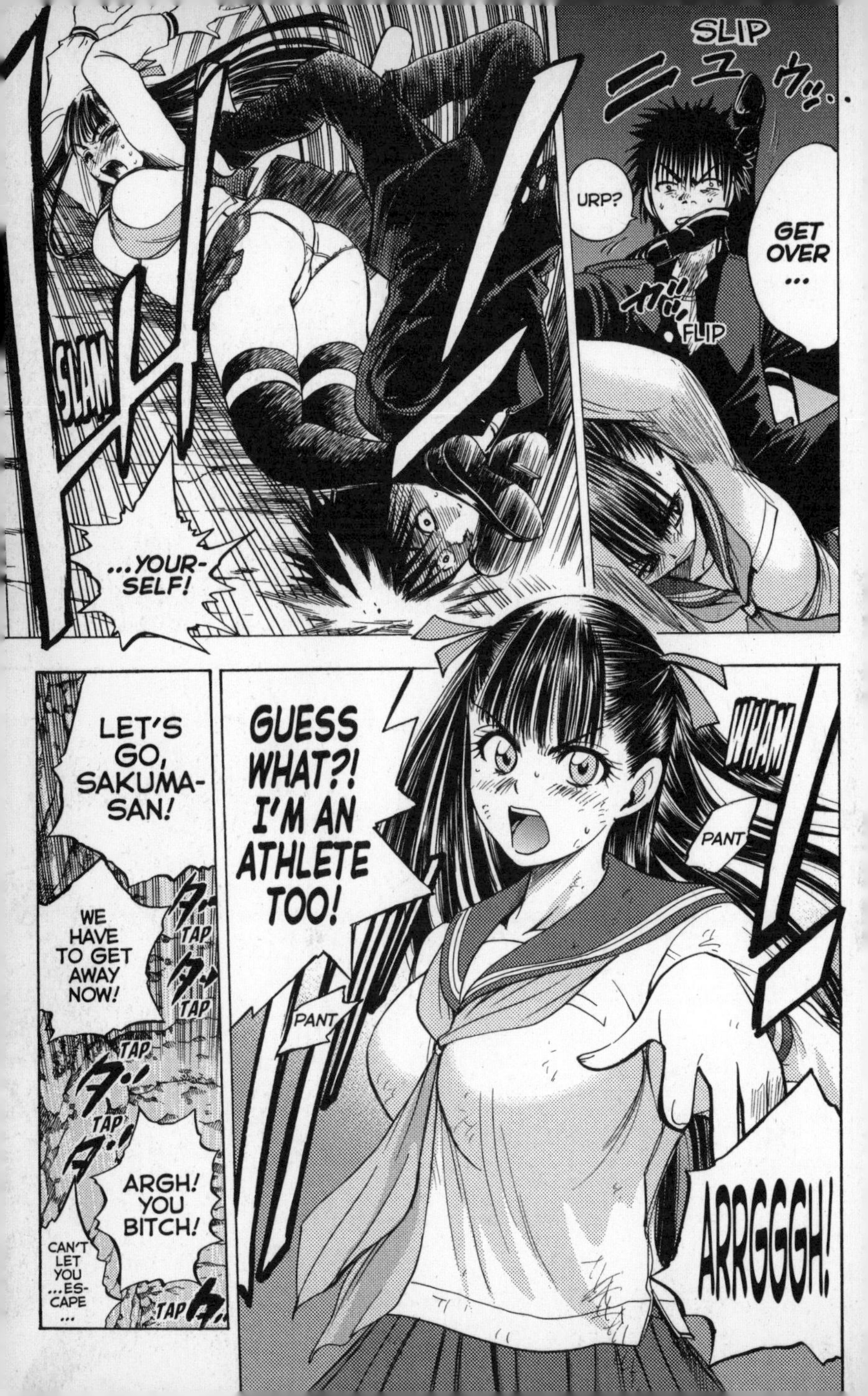
SLIP
URP?
GET OVER ...
FLIP
SLAM
...YOURSELF!
WHAM
PANT
GUESS WHAT?! I'M AN ATHLETE TOO!
PANT
ARRGGGH!
LET'S GO, SAKUMA-SAN!
WE HAVE TO GET AWAY NOW!
TAP
TAP
TAP
TAP
ARGH! YOU BITCH!
CAN'T LET YOU ...ES-CAPE ...
TAP

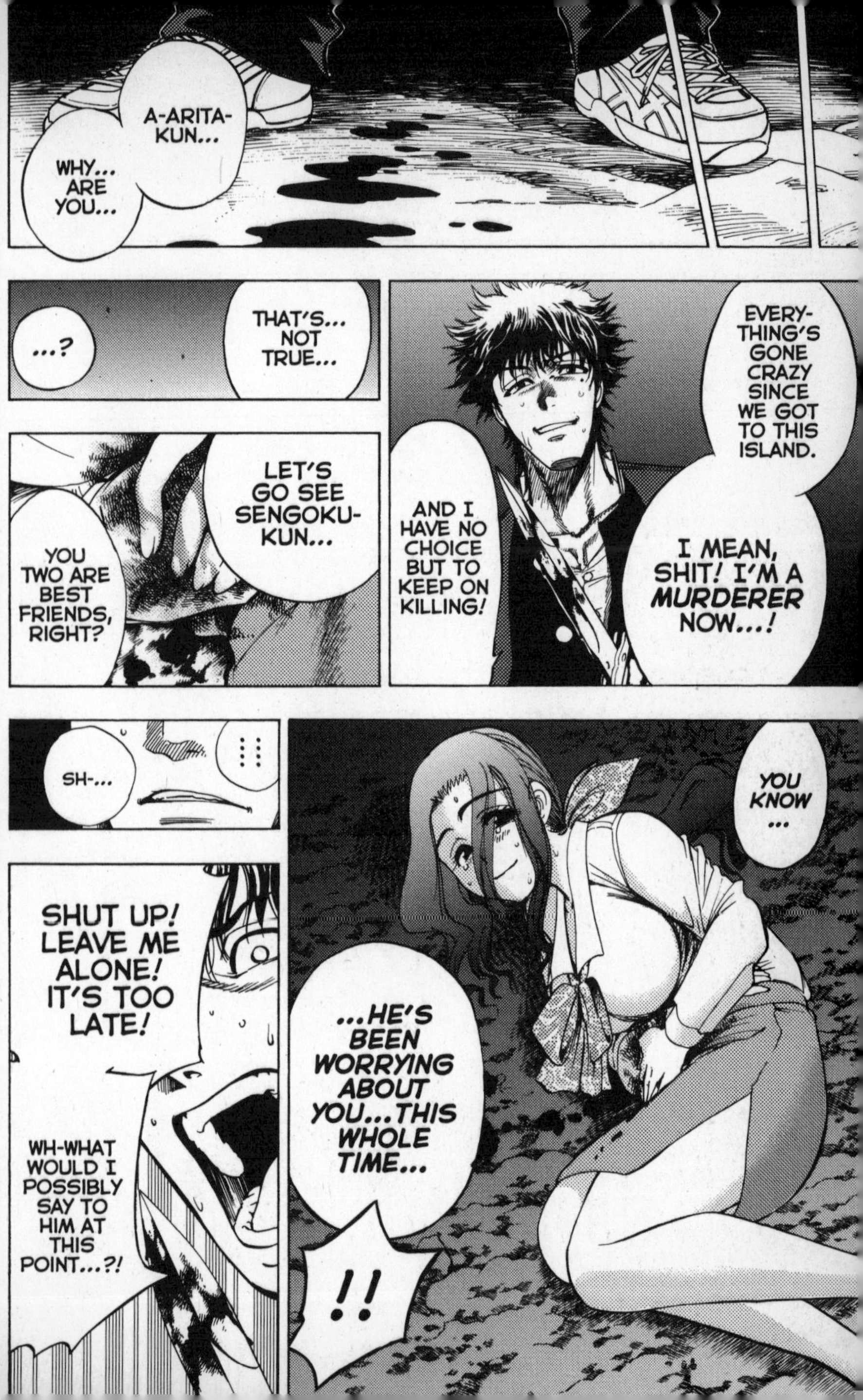
A-ARITA-KUN...
WHY... ARE YOU...
EVERY-THING'S GONE CRAZY SINCE WE GOT TO THIS ISLAND.
I MEAN, SHIT! I'M A *MURDERER* NOW...!
AND I HAVE NO CHOICE BUT TO KEEP ON KILLING!
THAT'S... NOT TRUE...
...?
LET'S GO SEE SENGOKU-KUN...
YOU TWO ARE BEST FRIENDS, RIGHT?
YOU KNOW ...
...HE'S BEEN WORRYING ABOUT YOU...THIS WHOLE TIME...
!!
...
SH-...
SHUT UP! LEAVE ME ALONE! IT'S TOO LATE!
WH-WHAT WOULD I POSSIBLY SAY TO HIM AT THIS POINT...?!

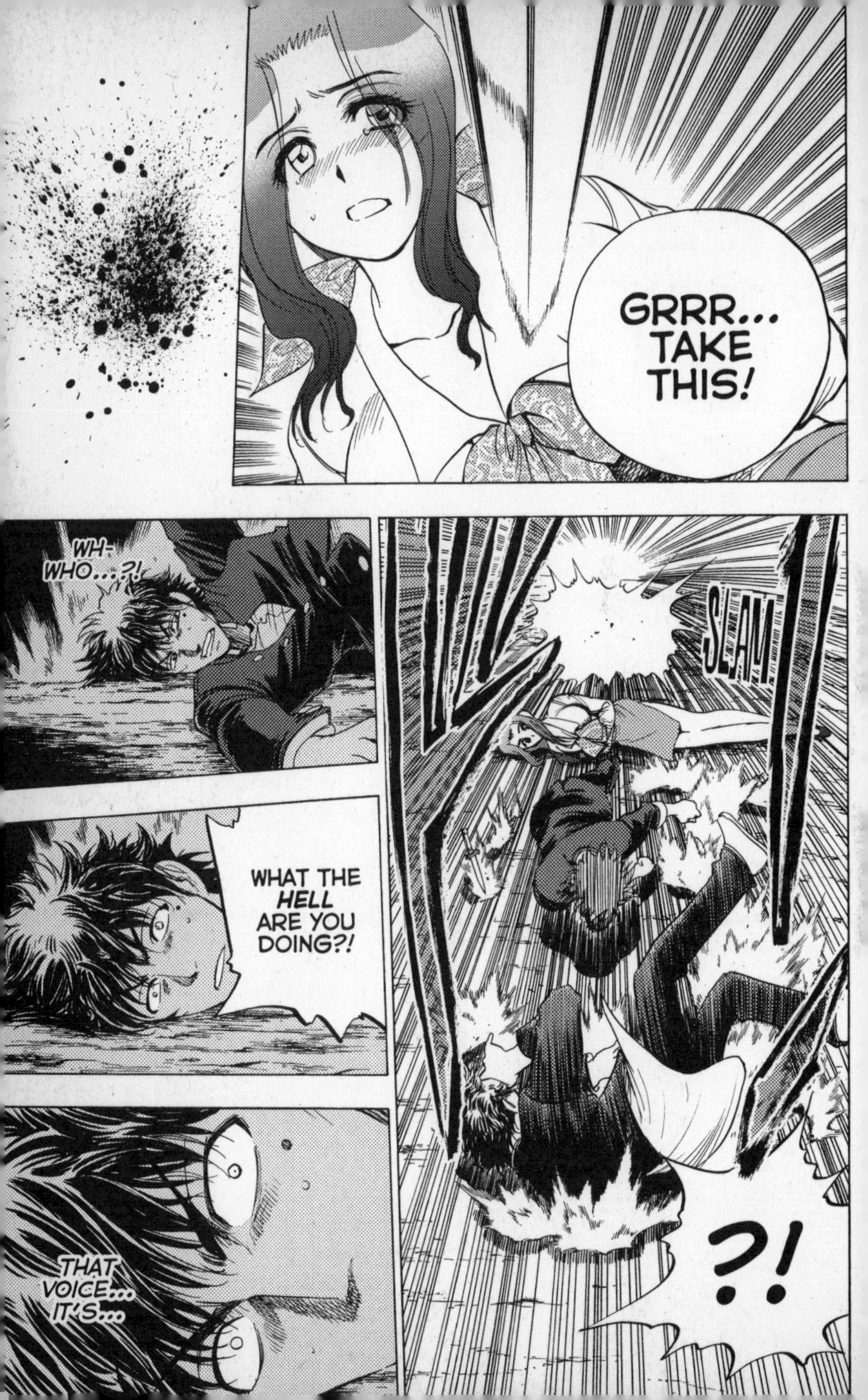
GRRR... TAKE THIS!
SLAM
?!
WH- WHO...?!
WHAT THE *HELL* ARE YOU DOING?!
THAT VOICE... IT'S...

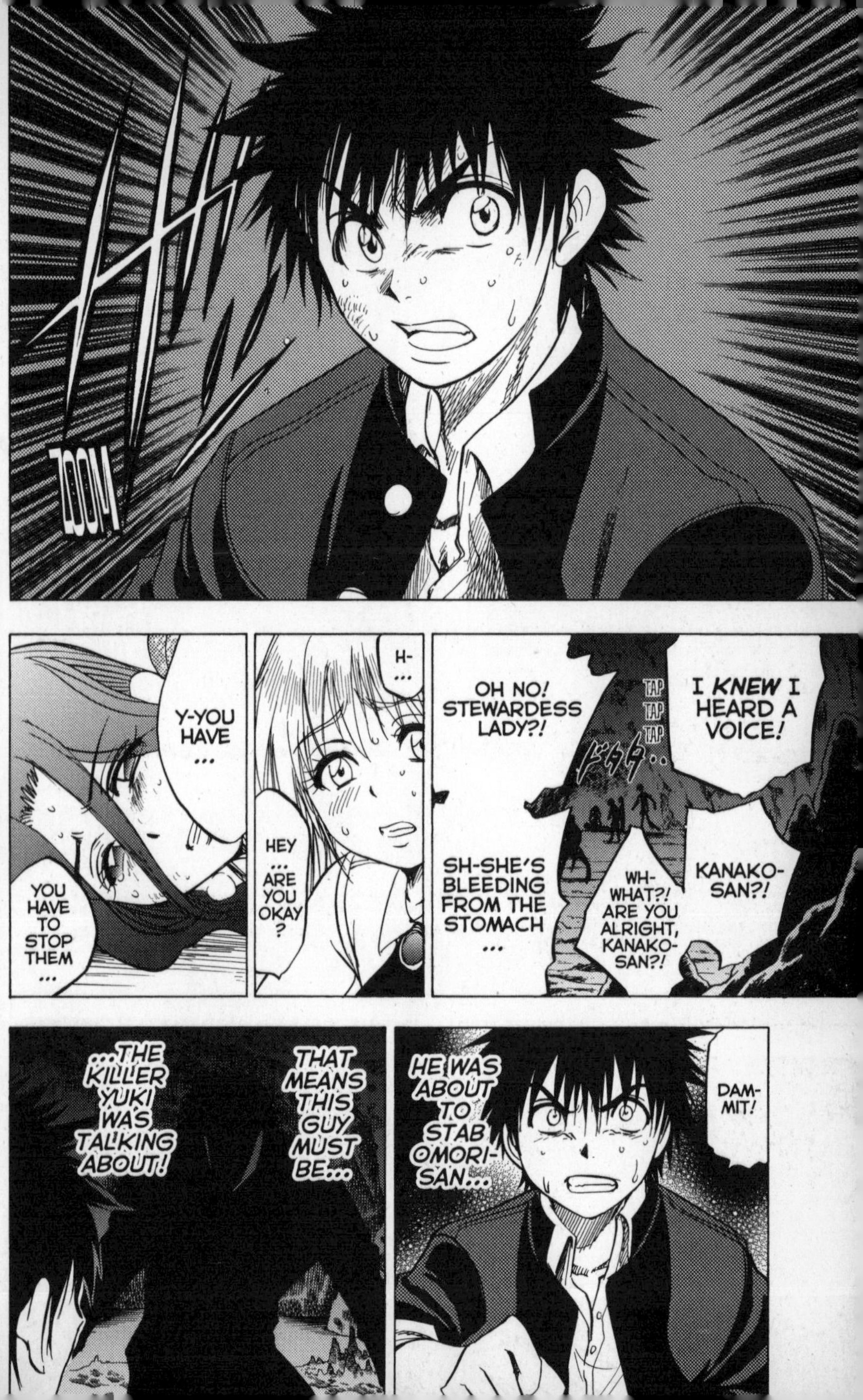
ZOOM
I KNEW I HEARD A VOICE!
TAP TAP TAP
ドタタ..
OH NO! STEWARDESS LADY?!
KANAKO-SAN?!
WH-WHAT?! ARE YOU ALRIGHT, KANAKO-SAN?!
SH-SHE'S BLEEDING FROM THE STOMACH...
H-...
HEY... ARE YOU OKAY?
Y-YOU HAVE...
YOU HAVE TO STOP THEM...
DAM-MIT!
HE WAS ABOUT TO STAB OMORI-SAN...
THAT MEANS THIS GUY MUST BE...
...THE KILLER YUKI WAS TALKING ABOUT!

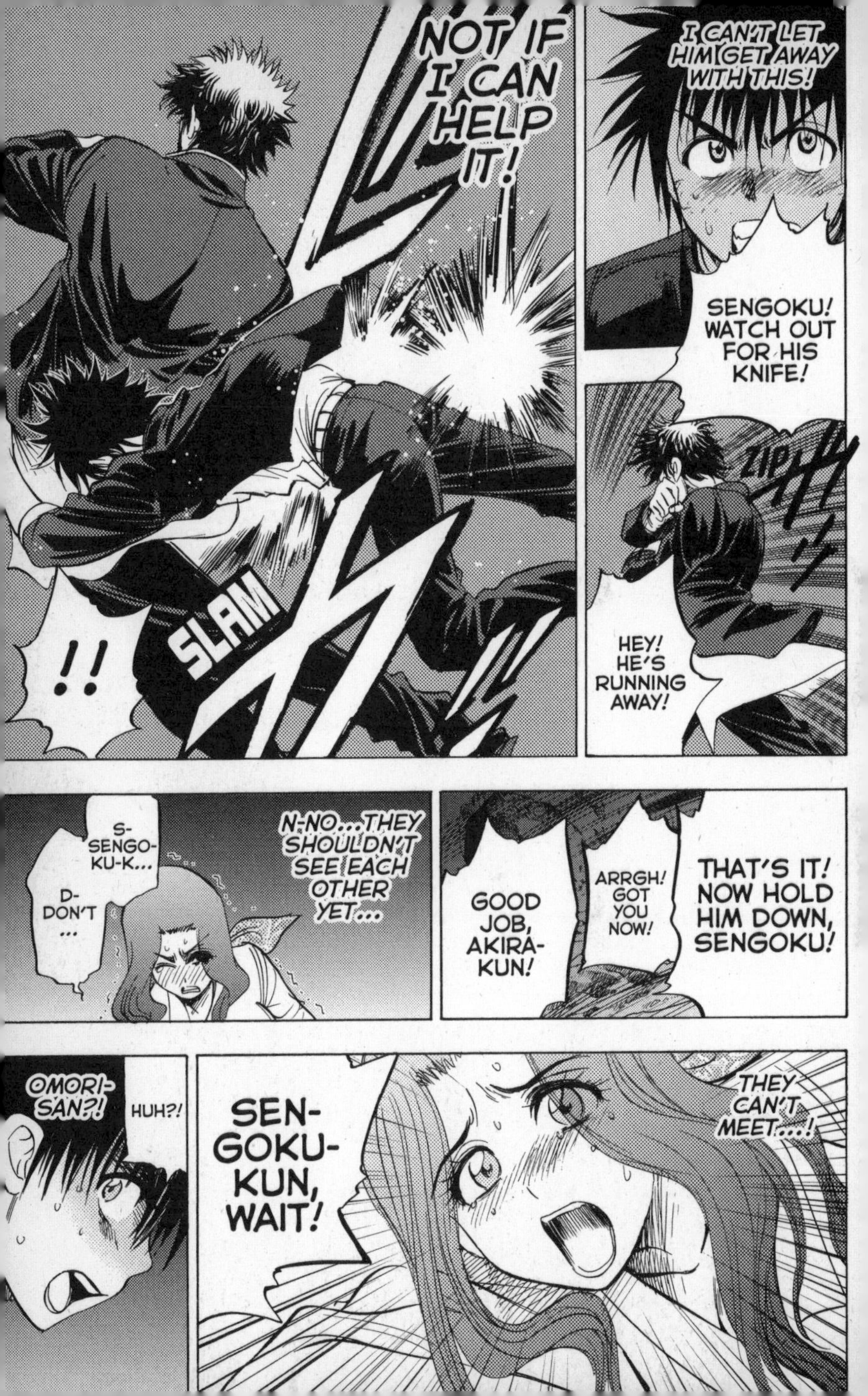
I CAN'T LET HIM GET AWAY WITH THIS!
SENGOKU! WATCH OUT FOR HIS KNIFE!
ZIP
HEY! HE'S RUNNING AWAY!
NOT IF I CAN HELP IT!
SLAM
!!
THAT'S IT! NOW HOLD HIM DOWN, SENGOKU!
ARRGH! GOT YOU NOW!
GOOD JOB, AKIRA-KUN!
N-NO...THEY SHOULDN'T SEE EACH OTHER YET...
S-SENGOKU-K...
D-DON'T...
THEY CAN'T MEET...!
SEN-GOKU-KUN, WAIT!
HUH?!
OMORI-SAN?!

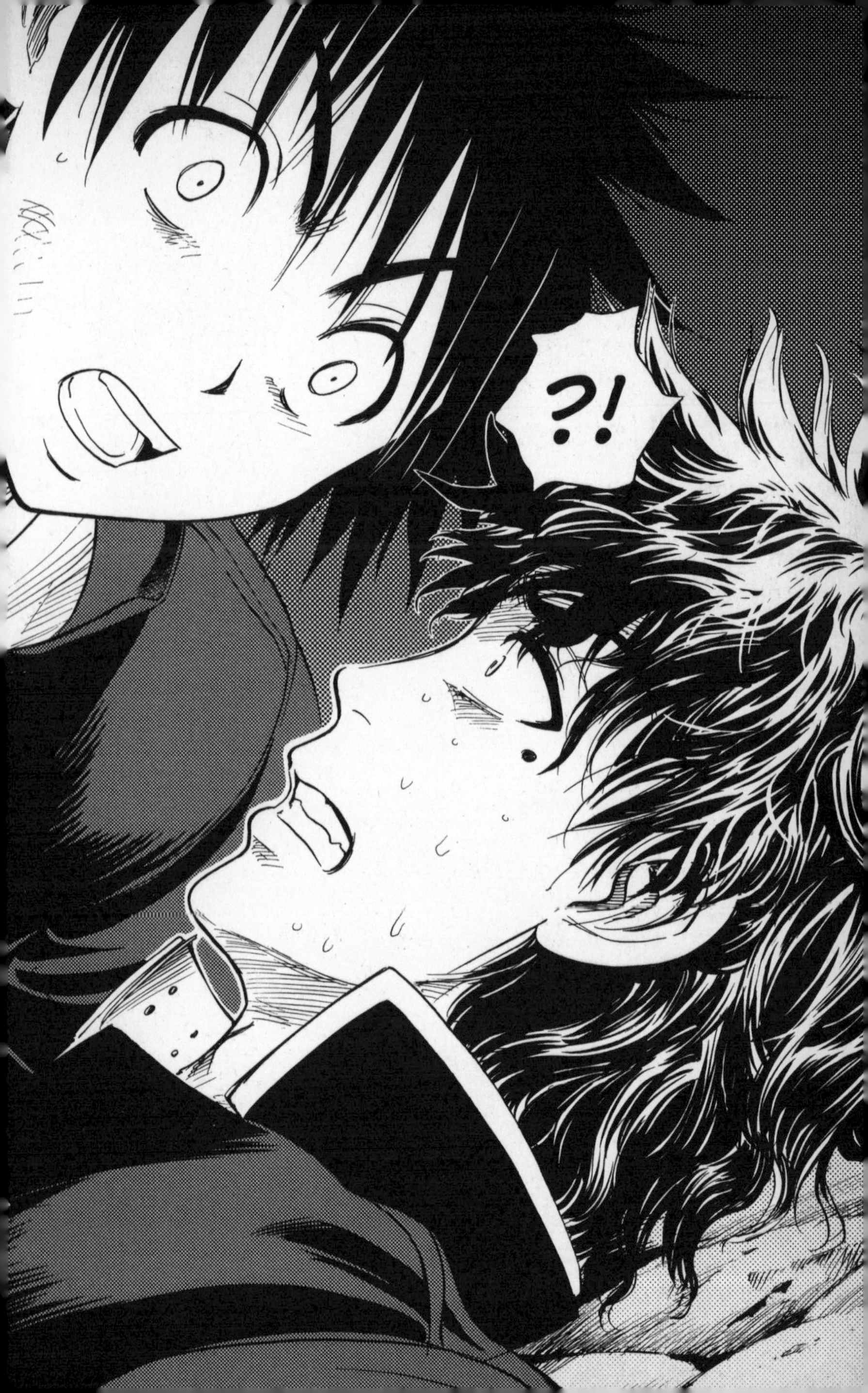
?!

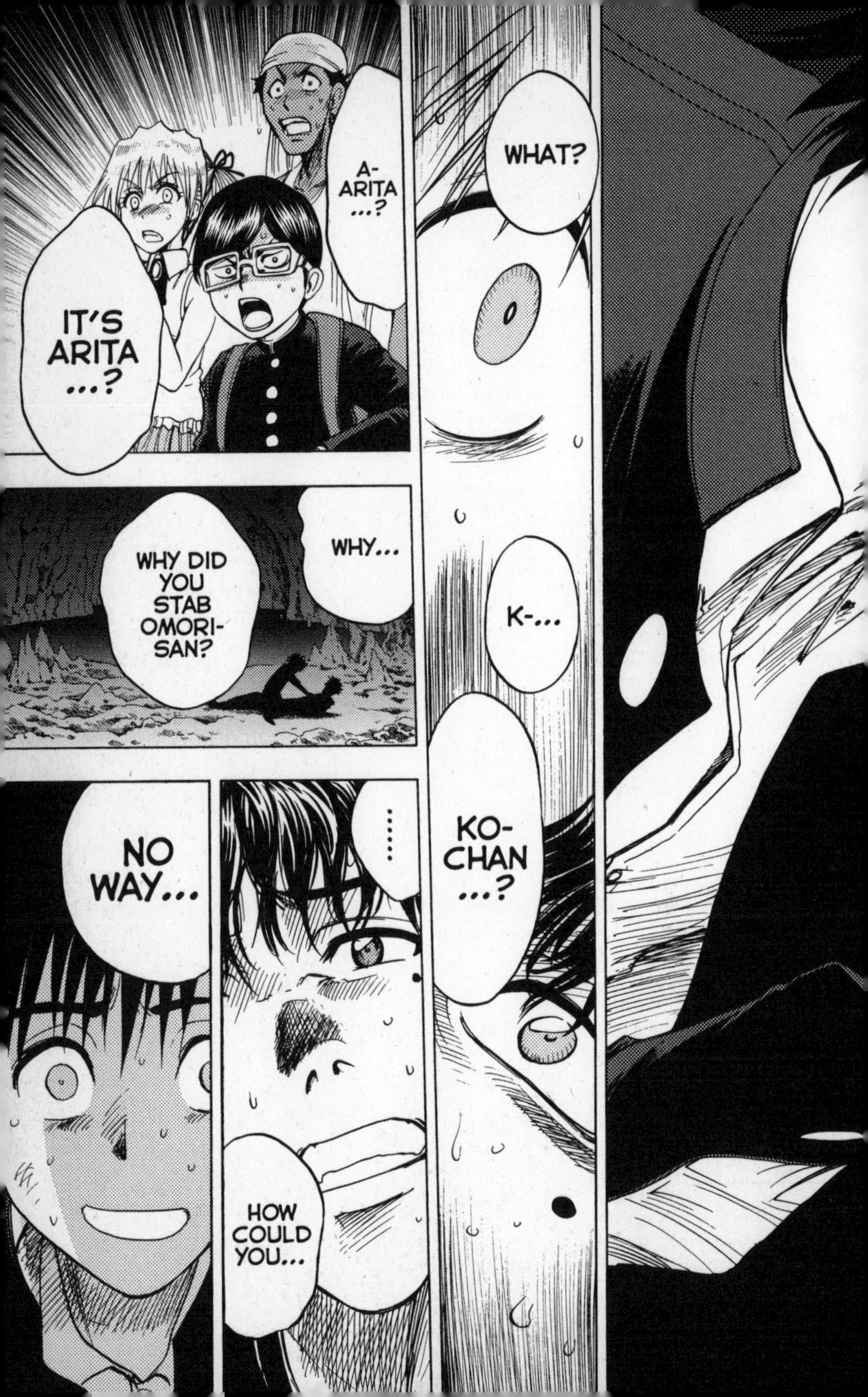
WHAT?
K-...
KO-CHAN ...?
A-ARITA ...?
IT'S ARITA ...?
WHY...
WHY DID YOU STAB OMORI-SAN?
......
HOW COULD YOU...
NO WAY...

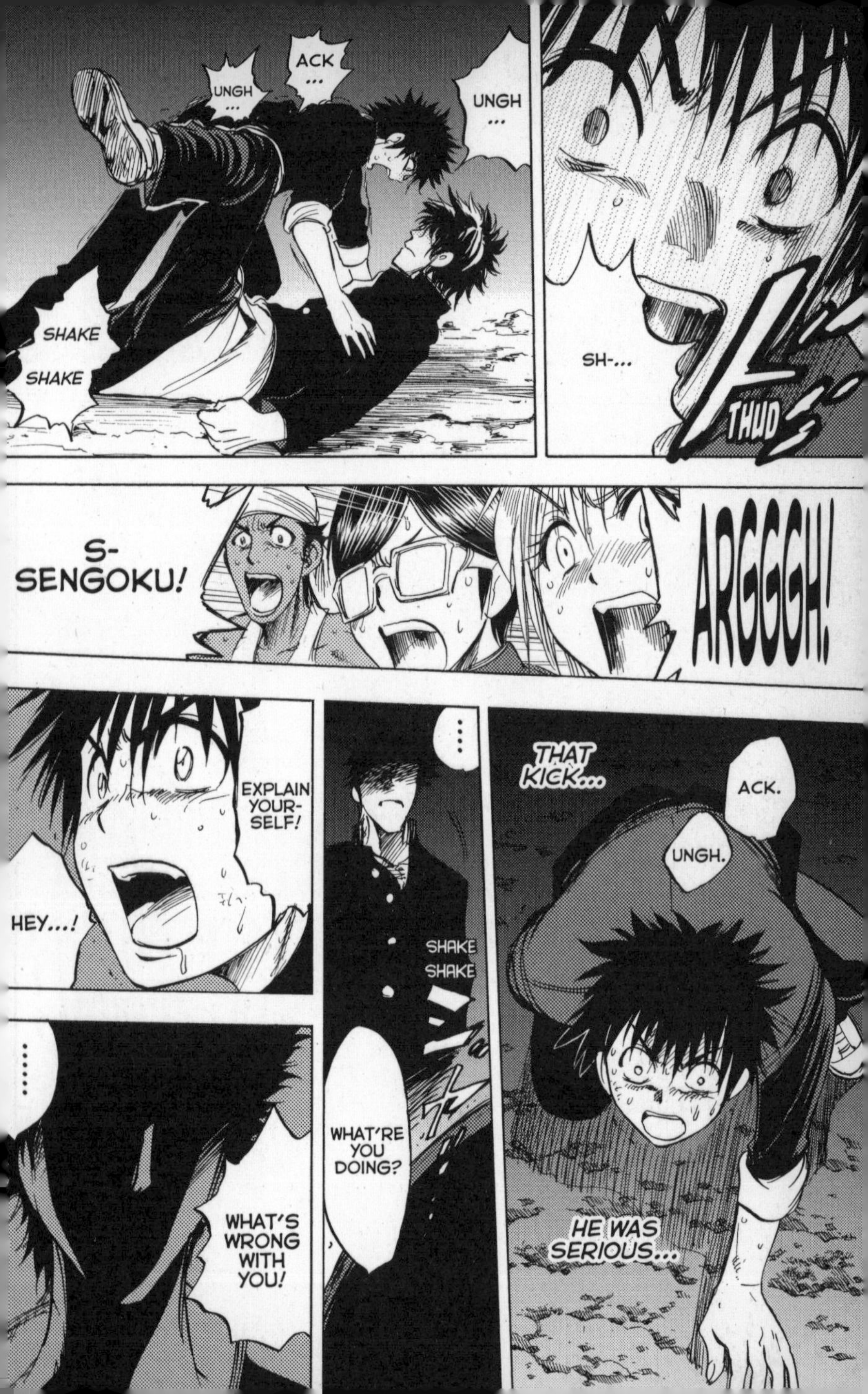
SH-...
THUD
UNGH ...
ACK ...
UNGH ...
SHAKE
SHAKE
ARGGGH!
S- SENGOKU!
ACK.
THAT KICK...
UNGH.
HE WAS SERIOUS...
....
SHAKE
SHAKE
WHAT'RE YOU DOING?
EXPLAIN YOURSELF!
HEY...!
......
WHAT'S WRONG WITH YOU!

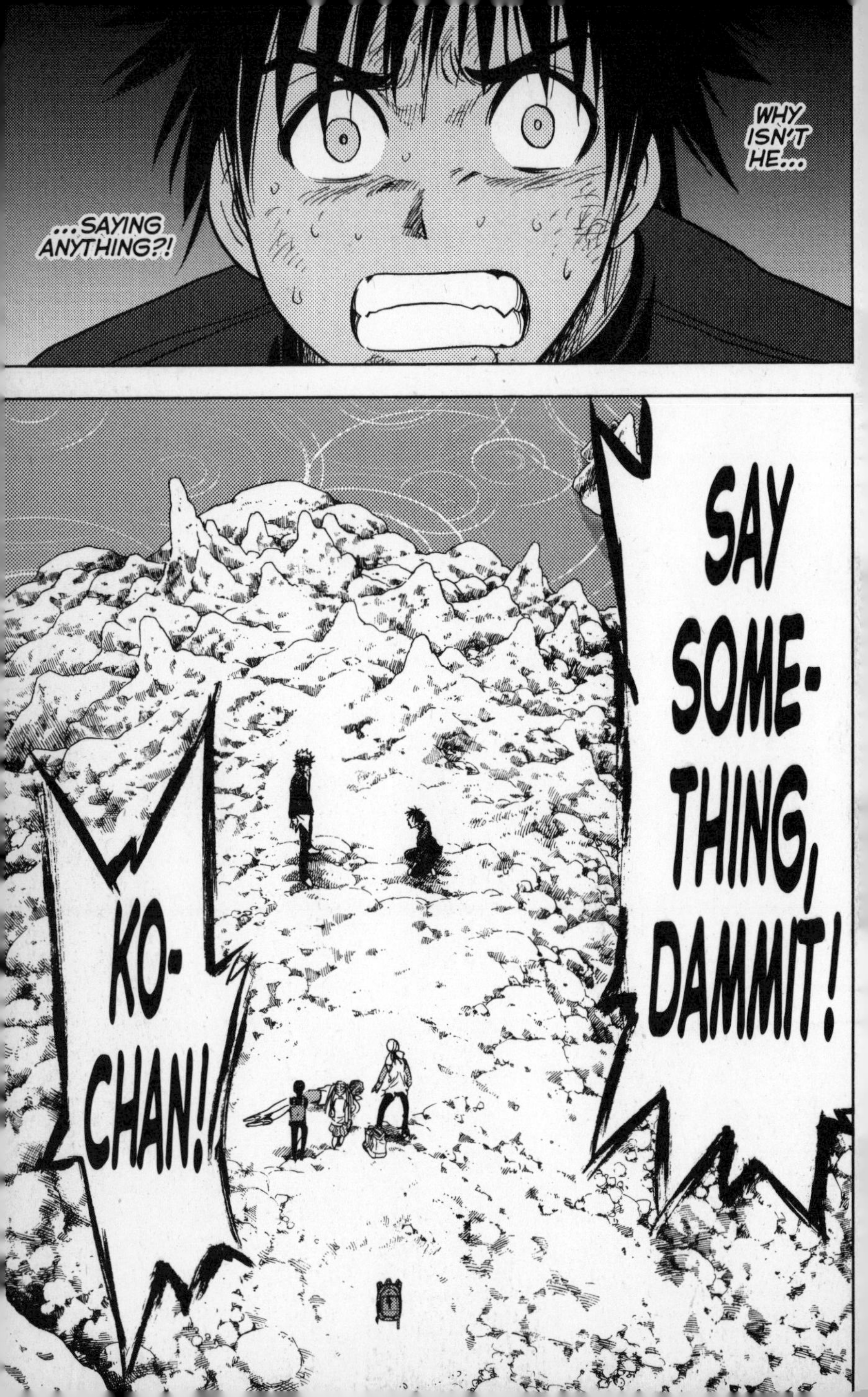
WHY ISN'T HE...
...SAYING ANYTHING?!
SAY SOME-THING, DAMMIT!
KO-CHAN!

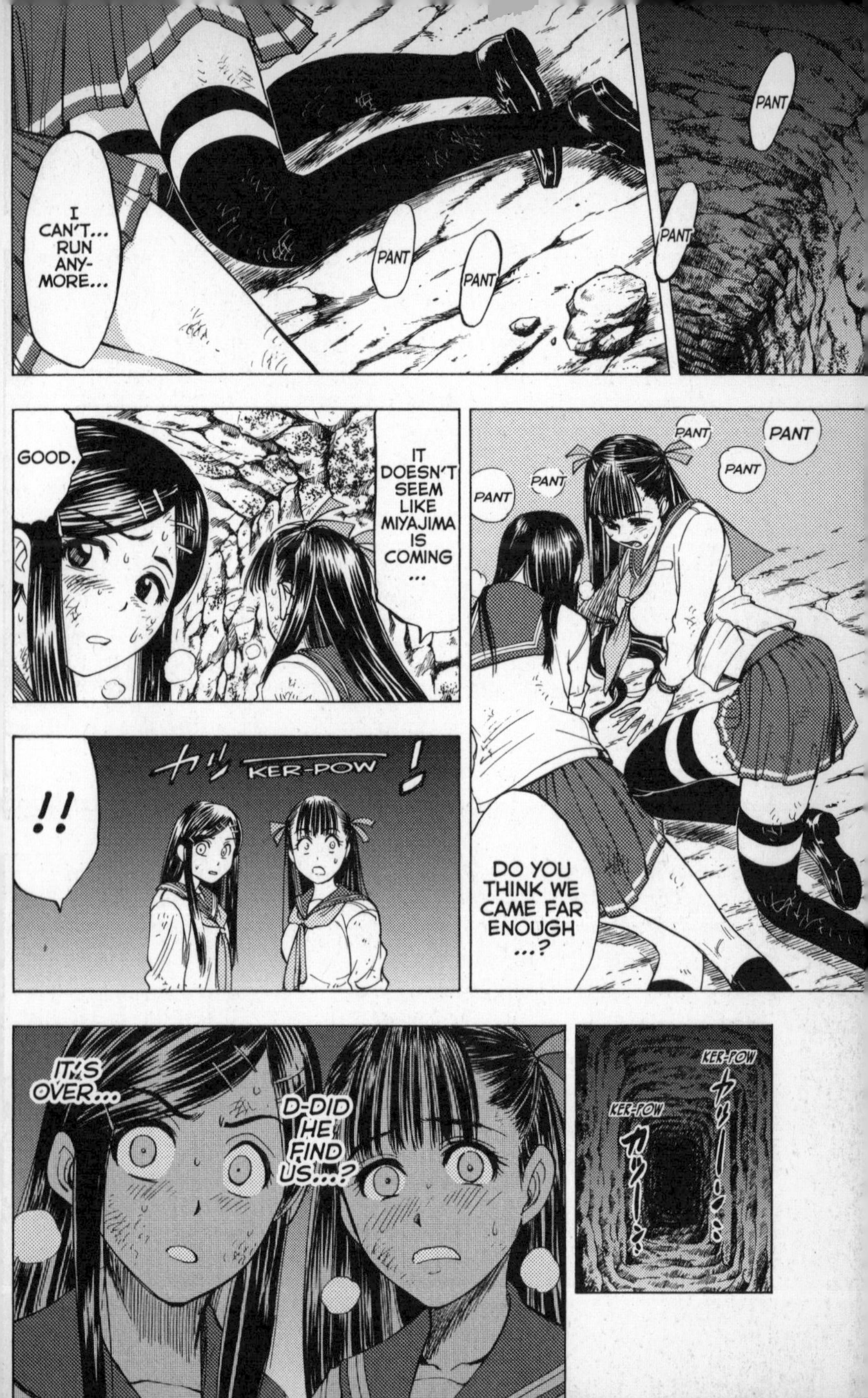
PANT
PANT
PANT
PANT
I CAN'T... RUN ANYMORE...
PANT
PANT
PANT
PANT
PANT
PANT
DO YOU THINK WE CAME FAR ENOUGH ...?
IT DOESN'T SEEM LIKE MIYAJIMA IS COMING ...
GOOD.
カッ KER-POW !
!!
KER-POW
KER-POW
D-DID HE FIND US...?
IT'S OVER...

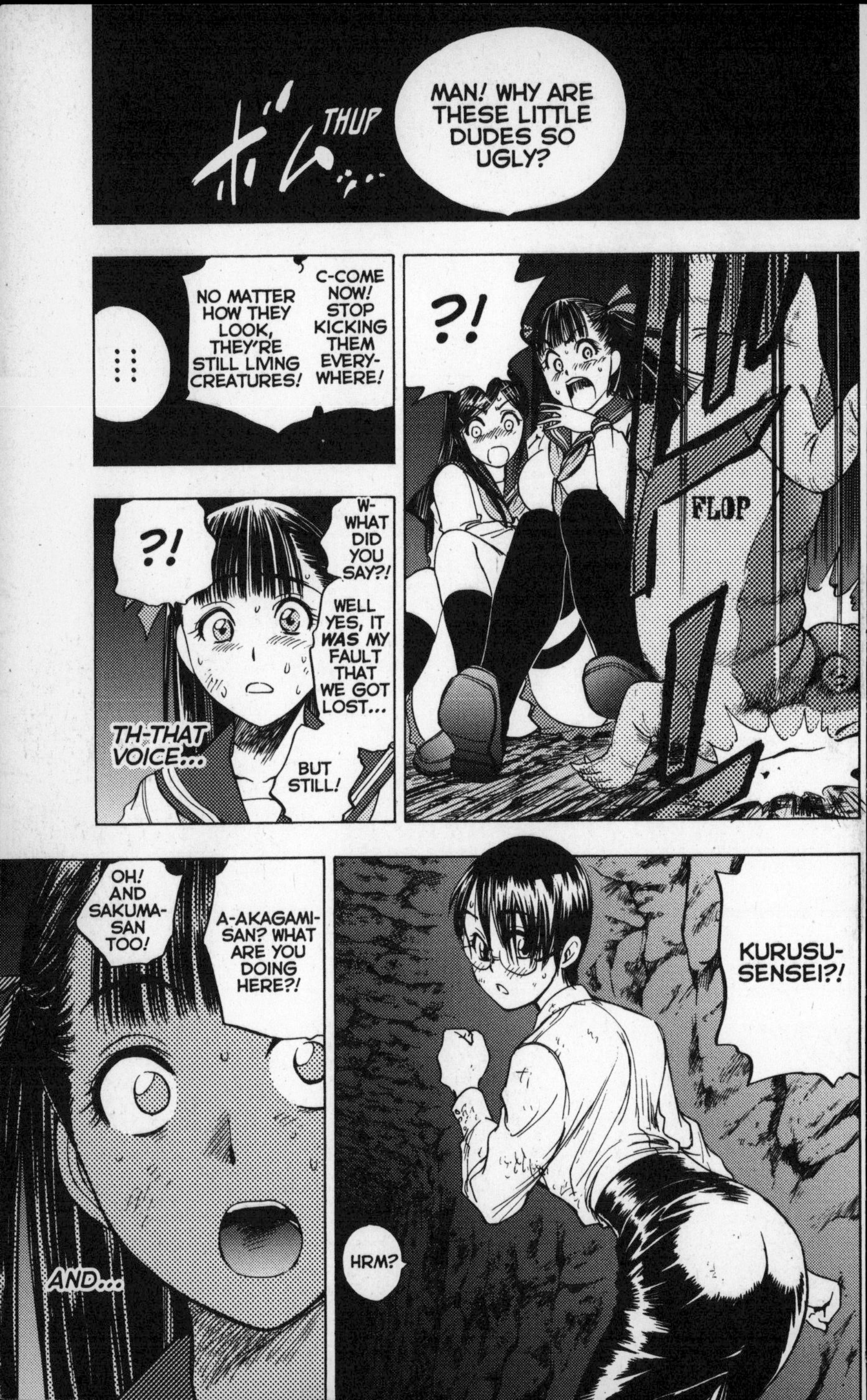
THUP
MAN! WHY ARE THESE LITTLE DUDES SO UGLY?
?!
FLOP
C-COME NOW! STOP KICKING THEM EVERYWHERE!
NO MATTER HOW THEY LOOK, THEY'RE STILL LIVING CREATURES!
......
W-WHAT DID YOU SAY?!
?!
WELL YES, IT WAS MY FAULT THAT WE GOT LOST...
BUT STILL!
TH-THAT VOICE...
KURUSU-SENSEI?!
HRM?
A-AKAGAMI-SAN? WHAT ARE YOU DOING HERE?!
OH! AND SAKUMA-SAN TOO!
AND...

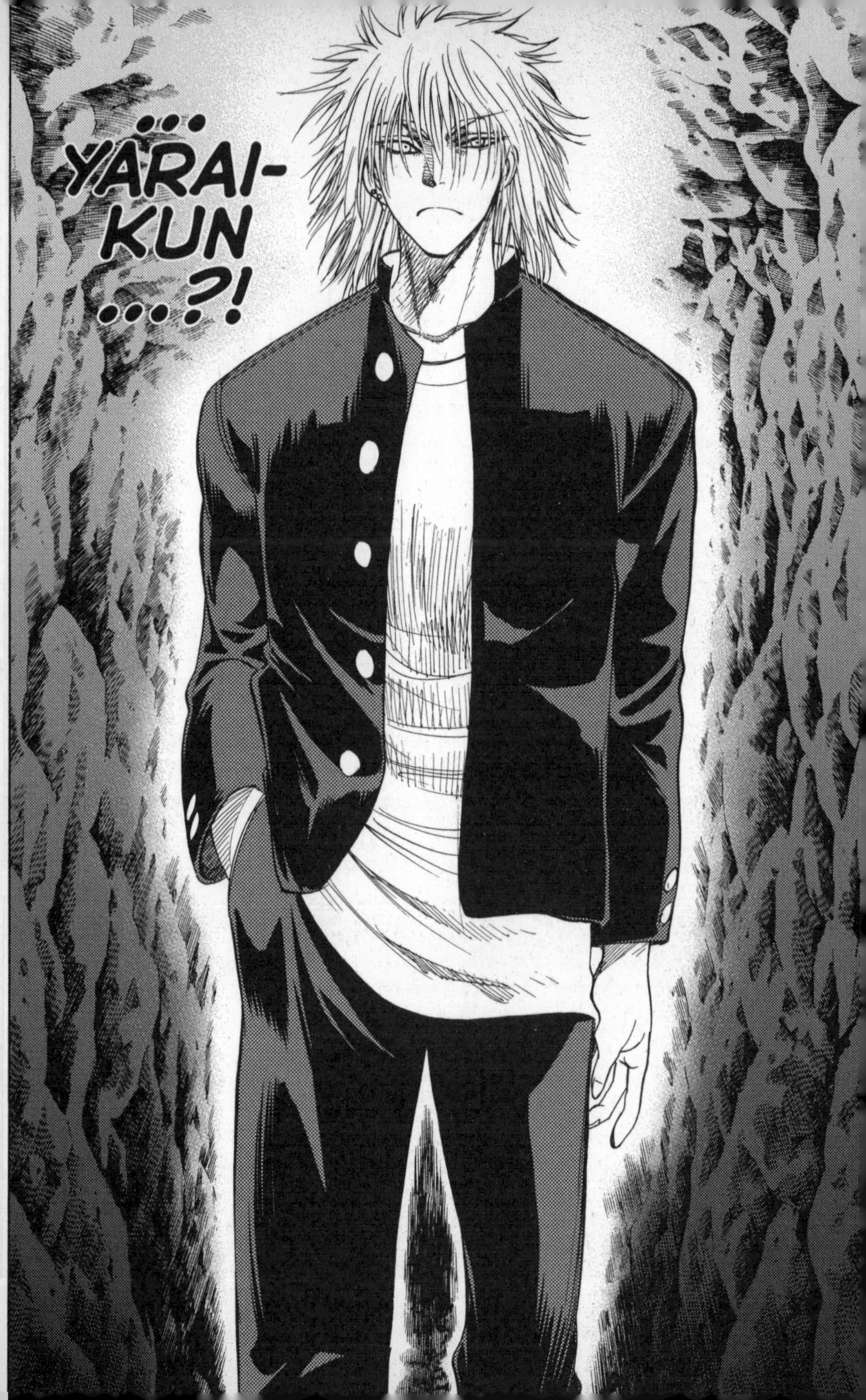
...YARAI-KUN ...?!

Episode 33 It's all or nothing! Stop him!

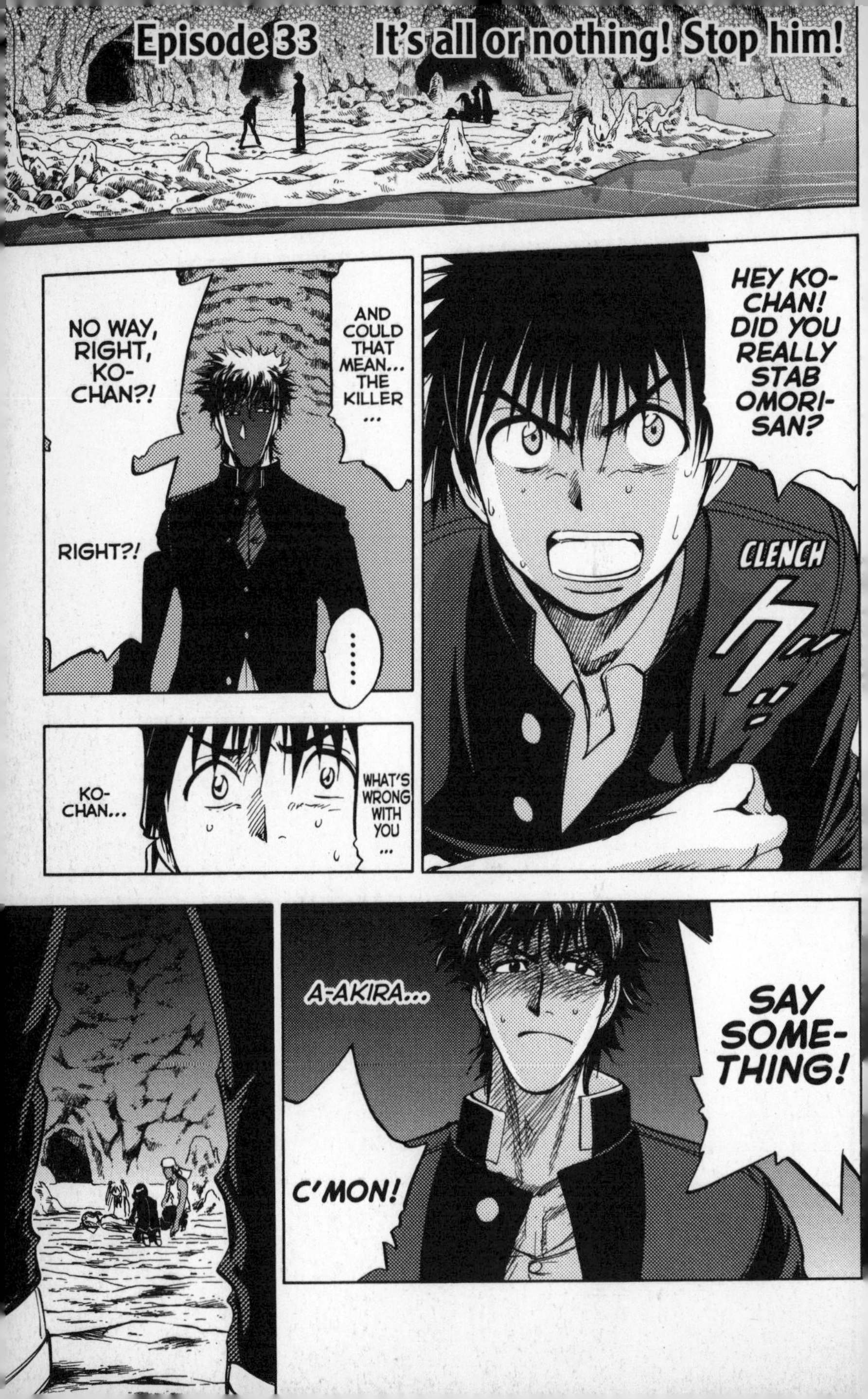
HEY KO-CHAN! DID YOU REALLY STAB OMORI-SAN?
CLENCH
AND COULD THAT MEAN... THE KILLER...
NO WAY, RIGHT, KO-CHAN?!
RIGHT?!
......
WHAT'S WRONG WITH YOU...
KO-CHAN...
SAY SOME-THING!
A-AKIRA...
C'MON!

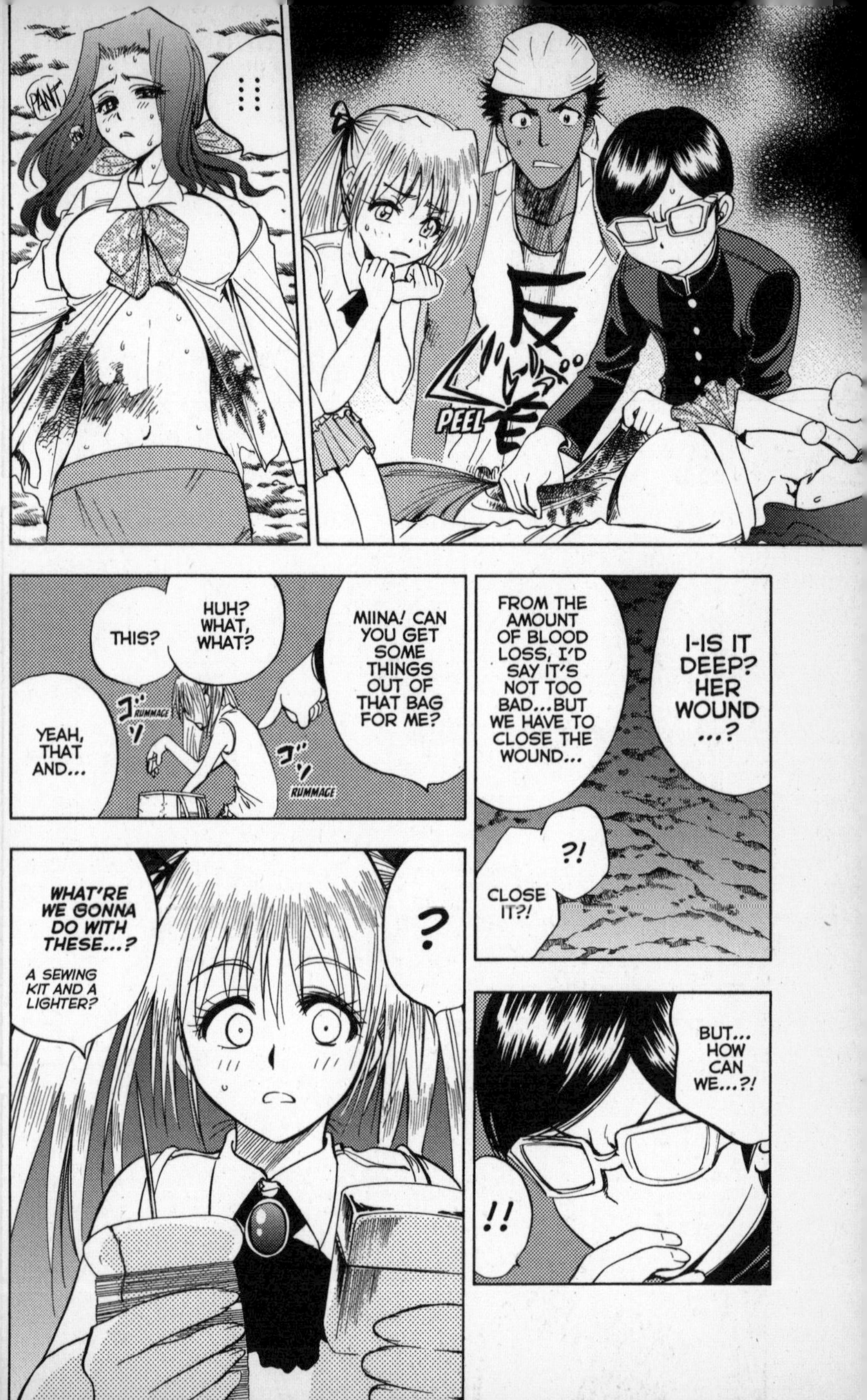
PEEL
PANT
I-IS IT DEEP? HER WOUND...?
FROM THE AMOUNT OF BLOOD LOSS, I'D SAY IT'S NOT TOO BAD...BUT WE HAVE TO CLOSE THE WOUND...
?!
CLOSE IT?!
MIINA! CAN YOU GET SOME THINGS OUT OF THAT BAG FOR ME?
HUH? WHAT, WHAT?
THIS?
RUMMAGE
YEAH, THAT AND...
RUMMAGE
BUT... HOW CAN WE...?!
!!
?
WHAT'RE WE GONNA DO WITH THESE...?
A SEWING KIT AND A LIGHTER?

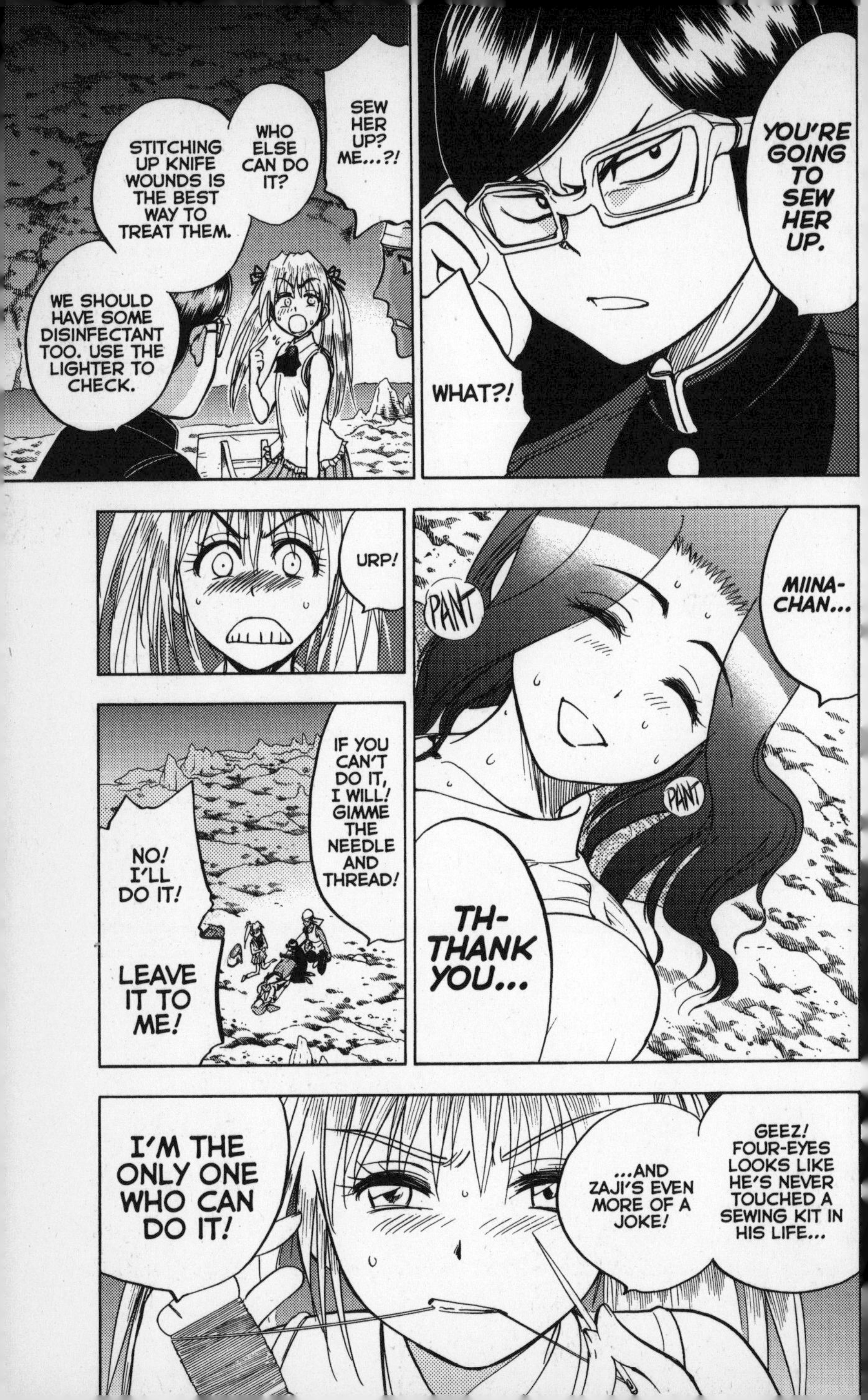
YOU'RE GOING TO SEW HER UP.
WHAT?!
SEW HER UP? ME...?!
WHO ELSE CAN DO IT?
STITCHING UP KNIFE WOUNDS IS THE BEST WAY TO TREAT THEM.
WE SHOULD HAVE SOME DISINFECTANT TOO. USE THE LIGHTER TO CHECK.
MIINA-CHAN...
PANT
PANT
TH-THANK YOU...
URP!
IF YOU CAN'T DO IT, I WILL! GIMME THE NEEDLE AND THREAD!
NO! I'LL DO IT!
LEAVE IT TO ME!
GEEZ! FOUR-EYES LOOKS LIKE HE'S NEVER TOUCHED A SEWING KIT IN HIS LIFE...
...AND ZAJI'S EVEN MORE OF A JOKE!
I'M THE ONLY ONE WHO CAN DO IT!

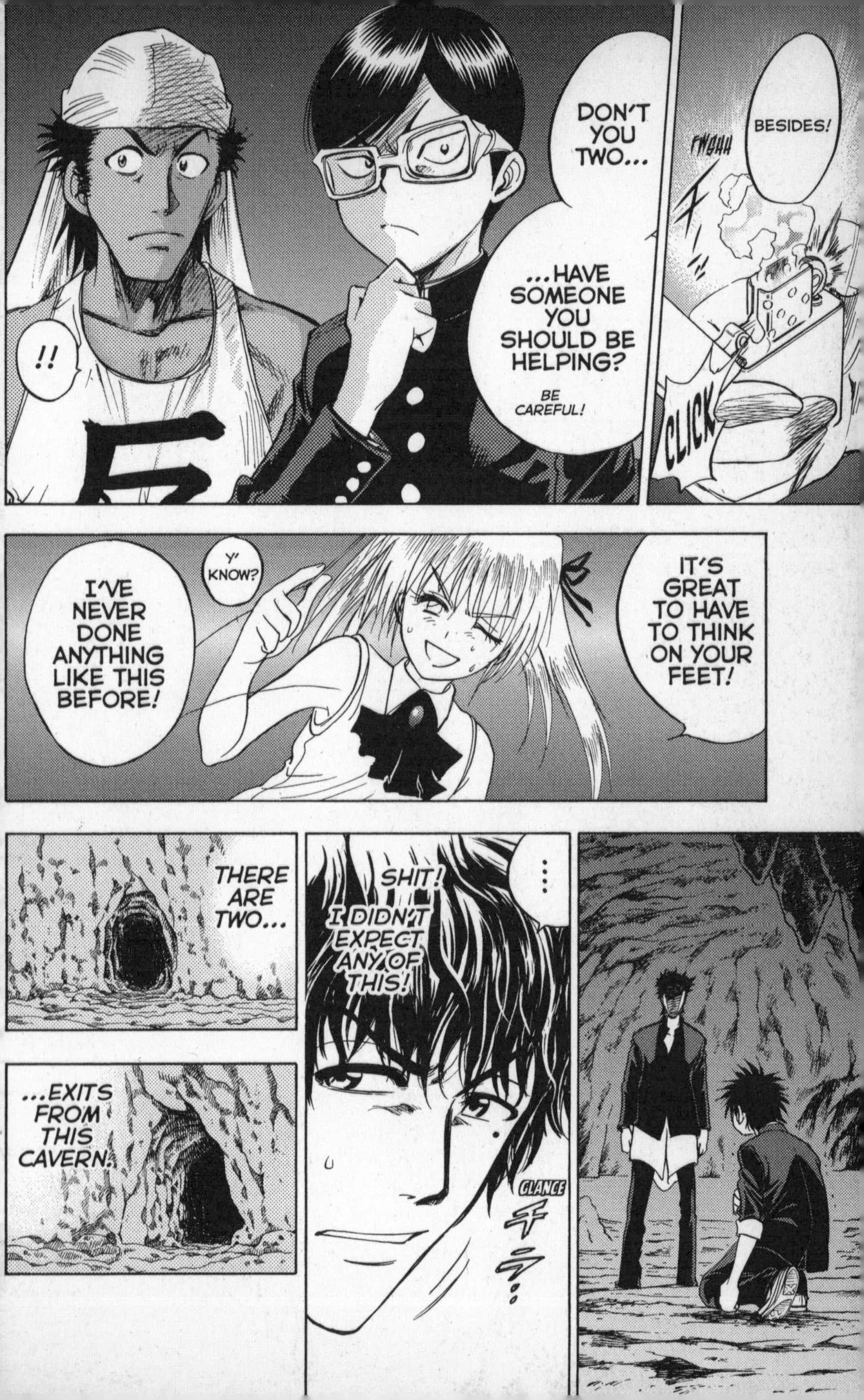
BESIDES!
FWSHH
CLICK
DON'T YOU TWO...
...HAVE SOMEONE YOU SHOULD BE HELPING?
BE CAREFUL!
!!
IT'S GREAT TO HAVE TO THINK ON YOUR FEET!
Y' KNOW?
I'VE NEVER DONE ANYTHING LIKE THIS BEFORE!
....
SHIT! I DIDN'T EXPECT ANY OF THIS!
GLANCE
THERE ARE TWO...
...EXITS FROM THIS CAVERN.

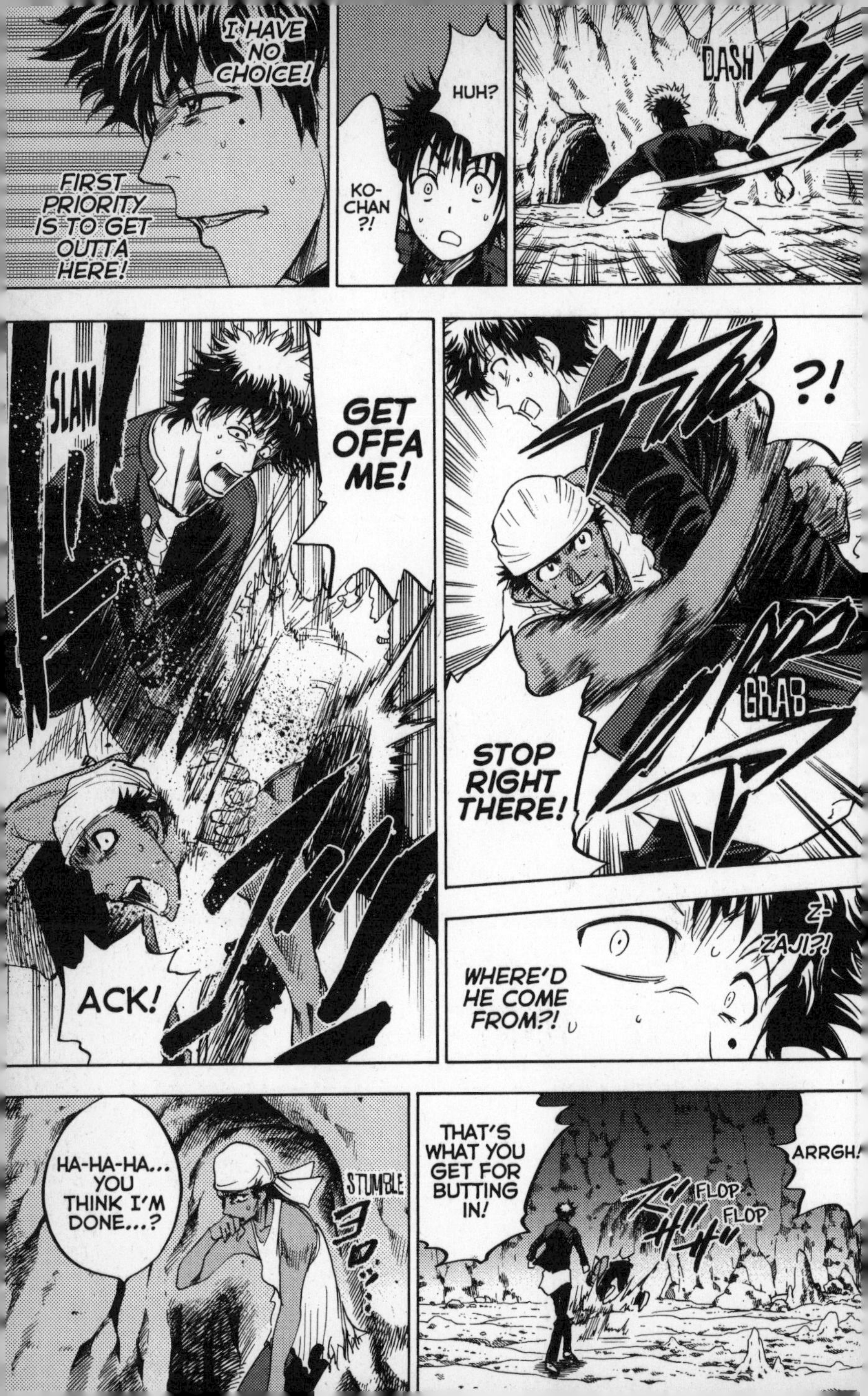
DASH
HUH?
KO-CHAN?!
I HAVE NO CHOICE!
FIRST PRIORITY IS TO GET OUTTA HERE!
?!
GRAB
STOP RIGHT THERE!
Z-ZAJI?!
WHERE'D HE COME FROM?!
GET OFFA ME!
SLAM
ACK!
ARRGH!
THAT'S WHAT YOU GET FOR BUTTING IN!
FLOP FLOP
STUMBLE
HA-HA-HA... YOU THINK I'M DONE...?

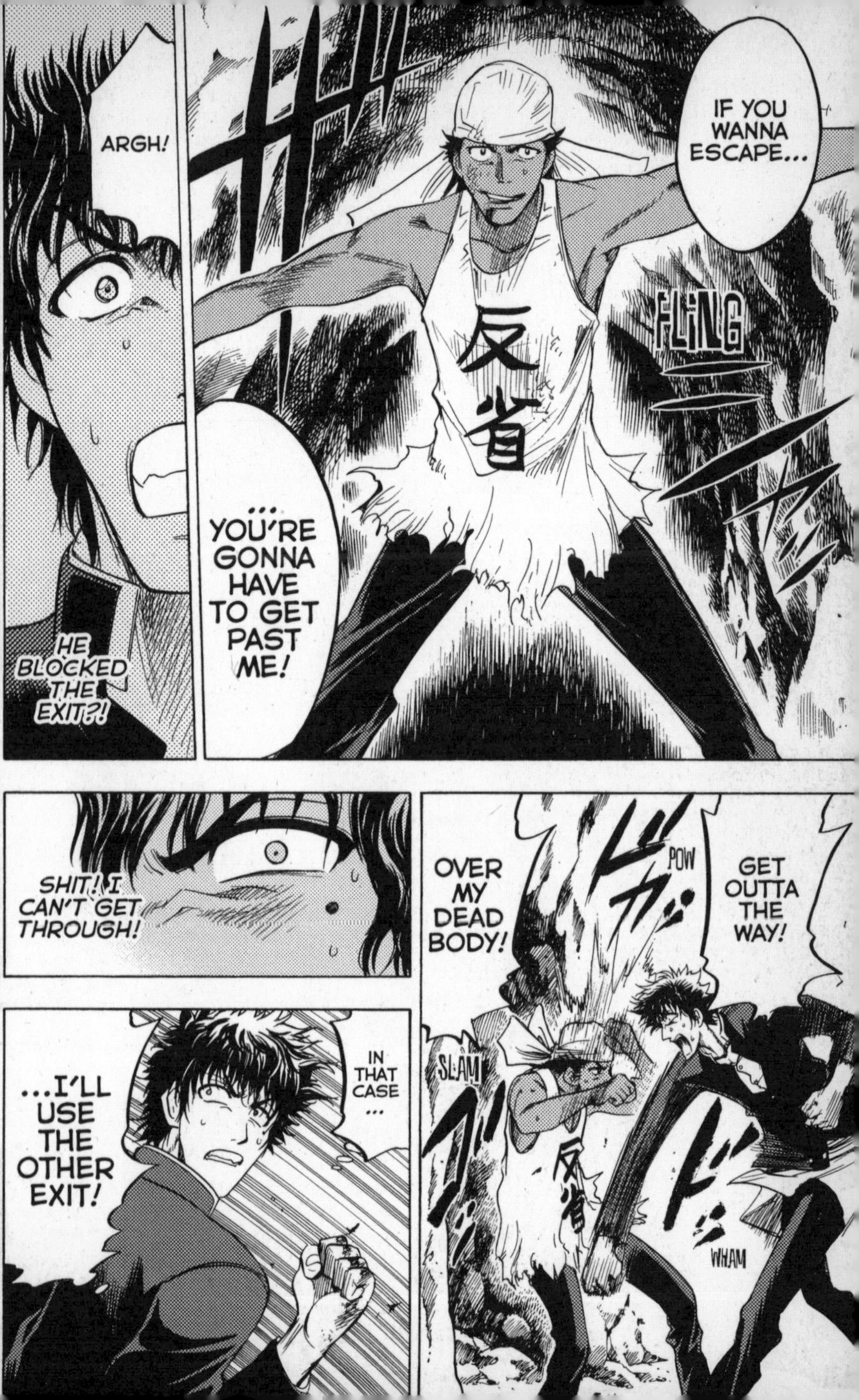
IF YOU WANNA ESCAPE...
FLING
...YOU'RE GONNA HAVE TO GET PAST ME!
ARGH!
HE BLOCKED THE EXIT?!
GET OUTTA THE WAY!
POW
OVER MY DEAD BODY!
SLAM
WHAM
SHIT! I CAN'T GET THROUGH!
IN THAT CASE...
...I'LL USE THE OTHER EXIT!

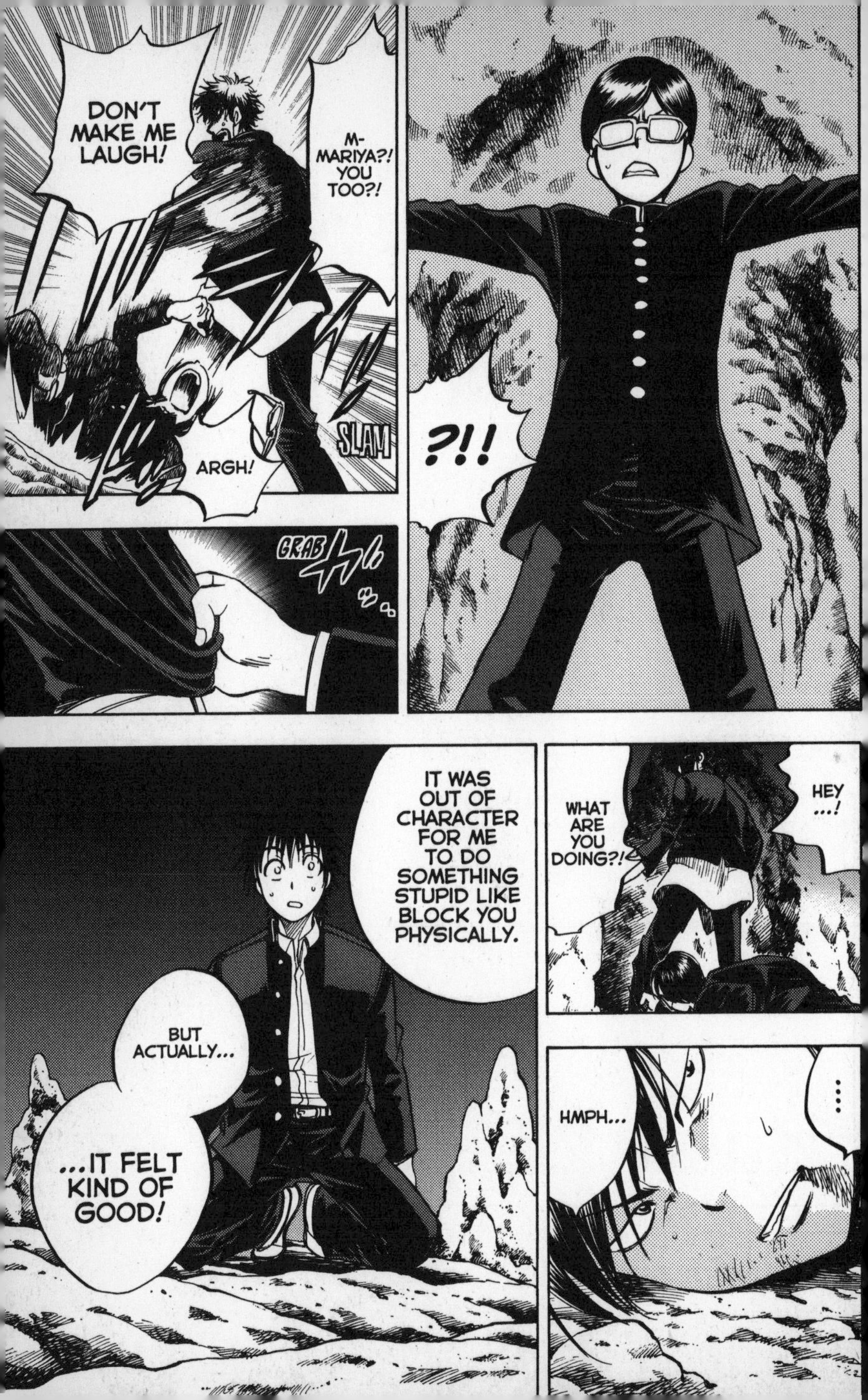
?!!
M-MARIYA?! YOU TOO?!
DON'T MAKE ME LAUGH!
SLAM
ARGH!
GRAB
HEY ...!
WHAT ARE YOU DOING?!
....
HMPH...
IT WAS OUT OF CHARACTER FOR ME TO DO SOMETHING STUPID LIKE BLOCK YOU PHYSICALLY.
BUT ACTUALLY...
...IT FELT KIND OF GOOD!

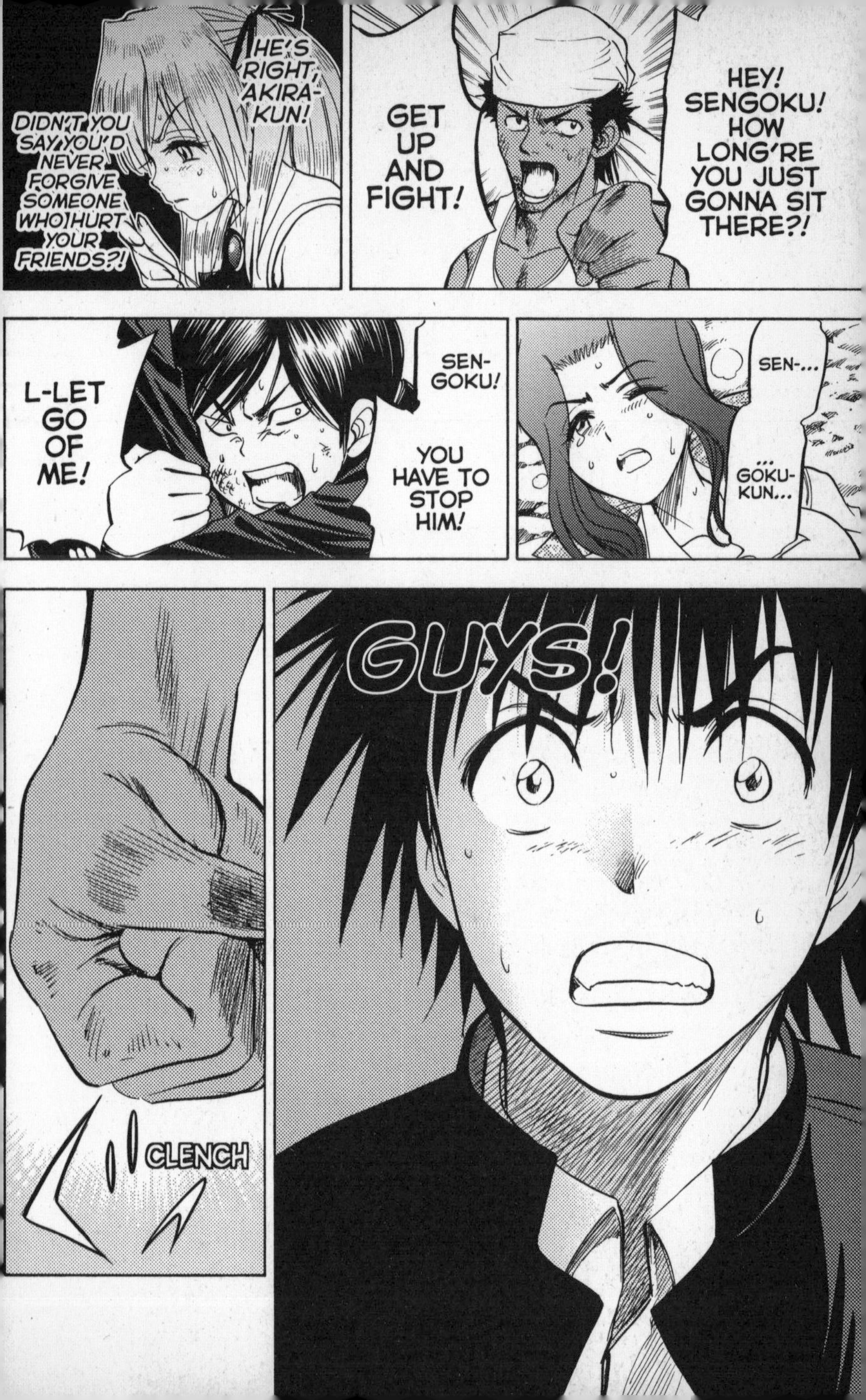
HEY! SENGOKU! HOW LONG'RE YOU JUST GONNA SIT THERE?!
GET UP AND FIGHT!
HE'S RIGHT, AKIRA-KUN!
DIDN'T YOU SAY YOU'D NEVER FORGIVE SOMEONE WHO HURT YOUR FRIENDS?!
SEN-...
...GOKU-KUN...
SEN-GOKU!
YOU HAVE TO STOP HIM!
L-LET GO OF ME!
GUYS!
CLENCH

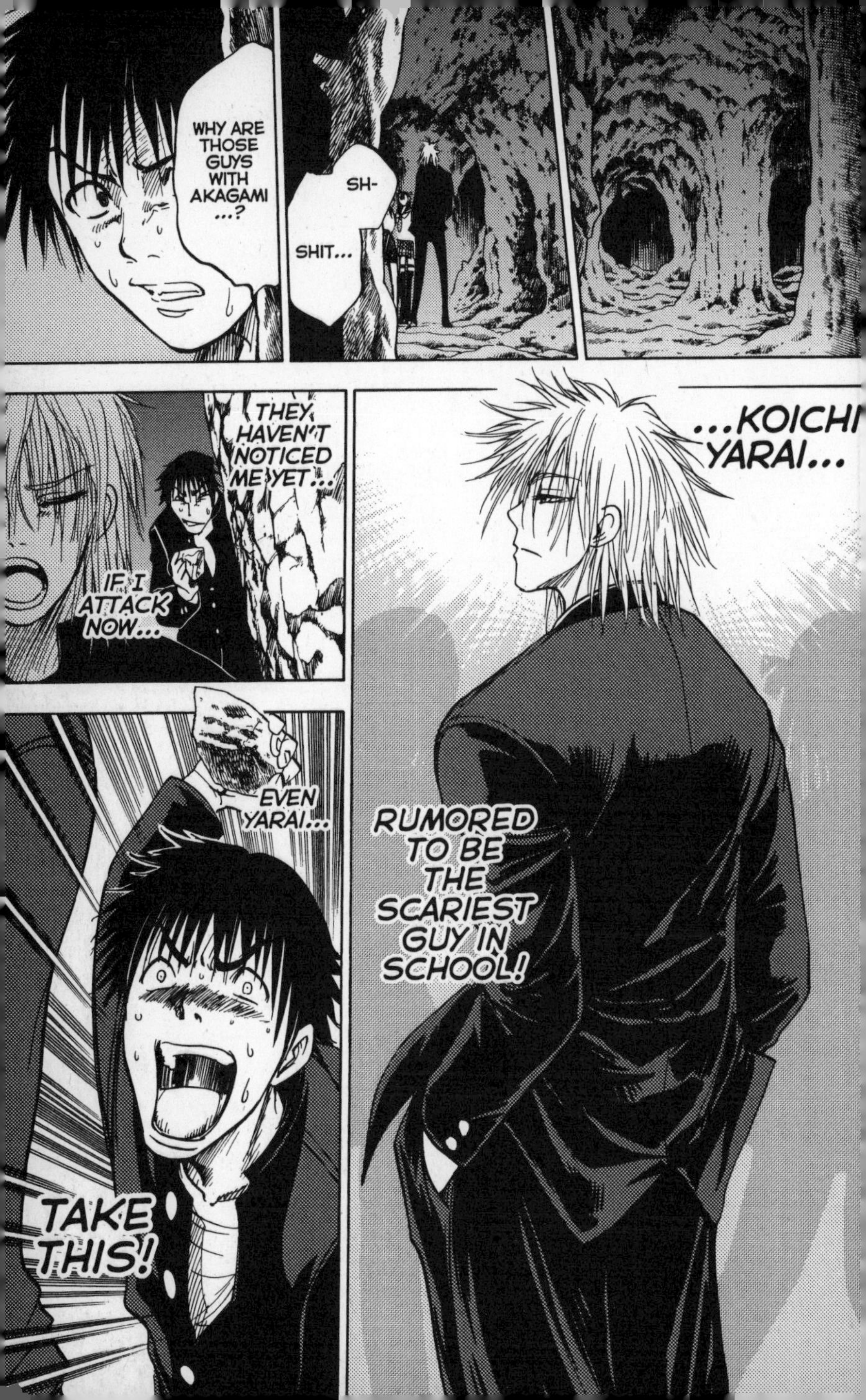
SH-
SHIT...
WHY ARE THOSE GUYS WITH AKAGAMI ...?
...KOICHI YARAI...
RUMORED TO BE THE SCARIEST GUY IN SCHOOL!
THEY HAVEN'T NOTICED ME YET...
IF I ATTACK NOW...
EVEN YARAI...
TAKE THIS!

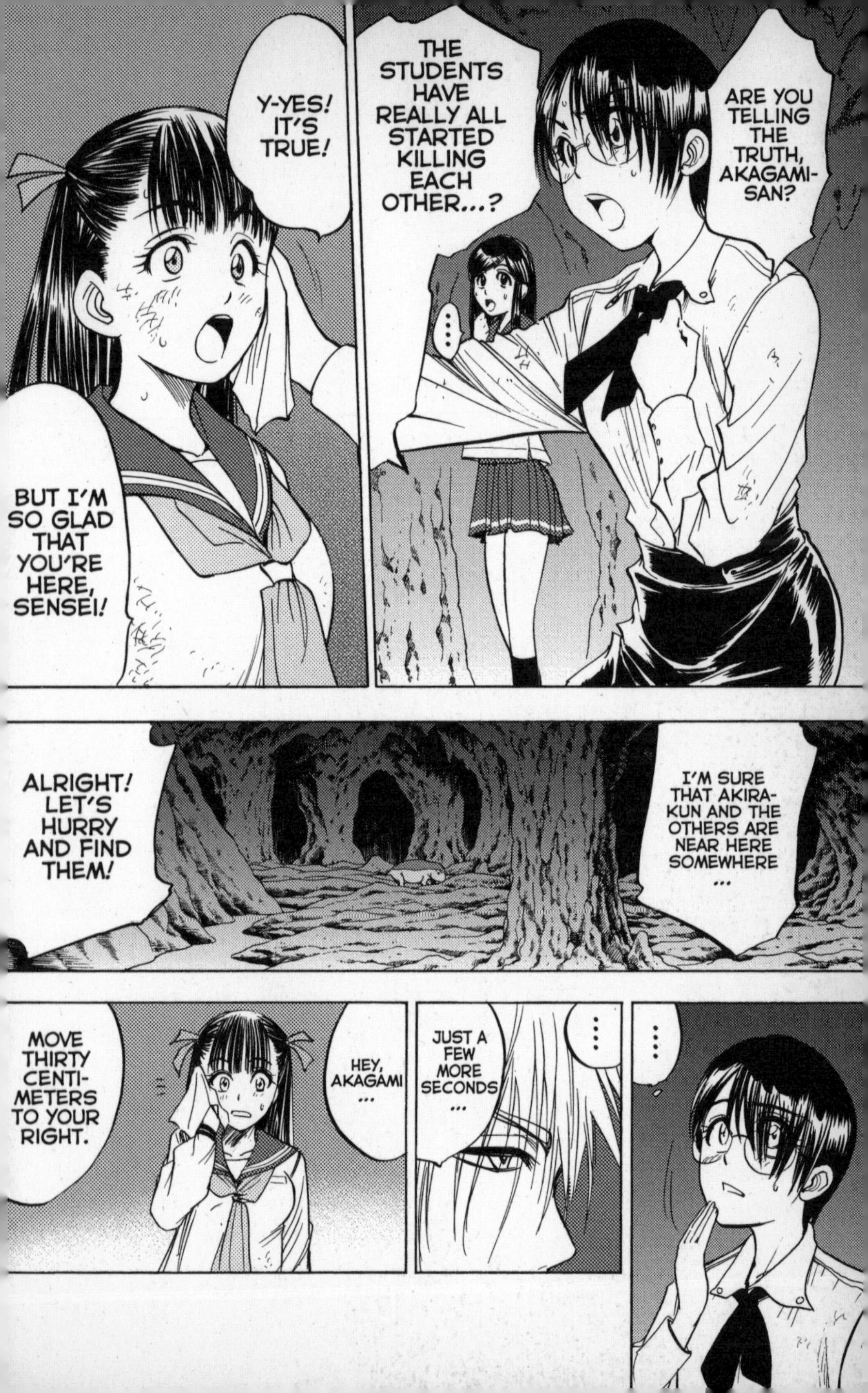
ARE YOU TELLING THE TRUTH, AKAGAMI-SAN?
THE STUDENTS HAVE REALLY ALL STARTED KILLING EACH OTHER...?
...
Y-YES! IT'S TRUE!
BUT I'M SO GLAD THAT YOU'RE HERE, SENSEI!
I'M SURE THAT AKIRA-KUN AND THE OTHERS ARE NEAR HERE SOMEWHERE...
ALRIGHT! LET'S HURRY AND FIND THEM!
...
...
JUST A FEW MORE SECONDS...
HEY, AKAGAMI...
MOVE THIRTY CENTIMETERS TO YOUR RIGHT.

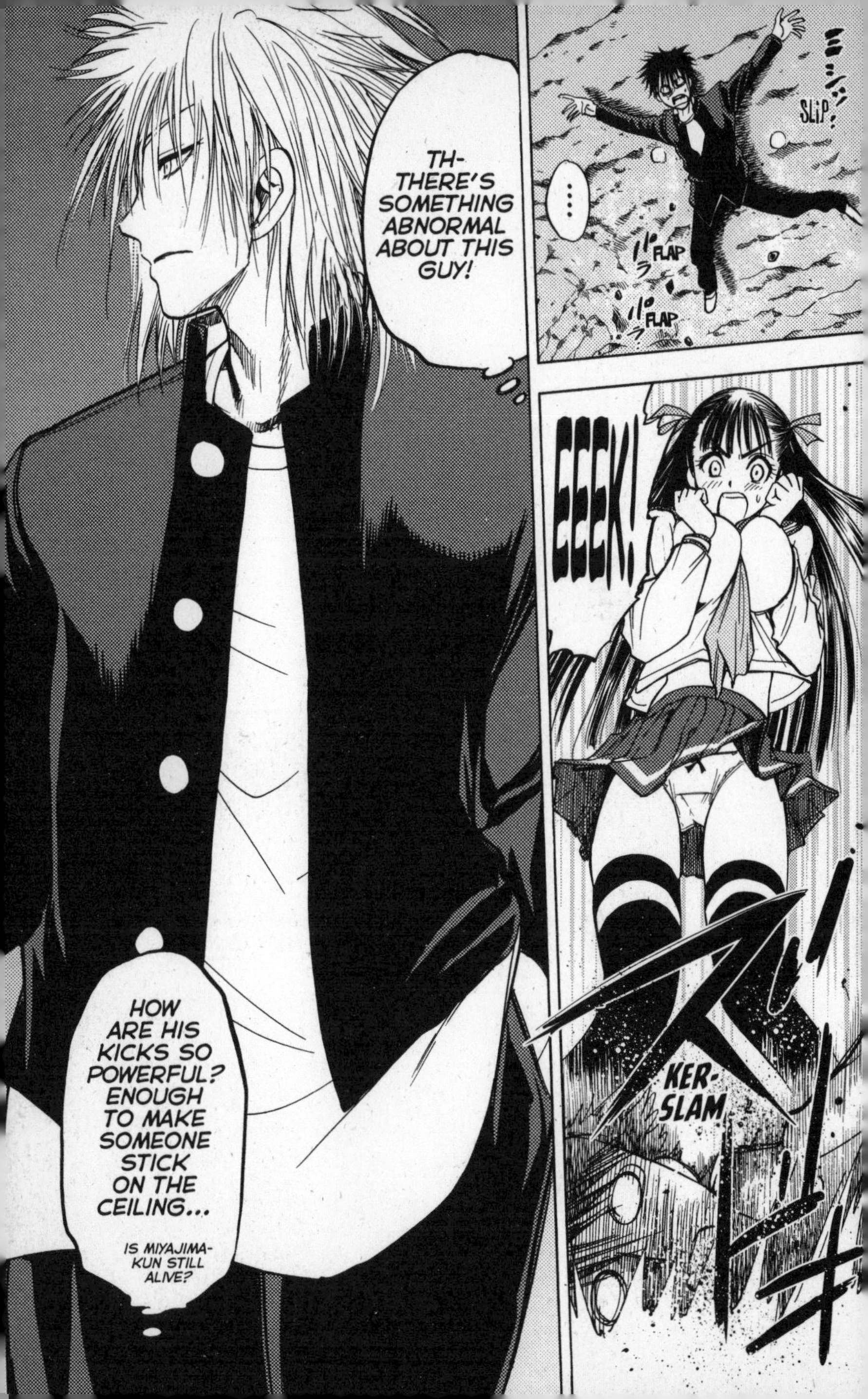
....
SLIP
FLAP
FLAP
EEEK!
KER-SLAM
TH- THERE'S SOMETHING ABNORMAL ABOUT THIS GUY!
HOW ARE HIS KICKS SO POWERFUL? ENOUGH TO MAKE SOMEONE STICK ON THE CEILING...
IS MIYAJIMA-KUN STILL ALIVE?

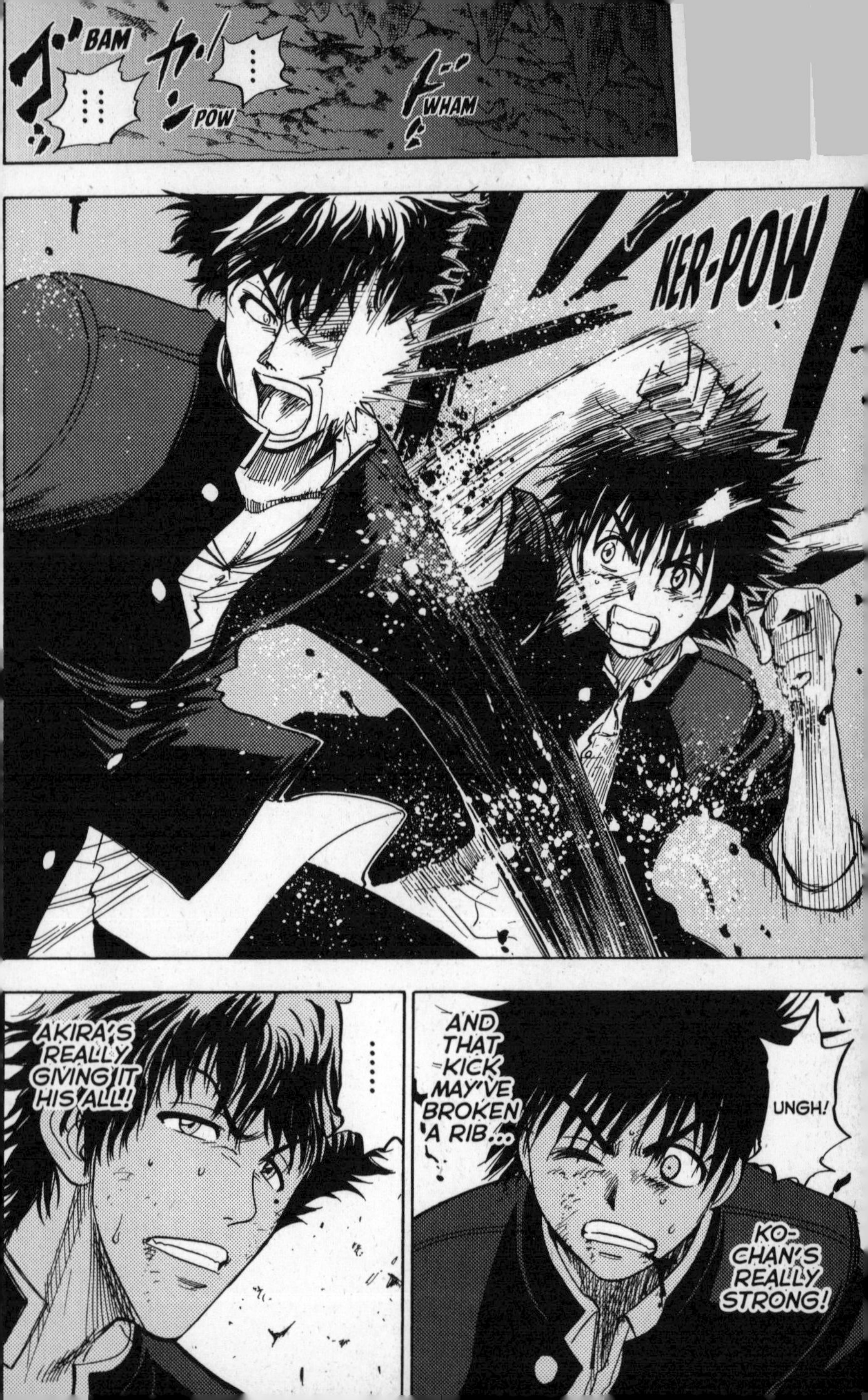
WHAM
...
POW
...
BAM
...
KER-POW
UNGH!
AND THAT KICK MAY'VE BROKEN A RIB...
KO-CHAN'S REALLY STRONG!
......
AKIRA'S REALLY GIVING IT HIS ALL!

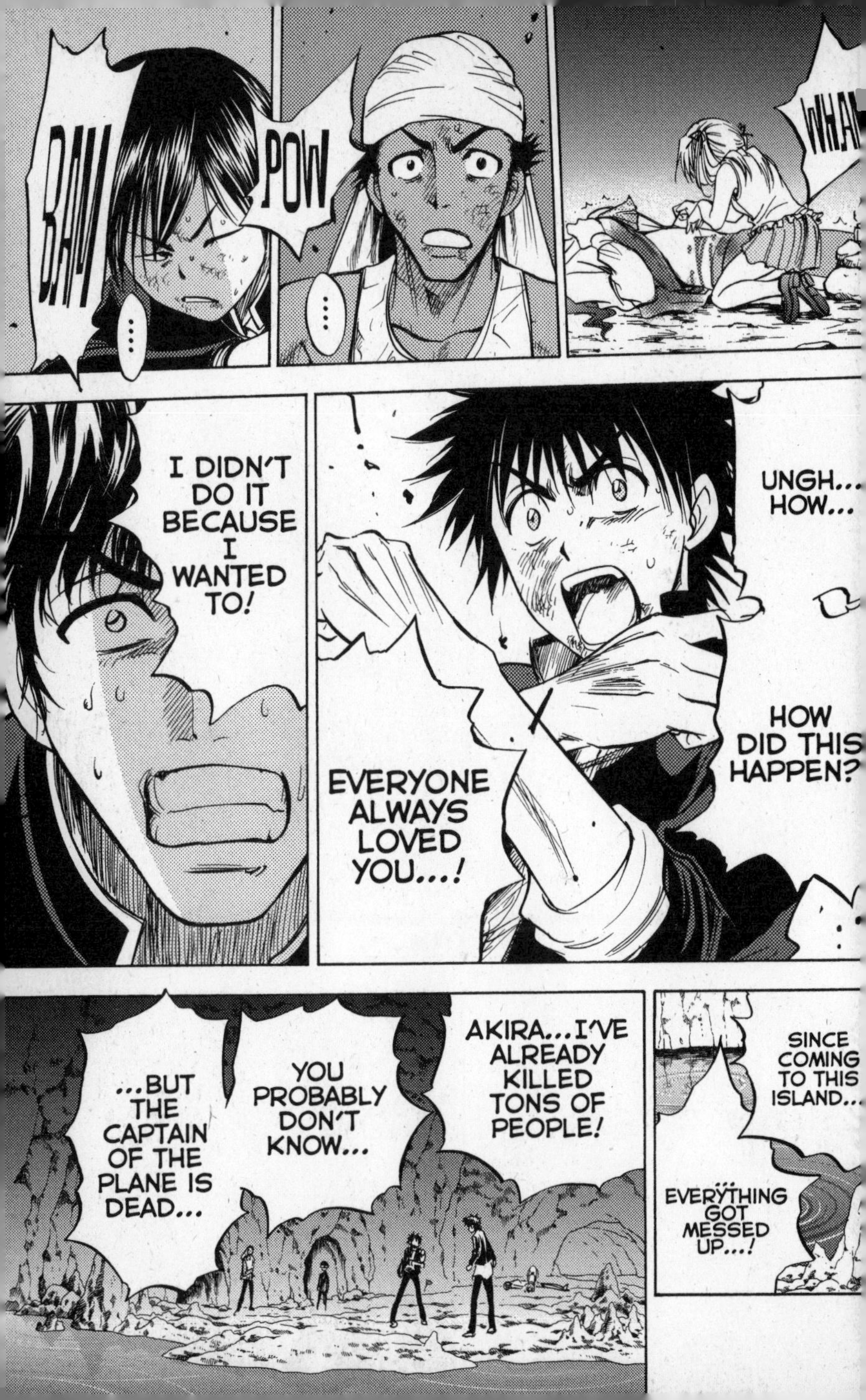
WHA
POW
....
BAM
....
UNGH... HOW...
HOW DID THIS HAPPEN?
EVERYONE ALWAYS LOVED YOU...!
I DIDN'T DO IT BECAUSE I WANTED TO!
SINCE COMING TO THIS ISLAND...
...EVERYTHING GOT MESSED UP...!
AKIRA...I'VE ALREADY KILLED TONS OF PEOPLE!
YOU PROBABLY DON'T KNOW...
...BUT THE CAPTAIN OF THE PLANE IS DEAD...

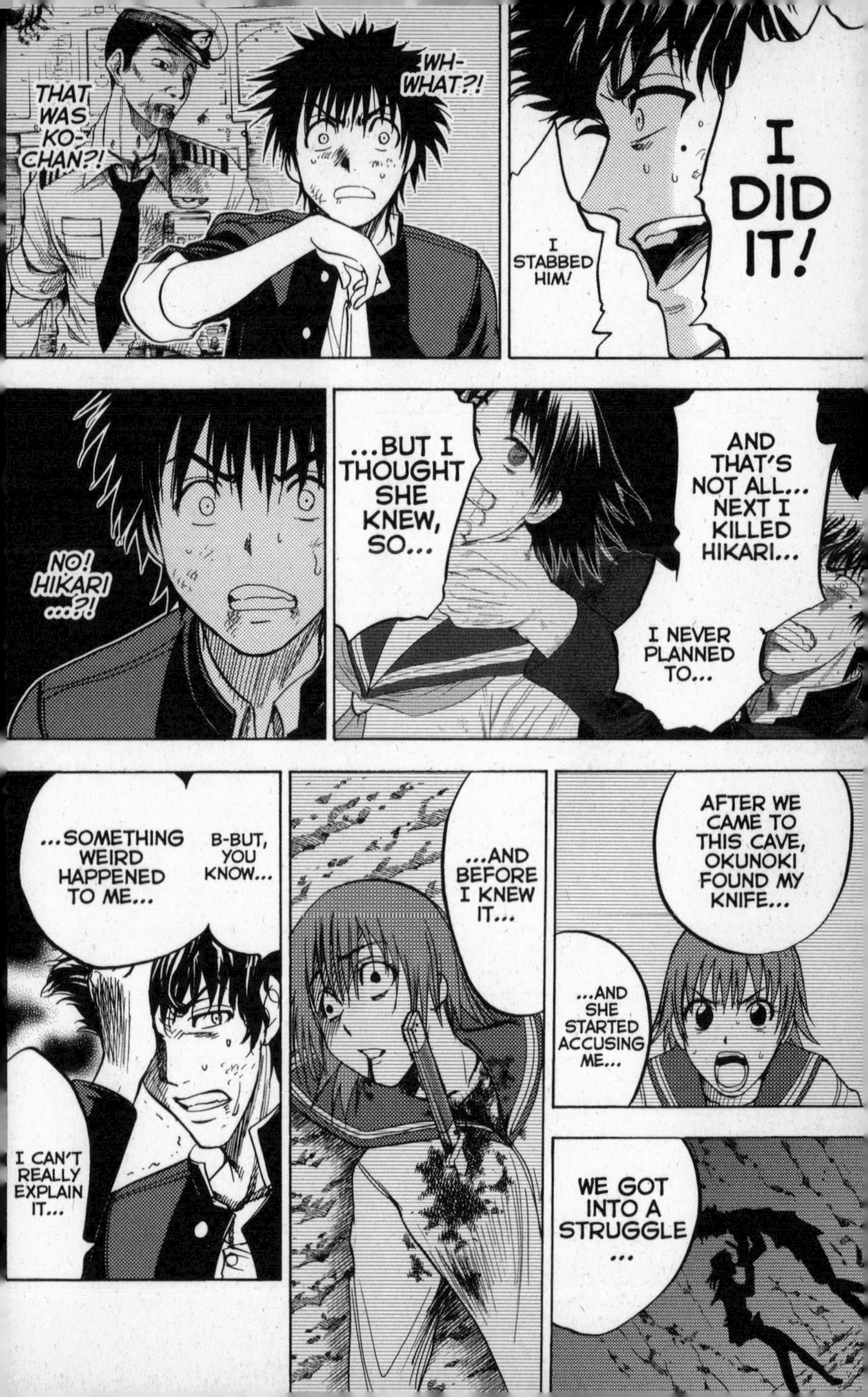
I DID IT!
I STABBED HIM!
WH-WHAT?!
THAT WAS KO-CHAN?!
AND THAT'S NOT ALL... NEXT I KILLED HIKARI...
I NEVER PLANNED TO...
...BUT I THOUGHT SHE KNEW, SO...
NO! HIKARI...?!
AFTER WE CAME TO THIS CAVE, OKUNOKI FOUND MY KNIFE...
...AND SHE STARTED ACCUSING ME...
WE GOT INTO A STRUGGLE ...
...AND BEFORE I KNEW IT...
B-BUT, YOU KNOW...
...SOMETHING WEIRD HAPPENED TO ME...
I CAN'T REALLY EXPLAIN IT...

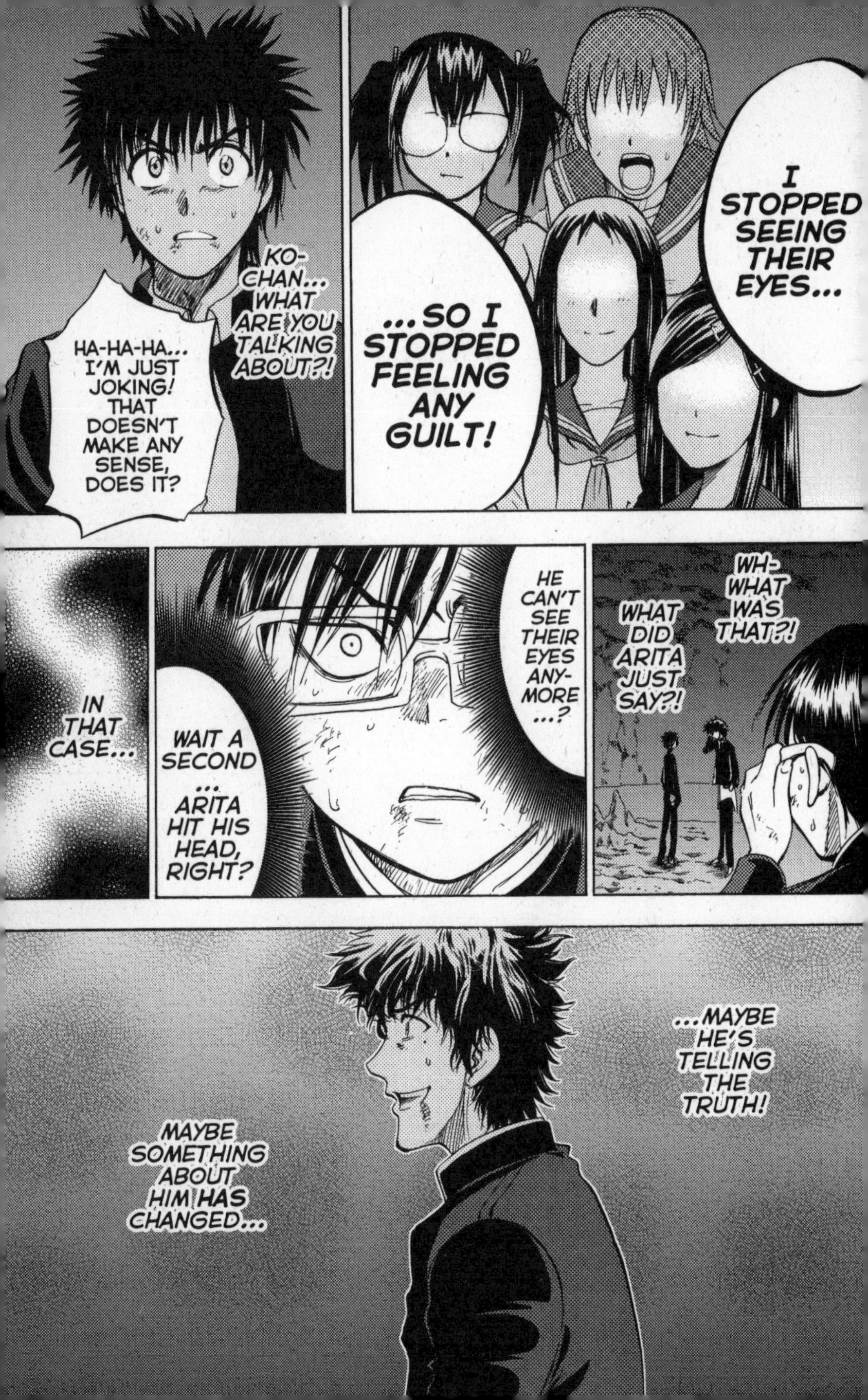
I STOPPED SEEING THEIR EYES...
...SO I STOPPED FEELING ANY GUILT!
KO-CHAN... WHAT ARE YOU TALKING ABOUT?!
HA-HA-HA... I'M JUST JOKING! THAT DOESN'T MAKE ANY SENSE, DOES IT?
WH-WHAT WAS THAT?!
WHAT DID ARITA JUST SAY?!
HE CAN'T SEE THEIR EYES ANY-MORE...?
WAIT A SECOND... ARITA HIT HIS HEAD, RIGHT?
IN THAT CASE...
...MAYBE HE'S TELLING THE TRUTH!
MAYBE SOMETHING ABOUT HIM HAS CHANGED...

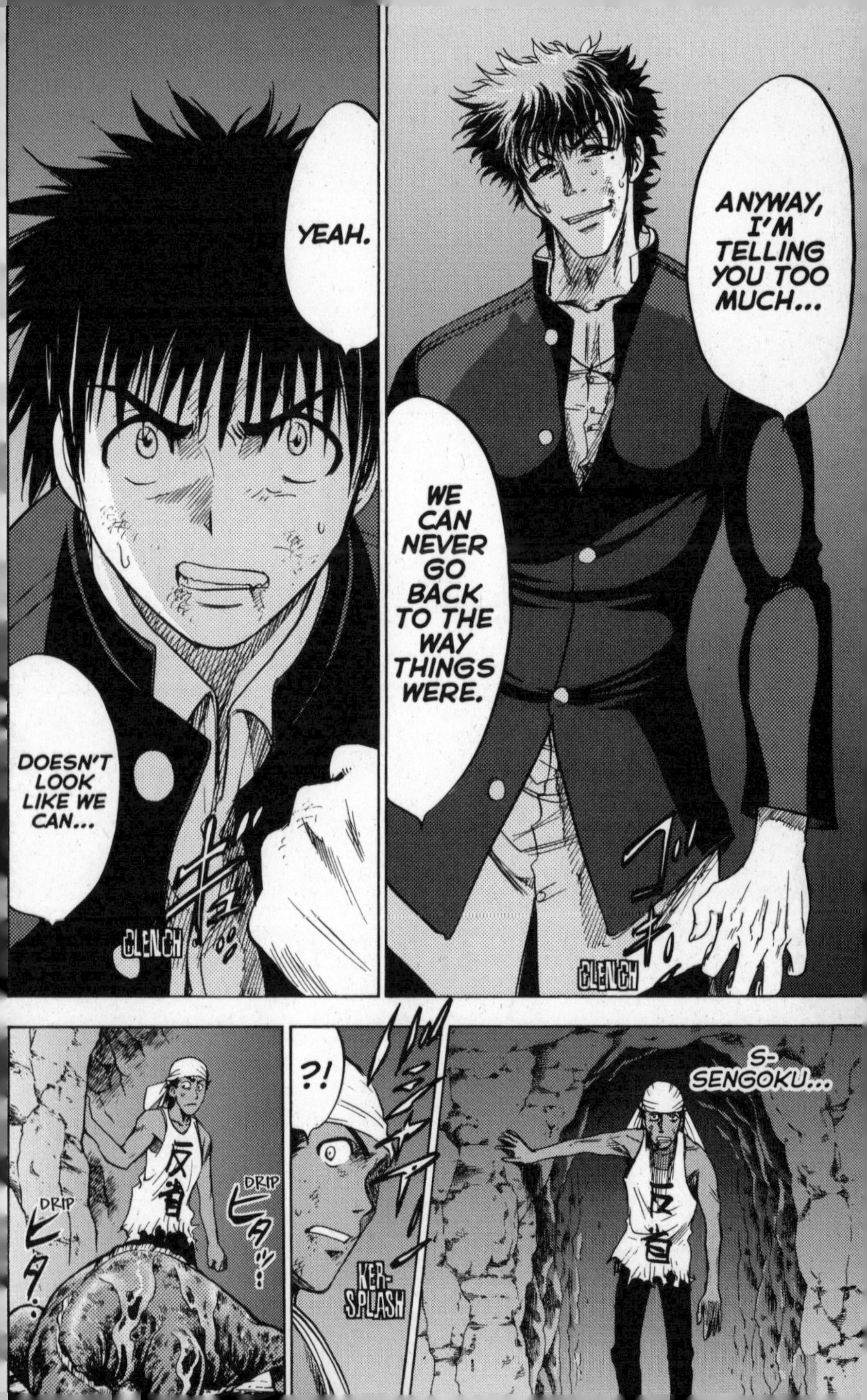
ANYWAY, I'M TELLING YOU TOO MUCH...
WE CAN NEVER GO BACK TO THE WAY THINGS WERE.
CLENCH
YEAH.
DOESN'T LOOK LIKE WE CAN...
CLENCH
S-SENGOKU...
?!
KER-SPLASH
DRIP
DRIP

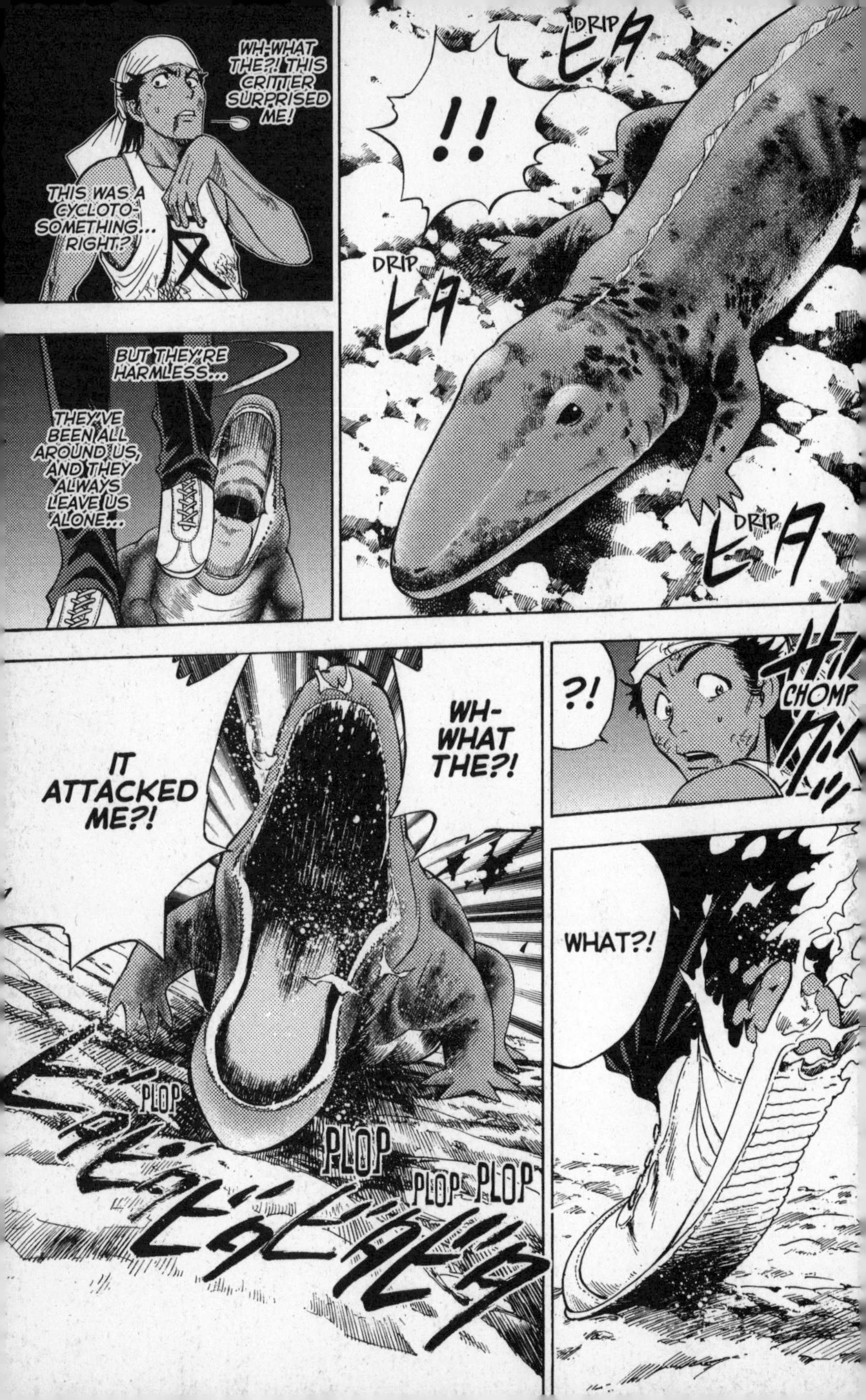
DRIP
!!
DRIP
DRIP
WH-WHAT THE?! THIS CRITTER SURPRISED ME!
THIS WAS A CYCLOTO-SOMETHING... RIGHT?
BUT THEY'RE HARMLESS...
THEY'VE BEEN ALL AROUND US, AND THEY ALWAYS LEAVE US ALONE...
?!
CHOMP
WHAT?!
WH-WHAT THE?!
IT ATTACKED ME?!
PLOP
PLOP
PLOP
PLOP

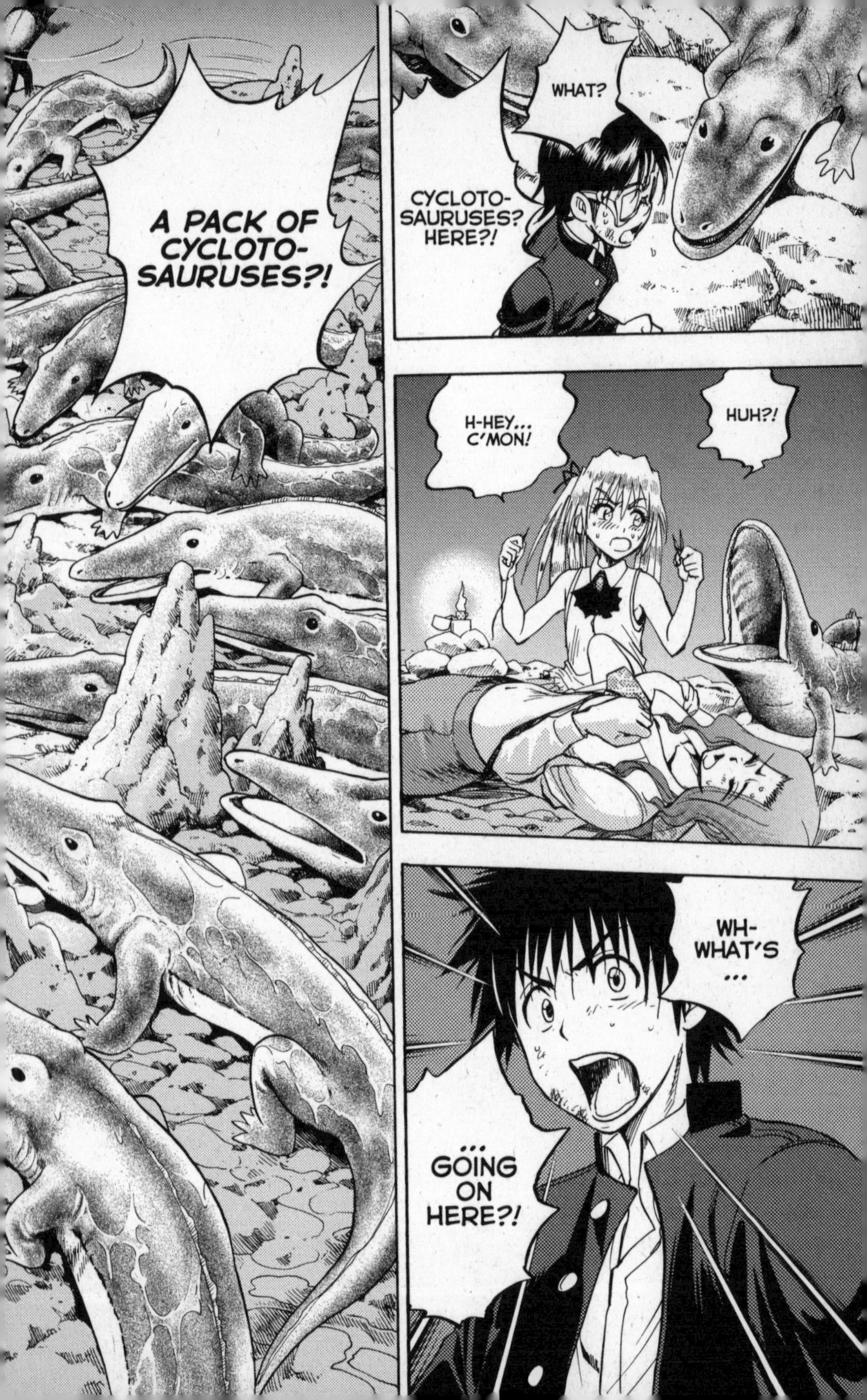
WHAT?
CYCLOTO-SAURUSES? HERE?!
HUH?!
H-HEY... C'MON!
WH-WHAT'S ...
... GOING ON HERE?!
A PACK OF CYCLOTO-SAURUSES?!

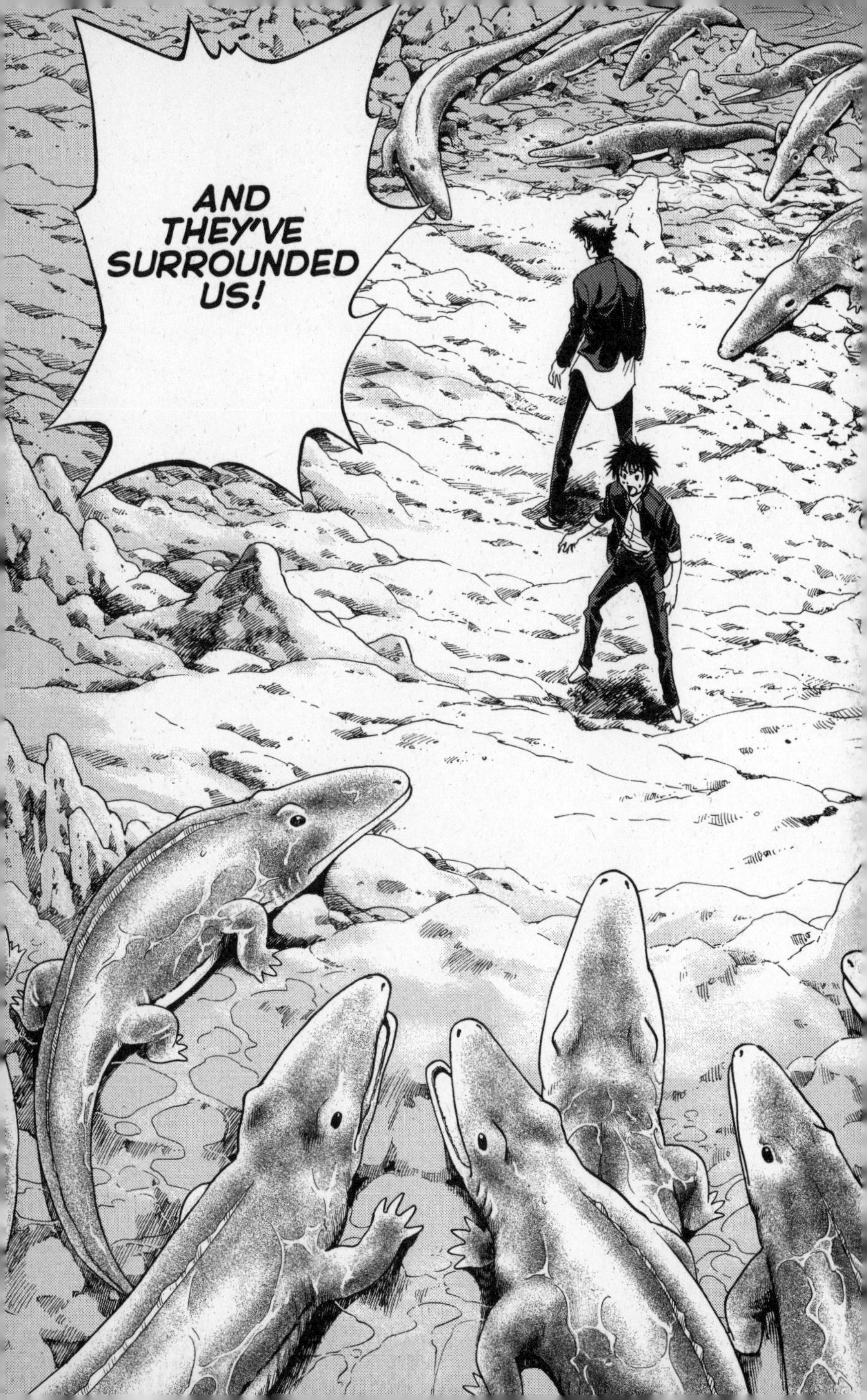
AND THEY'VE SURROUNDED US!

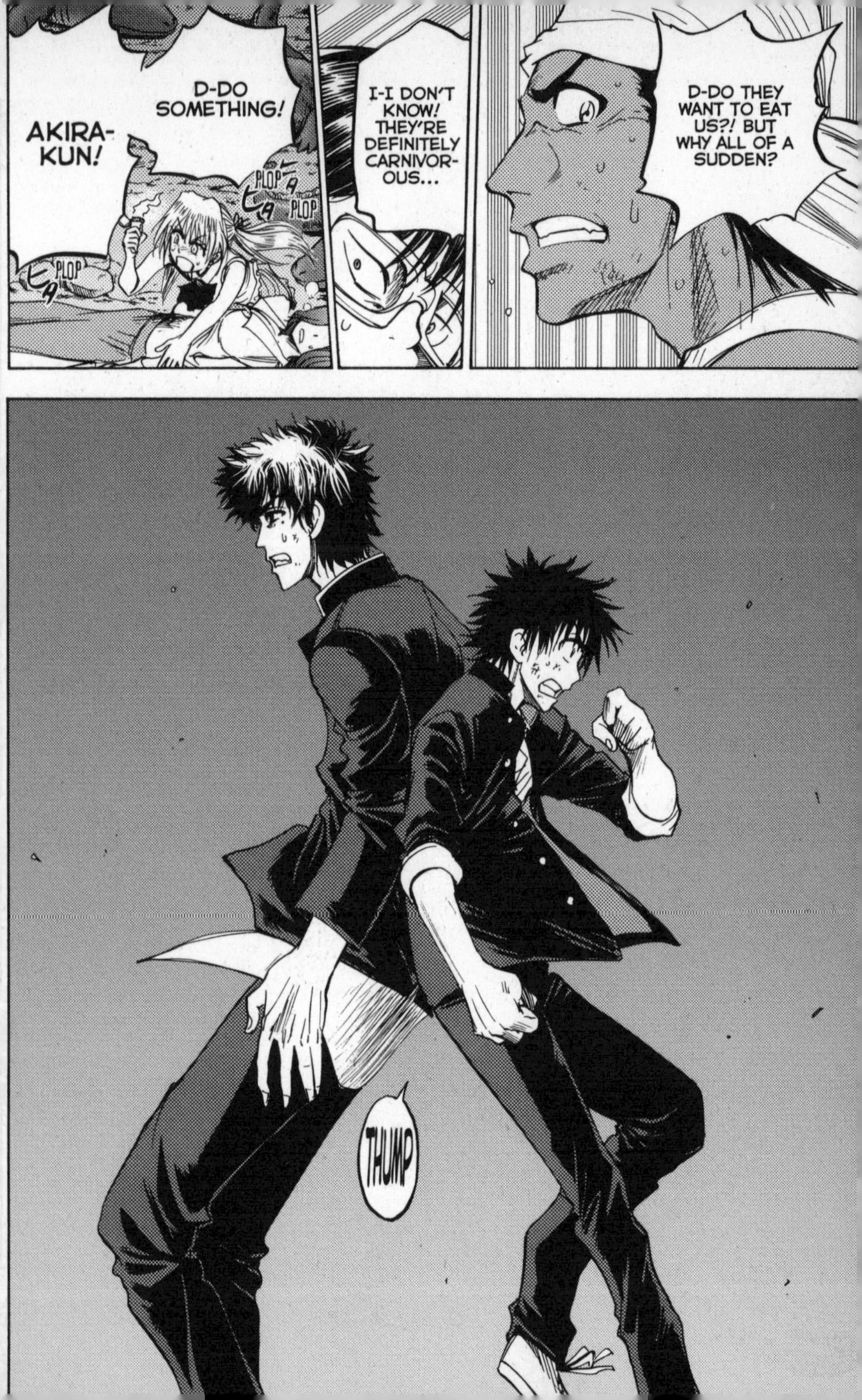
D-DO THEY WANT TO EAT US?! BUT WHY ALL OF A SUDDEN?
I-I DON'T KNOW! THEY'RE DEFINITELY CARNIVOROUS...
D-DO SOMETHING!
AKIRA-KUN!
PLOP
PLOP
PLOP
THUMP

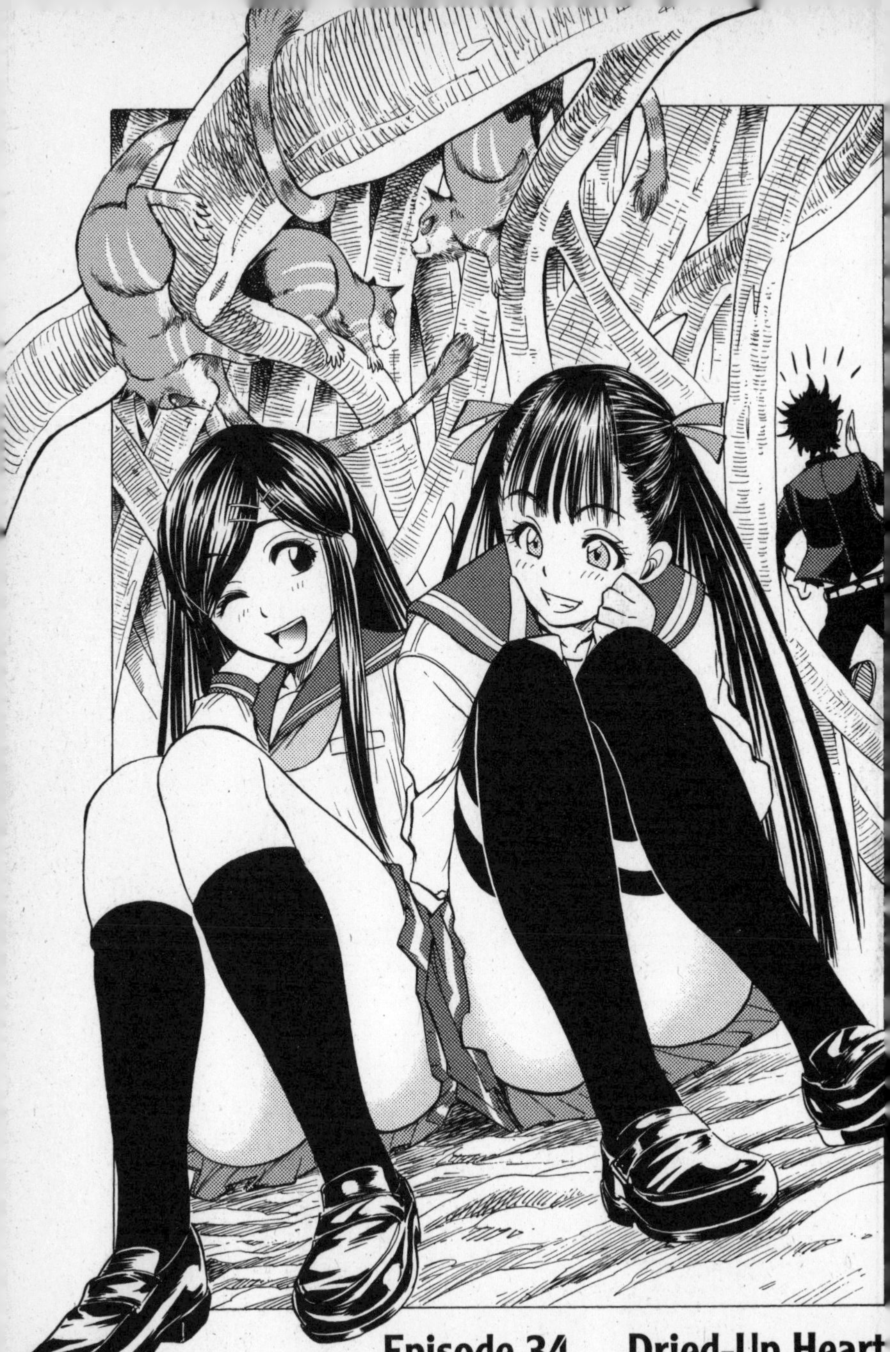

Episode 34 Dried-Up Heart

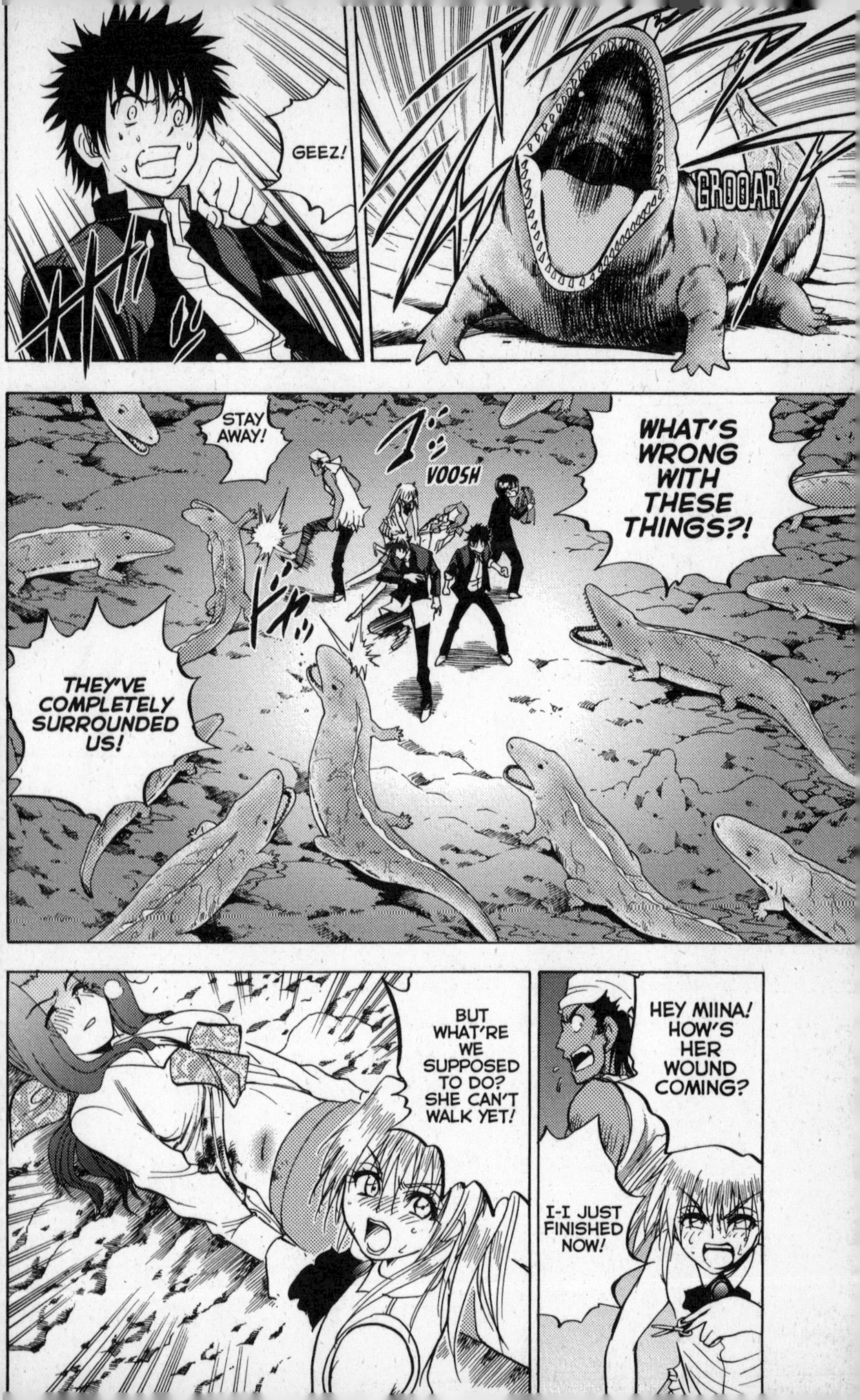
GROOAR
GEEZ!
WHAT'S WRONG WITH THESE THINGS?!
VOOSH
STAY AWAY!
THEY'VE COMPLETELY SURROUNDED US!
HEY MIINA! HOW'S HER WOUND COMING?
I-I JUST FINISHED NOW!
BUT WHAT'RE WE SUPPOSED TO DO? SHE CAN'T WALK YET!

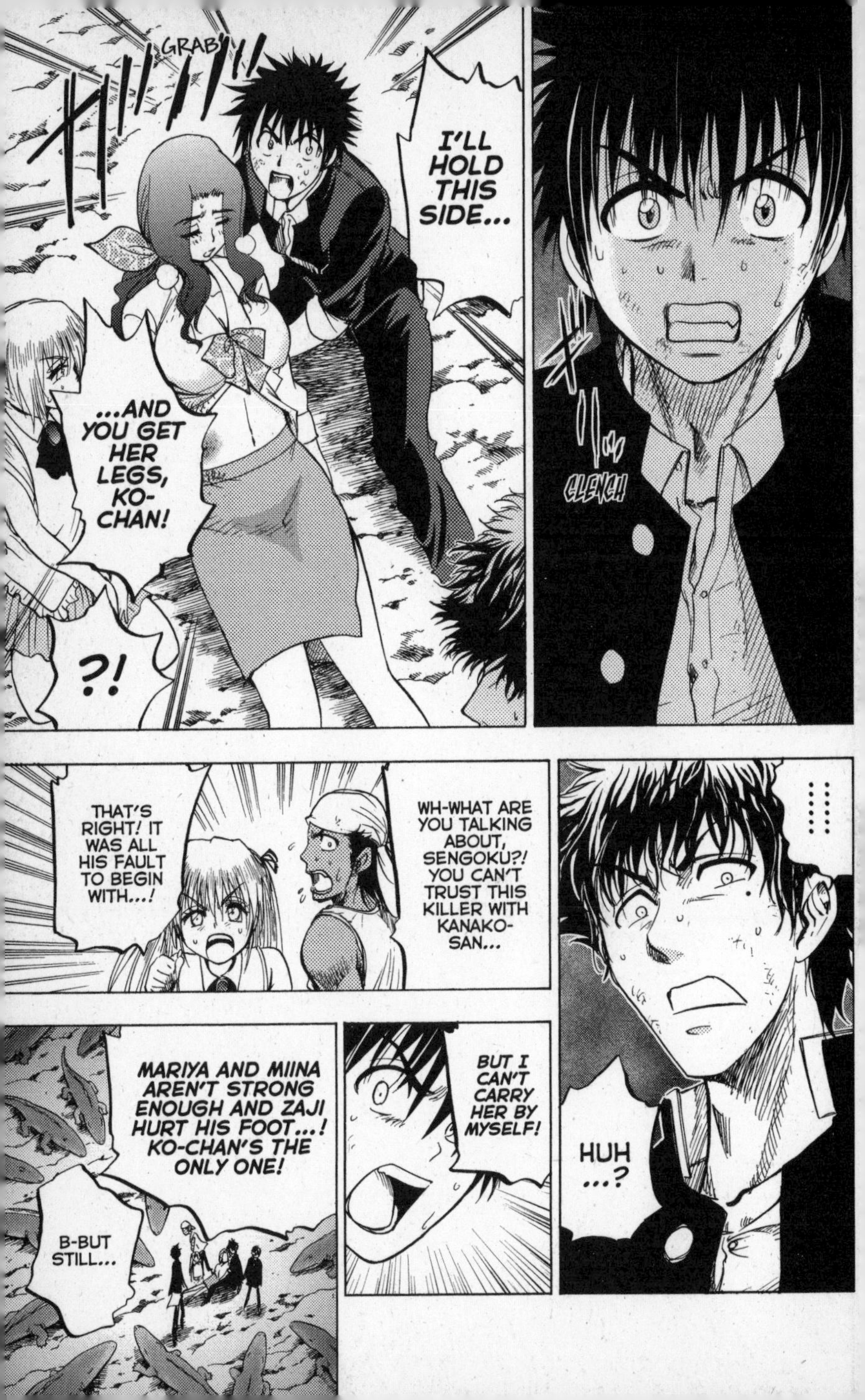
CLENCH
GRAB
I'LL HOLD THIS SIDE...
...AND YOU GET HER LEGS, KO-CHAN!
?!
......
HUH ...?
WH-WHAT ARE YOU TALKING ABOUT, SENGOKU?! YOU CAN'T TRUST THIS KILLER WITH KANAKO-SAN...
THAT'S RIGHT! IT WAS ALL HIS FAULT TO BEGIN WITH...!
BUT I CAN'T CARRY HER BY MYSELF!
MARIYA AND MIINA AREN'T STRONG ENOUGH AND ZAJI HURT HIS FOOT...! KO-CHAN'S THE ONLY ONE!
B-BUT STILL...

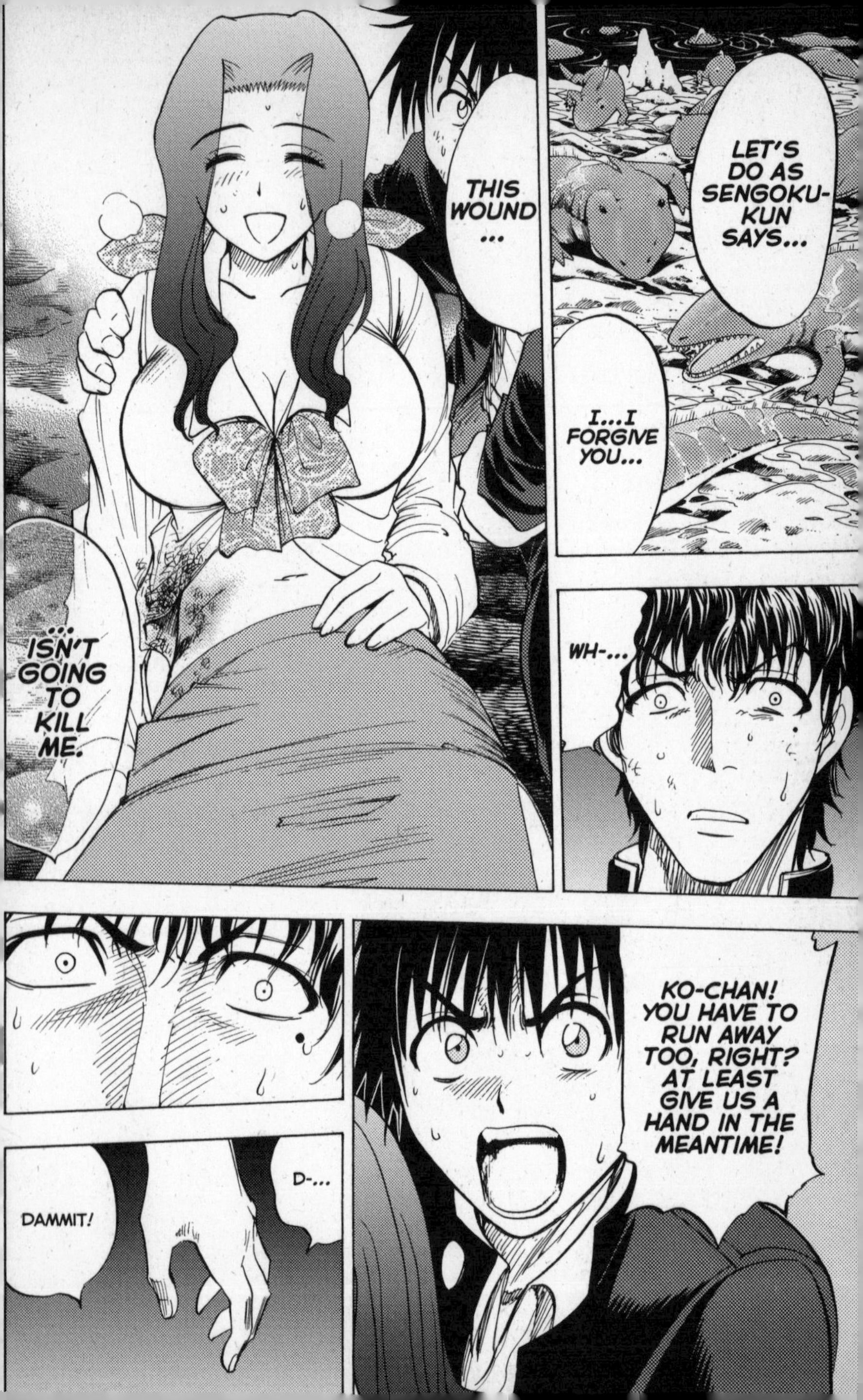
LET'S DO AS SENGOKU-KUN SAYS...
I...I FORGIVE YOU...
WH-...
THIS WOUND ...
...ISN'T GOING TO KILL ME.
KO-CHAN! YOU HAVE TO RUN AWAY TOO, RIGHT? AT LEAST GIVE US A HAND IN THE MEANTIME!
D-...
DAMMIT!

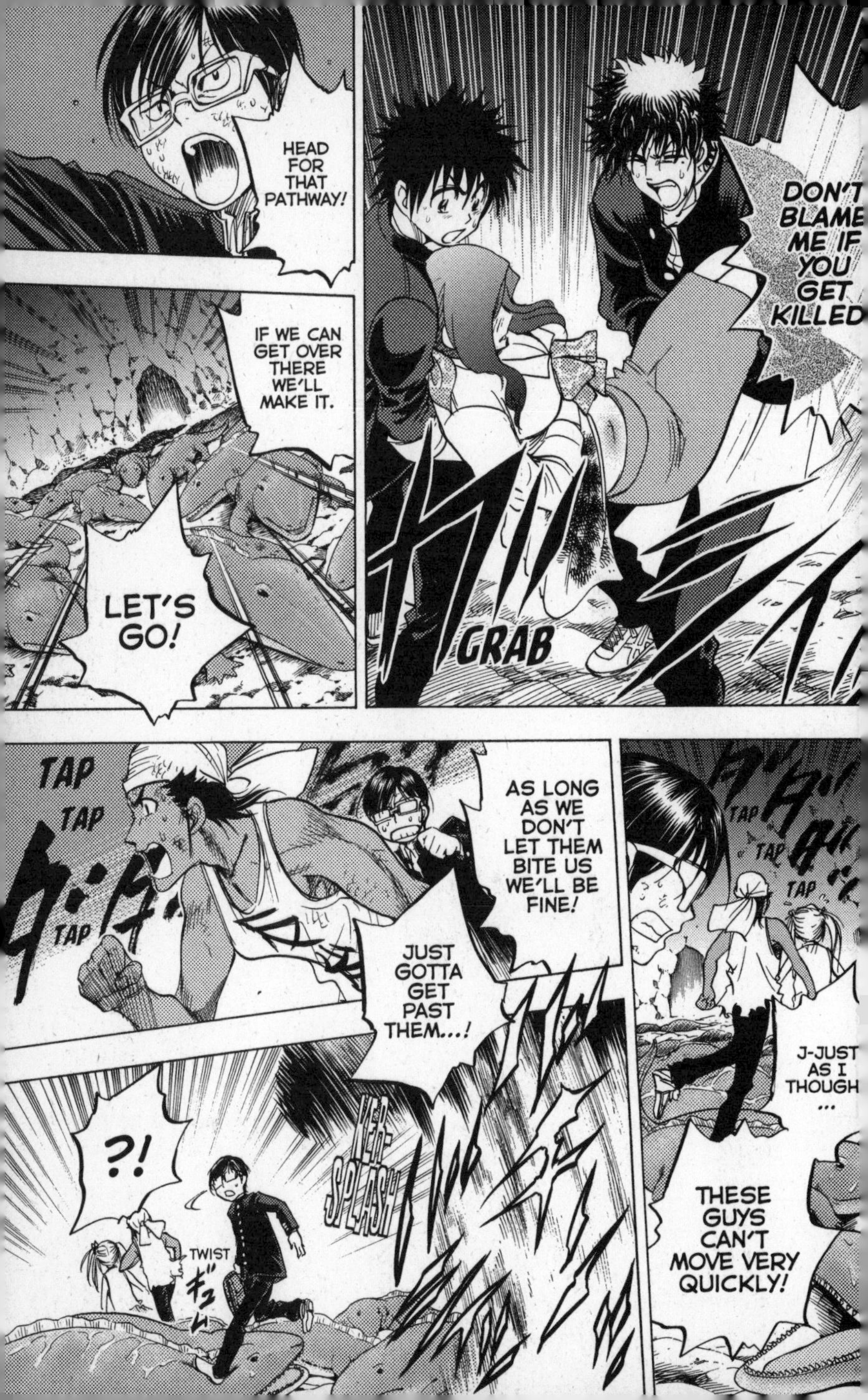

DON'T BLAME ME IF YOU GET KILLED
GRAB
HEAD FOR THAT PATHWAY!
IF WE CAN GET OVER THERE WE'LL MAKE IT.
LET'S GO!
TAP
TAP
TAP
J-JUST AS I THOUGH ...
THESE GUYS CAN'T MOVE VERY QUICKLY!
TAP
TAP
TAP
AS LONG AS WE DON'T LET THEM BITE US WE'LL BE FINE!
JUST GOTTA GET PAST THEM...!
SPLASH
?!
TWIST

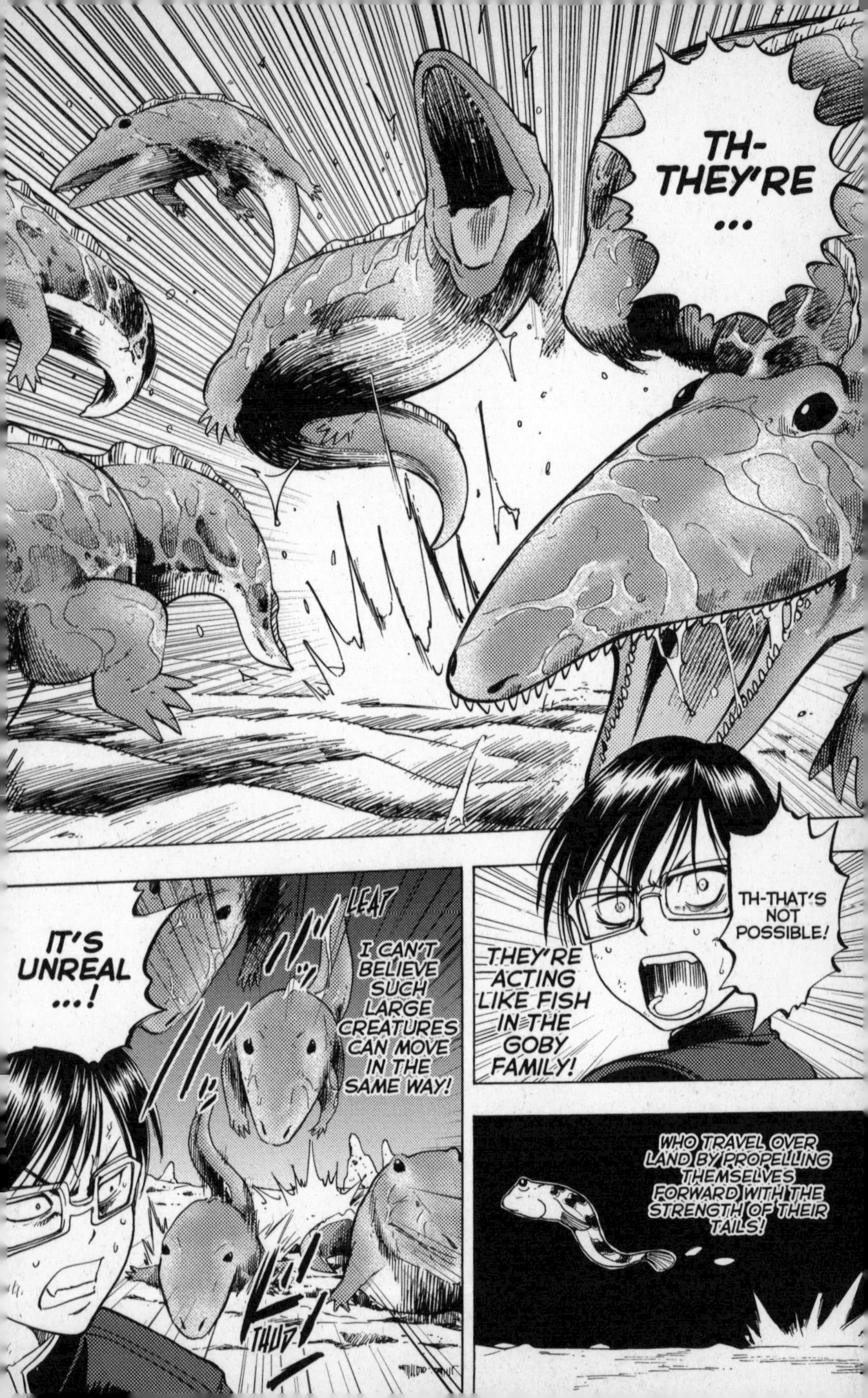
TH- THEY'RE ...
TH-THAT'S NOT POSSIBLE!
THEY'RE ACTING LIKE FISH IN THE GOBY FAMILY!
WHO TRAVEL OVER LAND BY PROPELLING THEMSELVES FORWARD WITH THE STRENGTH OF THEIR TAILS!
LEAP
I CAN'T BELIEVE SUCH LARGE CREATURES CAN MOVE IN THE SAME WAY!
IT'S UNREAL ...!
THUD

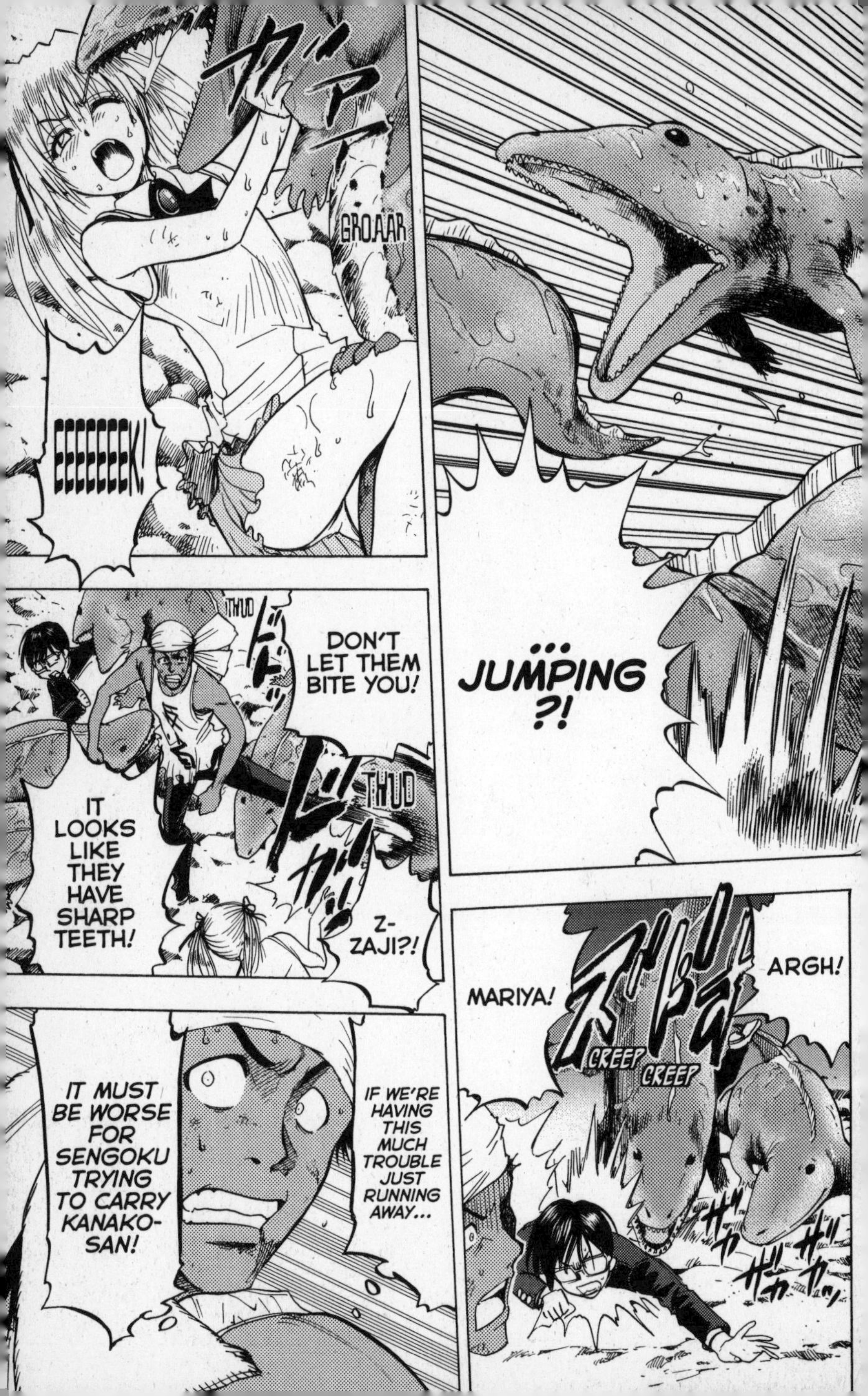
...JUMPING ?!
GROAAR
EEEEEEEK!
THUD
DON'T LET THEM BITE YOU!
THUD
Z-ZAJI?!
IT LOOKS LIKE THEY HAVE SHARP TEETH!
ARGH!
MARIYA!
CREEP CREEP
IF WE'RE HAVING THIS MUCH TROUBLE JUST RUNNING AWAY...
IT MUST BE WORSE FOR SENGOKU TRYING TO CARRY KANAKO-SAN!

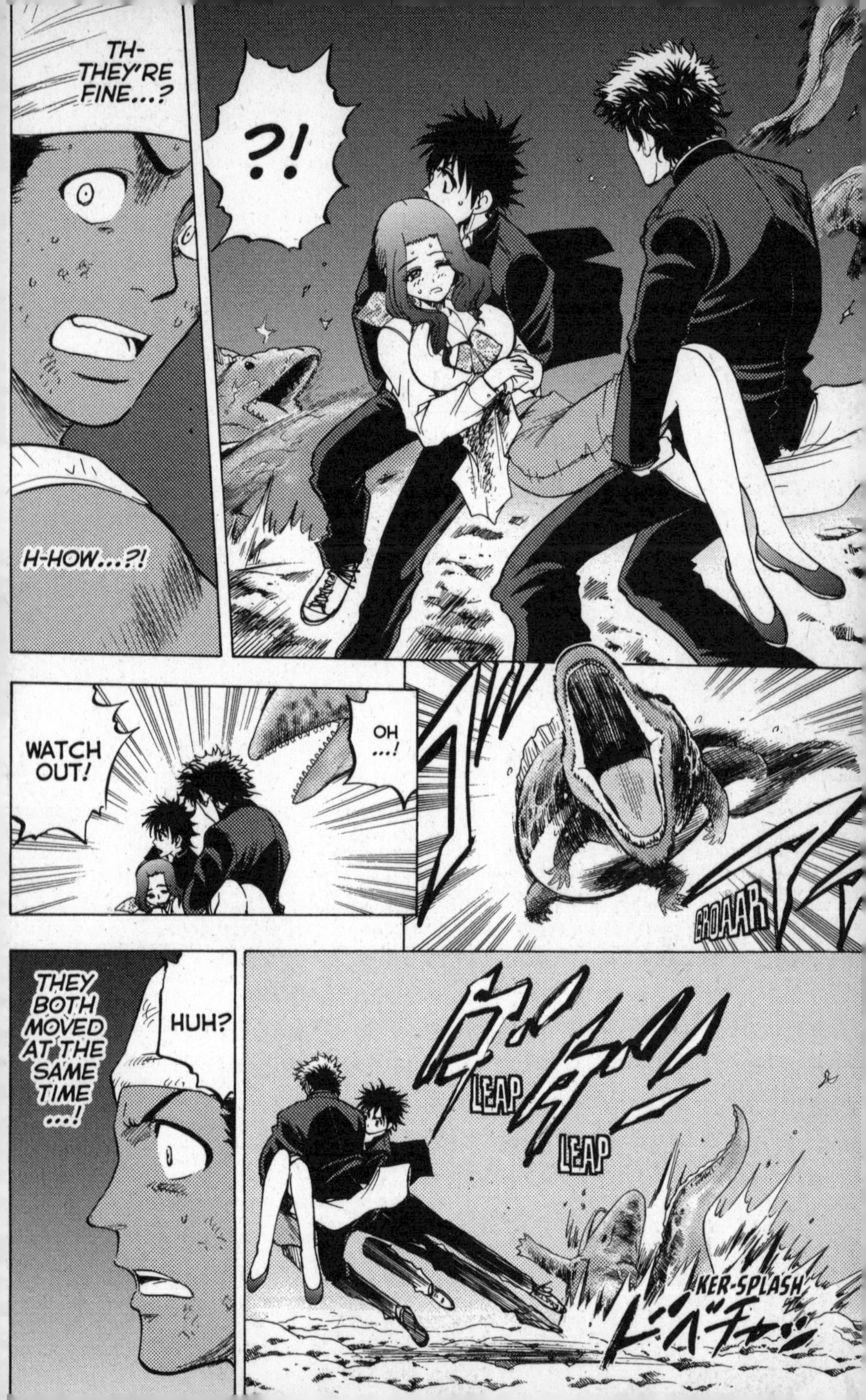
?!
TH-THEY'RE FINE...?
H-HOW...?!
GROAAR
OH ...!
WATCH OUT!
LEAP
LEAP
KER-SPLASH
HUH?
THEY BOTH MOVED AT THE SAME TIME ...!

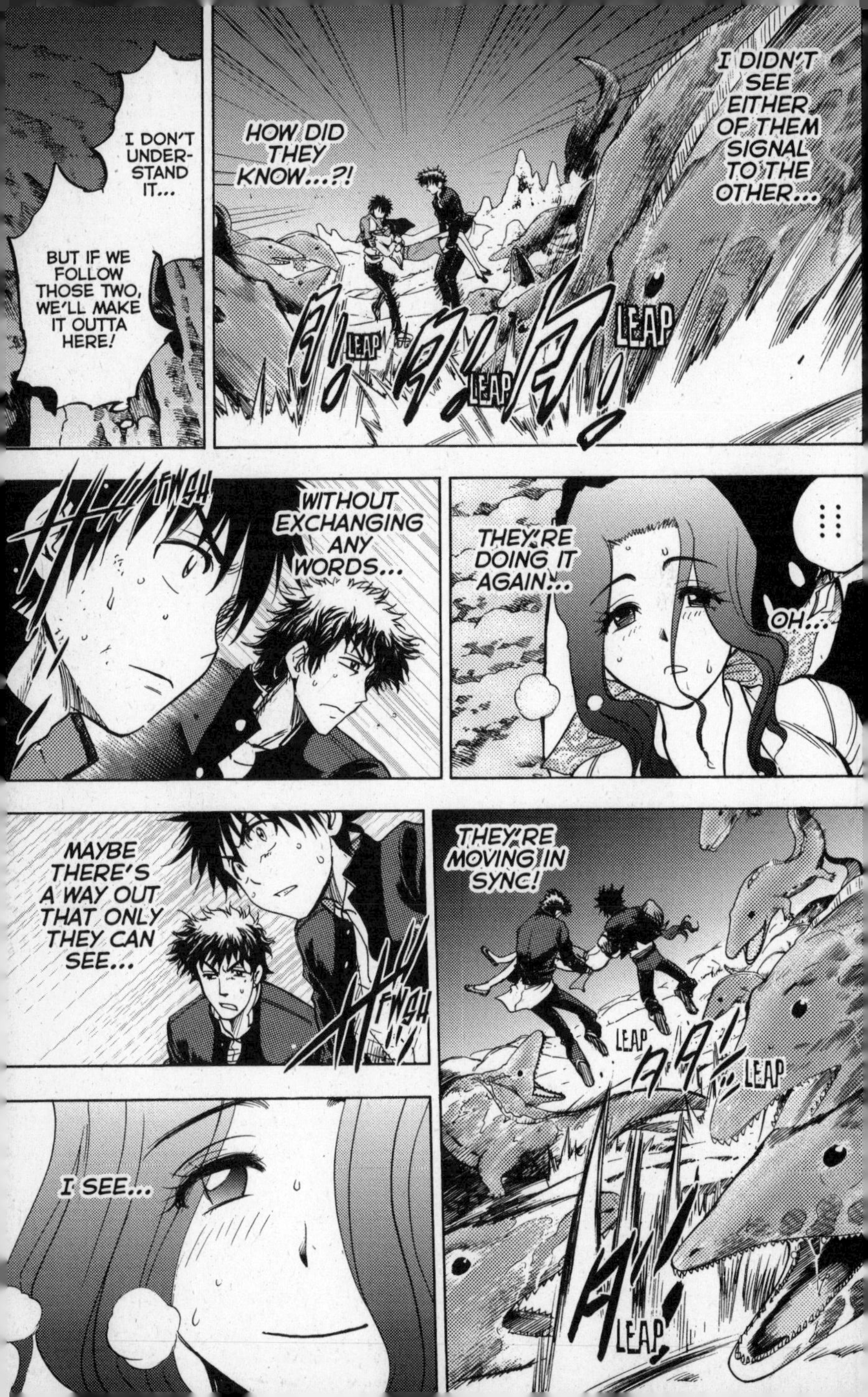
I DIDN'T SEE EITHER OF THEM SIGNAL TO THE OTHER...
HOW DID THEY KNOW...?!
LEAP
LEAP
LEAP
I DON'T UNDER-STAND IT...
BUT IF WE FOLLOW THOSE TWO, WE'LL MAKE IT OUTTA HERE!
......
OH...
THEY'RE DOING IT AGAIN...
FWSH
WITHOUT EXCHANGING ANY WORDS...
THEY'RE MOVING IN SYNC!
LEAP
LEAP
LEAP
MAYBE THERE'S A WAY OUT THAT ONLY THEY CAN SEE...
FWSH
I SEE...

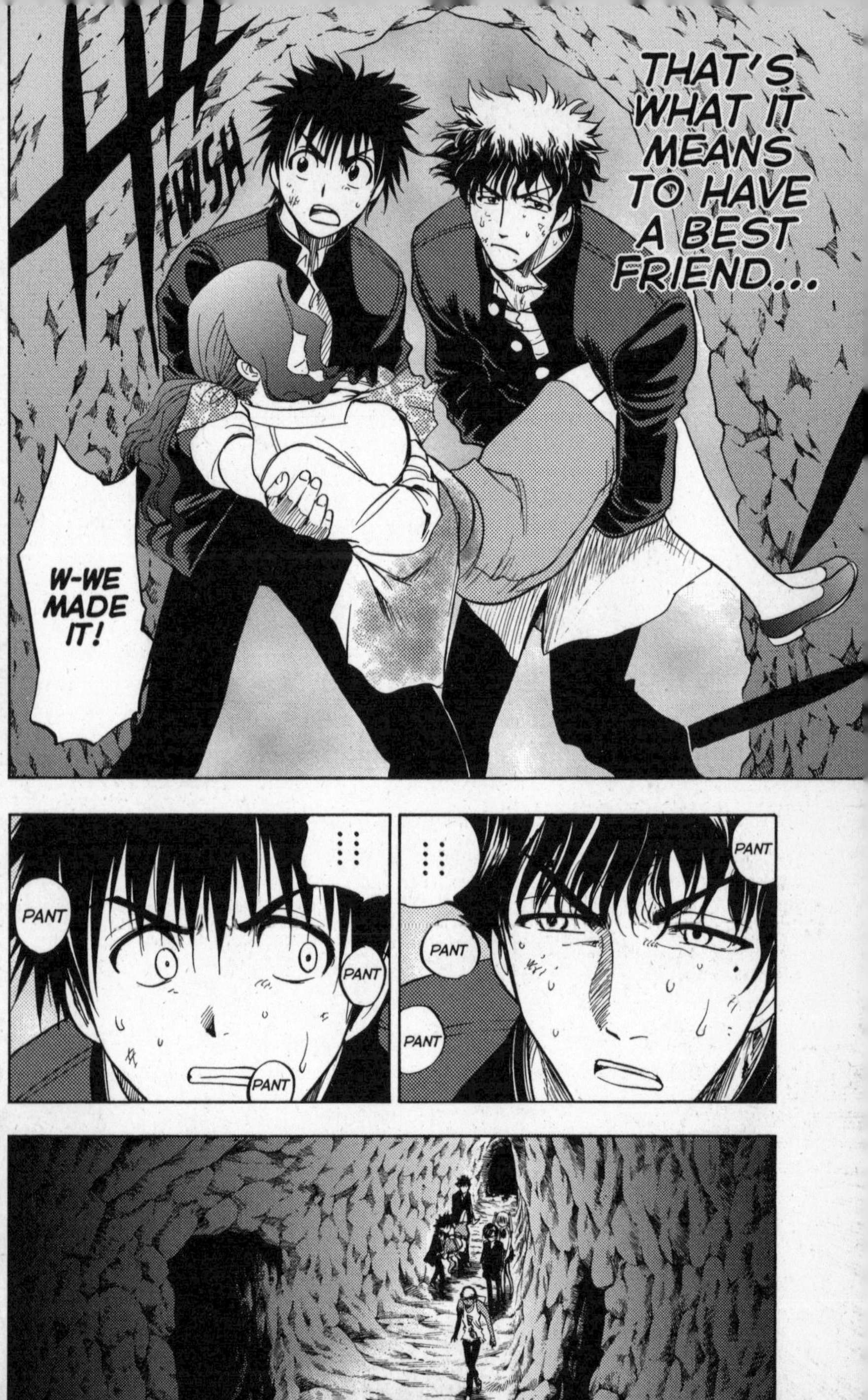
THAT'S WHAT IT MEANS TO HAVE A BEST FRIEND...
FWISH
W-WE MADE IT!
......
PANT
PANT
PANT
......
PANT
PANT
PANT

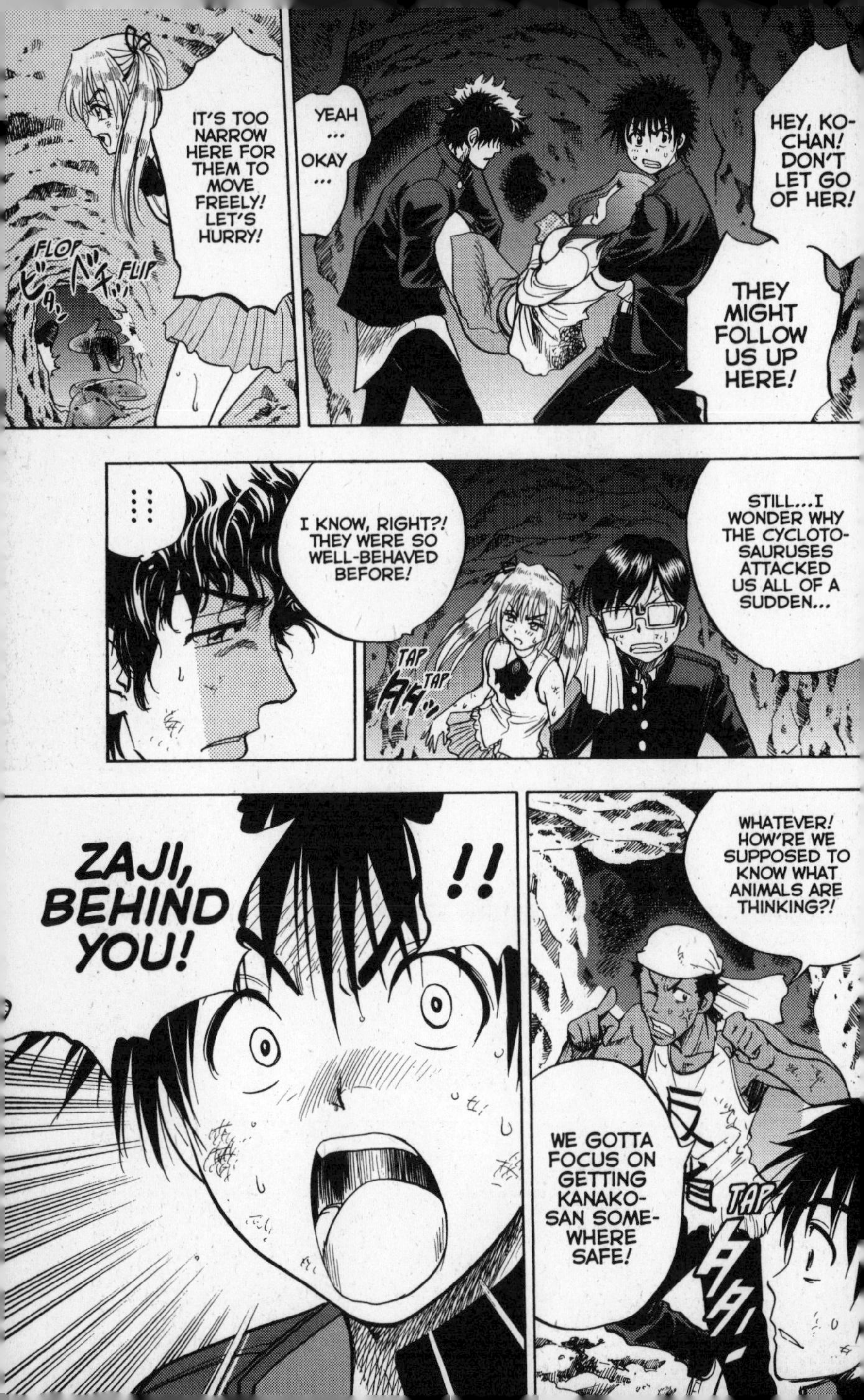
HEY, KO-CHAN! DON'T LET GO OF HER!
THEY MIGHT FOLLOW US UP HERE!
YEAH ... OKAY ...
IT'S TOO NARROW HERE FOR THEM TO MOVE FREELY! LET'S HURRY!
FLOP
FLIP
STILL...I WONDER WHY THE CYCLOTO-SAURUSES ATTACKED US ALL OF A SUDDEN...
I KNOW, RIGHT?! THEY WERE SO WELL-BEHAVED BEFORE!
TAP
TAP
......
WHATEVER! HOW'RE WE SUPPOSED TO KNOW WHAT ANIMALS ARE THINKING?!
WE GOTTA FOCUS ON GETTING KANAKO-SAN SOME-WHERE SAFE!
TAP
!!
ZAJI, BEHIND YOU!

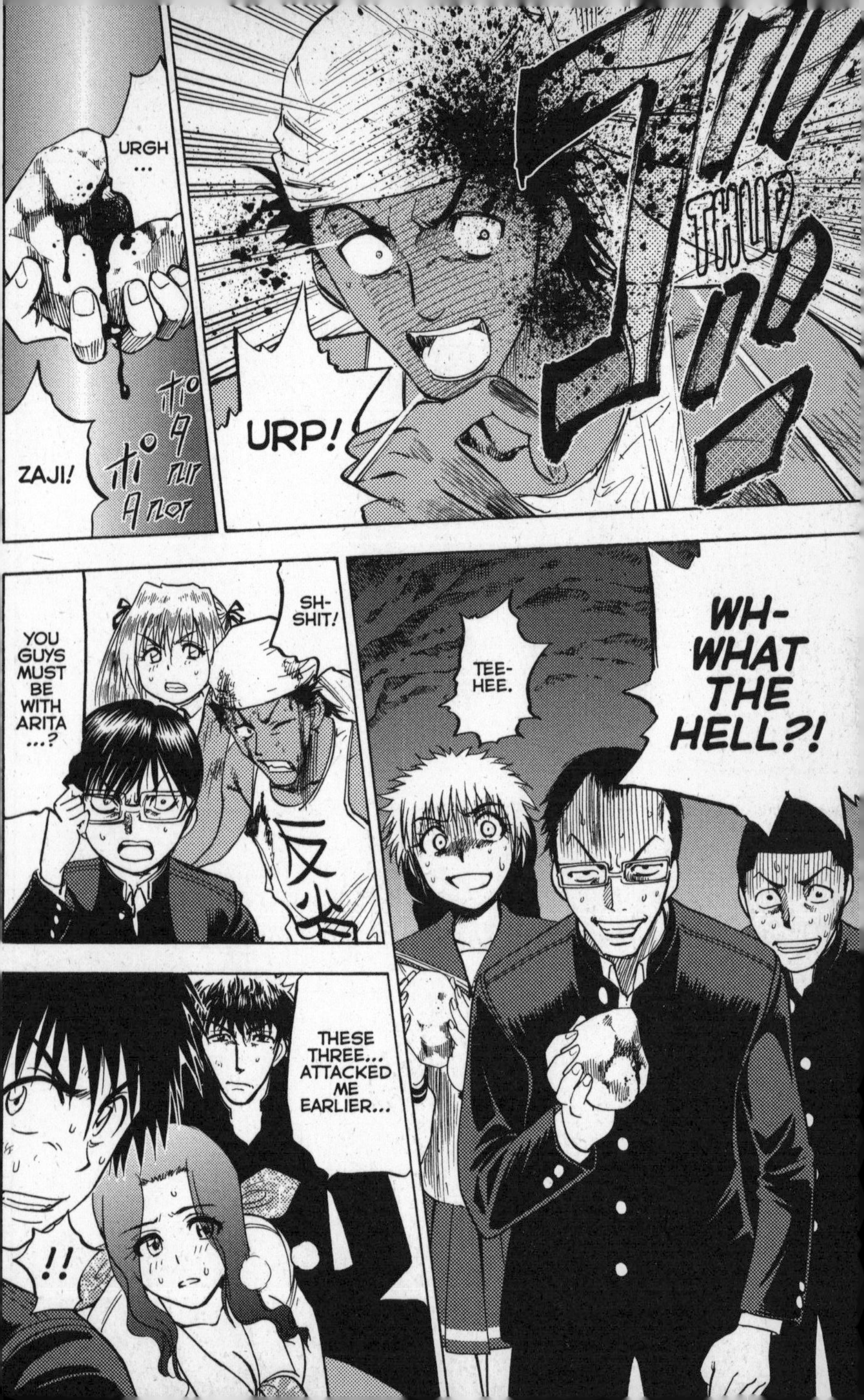
THUD
URP!
URGH
...
ZAJI!
ポタ plip
ポタ plop
WH-
WHAT
THE
HELL?!
TEE-
HEE.
SH-
SHIT!
YOU
GUYS
MUST
BE
WITH
ARITA
...?
THESE
THREE...
ATTACKED
ME
EARLIER...
!!

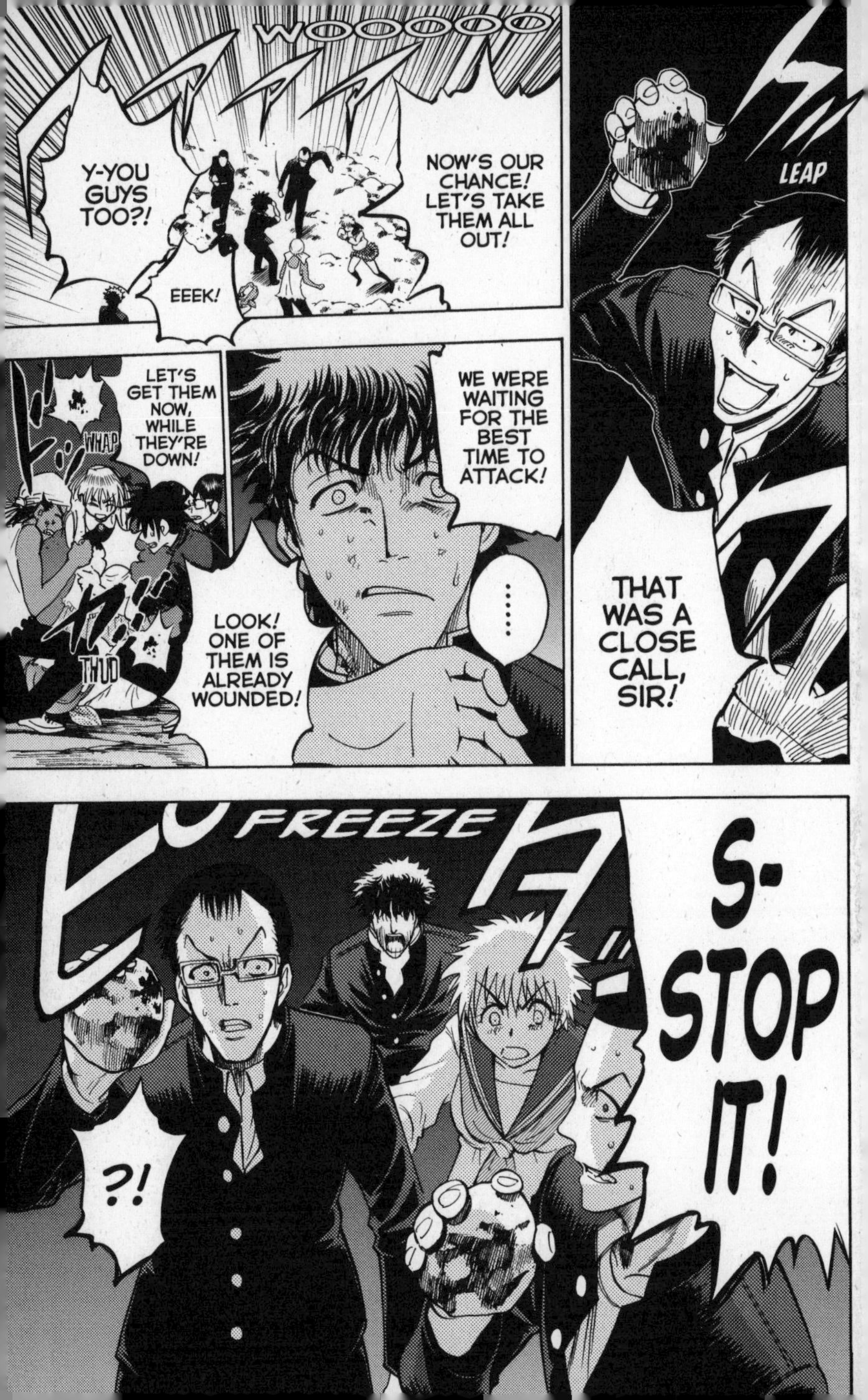
LEAP
THAT WAS A CLOSE CALL, SIR!
WOOOOO
NOW'S OUR CHANCE! LET'S TAKE THEM ALL OUT!
Y-YOU GUYS TOO?!
EEEK!
WE WERE WAITING FOR THE BEST TIME TO ATTACK!
......
LOOK! ONE OF THEM IS ALREADY WOUNDED!
LET'S GET THEM NOW, WHILE THEY'RE DOWN!
WHAP
THUD
S-STOP IT!
FREEZE
?!

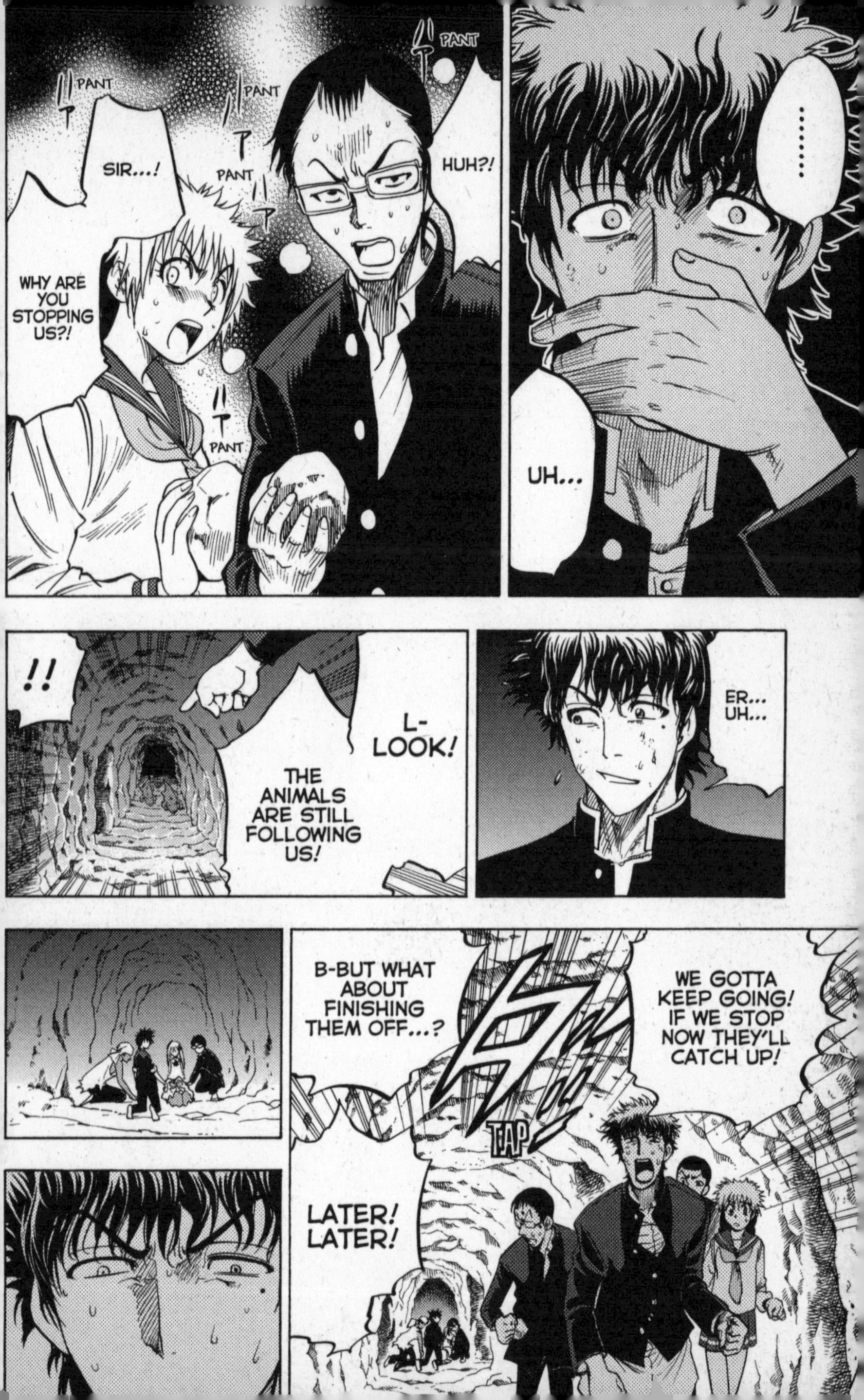
.....
UH...
PANT
HUH?!
PANT
PANT
SIR...!
WHY ARE YOU STOPPING US?!
PANT
PANT
ER... UH...
!!
L- LOOK!
THE ANIMALS ARE STILL FOLLOWING US!
WE GOTTA KEEP GOING! IF WE STOP NOW THEY'LL CATCH UP!
B-BUT WHAT ABOUT FINISHING THEM OFF...?
TAP
LATER! LATER!

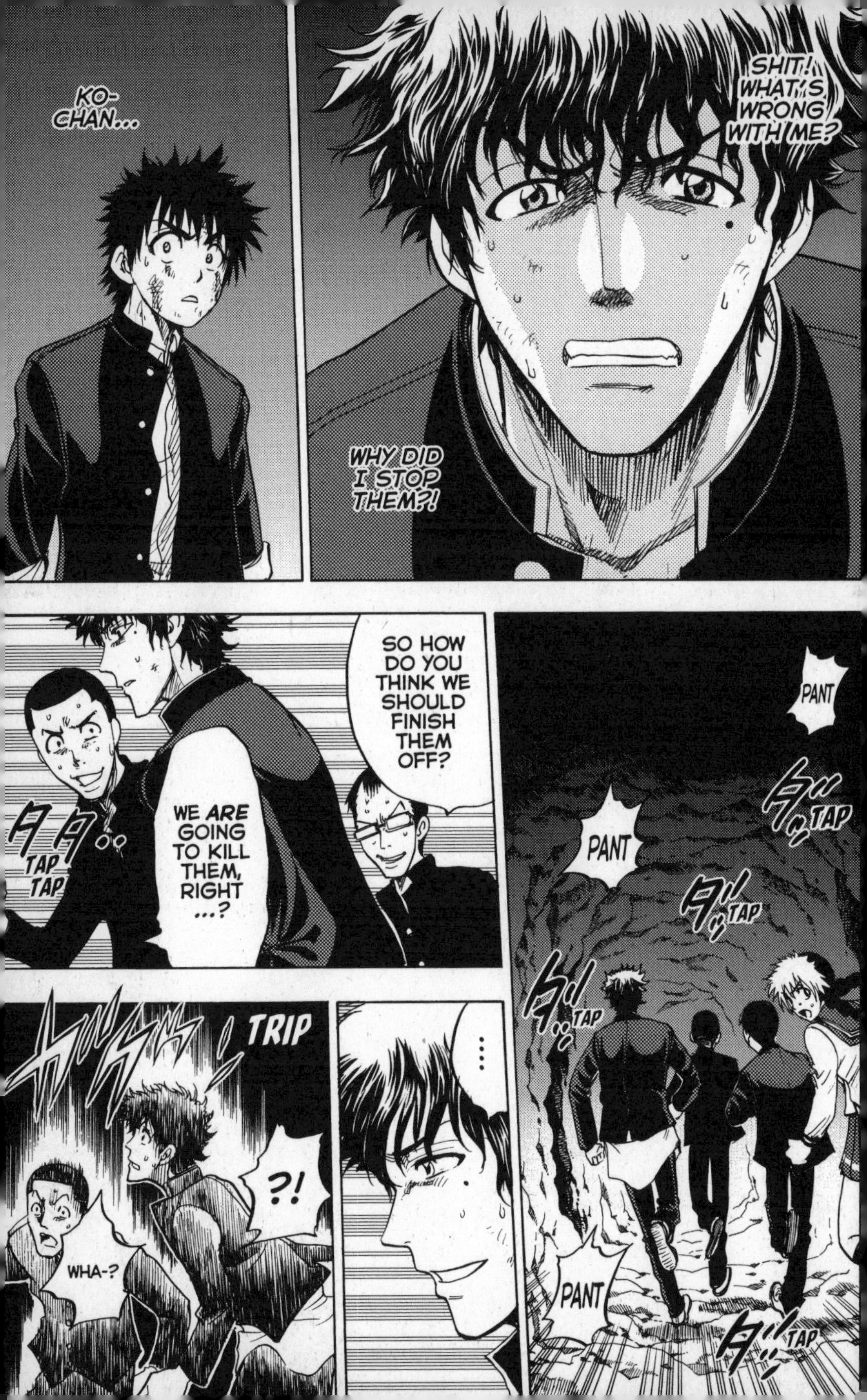
SHIT! WHAT'S WRONG WITH ME?
WHY DID I STOP THEM?!
KO-CHAN...
PANT
TAP
PANT
TAP
TAP
PANT
TAP
SO HOW DO YOU THINK WE SHOULD FINISH THEM OFF?
WE ARE GOING TO KILL THEM, RIGHT ...?
TAP TAP
....
TRIP
?!
WHA-?

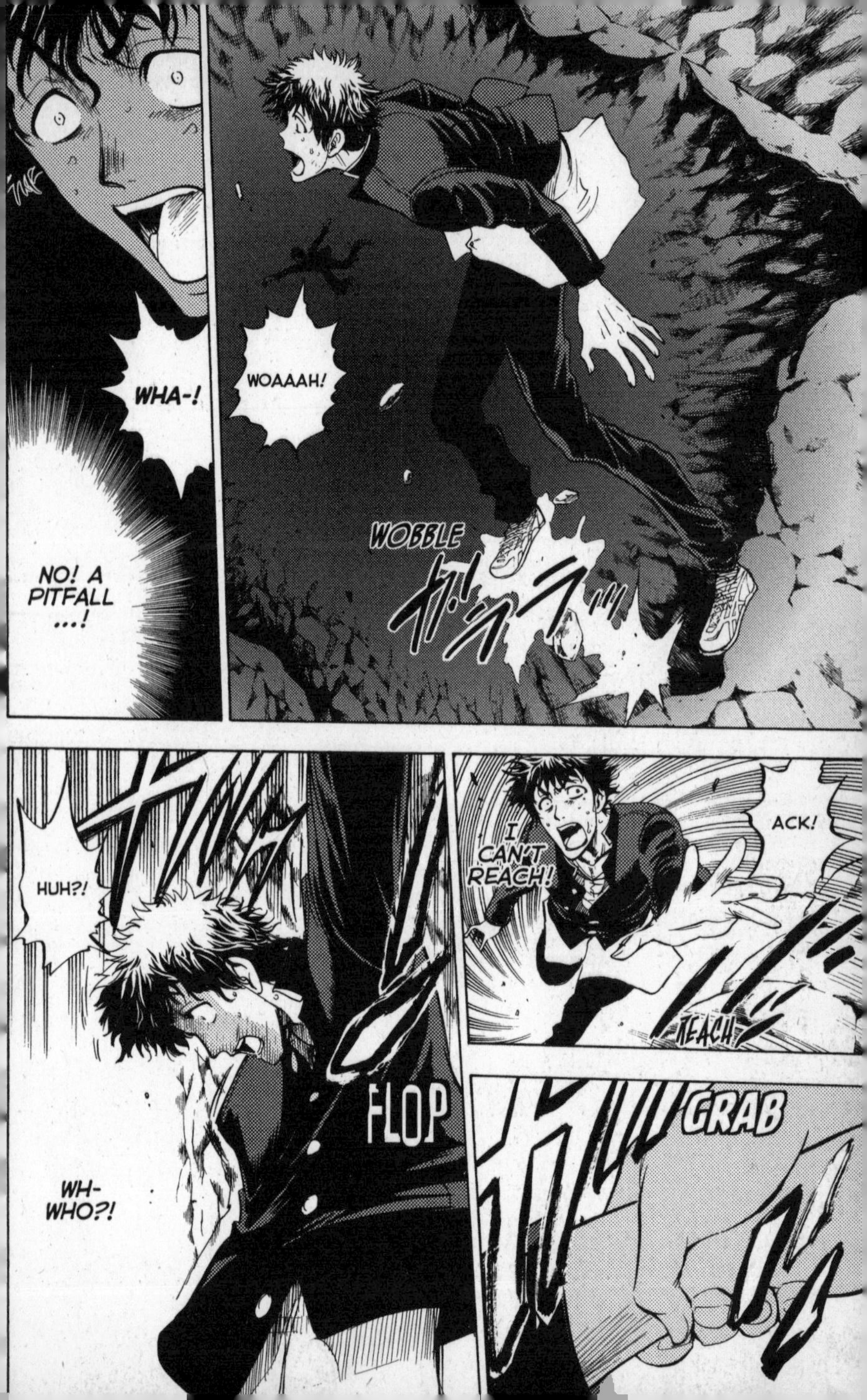
WOAAAH!
WOBBLE
WHA-!
NO! A PITFALL ...!
ACK!
I CAN'T REACH!
REACH
GRAB
HUH?!
FLOP
WH- WHO?!

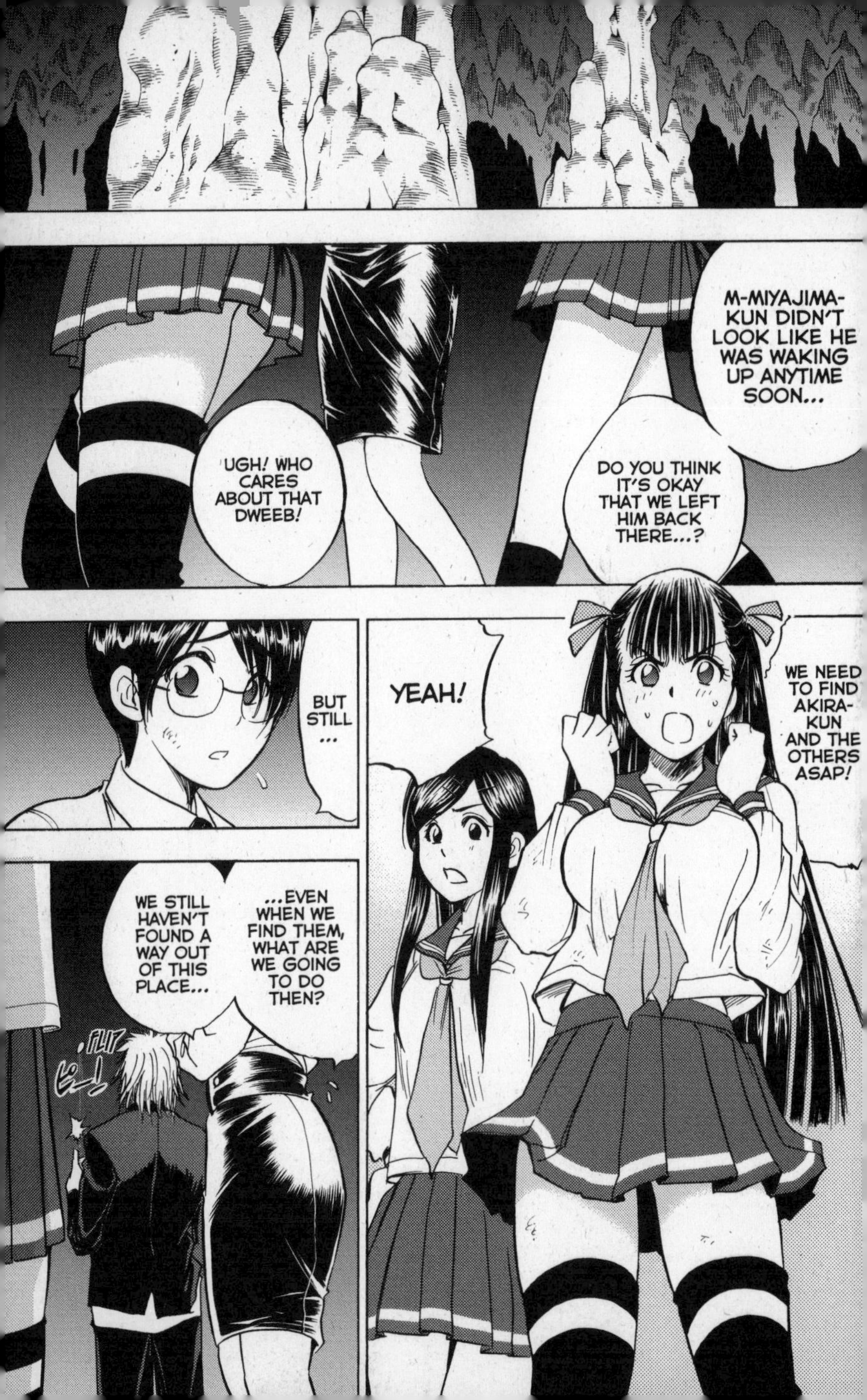
M-MIYAJIMA-KUN DIDN'T LOOK LIKE HE WAS WAKING UP ANYTIME SOON...
DO YOU THINK IT'S OKAY THAT WE LEFT HIM BACK THERE...?
UGH! WHO CARES ABOUT THAT DWEEB!
WE NEED TO FIND AKIRA-KUN AND THE OTHERS ASAP!
YEAH!
BUT STILL...
...EVEN WHEN WE FIND THEM, WHAT ARE WE GOING TO DO THEN?
WE STILL HAVEN'T FOUND A WAY OUT OF THIS PLACE...
FLIP

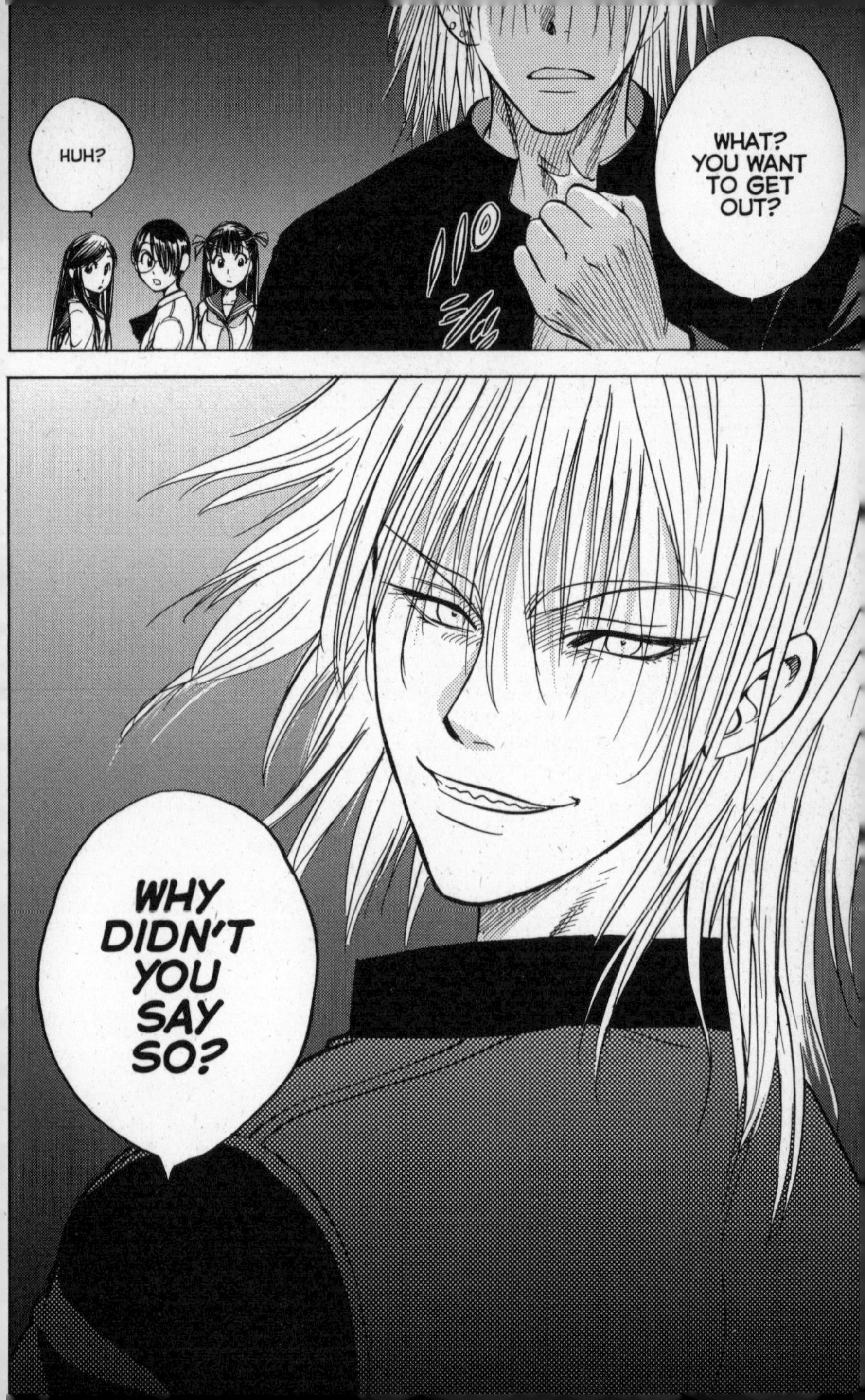
WHAT? YOU WANT TO GET OUT?
HUH?
WHY DIDN'T YOU SAY SO?

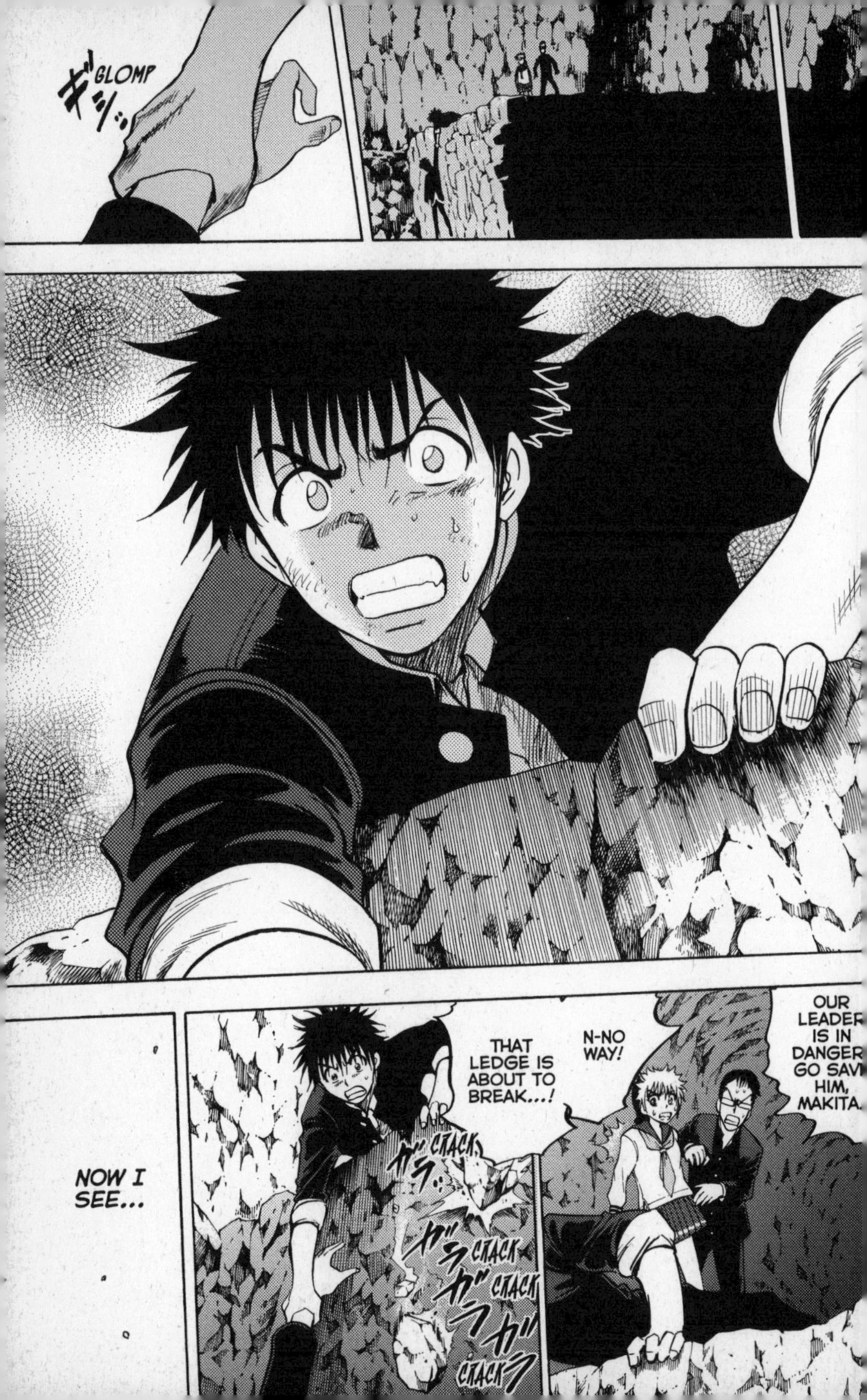

GLOMP
OUR LEADER IS IN DANGER GO SAV HIM, MAKITA.
N-NO WAY!
THAT LEDGE IS ABOUT TO BREAK...!
CRACK
CRACK
CRACK
CRACK
NOW I SEE...

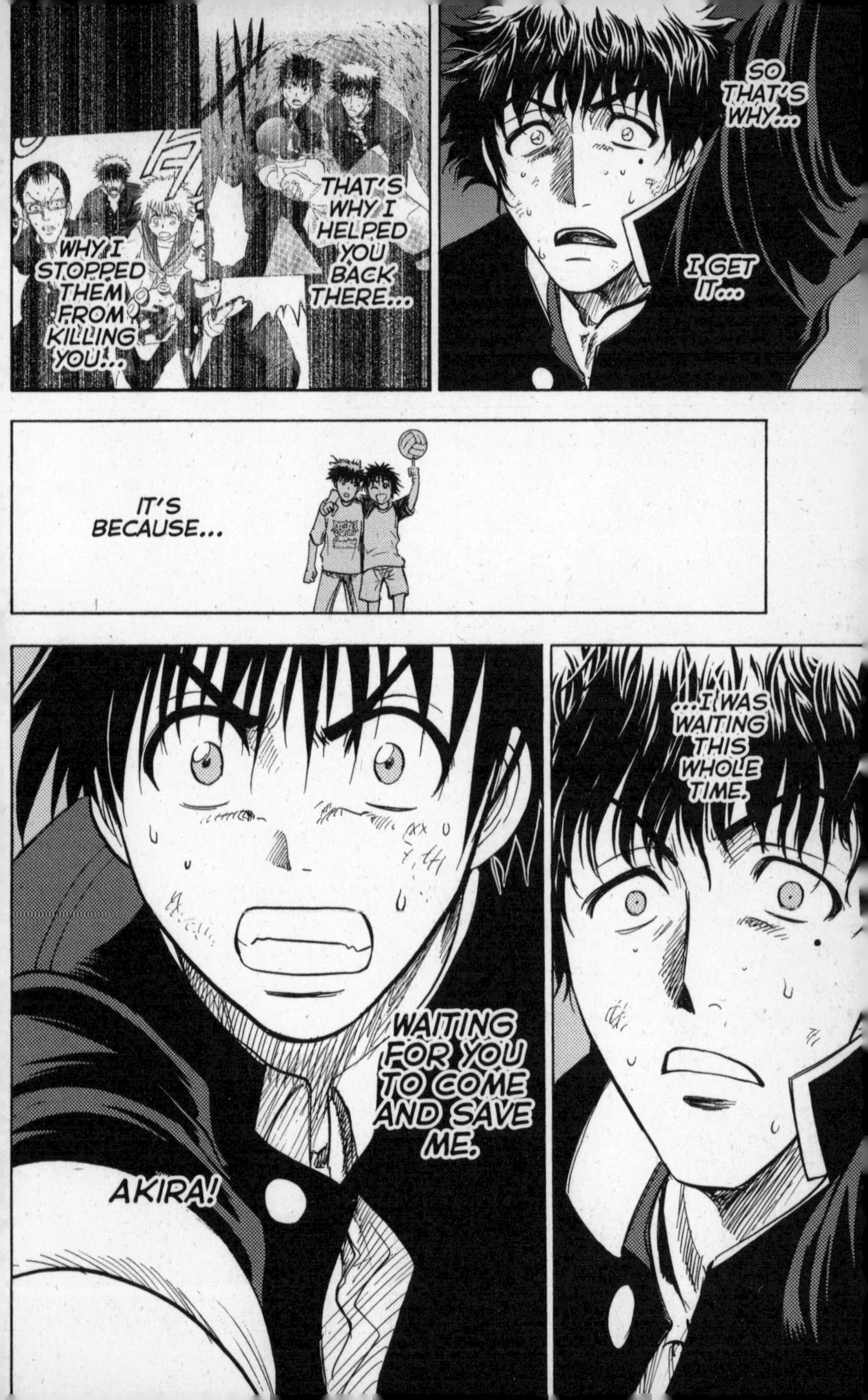
SO THAT'S WHY...
I GET IT...
THAT'S WHY I HELPED YOU BACK THERE...
WHY I STOPPED THEM FROM KILLING YOU...
IT'S BECAUSE...
...I WAS WAITING THIS WHOLE TIME.
WAITING FOR YOU TO COME AND SAVE ME.
AKIRA!

Episode 35 Assembly

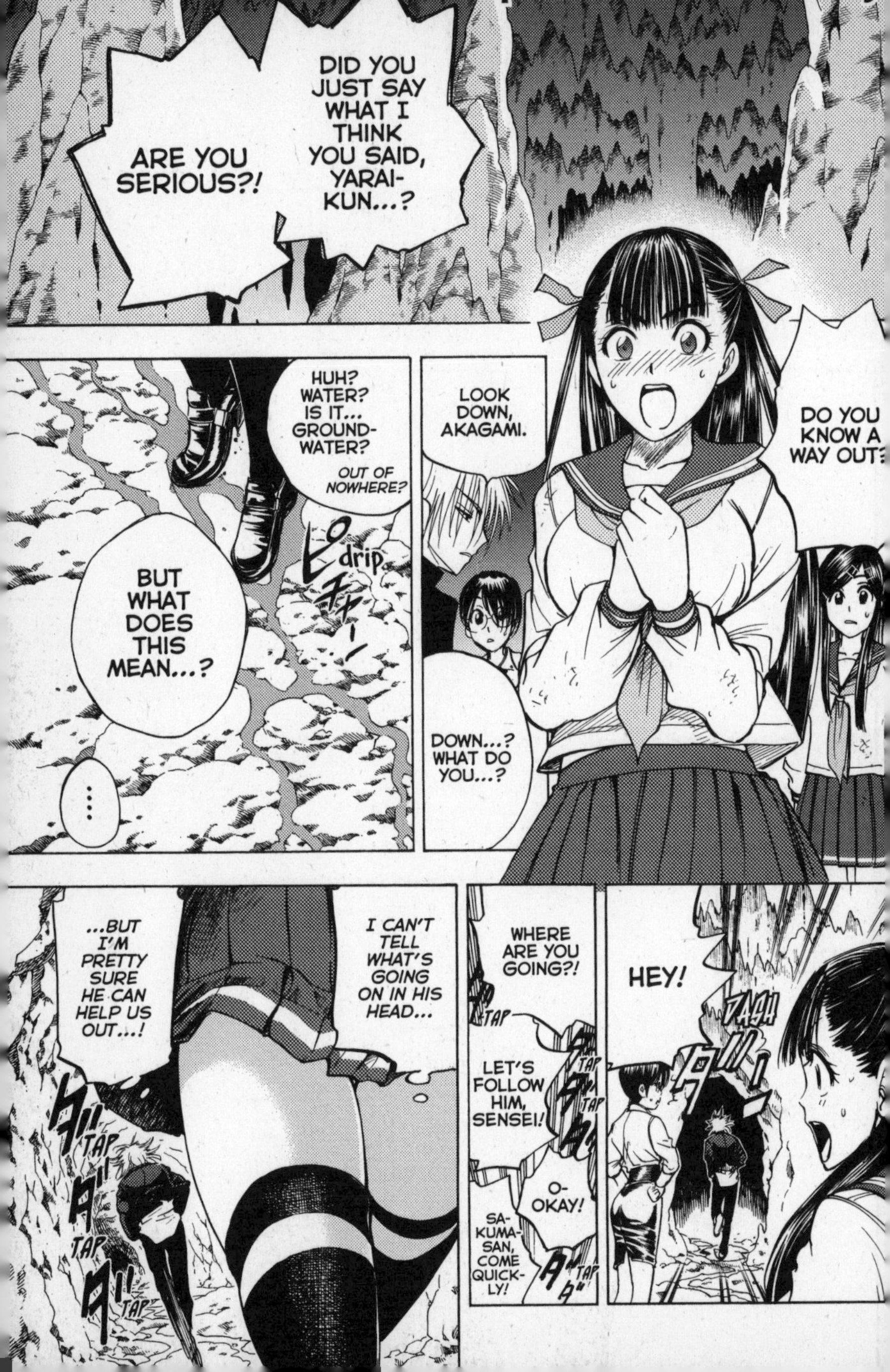
DID YOU JUST SAY WHAT I THINK YOU SAID, YARAI-KUN...?
ARE YOU SERIOUS?!
DO YOU KNOW A WAY OUT!?
LOOK DOWN, AKAGAMI.
DOWN...? WHAT DO YOU...?
HUH? WATER? IS IT... GROUND-WATER?
OUT OF NOWHERE?
drip
BUT WHAT DOES THIS MEAN...?
......
HEY!
DASH
WHERE ARE YOU GOING?!
TAP
LET'S FOLLOW HIM, SENSEI!
TAP
TAP
O-OKAY!
SAKUMA-SAN, COME QUICKLY!
TAP
I CAN'T TELL WHAT'S GOING ON IN HIS HEAD...
...BUT I'M PRETTY SURE HE CAN HELP US OUT...!
TAP
TAP
TAP

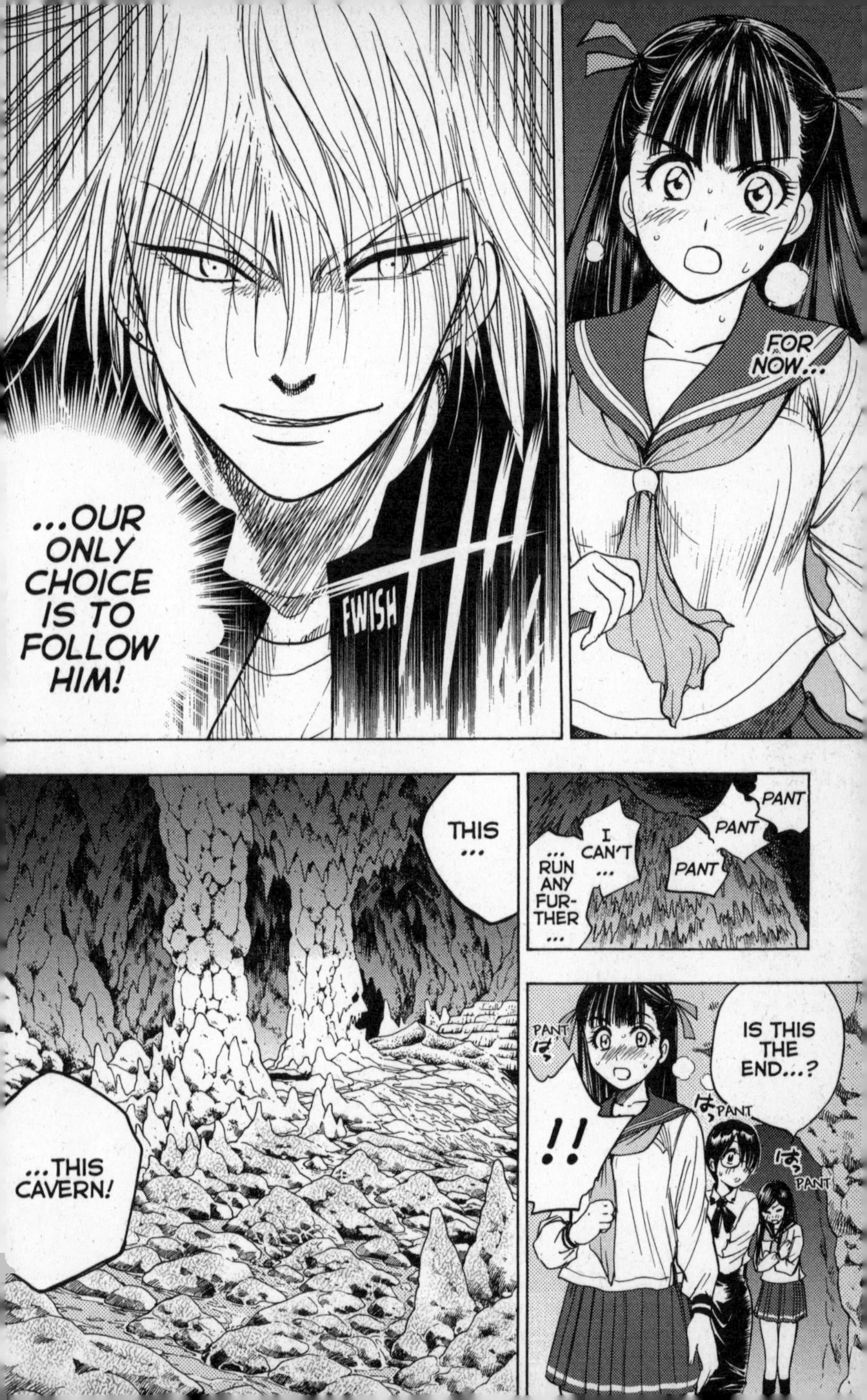
FOR NOW...
...OUR ONLY CHOICE IS TO FOLLOW HIM!
FWISH
PANT
PANT
PANT
I CAN'T...
...RUN ANY FURTHER...
IS THIS THE END...?
PANT
PANT
PANT
!!
THIS...
...THIS CAVERN!

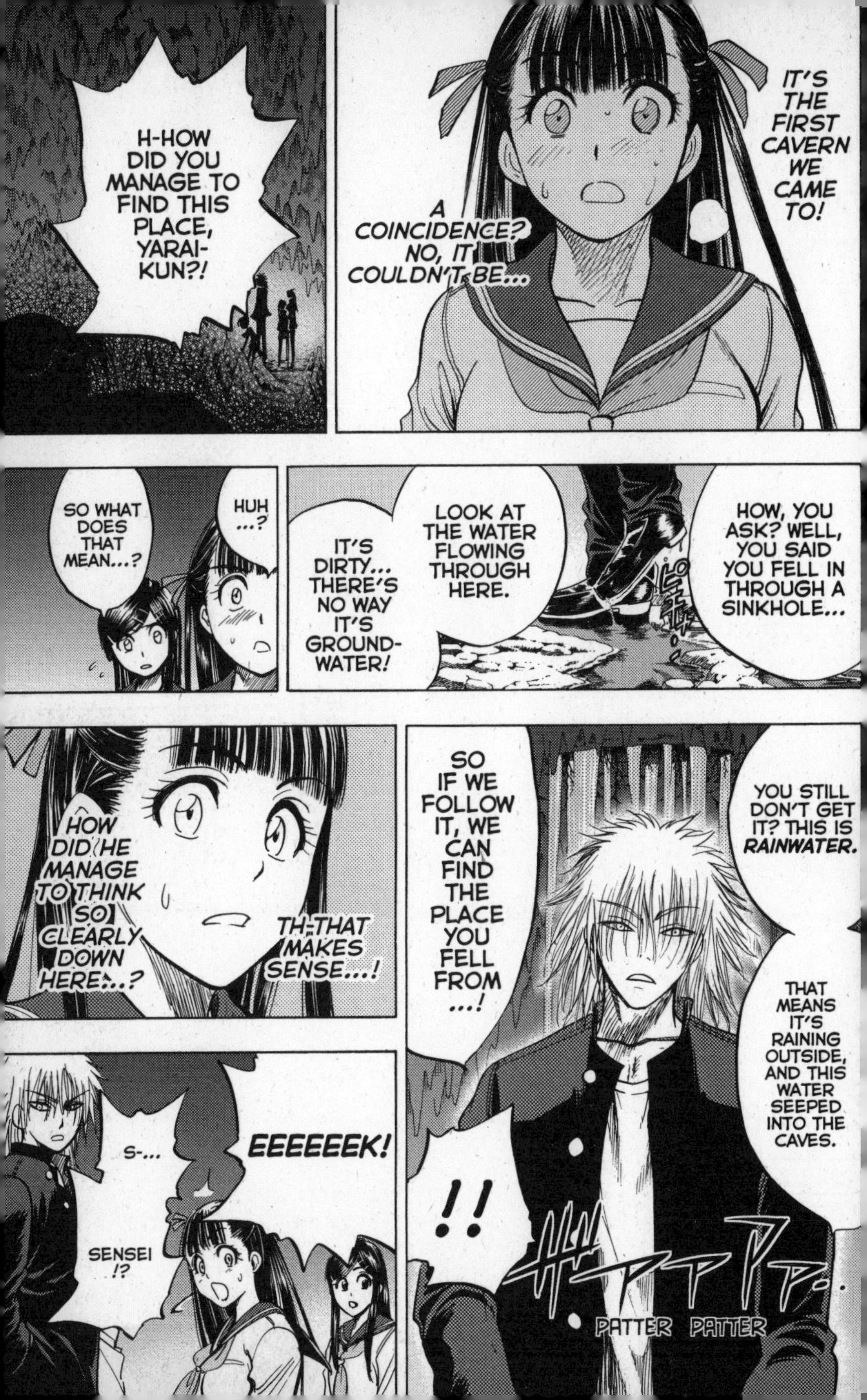
IT'S THE FIRST CAVERN WE CAME TO!
A COINCIDENCE? NO, IT COULDN'T BE...
H-HOW DID YOU MANAGE TO FIND THIS PLACE, YARAI-KUN?!
HOW, YOU ASK? WELL, YOU SAID YOU FELL IN THROUGH A SINKHOLE...
LOOK AT THE WATER FLOWING THROUGH HERE.
IT'S DIRTY... THERE'S NO WAY IT'S GROUND-WATER!
HUH ...?
SO WHAT DOES THAT MEAN...?
YOU STILL DON'T GET IT? THIS IS **RAINWATER.**
THAT MEANS IT'S RAINING OUTSIDE, AND THIS WATER SEEPED INTO THE CAVES.
SO IF WE FOLLOW IT, WE CAN FIND THE PLACE YOU FELL FROM ...!
!!
PATTER PATTER
TH-THAT MAKES SENSE...!
HOW DID HE MANAGE TO THINK SO CLEARLY DOWN HERE...?
EEEEEEK!
S-...
SENSEI !?

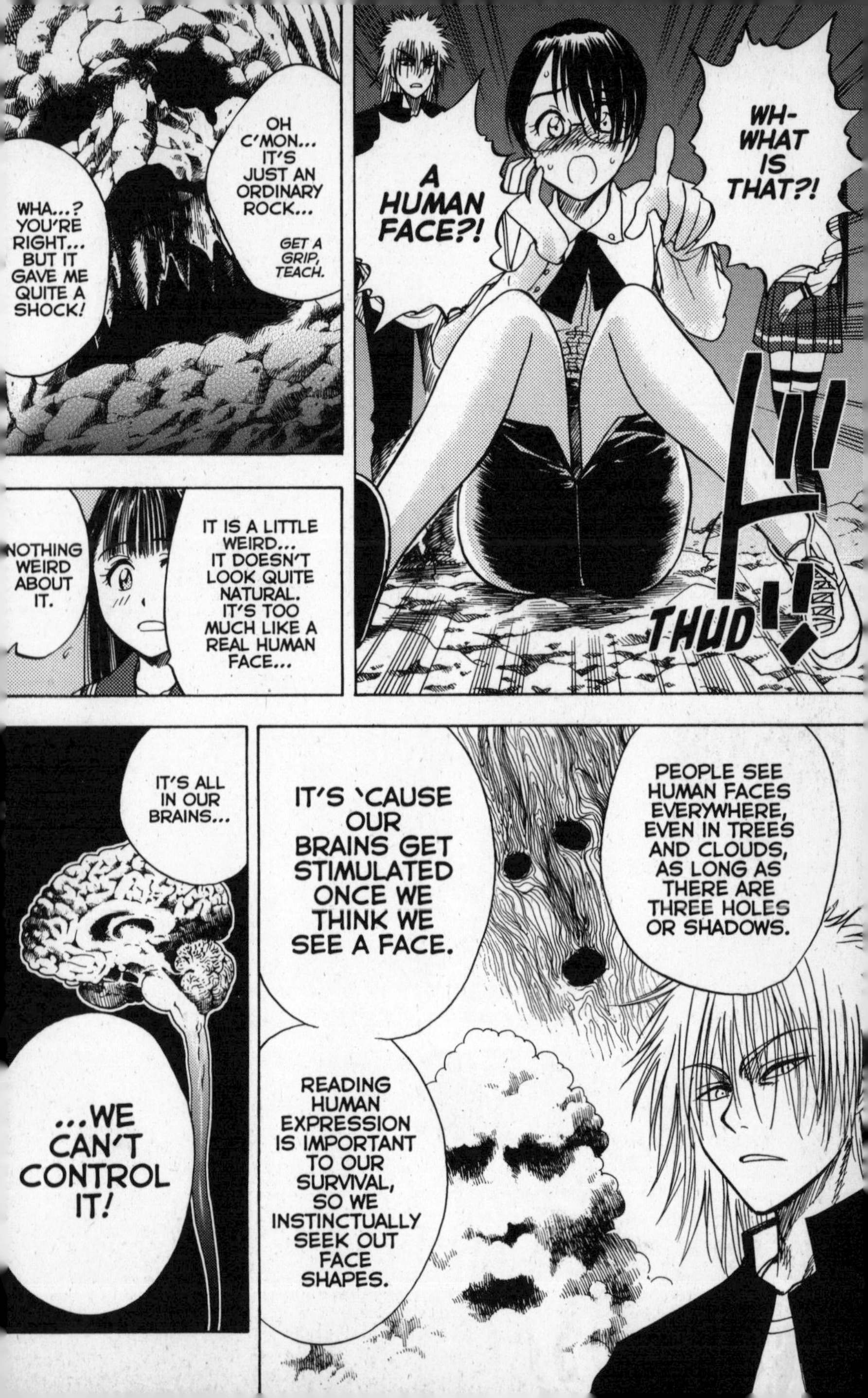
WH- WHAT IS THAT?!
A HUMAN FACE?!
THUD
OH C'MON... IT'S JUST AN ORDINARY ROCK...
GET A GRIP, TEACH.
WHA...? YOU'RE RIGHT... BUT IT GAVE ME QUITE A SHOCK!
IT IS A LITTLE WEIRD... IT DOESN'T LOOK QUITE NATURAL. IT'S TOO MUCH LIKE A REAL HUMAN FACE...
NOTHING WEIRD ABOUT IT.
PEOPLE SEE HUMAN FACES EVERYWHERE, EVEN IN TREES AND CLOUDS, AS LONG AS THERE ARE THREE HOLES OR SHADOWS.
IT'S `CAUSE OUR BRAINS GET STIMULATED ONCE WE THINK WE SEE A FACE.
READING HUMAN EXPRESSION IS IMPORTANT TO OUR SURVIVAL, SO WE INSTINCTUALLY SEEK OUT FACE SHAPES.
IT'S ALL IN OUR BRAINS...
...WE CAN'T CONTROL IT!

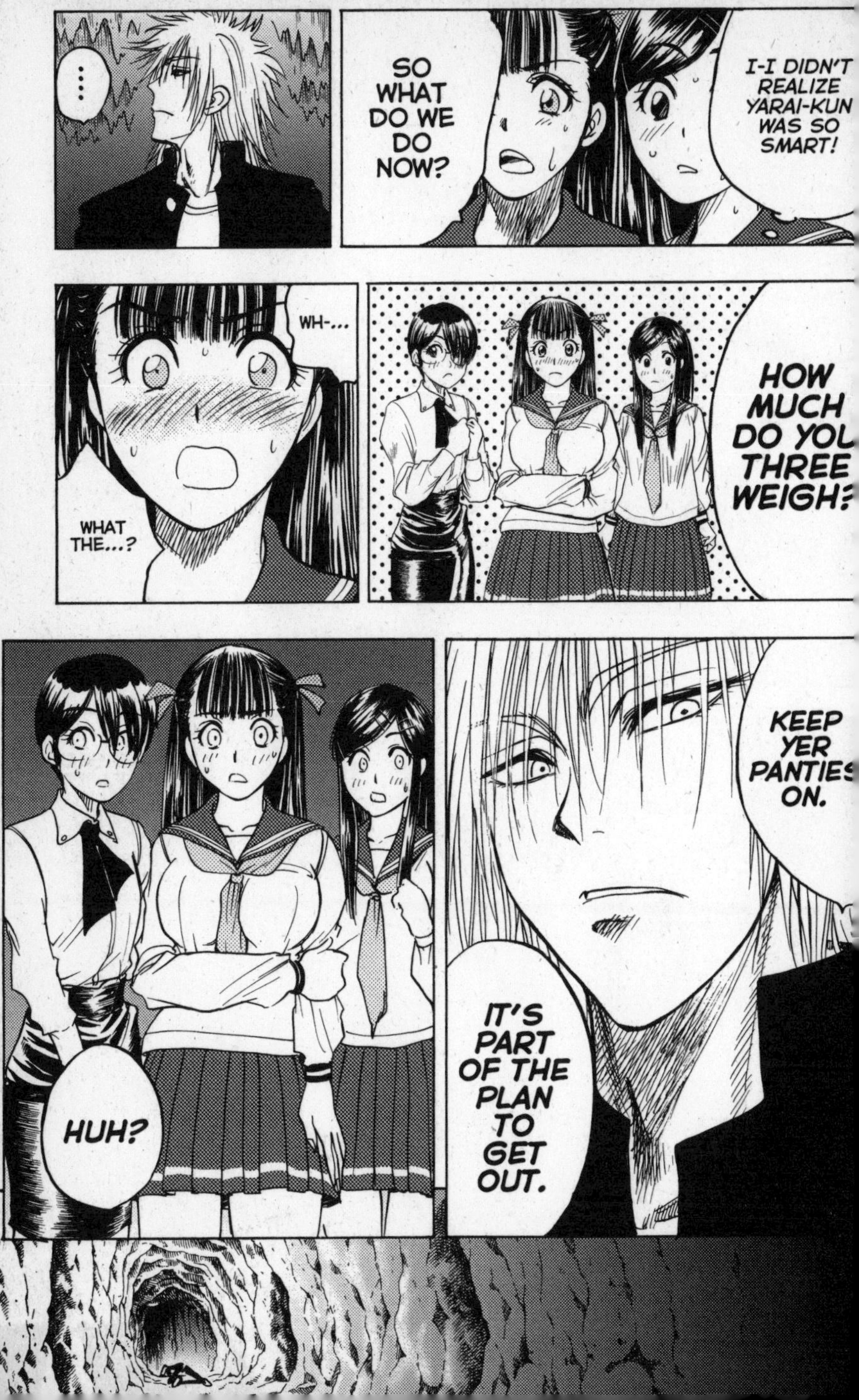
I-I DIDN'T REALIZE YARAI-KUN WAS SO SMART!
SO WHAT DO WE DO NOW?
....
HOW MUCH DO YOU THREE WEIGH?
WH-...
WHAT THE...?
KEEP YER PANTIES ON.
IT'S PART OF THE PLAN TO GET OUT.
HUH?

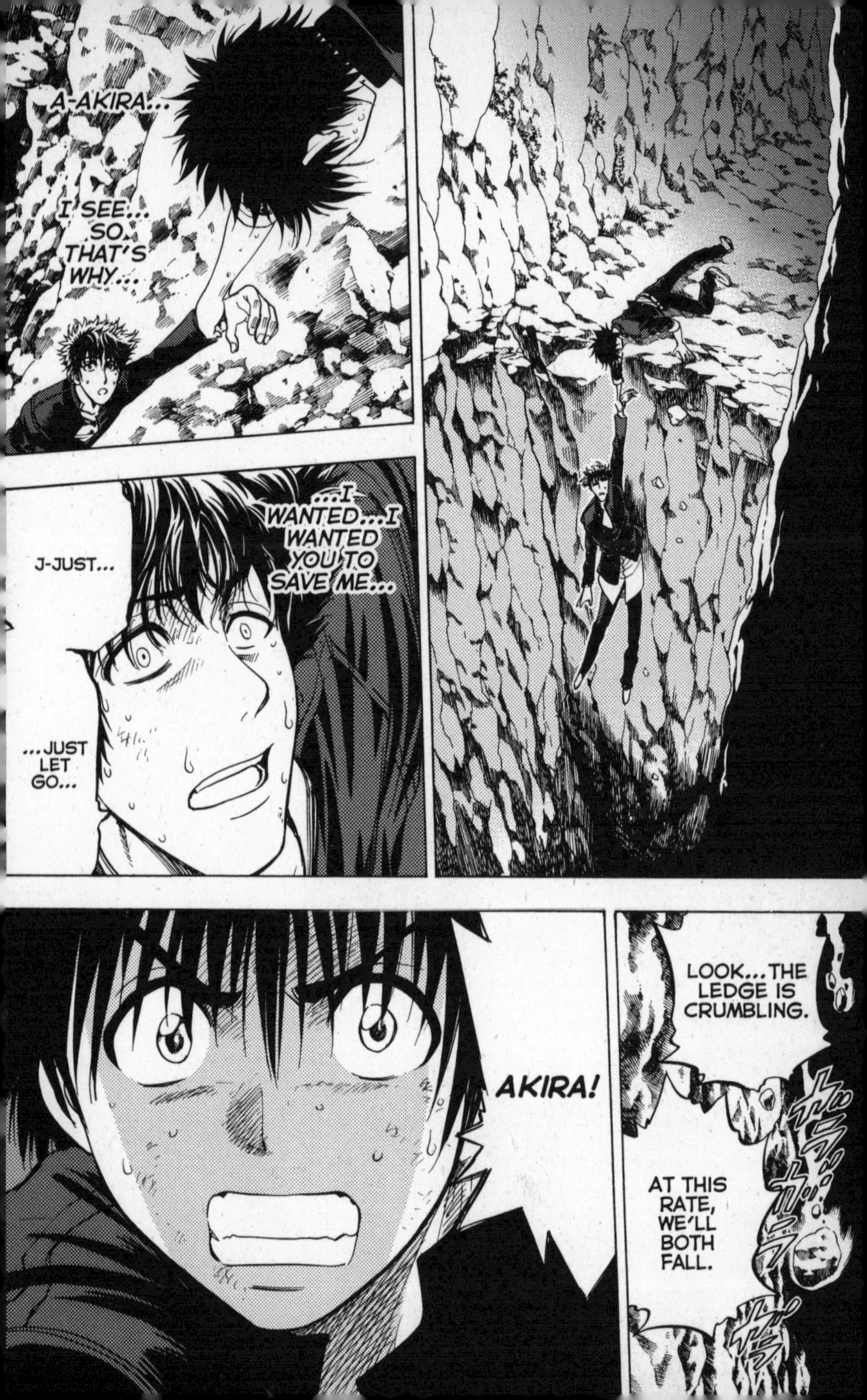
A-AKIRA...
I SEE... SO. THAT'S WHY...
...I WANTED...I WANTED YOU TO SAVE ME...
J-JUST...
...JUST LET GO...
LOOK...THE LEDGE IS CRUMBLING.
AT THIS RATE, WE'LL BOTH FALL.
AKIRA!

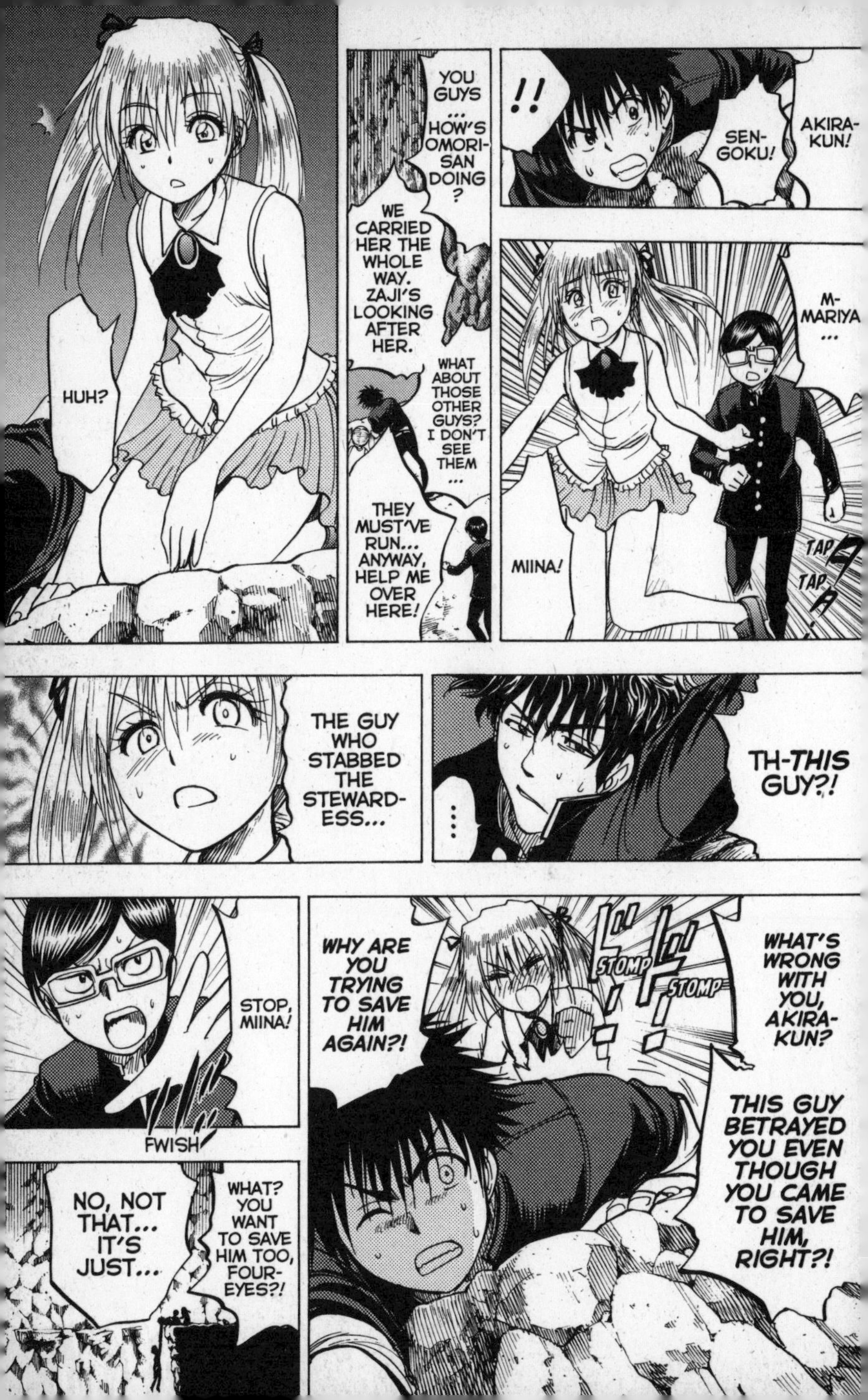
AKIRA-KUN!
SEN-GOKU!
!!
M-MARIYA...
TAP TAP
MIINA!
YOU GUYS... HOW'S OMORI-SAN DOING?
WE CARRIED HER THE WHOLE WAY. ZAJI'S LOOKING AFTER HER.
WHAT ABOUT THOSE OTHER GUYS? I DON'T SEE THEM...
THEY MUST'VE RUN... ANYWAY, HELP ME OVER HERE!
HUH?
TH-THIS GUY?!
....
THE GUY WHO STABBED THE STEWARDESS...
WHAT'S WRONG WITH YOU, AKIRA-KUN?
WHY ARE YOU TRYING TO SAVE HIM AGAIN?!
STOMP STOMP
THIS GUY BETRAYED YOU EVEN THOUGH YOU CAME TO SAVE HIM, RIGHT?!
STOP, MIINA!
FWISH
WHAT? YOU WANT TO SAVE HIM TOO, FOUR-EYES?!
NO, NOT THAT... IT'S JUST...

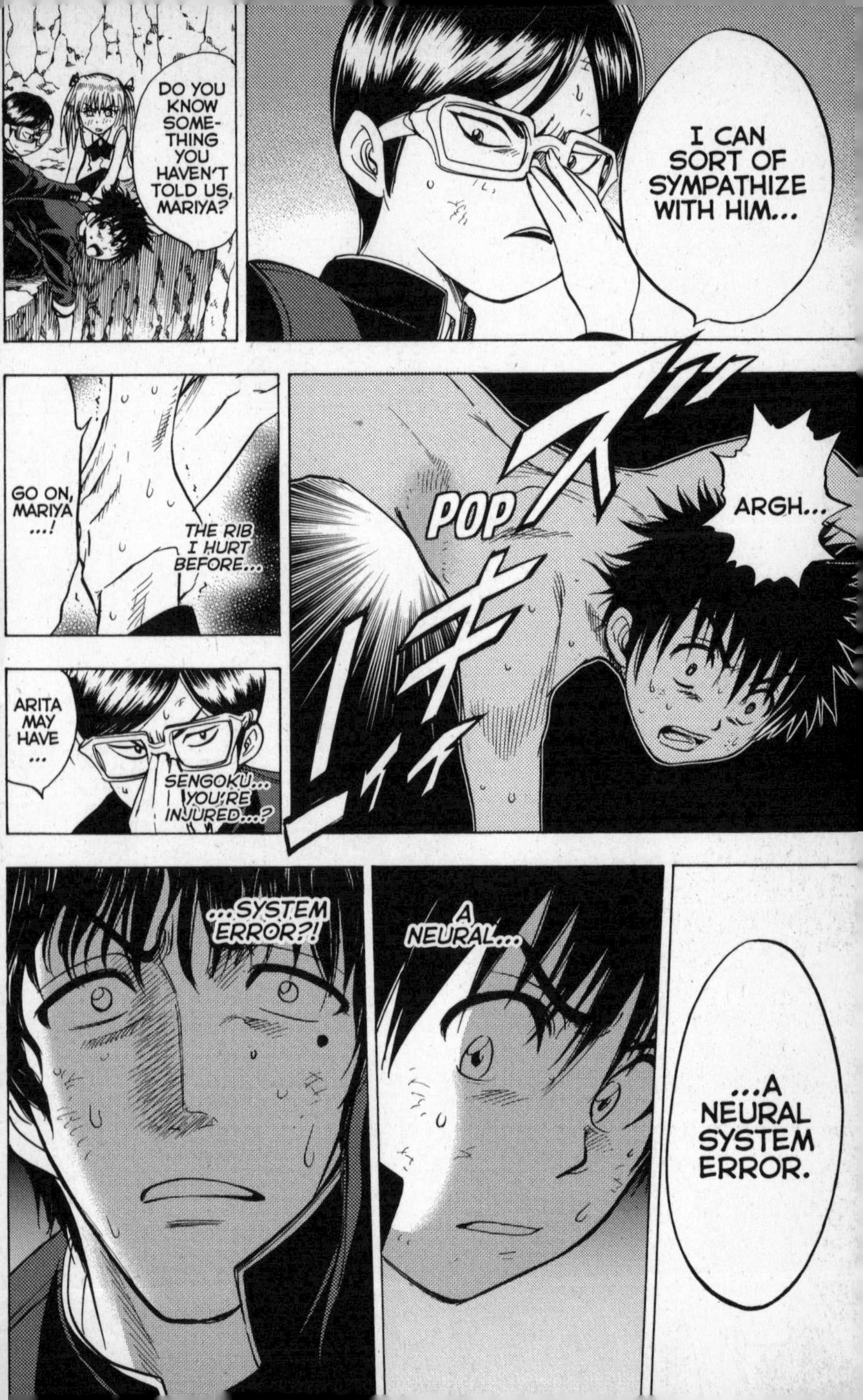
I CAN SORT OF SYMPATHIZE WITH HIM...
DO YOU KNOW SOME-THING YOU HAVEN'T TOLD US, MARIYA?
POP
ARGH...
THE RIB I HURT BEFORE...
GO ON, MARIYA...!
SENGOKU... YOU'RE INJURED...?
ARITA MAY HAVE...
...A NEURAL SYSTEM ERROR.
A NEURAL...
...SYSTEM ERROR?!

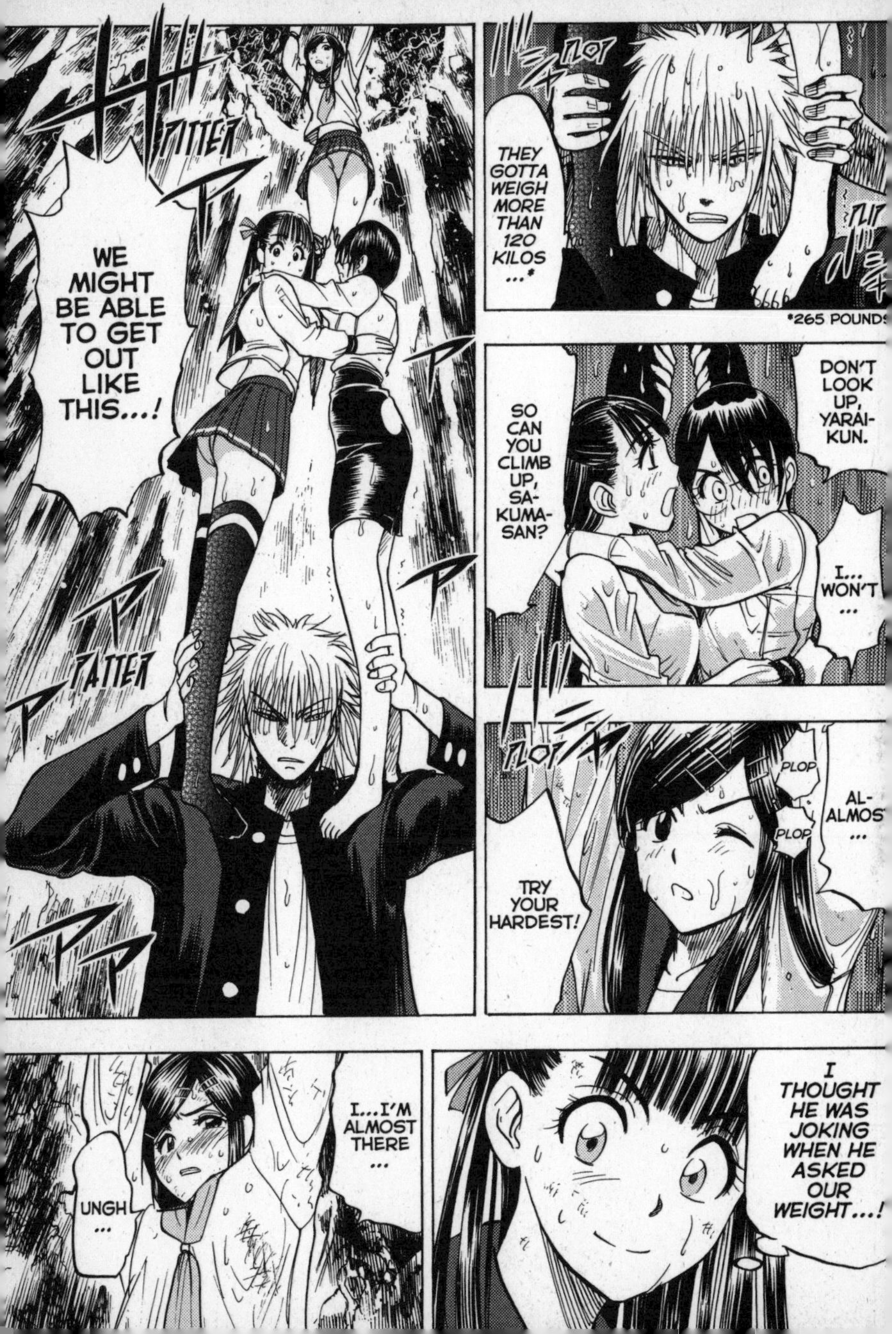
THEY GOTTA WEIGH MORE THAN 120 KILOS...*
*265 POUNDS
DON'T LOOK UP, YARAI-KUN.
SO CAN YOU CLIMB UP, SA-KUMA-SAN?
I... WON'T ...
PLOP
AL- ALMOST ...
PLOP
TRY YOUR HARDEST!
PATTER
WE MIGHT BE ABLE TO GET OUT LIKE THIS...!
PATTER
I THOUGHT HE WAS JOKING WHEN HE ASKED OUR WEIGHT...!
I...I'M ALMOST THERE ...
UNGH ...

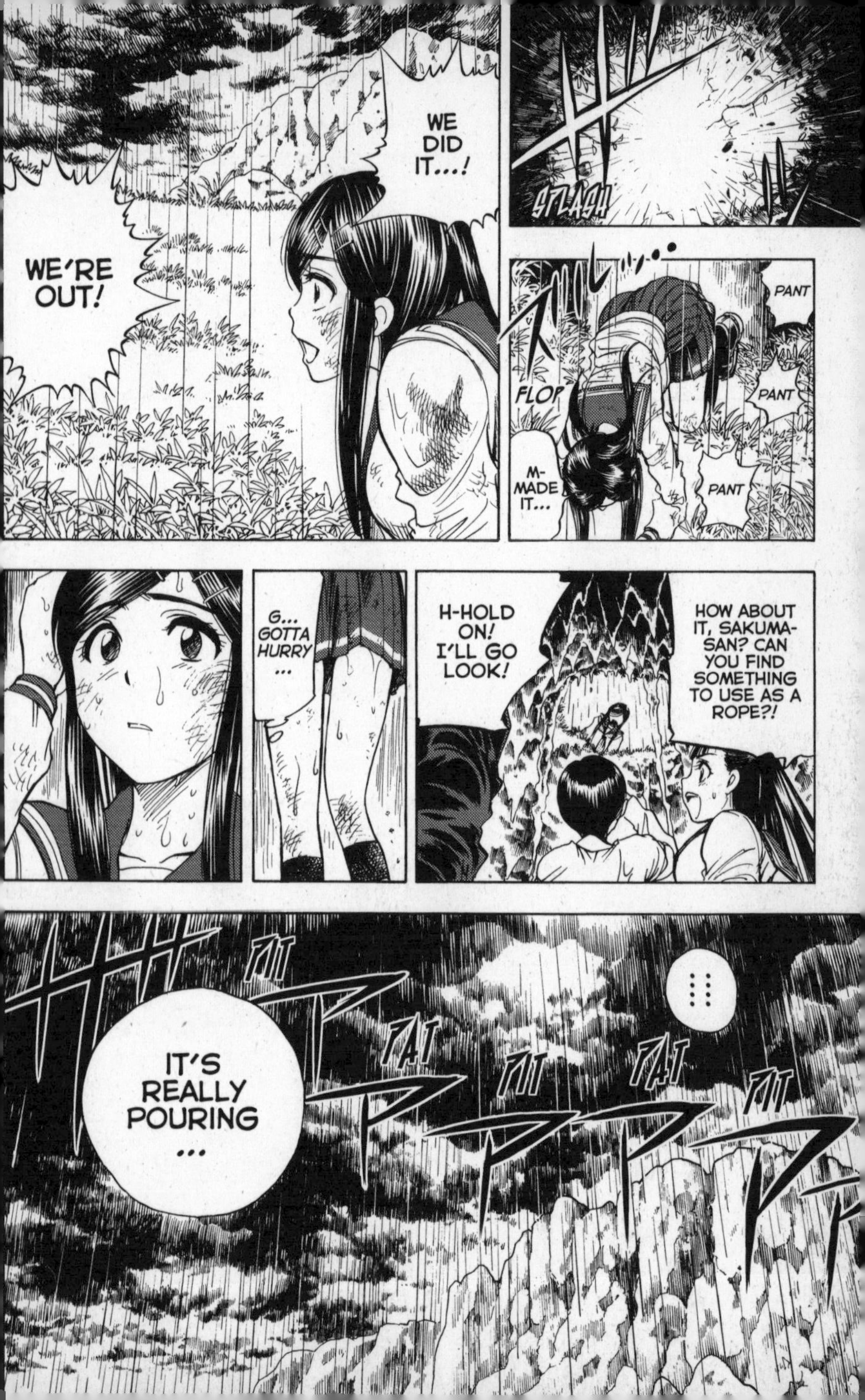
SPLASH
PANT
PANT
FLOP
M-MADE IT...
PANT
WE DID IT...!
WE'RE OUT!
HOW ABOUT IT, SAKUMA-SAN? CAN YOU FIND SOMETHING TO USE AS A ROPE?!
H-HOLD ON! I'LL GO LOOK!
G... GOTTA HURRY...
......
PAT
PAT
PAT
PAT
PAT
IT'S REALLY POURING...

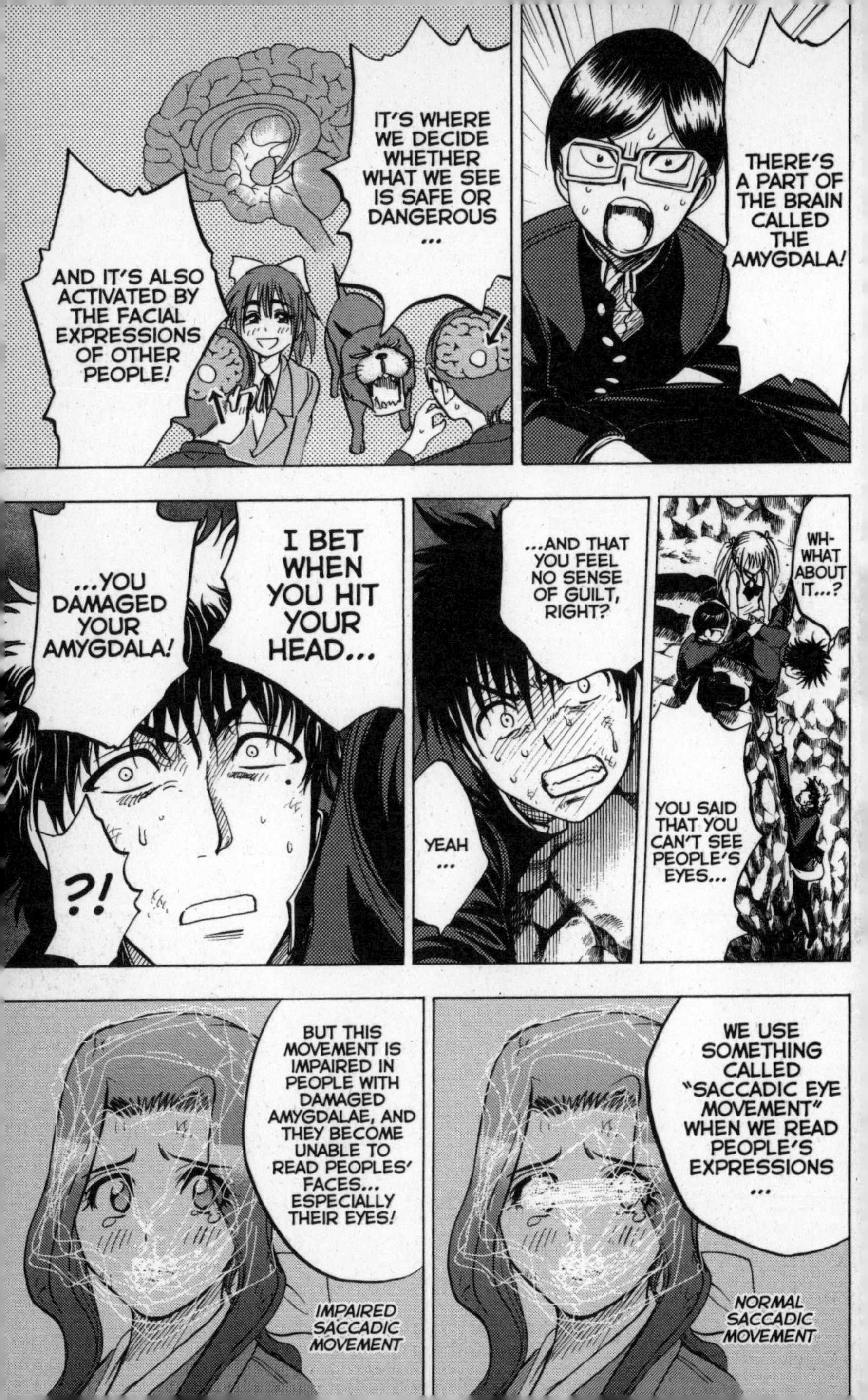
THERE'S A PART OF THE BRAIN CALLED THE AMYGDALA!
IT'S WHERE WE DECIDE WHETHER WHAT WE SEE IS SAFE OR DANGEROUS ...
AND IT'S ALSO ACTIVATED BY THE FACIAL EXPRESSIONS OF OTHER PEOPLE!
WH- WHAT ABOUT IT...?
YOU SAID THAT YOU CAN'T SEE PEOPLE'S EYES...
...AND THAT YOU FEEL NO SENSE OF GUILT, RIGHT?
YEAH ...
I BET WHEN YOU HIT YOUR HEAD...
...YOU DAMAGED YOUR AMYGDALA!
?!
WE USE SOMETHING CALLED "SACCADIC EYE MOVEMENT" WHEN WE READ PEOPLE'S EXPRESSIONS ...
NORMAL SACCADIC MOVEMENT
BUT THIS MOVEMENT IS IMPAIRED IN PEOPLE WITH DAMAGED AMYGDALAE, AND THEY BECOME UNABLE TO READ PEOPLES' FACES... ESPECIALLY THEIR EYES!
IMPAIRED SACCADIC MOVEMENT

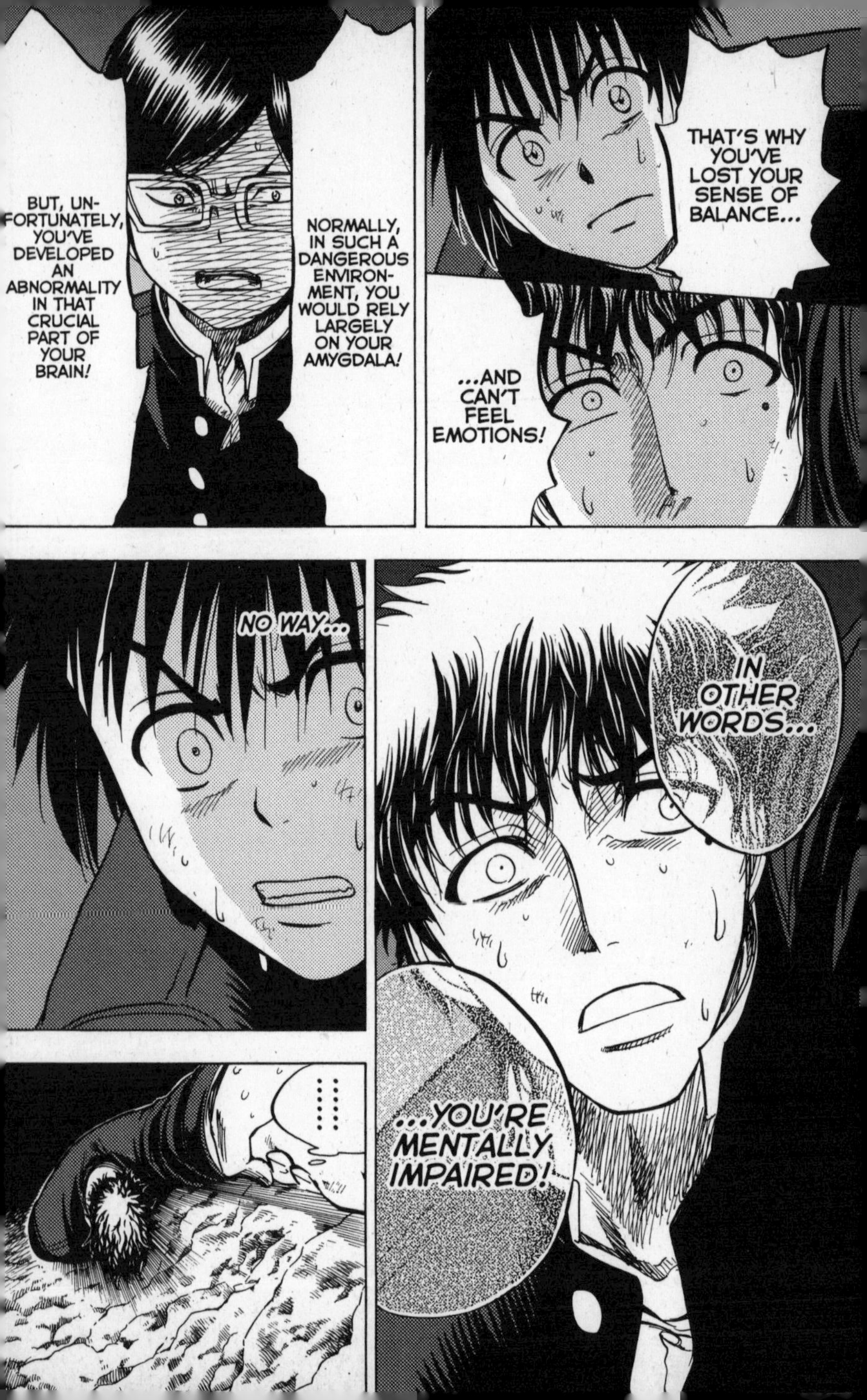
NORMALLY, IN SUCH A DANGEROUS ENVIRON-MENT, YOU WOULD RELY LARGELY ON YOUR AMYGDALA!
BUT, UN-FORTUNATELY, YOU'VE DEVELOPED AN ABNORMALITY IN THAT CRUCIAL PART OF YOUR BRAIN!
THAT'S WHY YOU'VE LOST YOUR SENSE OF BALANCE...
...AND CAN'T FEEL EMOTIONS!
IN OTHER WORDS...
...YOU'RE MENTALLY IMPAIRED!
NO WAY...

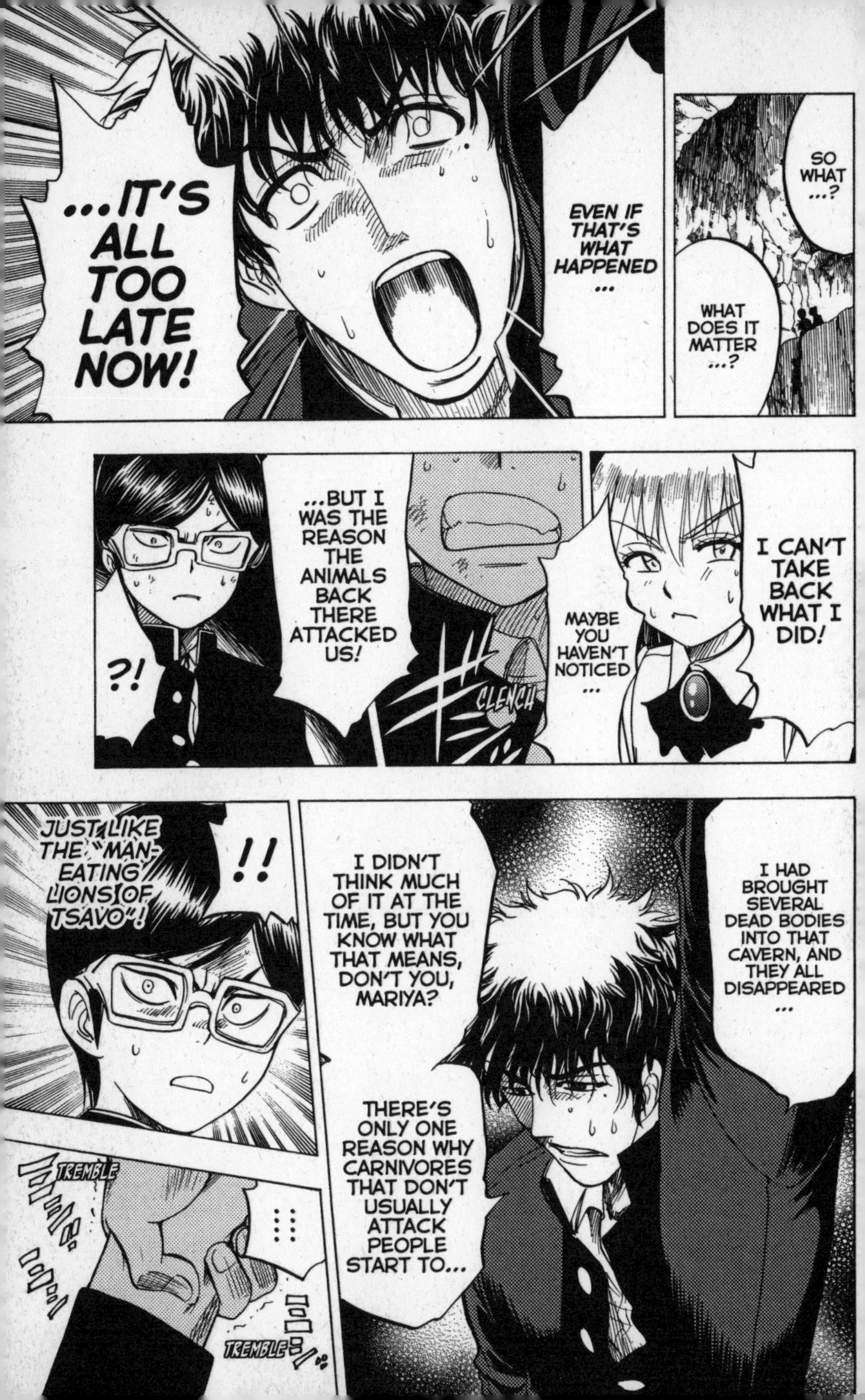
SO WHAT ...?
WHAT DOES IT MATTER ...?
EVEN IF THAT'S WHAT HAPPENED ...
...IT'S ALL TOO LATE NOW!
I CAN'T TAKE BACK WHAT I DID!
MAYBE YOU HAVEN'T NOTICED ...
...BUT I WAS THE REASON THE ANIMALS BACK THERE ATTACKED US!
CLENCH
?!
I HAD BROUGHT SEVERAL DEAD BODIES INTO THAT CAVERN, AND THEY ALL DISAPPEARED ...
I DIDN'T THINK MUCH OF IT AT THE TIME, BUT YOU KNOW WHAT THAT MEANS, DON'T YOU, MARIYA?
THERE'S ONLY ONE REASON WHY CARNIVORES THAT DON'T USUALLY ATTACK PEOPLE START TO...
JUST LIKE THE "MAN-EATING LIONS OF TSAVO"!
!!
TREMBLE
......
TREMBLE

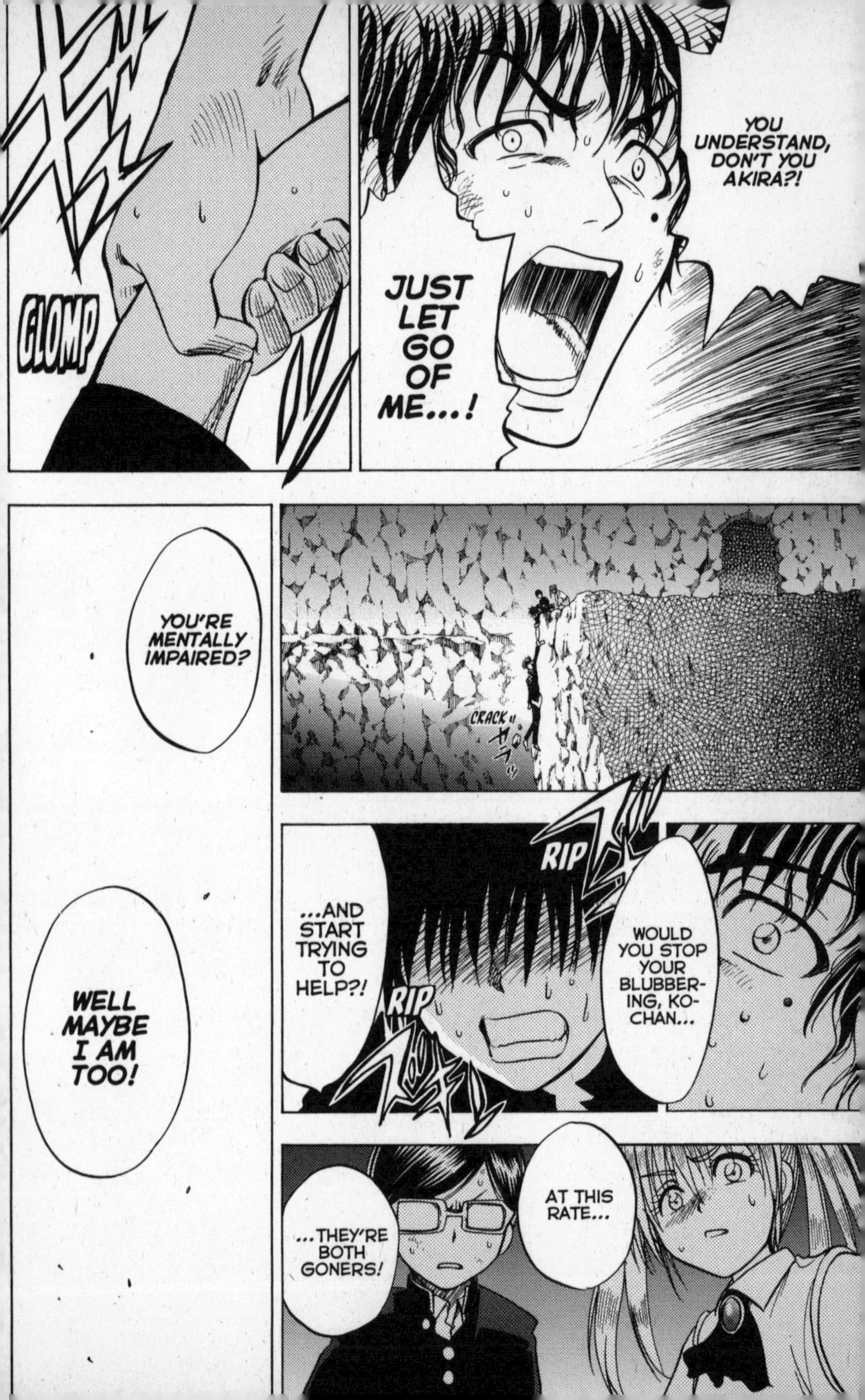
YOU UNDERSTAND, DON'T YOU AKIRA?!
JUST LET GO OF ME...!
GLOMP
CRACK
WOULD YOU STOP YOUR BLUBBER-ING, KO-CHAN...
RIP
...AND START TRYING TO HELP?!
RIP
AT THIS RATE...
...THEY'RE BOTH GONERS!
YOU'RE MENTALLY IMPAIRED?
WELL MAYBE I AM TOO!

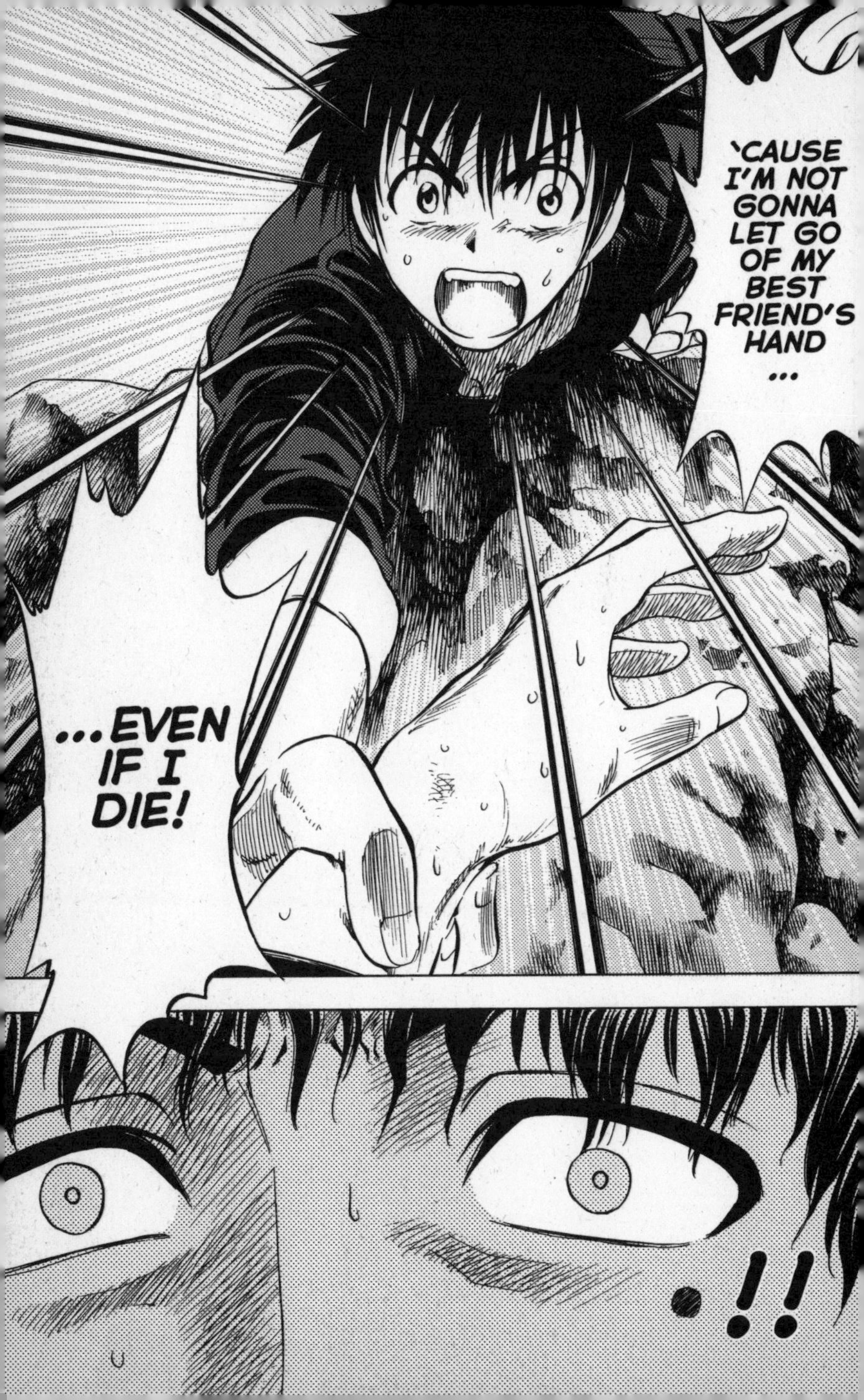
'CAUSE I'M NOT GONNA LET GO OF MY BEST FRIEND'S HAND ...
...EVEN IF I DIE!
.!!

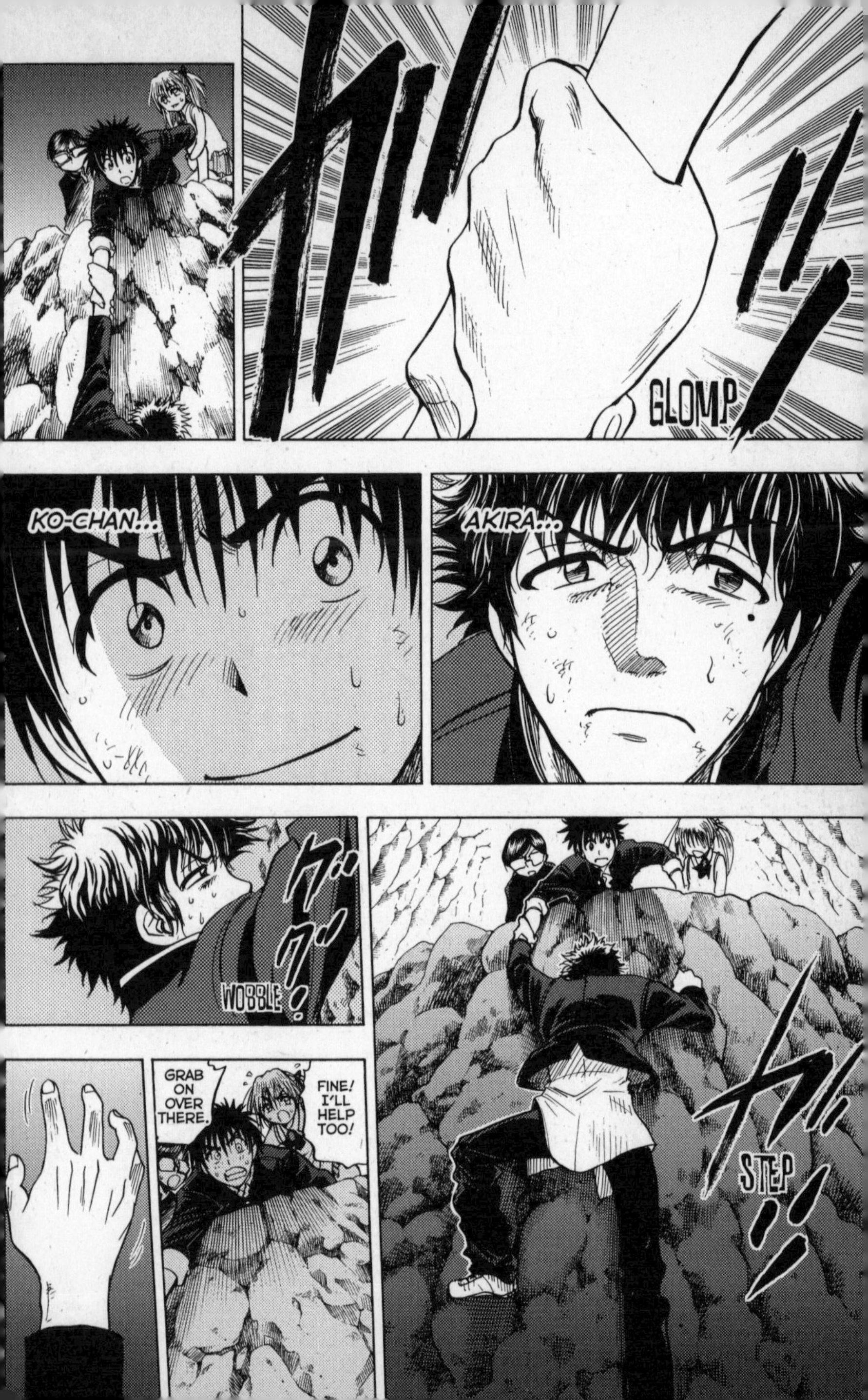
GLOMP
AKIRA...
KO-CHAN...
STEP
WOBBLE
FINE! I'LL HELP TOO!
GRAB ON OVER THERE.

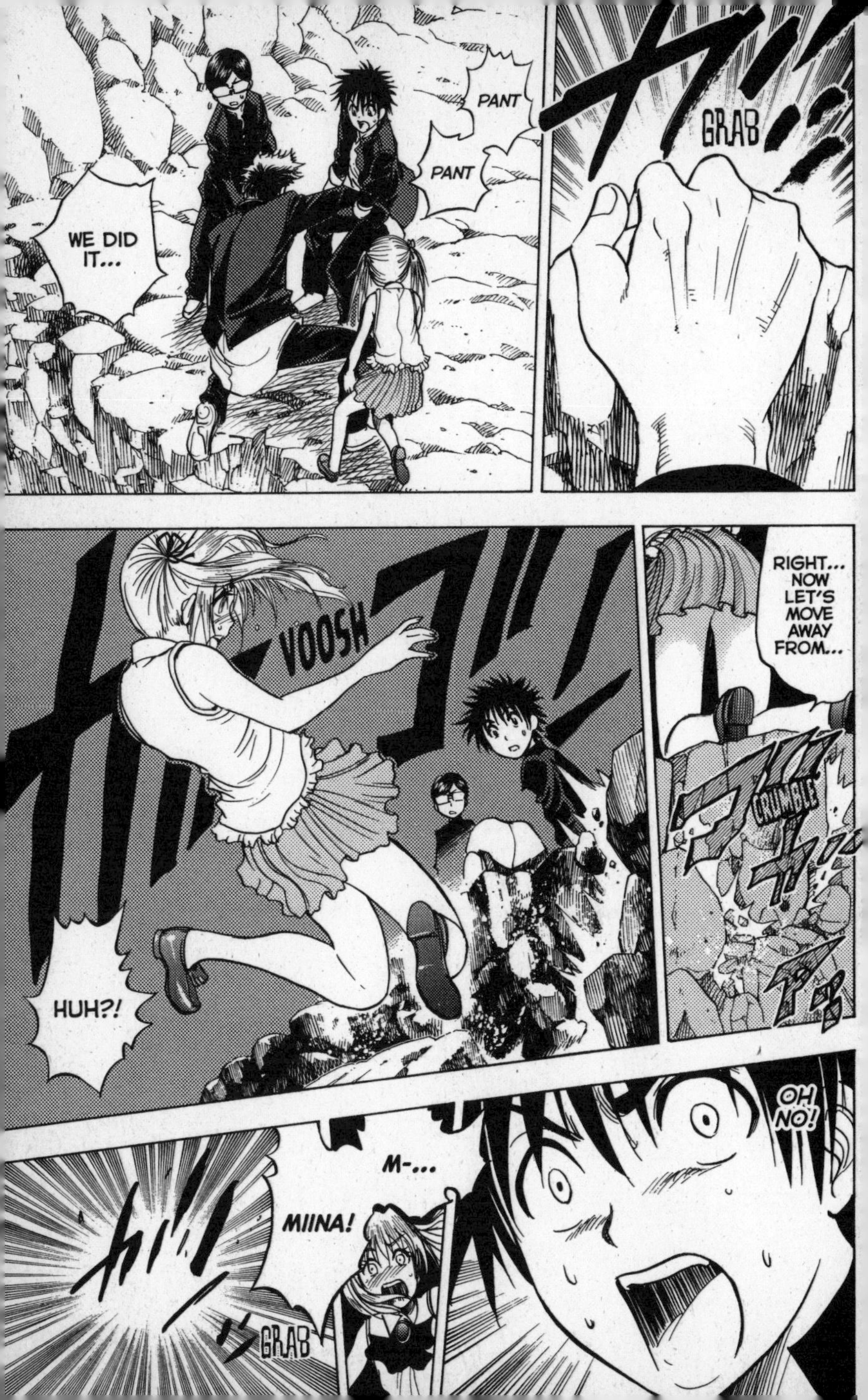
GRAB
PANT
PANT
WE DID IT...
RIGHT... NOW LET'S MOVE AWAY FROM...
CRUMBLE
VOOSH
HUH?!
OH NO!
M-...
MIINA!
GRAB

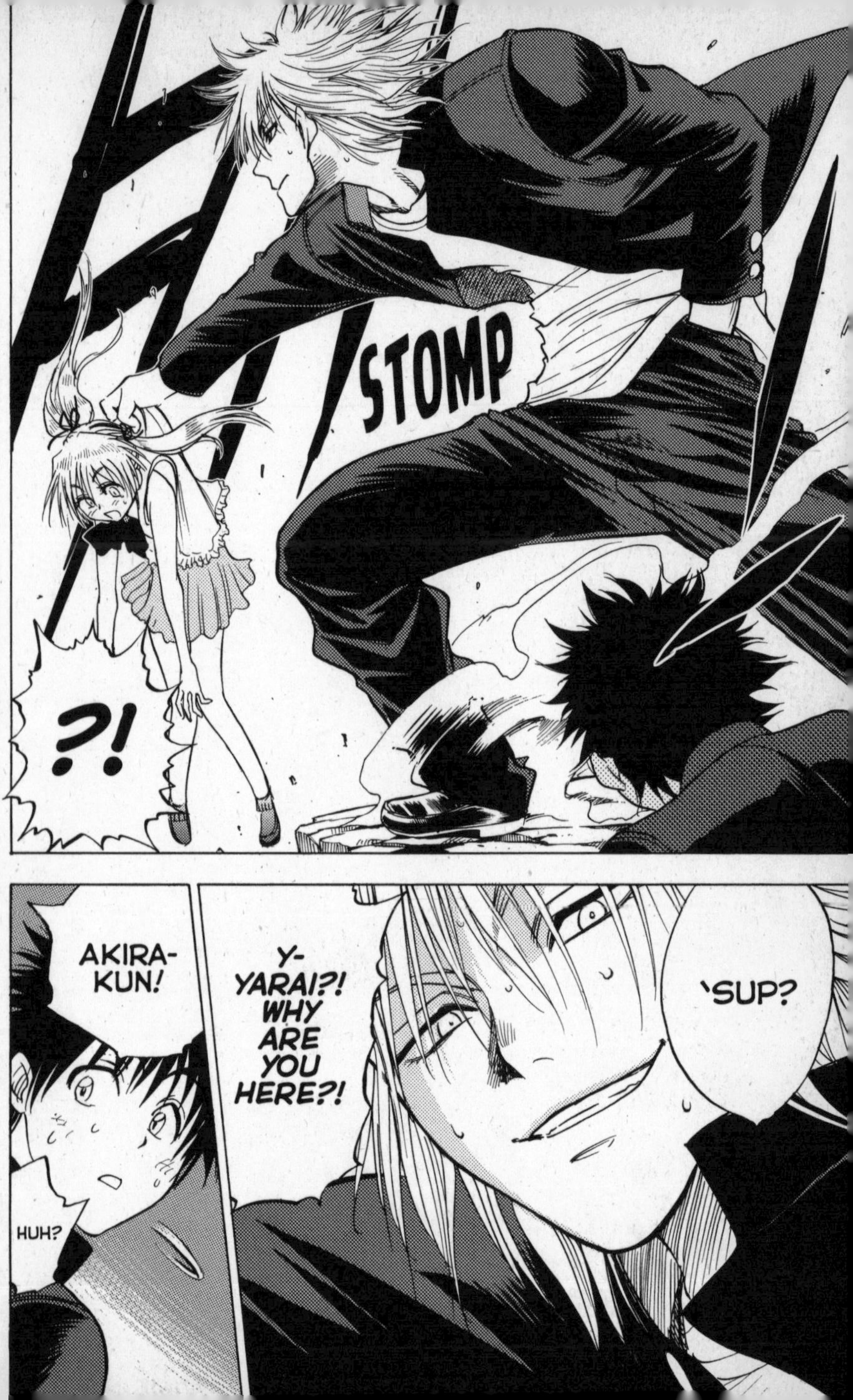
STOMP
?!
'SUP?
Y-YARAI?! WHY ARE YOU HERE?!
AKIRA-KUN!
HUH?

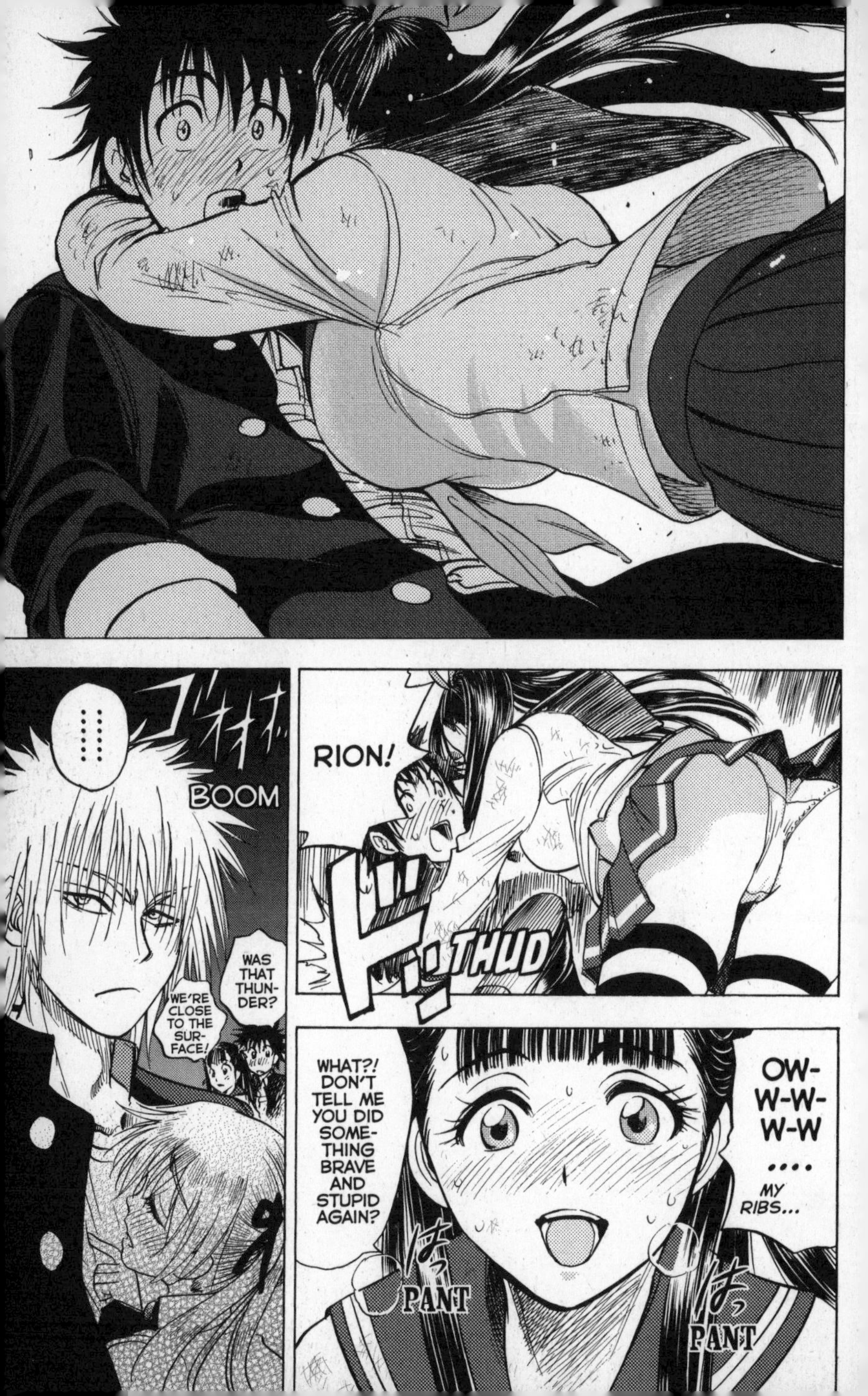
RION!
THUD
OW-W-W-W-W....
MY RIBS...
WHAT?! DON'T TELL ME YOU DID SOMETHING BRAVE AND STUPID AGAIN?
PANT
PANT
......
BOOM
WAS THAT THUNDER?
WE'RE CLOSE TO THE SURFACE!

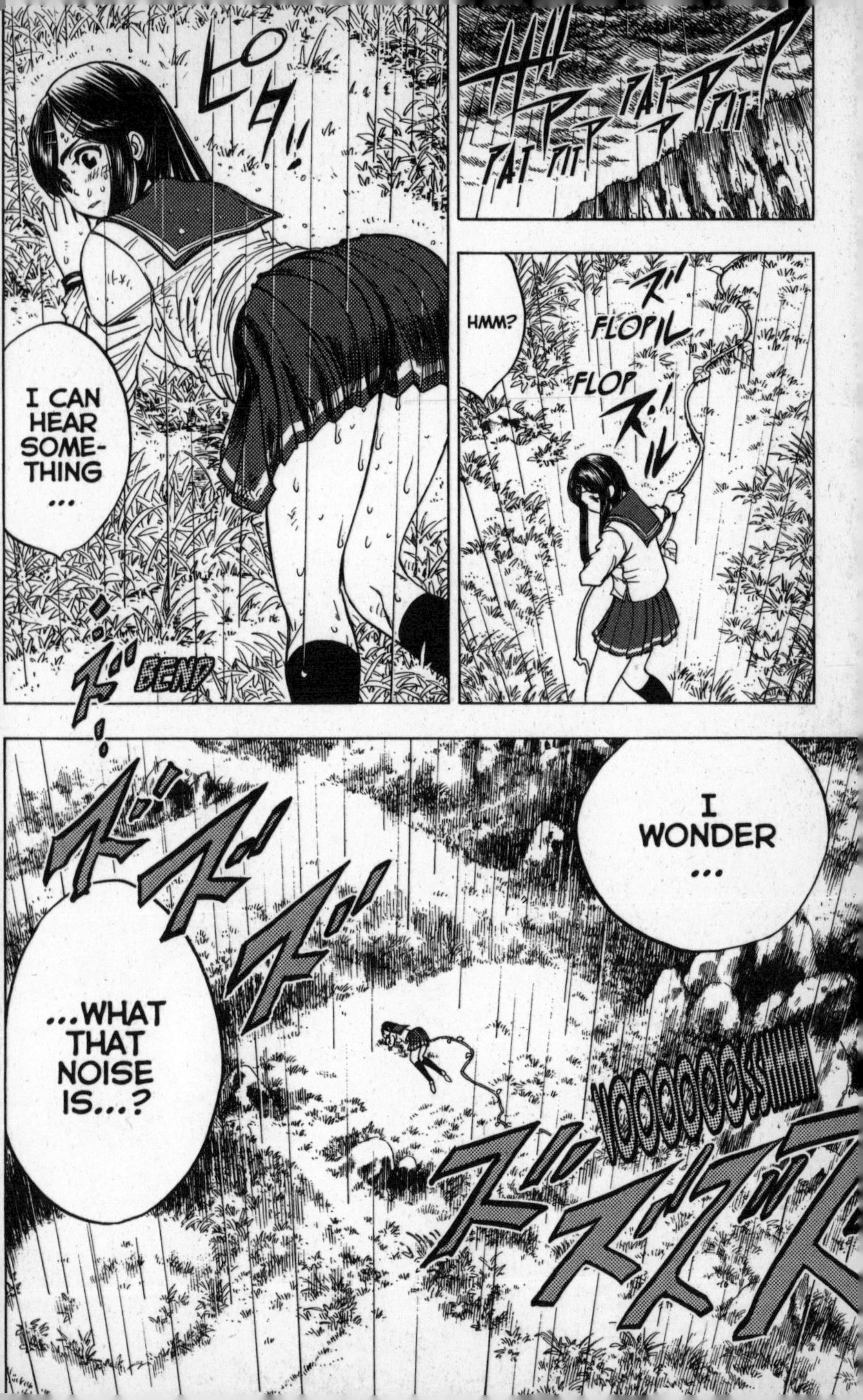
PAT PIT PAT PIT PAT PIT
HMM?
FLOP
FLOP
I CAN HEAR SOME-THING ...
BEND
I WONDER ...
...WHAT THAT NOISE IS...?
VOOOOOOOSSHHH

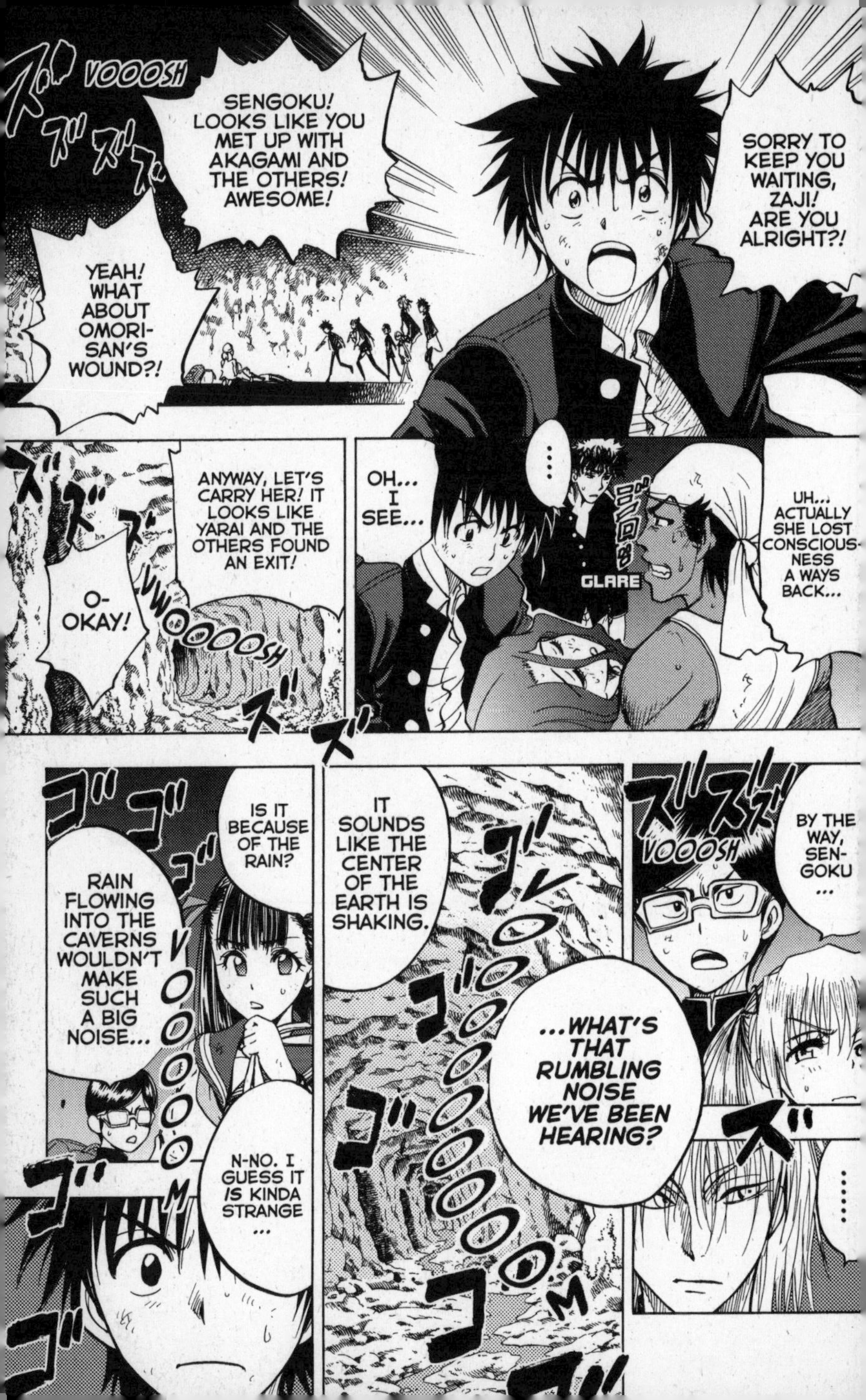
SORRY TO KEEP YOU WAITING, ZAJI! ARE YOU ALRIGHT?!
VOOOSH
SENGOKU! LOOKS LIKE YOU MET UP WITH AKAGAMI AND THE OTHERS! AWESOME!
YEAH! WHAT ABOUT OMORI-SAN'S WOUND?!
UH... ACTUALLY SHE LOST CONSCIOUSNESS A WAYS BACK...
....
GLARE
OH... I SEE...
ANYWAY, LET'S CARRY HER! IT LOOKS LIKE YARAI AND THE OTHERS FOUND AN EXIT!
O-OKAY!
VWOOOOOSH
BY THE WAY, SENGOKU...
VOOOSH
...WHAT'S THAT RUMBLING NOISE WE'VE BEEN HEARING?
......
IT SOUNDS LIKE THE CENTER OF THE EARTH IS SHAKING.
IS IT BECAUSE OF THE RAIN?
RAIN FLOWING INTO THE CAVERNS WOULDN'T MAKE SUCH A BIG NOISE...
N-NO. I GUESS IT IS KINDA STRANGE...

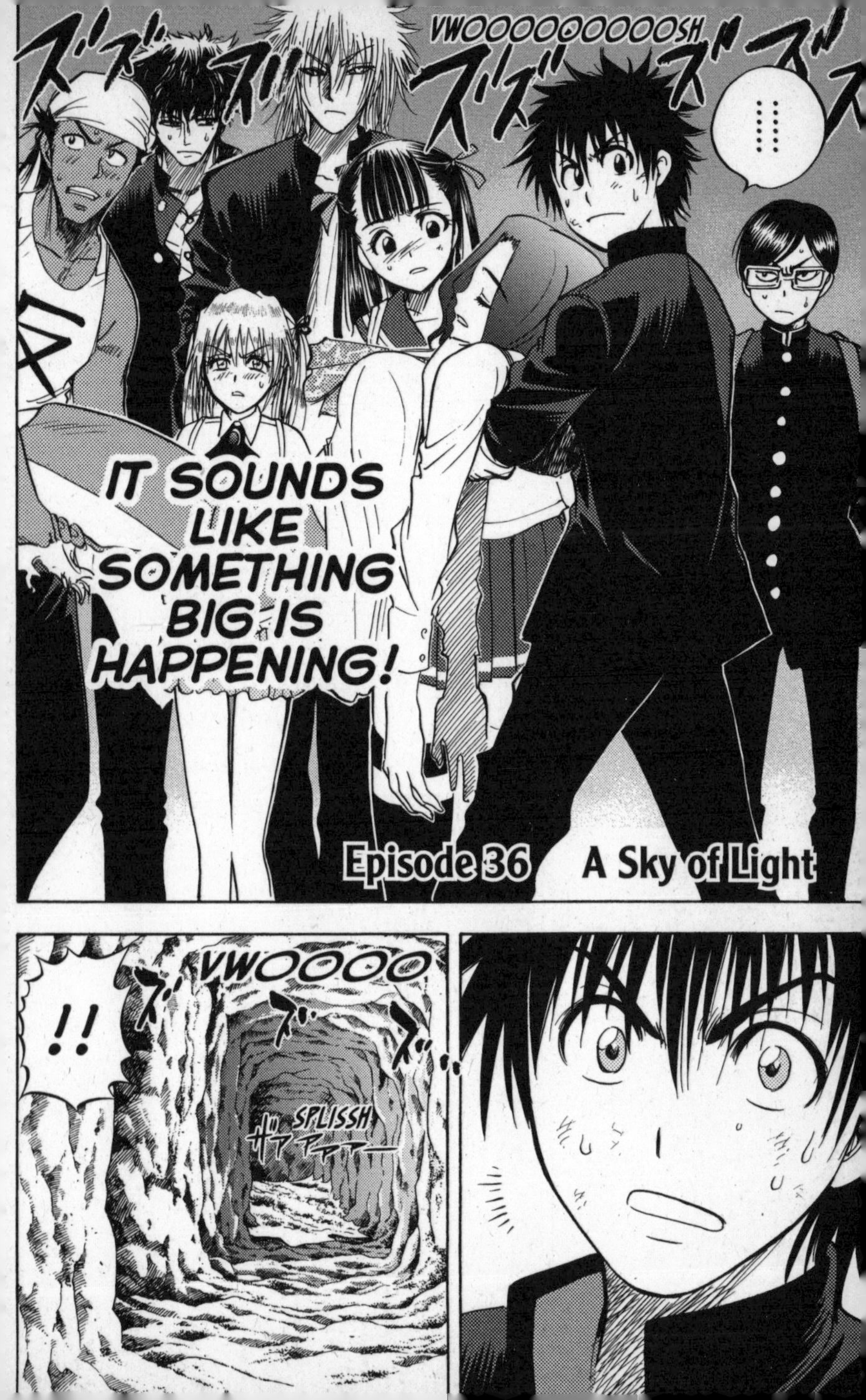
VWOOOOOOOOOOSH
......
IT SOUNDS LIKE SOMETHING BIG IS HAPPENING!
Episode 36 A Sky of Light
VWOOOOO
!!
SPLISSH

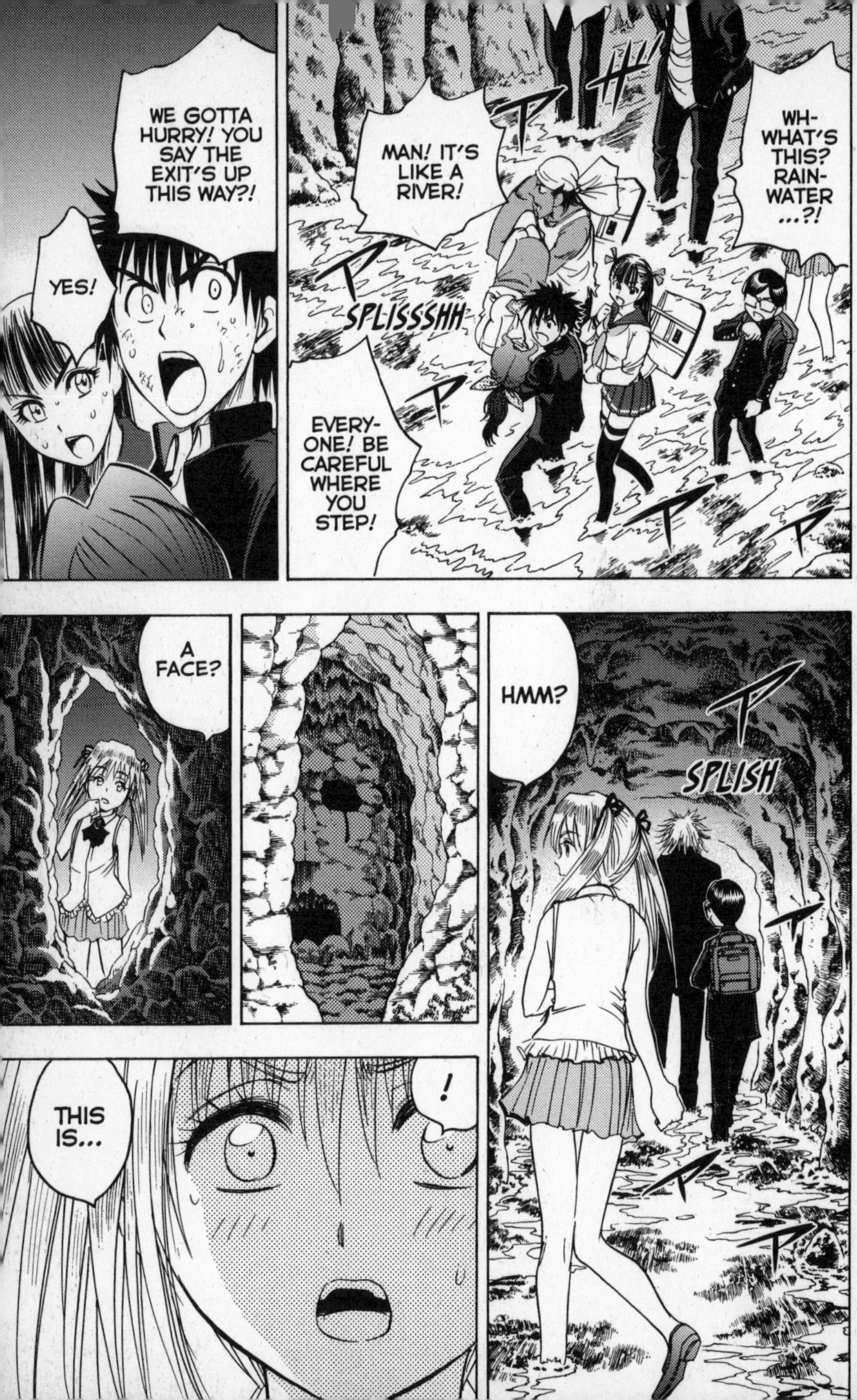
WH- WHAT'S THIS? RAIN-WATER ...?!
MAN! IT'S LIKE A RIVER!
SPLISSSHH
EVERY-ONE! BE CAREFUL WHERE YOU STEP!
WE GOTTA HURRY! YOU SAY THE EXIT'S UP THIS WAY?!
YES!
HMM?
SPLISH
A FACE?
!
THIS IS...

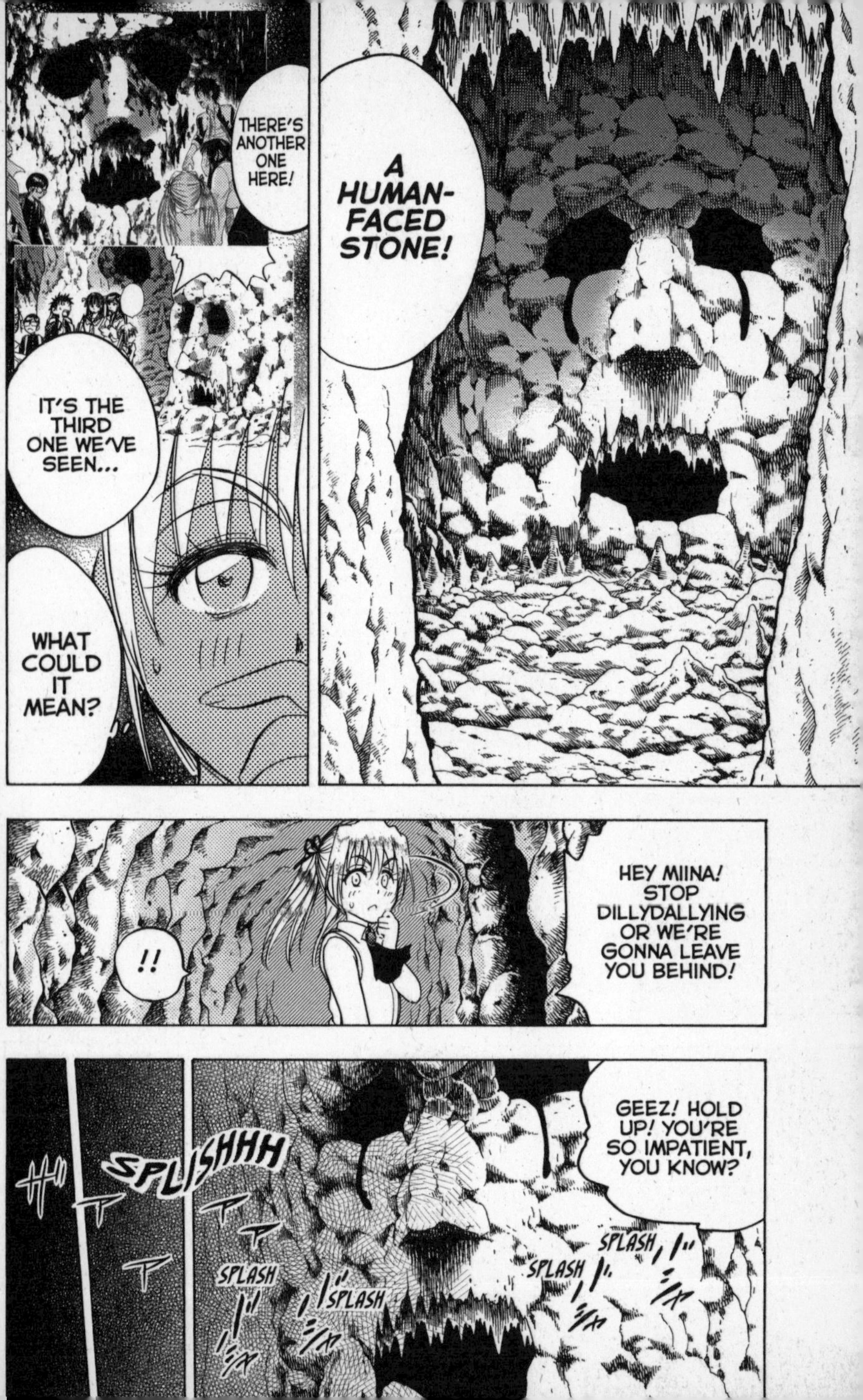

A HUMAN-FACED STONE!
THERE'S ANOTHER ONE HERE!
IT'S THE THIRD ONE WE'VE SEEN...
WHAT COULD IT MEAN?
HEY MIINA! STOP DILLYDALLYING OR WE'RE GONNA LEAVE YOU BEHIND!
!!
GEEZ! HOLD UP! YOU'RE SO IMPATIENT, YOU KNOW?
SPLASH
SPLASH
SPLASH
SPLASH
SPLISHHH

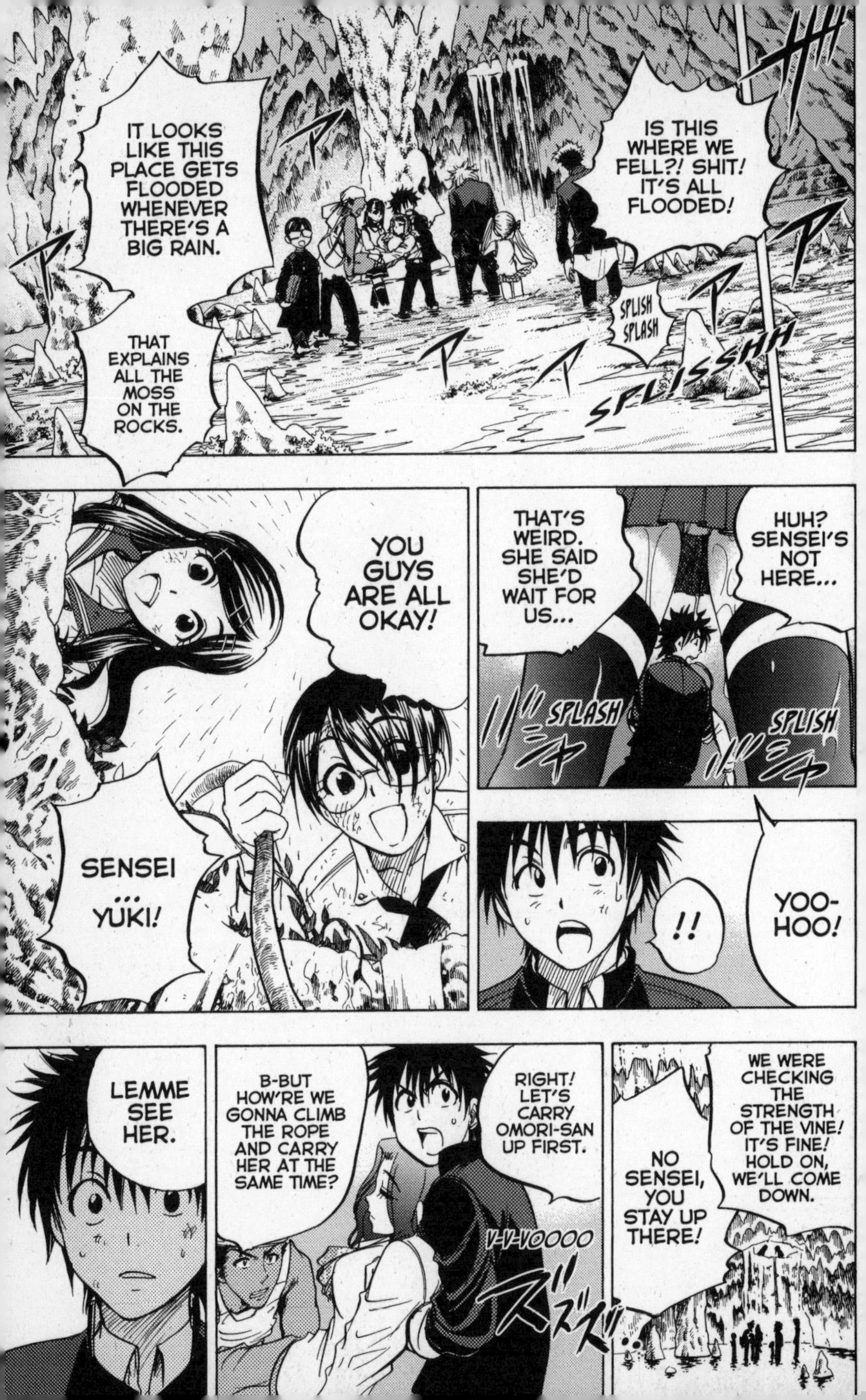
IS THIS WHERE WE FELL?! SHIT! IT'S ALL FLOODED!
SPLISSHH
SPLISH SPLASH
IT LOOKS LIKE THIS PLACE GETS FLOODED WHENEVER THERE'S A BIG RAIN.
THAT EXPLAINS ALL THE MOSS ON THE ROCKS.
HUH? SENSEI'S NOT HERE...
THAT'S WEIRD. SHE SAID SHE'D WAIT FOR US...
SPLISH
SPLASH
YOO-HOO!
!!
YOU GUYS ARE ALL OKAY!
SENSEI ... YUKI!
WE WERE CHECKING THE STRENGTH OF THE VINE! IT'S FINE! HOLD ON, WE'LL COME DOWN.
NO SENSEI, YOU STAY UP THERE!
RIGHT! LET'S CARRY OMORI-SAN UP FIRST.
B-BUT HOW'RE WE GONNA CLIMB THE ROPE AND CARRY HER AT THE SAME TIME?
V-V-VOOOO
LEMME SEE HER.

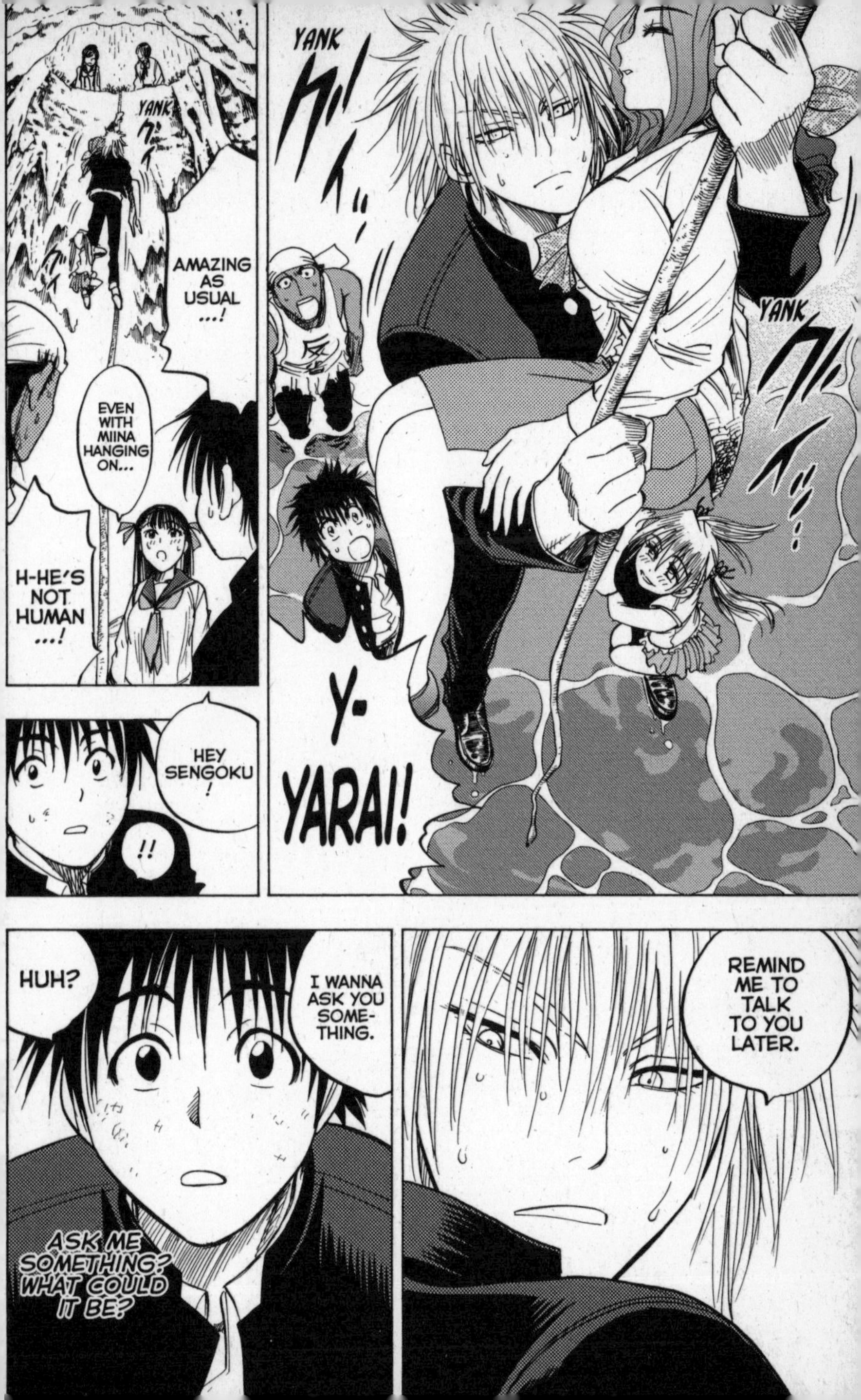
YANK
YANK
Y- YARAI!
YANK
AMAZING AS USUAL ...!
EVEN WITH MIINA HANGING ON...
H-HE'S NOT HUMAN ...!
HEY SENGOKU!
!!
REMIND ME TO TALK TO YOU LATER.
I WANNA ASK YOU SOME-THING.
HUH?
ASK ME SOMETHING? WHAT COULD IT BE?

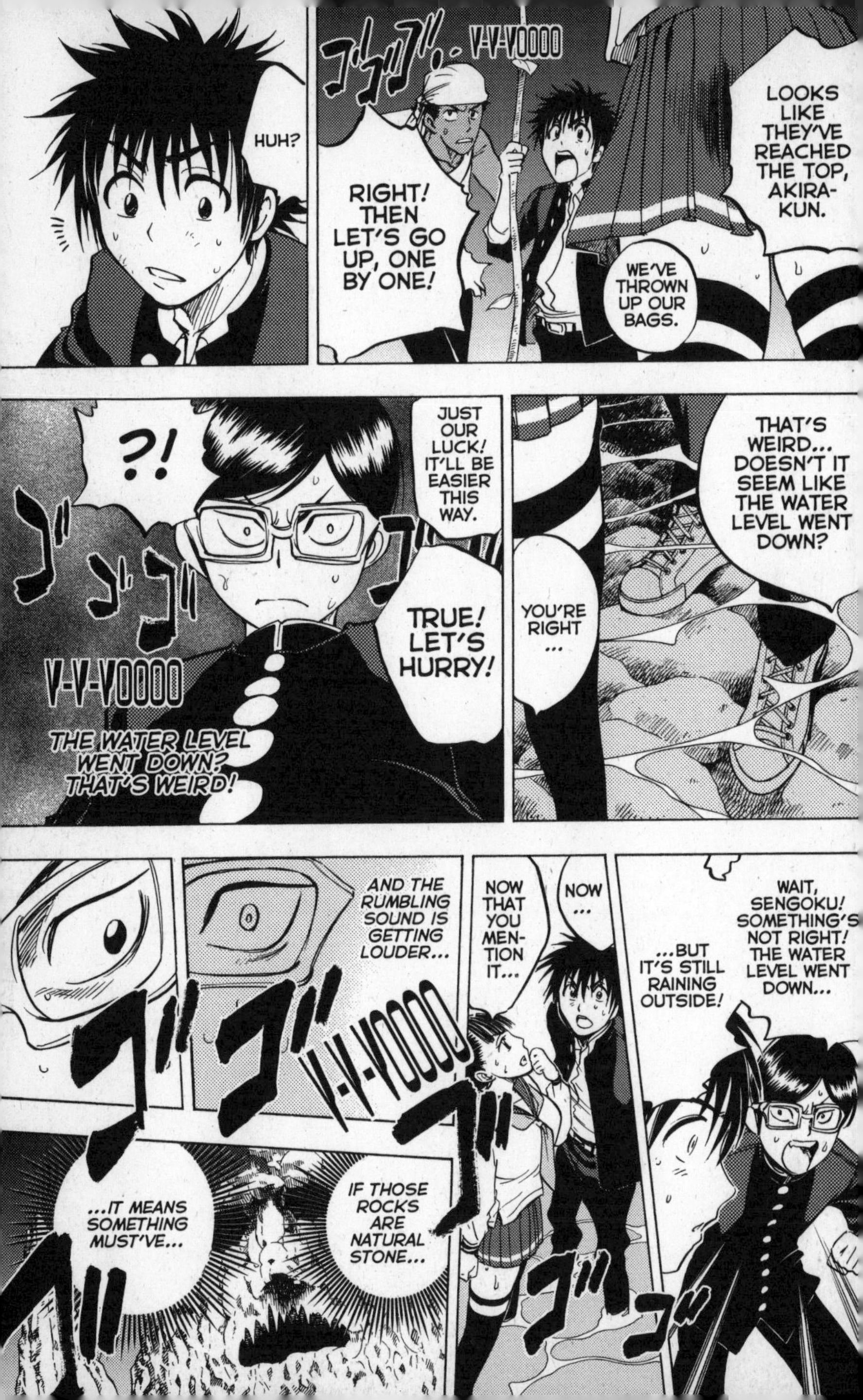
LOOKS LIKE THEY'VE REACHED THE TOP, AKIRA-KUN.
WE'VE THROWN UP OUR BAGS.
V-V-VOOOO
RIGHT! THEN LET'S GO UP, ONE BY ONE!
HUH?
THAT'S WEIRD... DOESN'T IT SEEM LIKE THE WATER LEVEL WENT DOWN?
YOU'RE RIGHT ...
JUST OUR LUCK! IT'LL BE EASIER THIS WAY.
TRUE! LET'S HURRY!
?!
V-V-VOOOO
THE WATER LEVEL WENT DOWN? THAT'S WEIRD!
WAIT, SENGOKU! SOMETHING'S NOT RIGHT! THE WATER LEVEL WENT DOWN...
...BUT IT'S STILL RAINING OUTSIDE!
NOW ...
NOW THAT YOU MEN-TION IT...
AND THE RUMBLING SOUND IS GETTING LOUDER...
V-V-VOOOO
IF THOSE ROCKS ARE NATURAL STONE...
...IT MEANS SOMETHING MUST'VE...

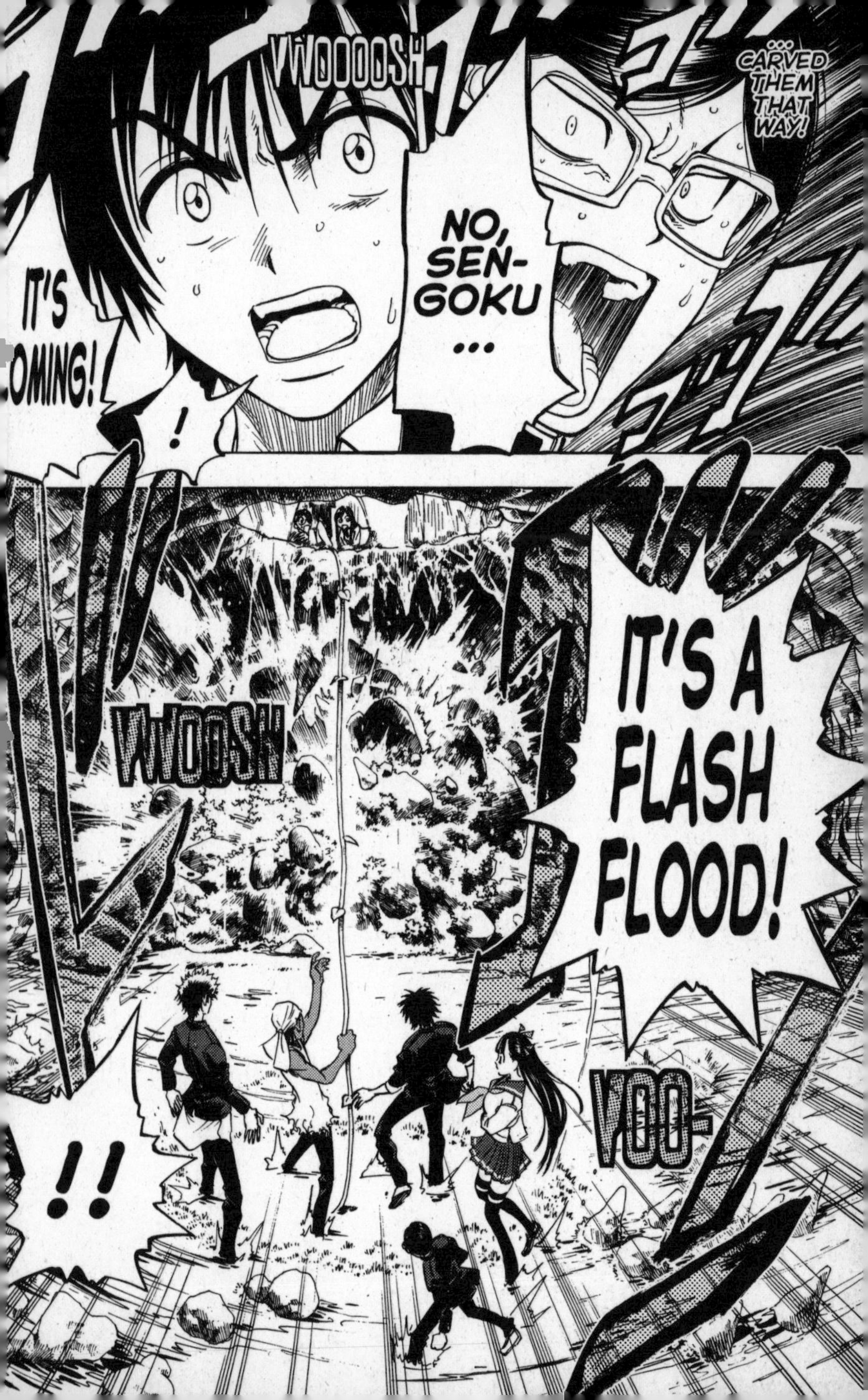

...CARVED THEM THAT WAY!
NO, SEN-GOKU...
VWOOOOSH
!
IT'S OMING!
IT'S A FLASH FLOOD!
VOO-
VWOOSH
!!

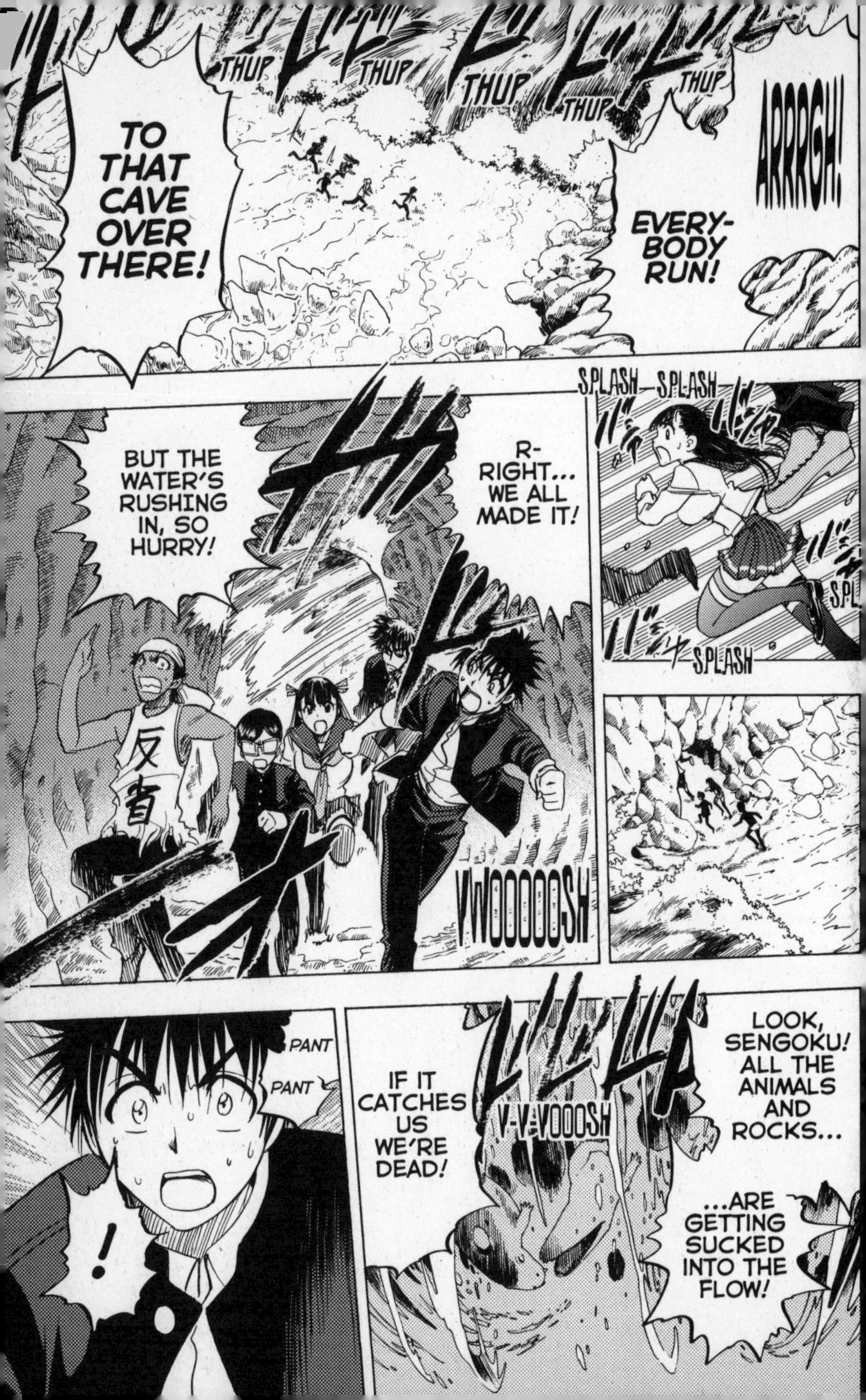
ARRRGH!
THUP
THUP
THUP
THUP
THUP
THUP
EVERY-BODY RUN!
TO THAT CAVE OVER THERE!
SPLASH SPLASH
SPL
SPLASH
R-RIGHT... WE ALL MADE IT!
BUT THE WATER'S RUSHING IN, SO HURRY!
VWOOOOOSH
LOOK, SENGOKU! ALL THE ANIMALS AND ROCKS...
...ARE GETTING SUCKED INTO THE FLOW!
V-V-VOOOSH
IF IT CATCHES US WE'RE DEAD!
PANT
PANT
!

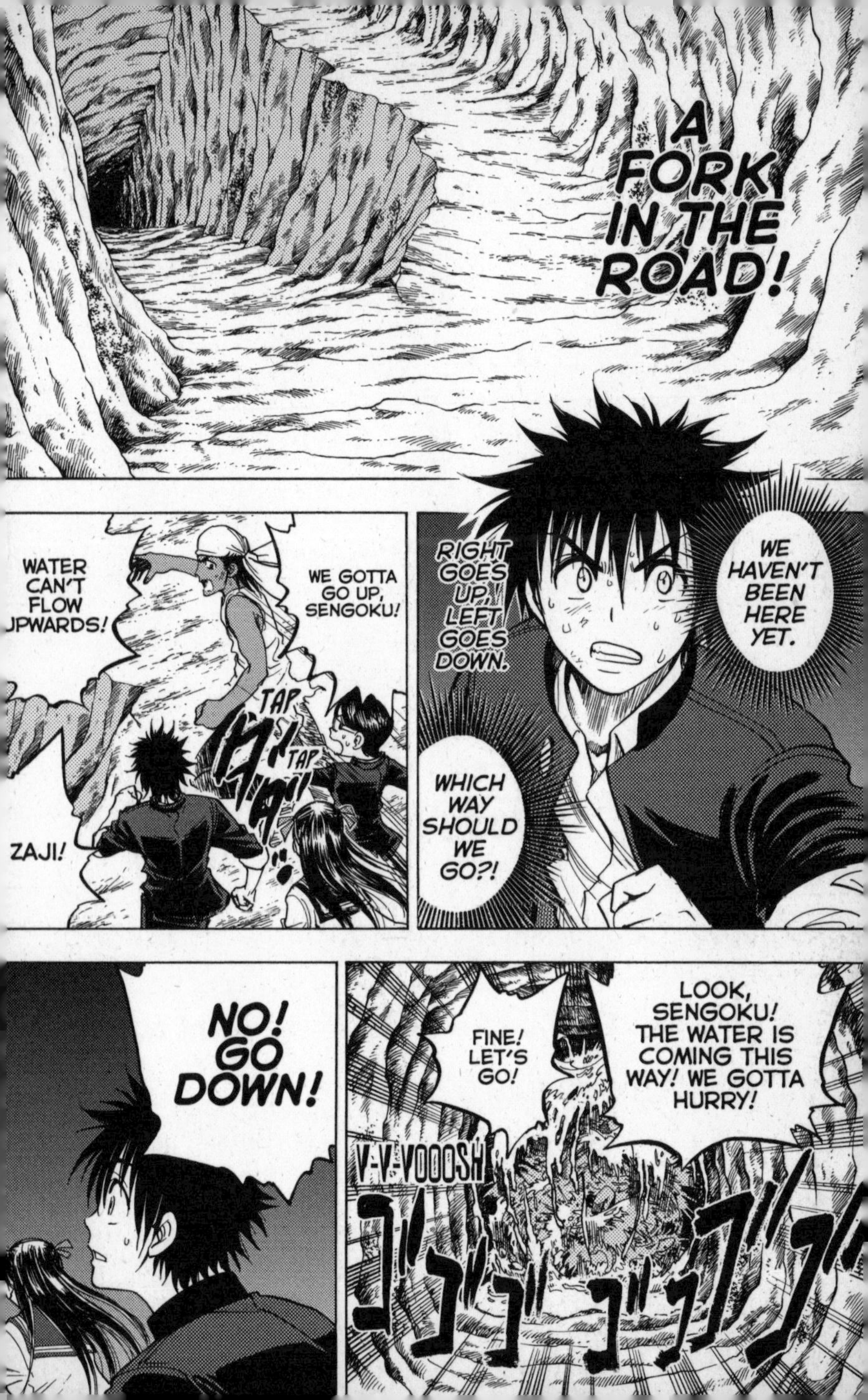

A FORK IN THE ROAD!
WE HAVEN'T BEEN HERE YET.
RIGHT GOES UP, LEFT GOES DOWN.
WHICH WAY SHOULD WE GO?!
WE GOTTA GO UP, SENGOKU!
WATER CAN'T FLOW UPWARDS!
TAP
TAP
ZAJI!
LOOK, SENGOKU! THE WATER IS COMING THIS WAY! WE GOTTA HURRY!
FINE! LET'S GO!
V-V-VOOOSH
NO! GO DOWN!

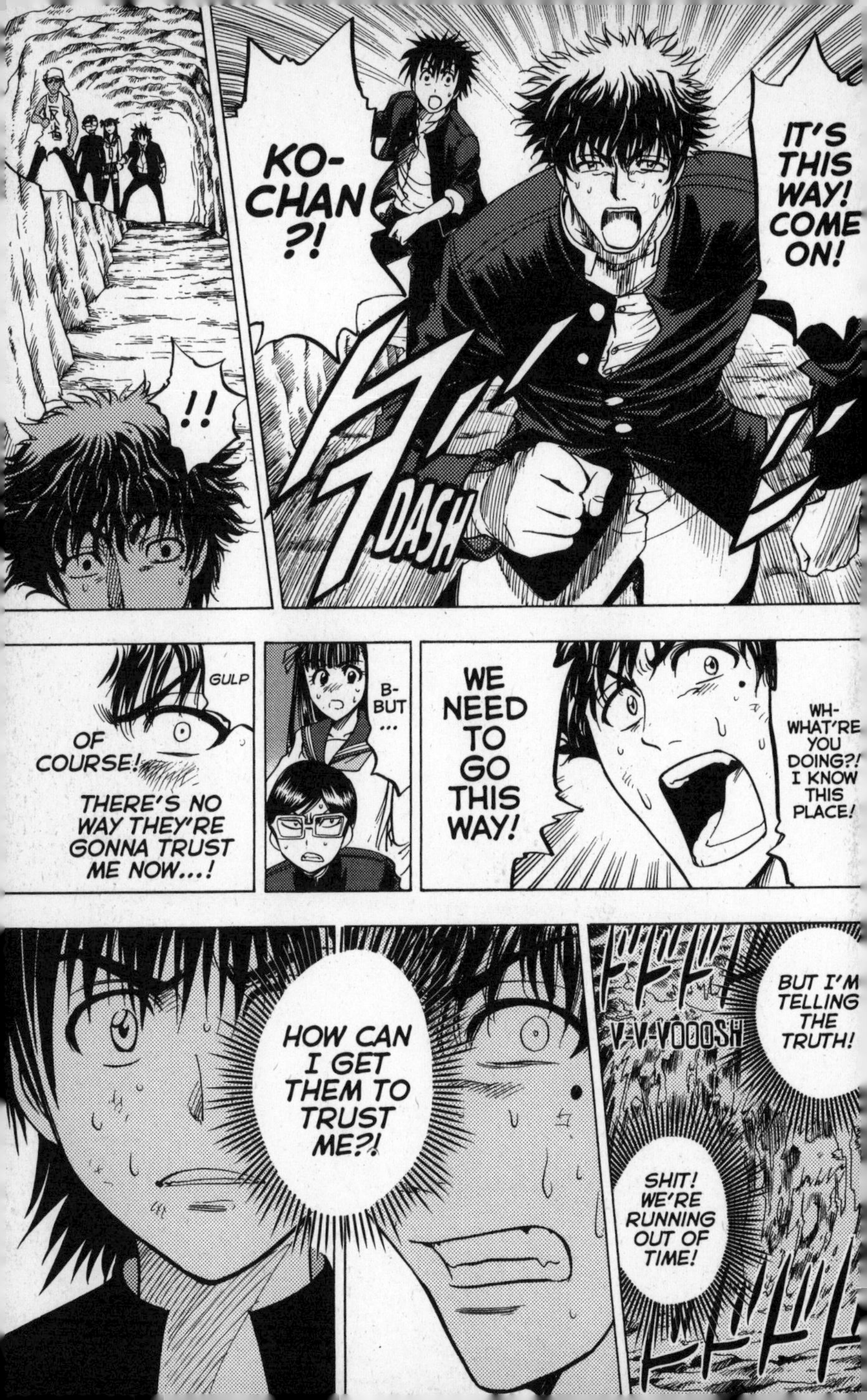
IT'S THIS WAY! COME ON!
KO-CHAN?!
DASH
!!
WH-WHAT'RE YOU DOING?! I KNOW THIS PLACE!
WE NEED TO GO THIS WAY!
B-BUT...
GULP
OF COURSE!
THERE'S NO WAY THEY'RE GONNA TRUST ME NOW...!
BUT I'M TELLING THE TRUTH!
V-V-VOOOSH
SHIT! WE'RE RUNNING OUT OF TIME!
HOW CAN I GET THEM TO TRUST ME?!

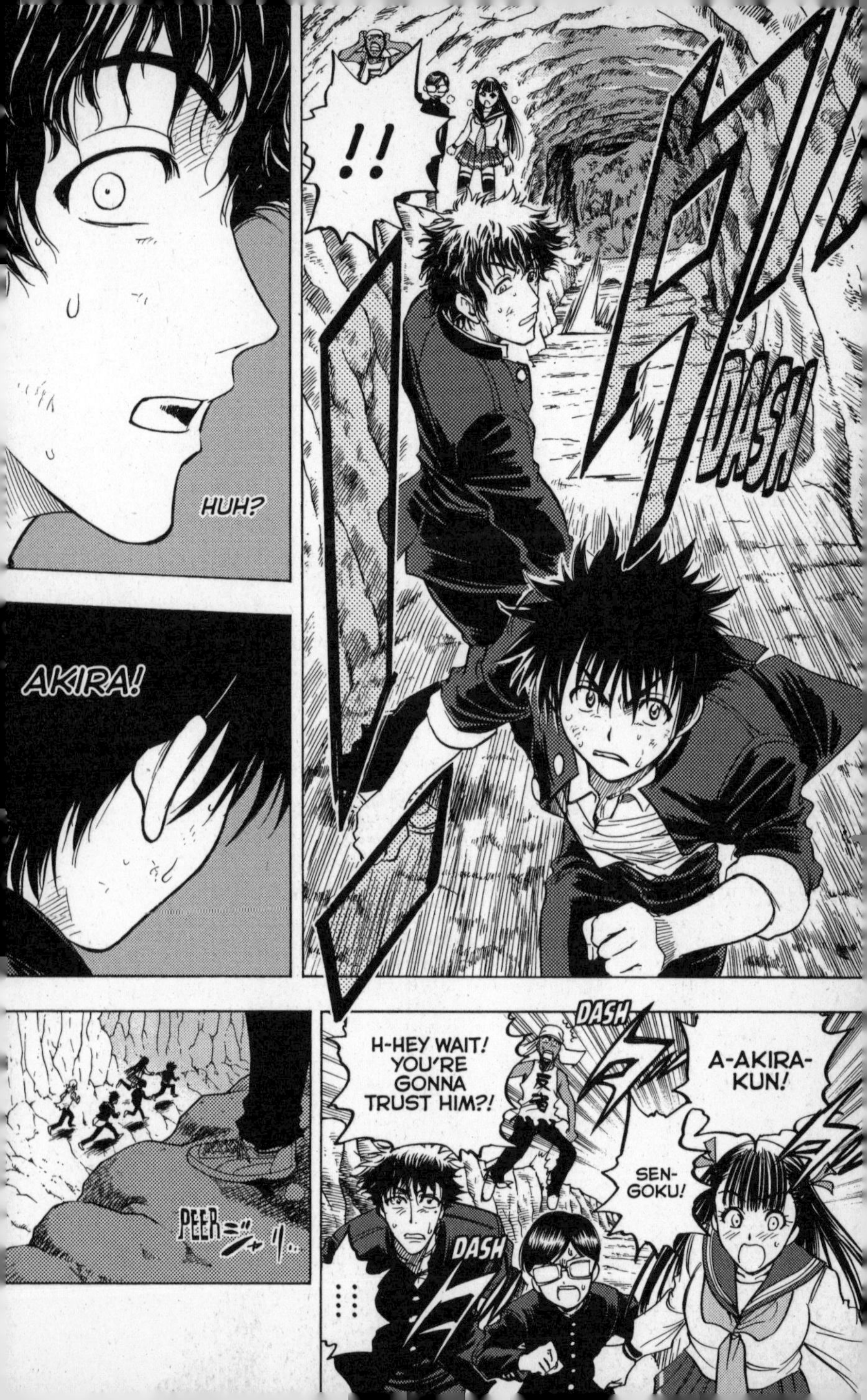
!!
DASH
HUH?
AKIRA!
A-AKIRA-KUN!
DASH
H-HEY WAIT! YOU'RE GONNA TRUST HIM?!
SEN-GOKU!
DASH
PEER

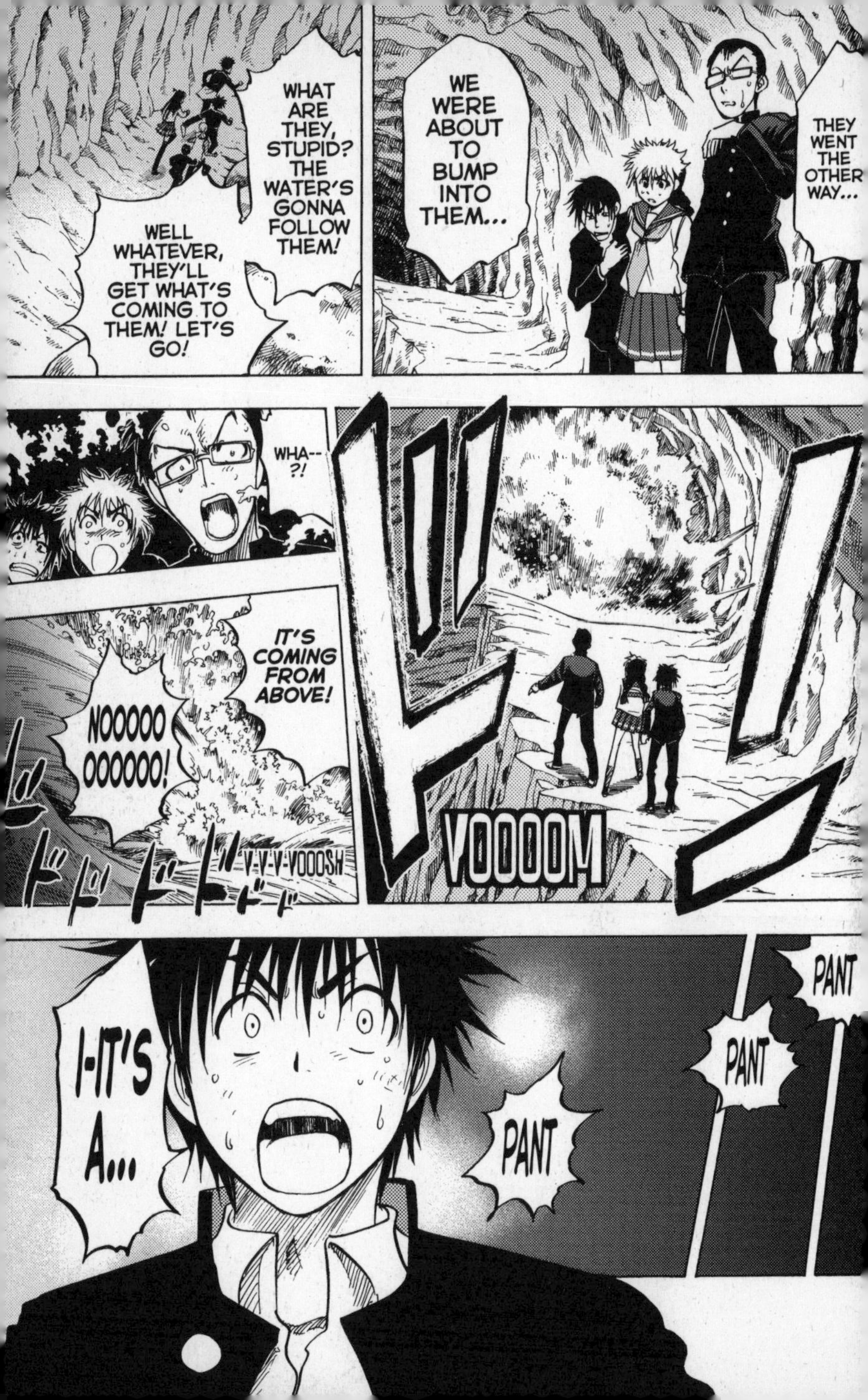
THEY WENT THE OTHER WAY...
WE WERE ABOUT TO BUMP INTO THEM...
WHAT ARE THEY, STUPID? THE WATER'S GONNA FOLLOW THEM!
WELL WHATEVER, THEY'LL GET WHAT'S COMING TO THEM! LET'S GO!
VOOOOM
WHA--?!
IT'S COMING FROM ABOVE!
NOOOOOOOOOOO!
V-V-V-VOOOSH
PANT
PANT
PANT
I-IT'S A...

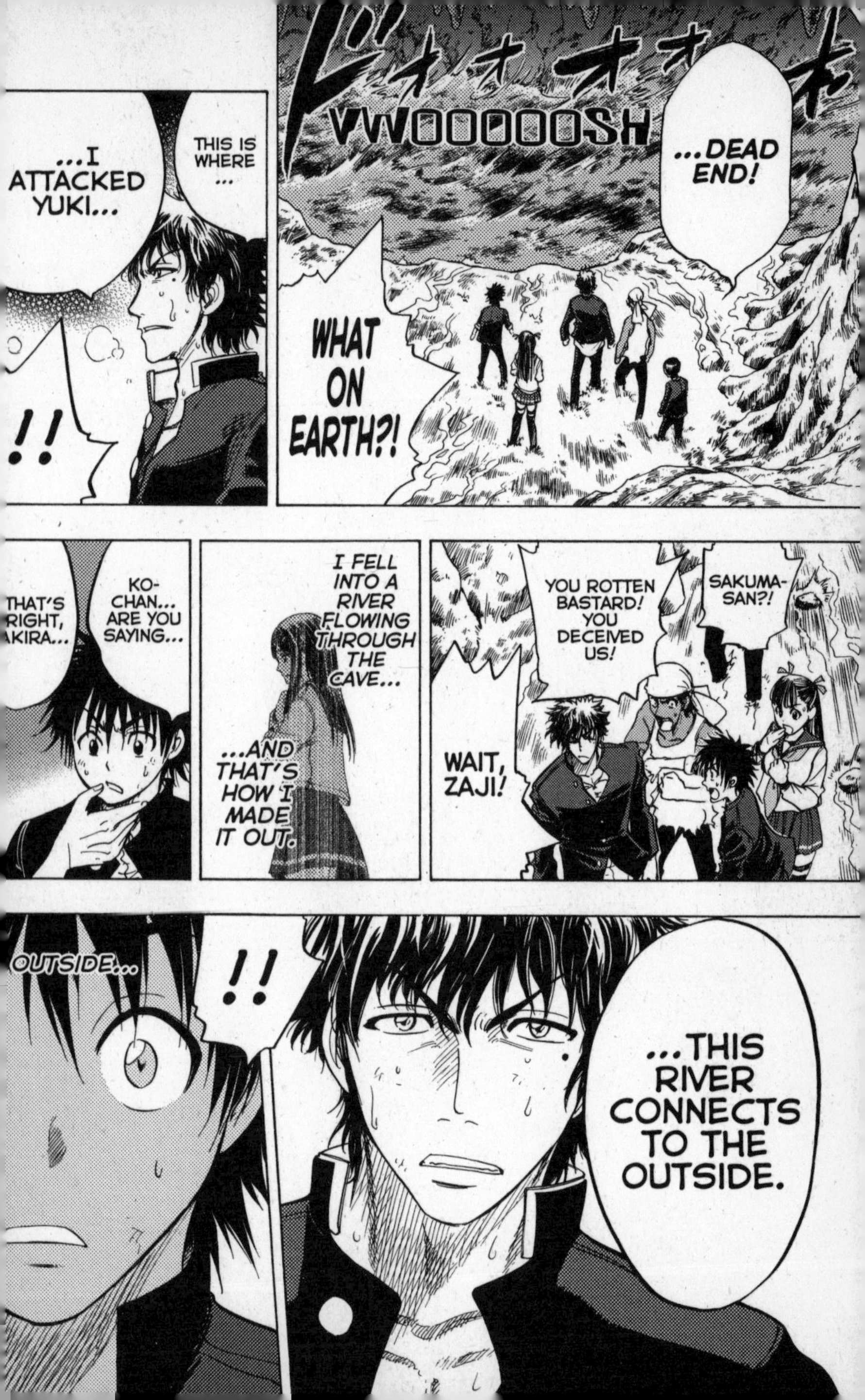
VWOOOOOOSH
...DEAD END!
WHAT ON EARTH?!
THIS IS WHERE ...
...I ATTACKED YUKI...
!!
SAKUMA-SAN?!
YOU ROTTEN BASTARD! YOU DECEIVED US!
WAIT, ZAJI!
I FELL INTO A RIVER FLOWING THROUGH THE CAVE...
...AND THAT'S HOW I MADE IT OUT.
KO-CHAN... ARE YOU SAYING...
THAT'S RIGHT, AKIRA...
...THIS RIVER CONNECTS TO THE OUTSIDE.
!!
OUTSIDE...

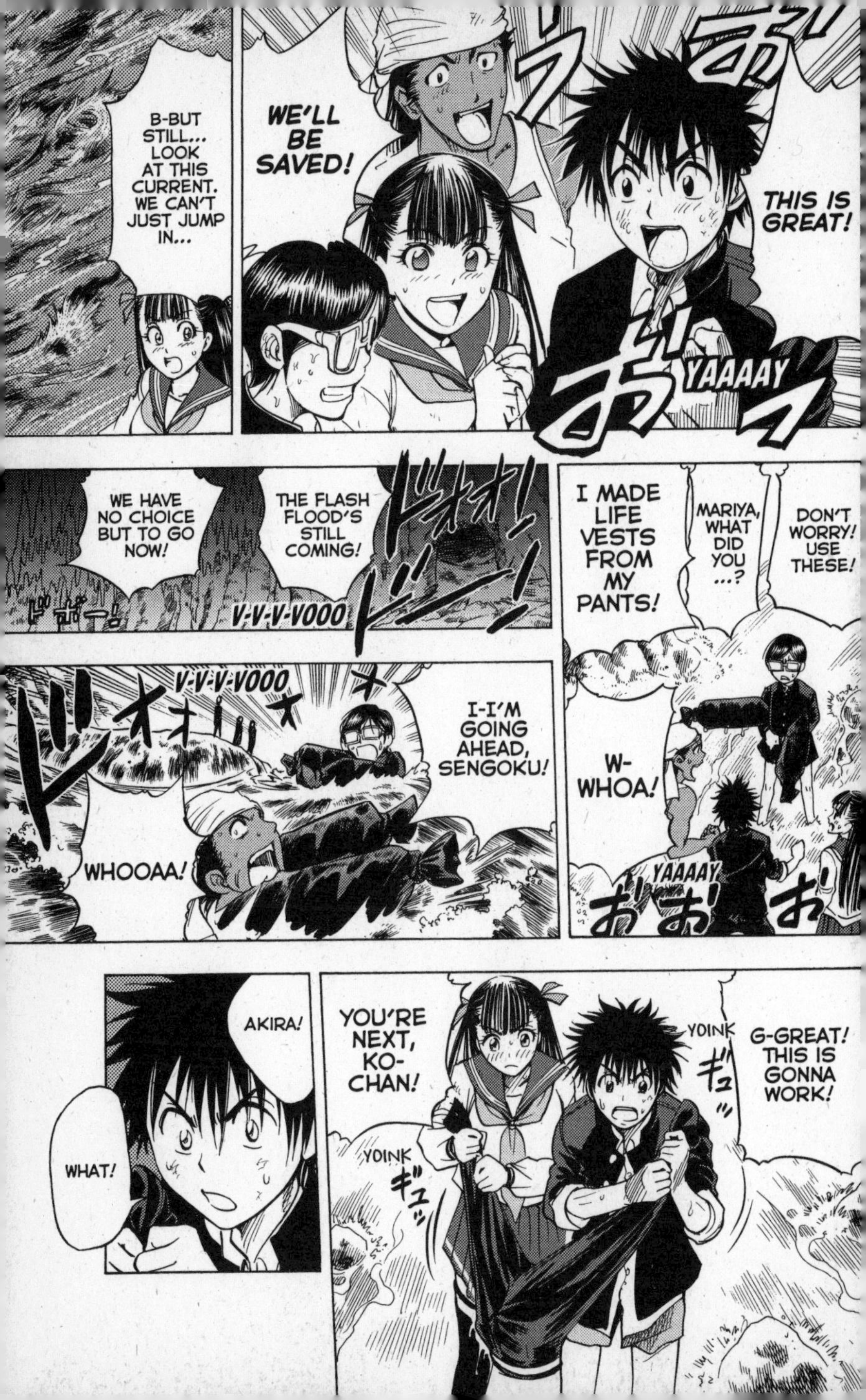
THIS IS GREAT!
WE'LL BE SAVED!
YAAAAY
B-BUT STILL... LOOK AT THIS CURRENT. WE CAN'T JUST JUMP IN...
DON'T WORRY! USE THESE!
MARIYA, WHAT DID YOU ...?
I MADE LIFE VESTS FROM MY PANTS!
W-WHOA!
YAAAAY
THE FLASH FLOOD'S STILL COMING!
V-V-V-VOOO
WE HAVE NO CHOICE BUT TO GO NOW!
I-I'M GOING AHEAD, SENGOKU!
V-V-V-VOOO
WHOOAA!
G-GREAT! THIS IS GONNA WORK!
YOINK
YOU'RE NEXT, KO-CHAN!
YOINK
AKIRA!
WHAT!

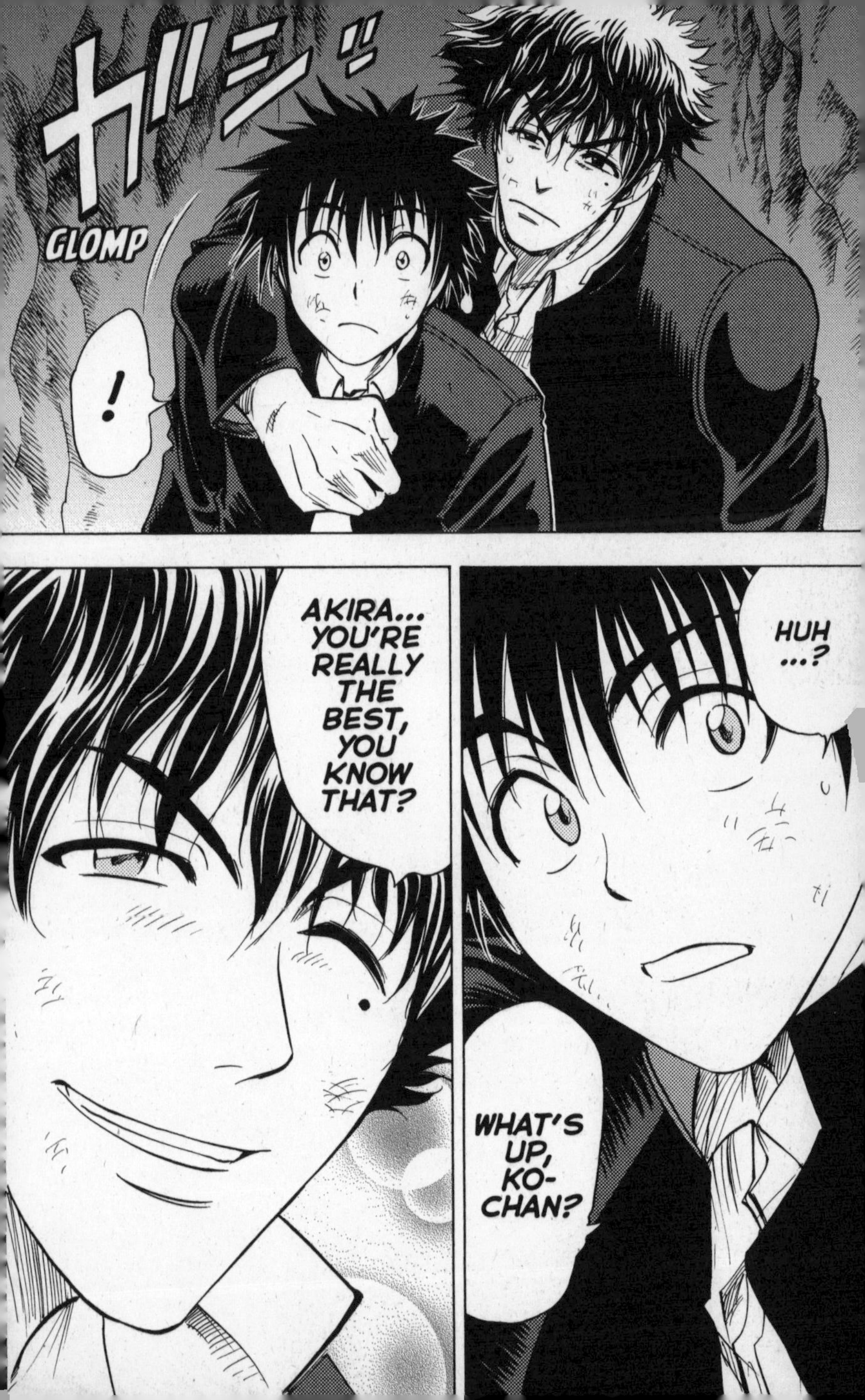
ガシッ
GLOMP
!
HUH ...?
WHAT'S UP, KO-CHAN?
AKIRA... YOU'RE REALLY THE BEST, YOU KNOW THAT?

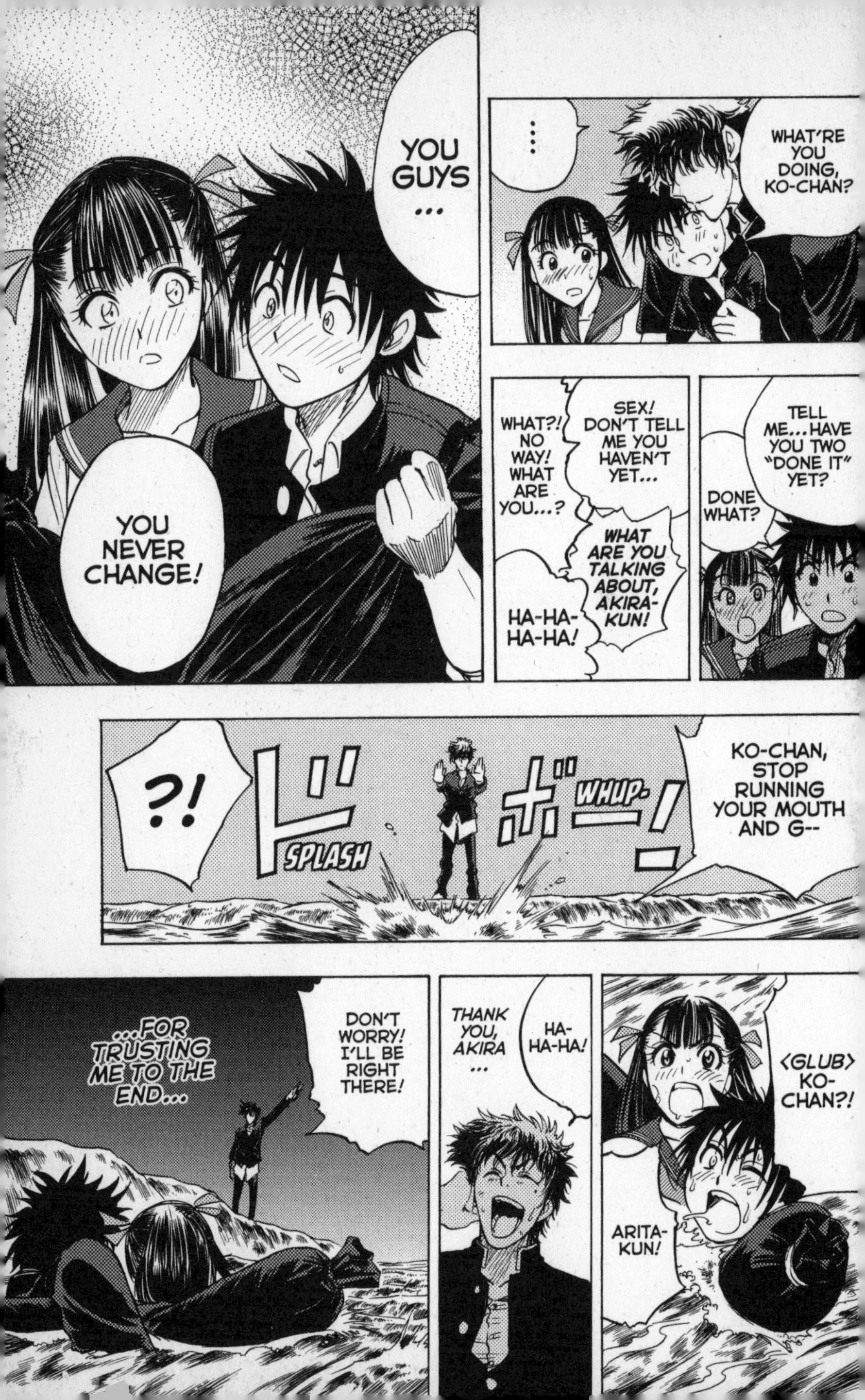

WHAT'RE YOU DOING, KO-CHAN?
....
TELL ME...HAVE YOU TWO "DONE IT" YET?
DONE WHAT?
SEX! DON'T TELL ME YOU HAVEN'T YET...
WHAT?! NO WAY! WHAT ARE YOU...?
WHAT ARE YOU TALKING ABOUT, AKIRA-KUN!
HA-HA-HA-HA!
YOU GUYS...
YOU NEVER CHANGE!
KO-CHAN, STOP RUNNING YOUR MOUTH AND G--
WHUP
SPLASH
?!
<GLUB> KO-CHAN?!
ARITA-KUN!
HA-HA-HA!
THANK YOU, AKIRA...
DON'T WORRY! I'LL BE RIGHT THERE!
...FOR TRUSTING ME TO THE END...

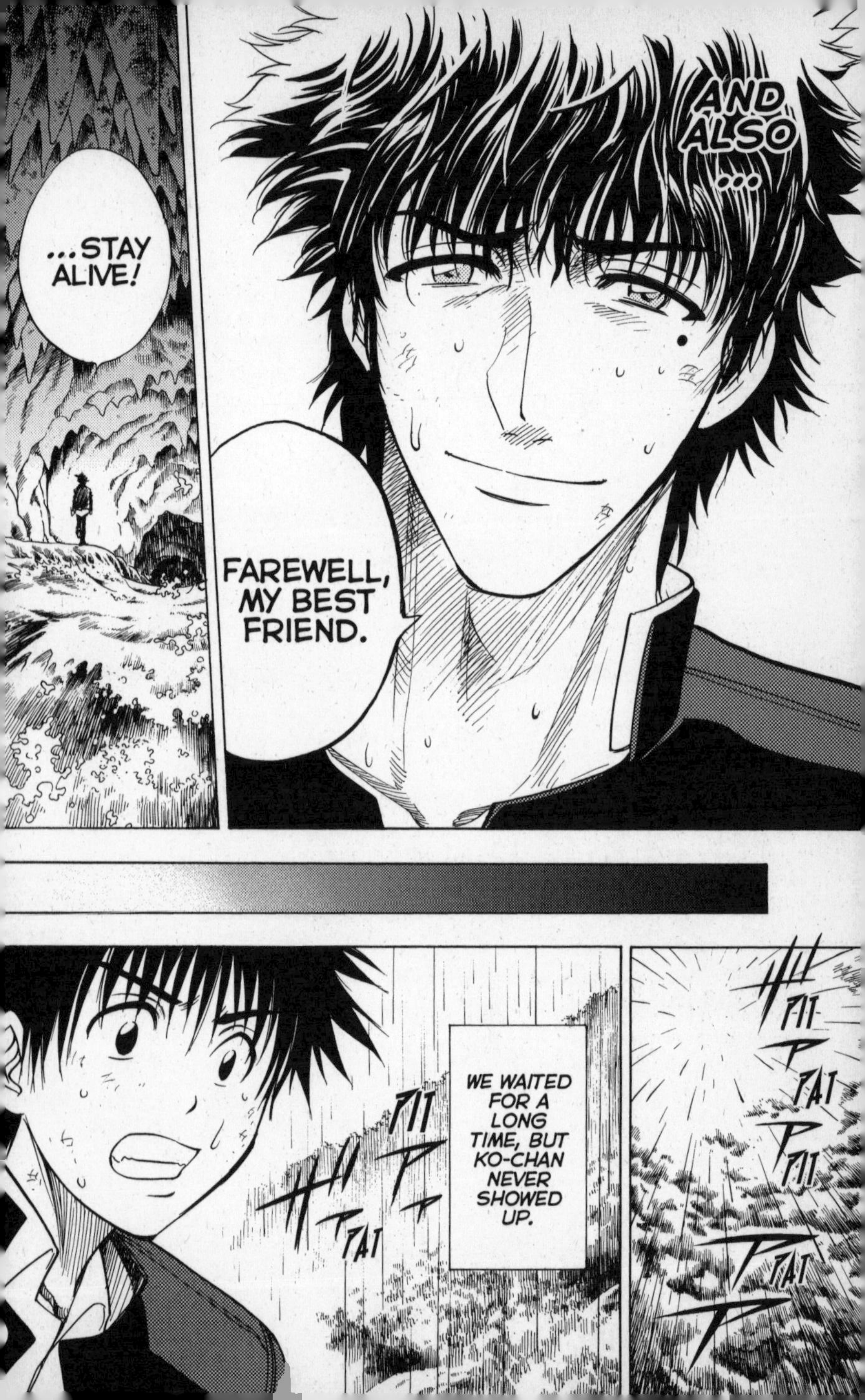
AND ALSO ...
FAREWELL, MY BEST FRIEND.
...STAY ALIVE!
PIT
PAT
PIT
PAT
WE WAITED FOR A LONG TIME, BUT KO-CHAN NEVER SHOWED UP.
PIT
PAT

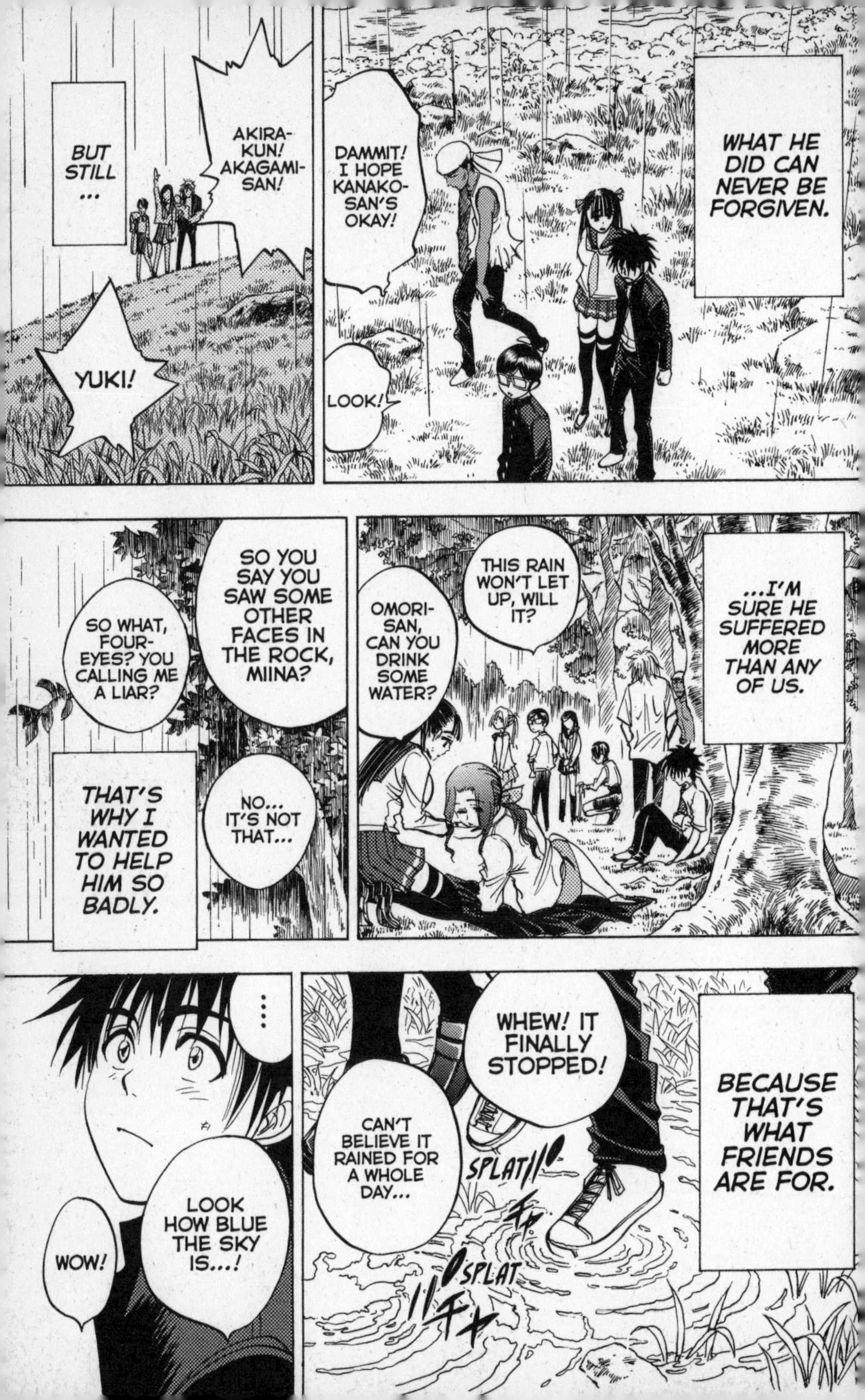
WHAT HE DID CAN NEVER BE FORGIVEN.
DAMMIT! I HOPE KANAKO-SAN'S OKAY!
LOOK!
AKIRA-KUN! AKAGAMI-SAN!
BUT STILL ...
YUKI!
...I'M SURE HE SUFFERED MORE THAN ANY OF US.
THIS RAIN WON'T LET UP, WILL IT?
OMORI-SAN, CAN YOU DRINK SOME WATER?
SO YOU SAY YOU SAW SOME OTHER FACES IN THE ROCK, MIINA?
SO WHAT, FOUR-EYES? YOU CALLING ME A LIAR?
NO... IT'S NOT THAT...
THAT'S WHY I WANTED TO HELP HIM SO BADLY.
BECAUSE THAT'S WHAT FRIENDS ARE FOR.
WHEW! IT FINALLY STOPPED!
CAN'T BELIEVE IT RAINED FOR A WHOLE DAY...
SPLAT
SPLAT
....
LOOK HOW BLUE THE SKY IS...!
WOW!

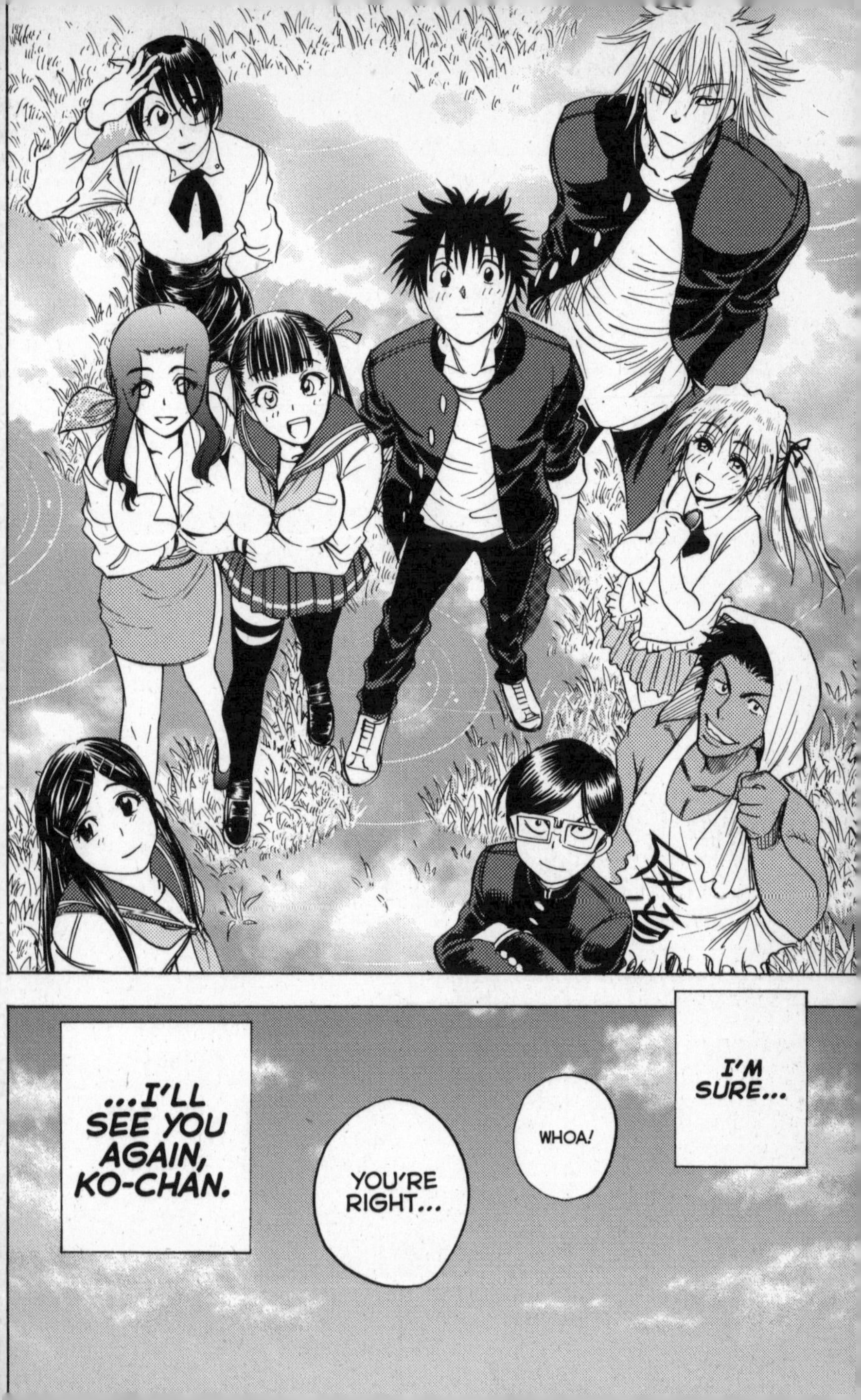
I'M SURE...
WHOA!
YOU'RE RIGHT...
...I'LL SEE YOU AGAIN, KO-CHAN.

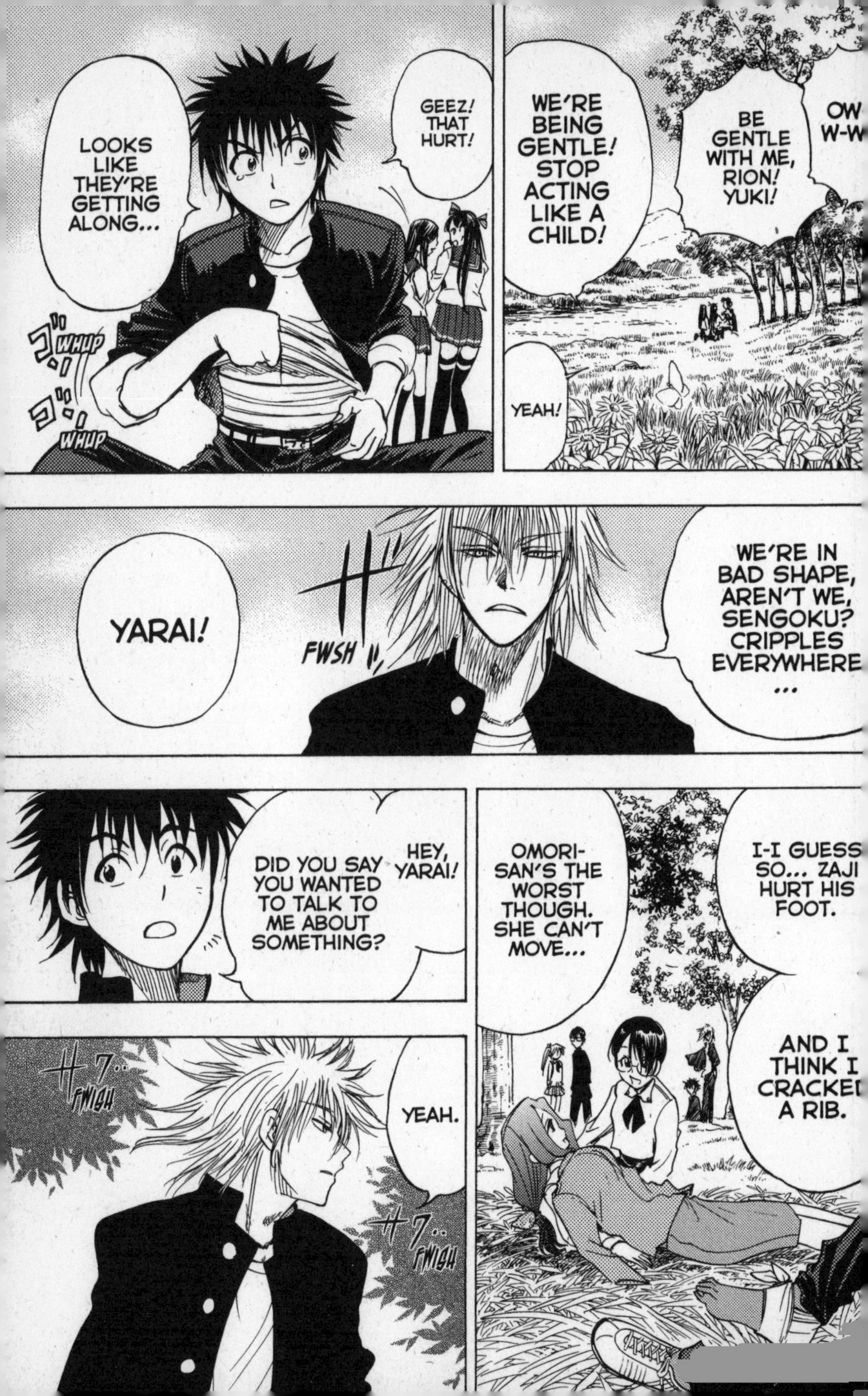
OW W-W
BE GENTLE WITH ME, RION! YUKI!
WE'RE BEING GENTLE! STOP ACTING LIKE A CHILD!
YEAH!
GEEZ! THAT HURT!
LOOKS LIKE THEY'RE GETTING ALONG...
WHUP
WHUP
WE'RE IN BAD SHAPE, AREN'T WE, SENGOKU? CRIPPLES EVERYWHERE...
FWSH
YARAI!
I-I GUESS SO... ZAJI HURT HIS FOOT.
AND I THINK I CRACKED A RIB.
OMORI-SAN'S THE WORST THOUGH. SHE CAN'T MOVE...
HEY, YARAI!
DID YOU SAY YOU WANTED TO TALK TO ME ABOUT SOMETHING?
YEAH.
FWISH
FWISH

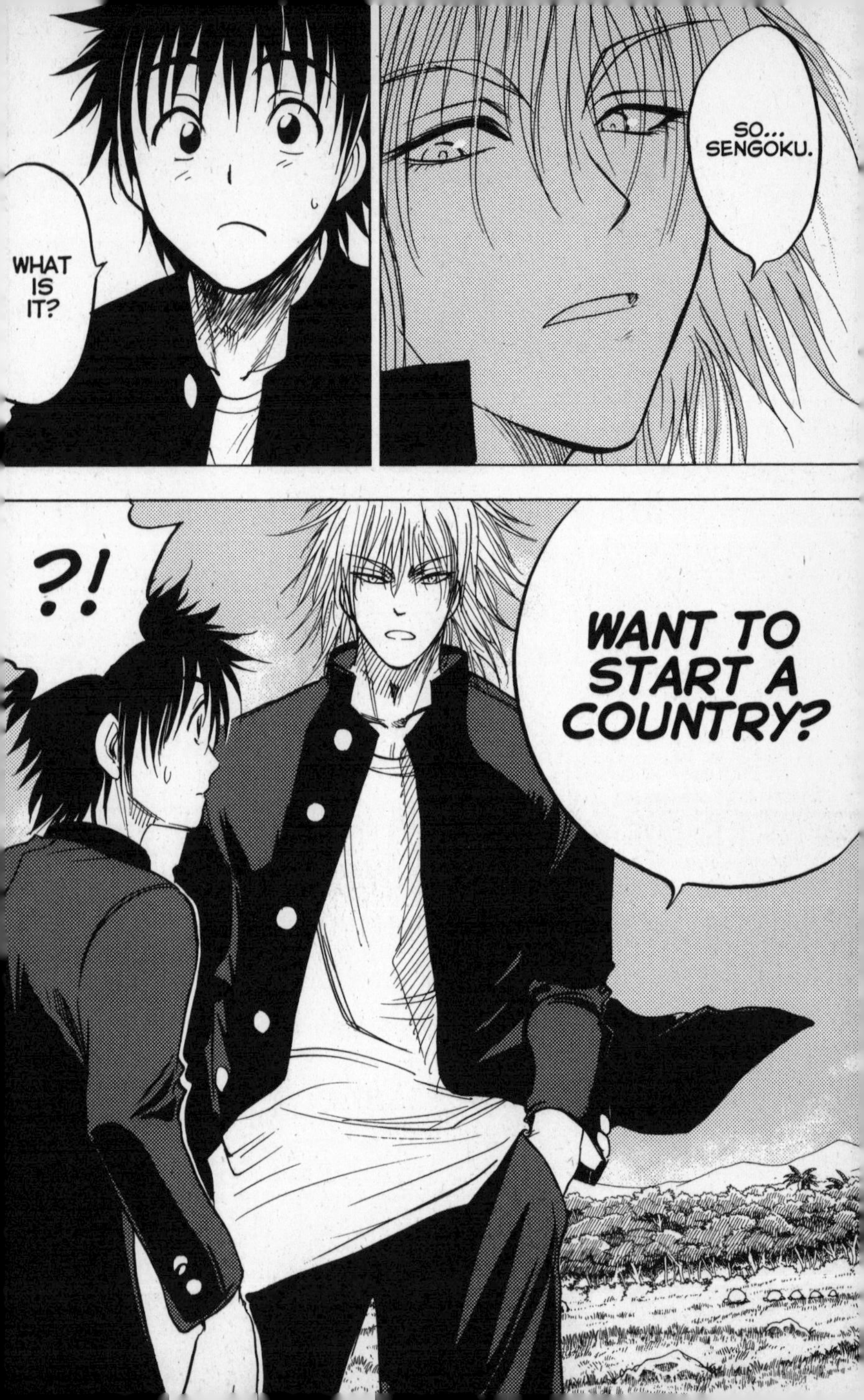
SO... SENGOKU.
WHAT IS IT?
WANT TO START A COUNTRY?
?!

Episode 37 A Country of Children

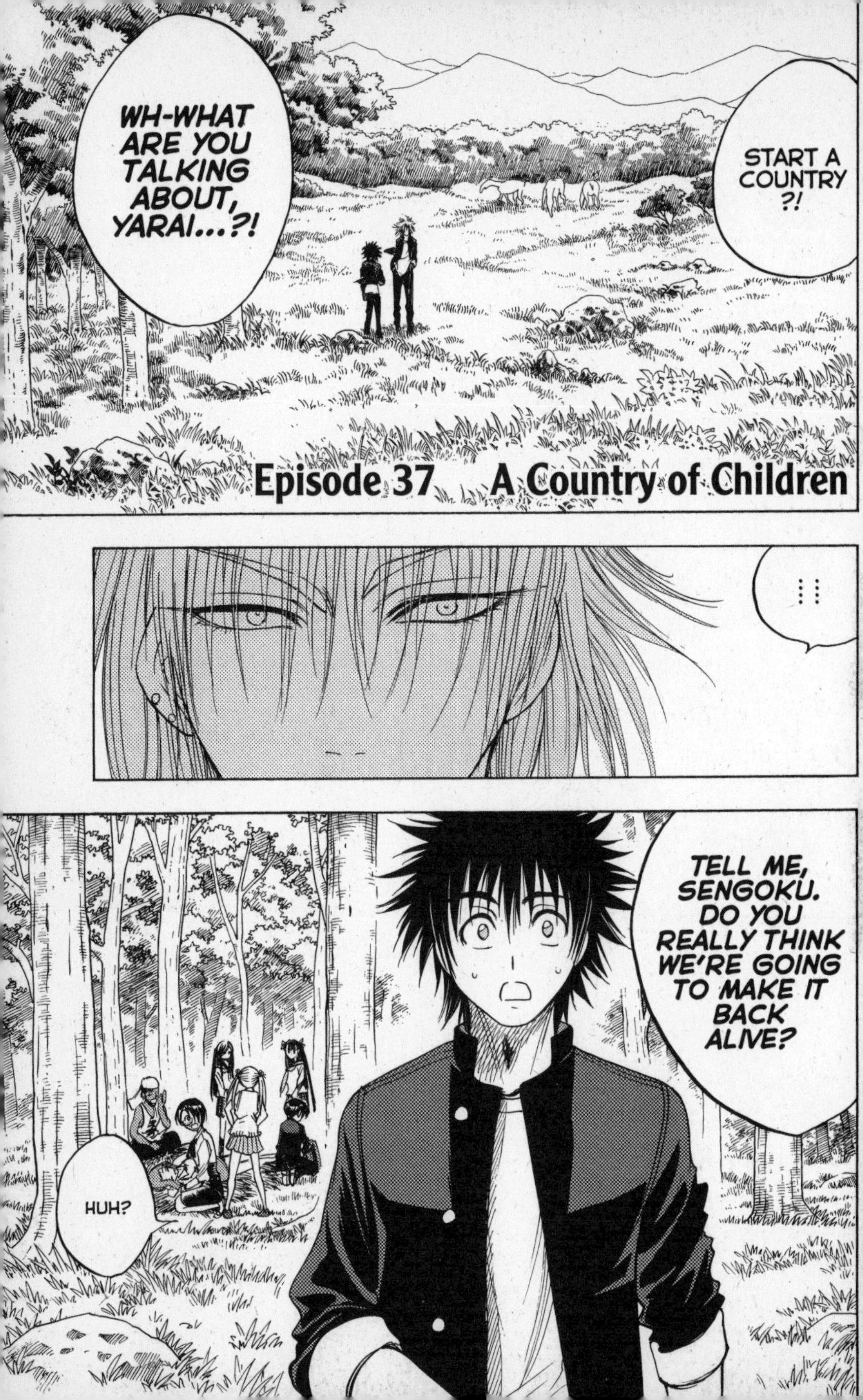
START A COUNTRY?!
WH-WHAT ARE YOU TALKING ABOUT, YARAI...?!
...
TELL ME, SENGOKU. DO YOU REALLY THINK WE'RE GOING TO MAKE IT BACK ALIVE?
HUH?

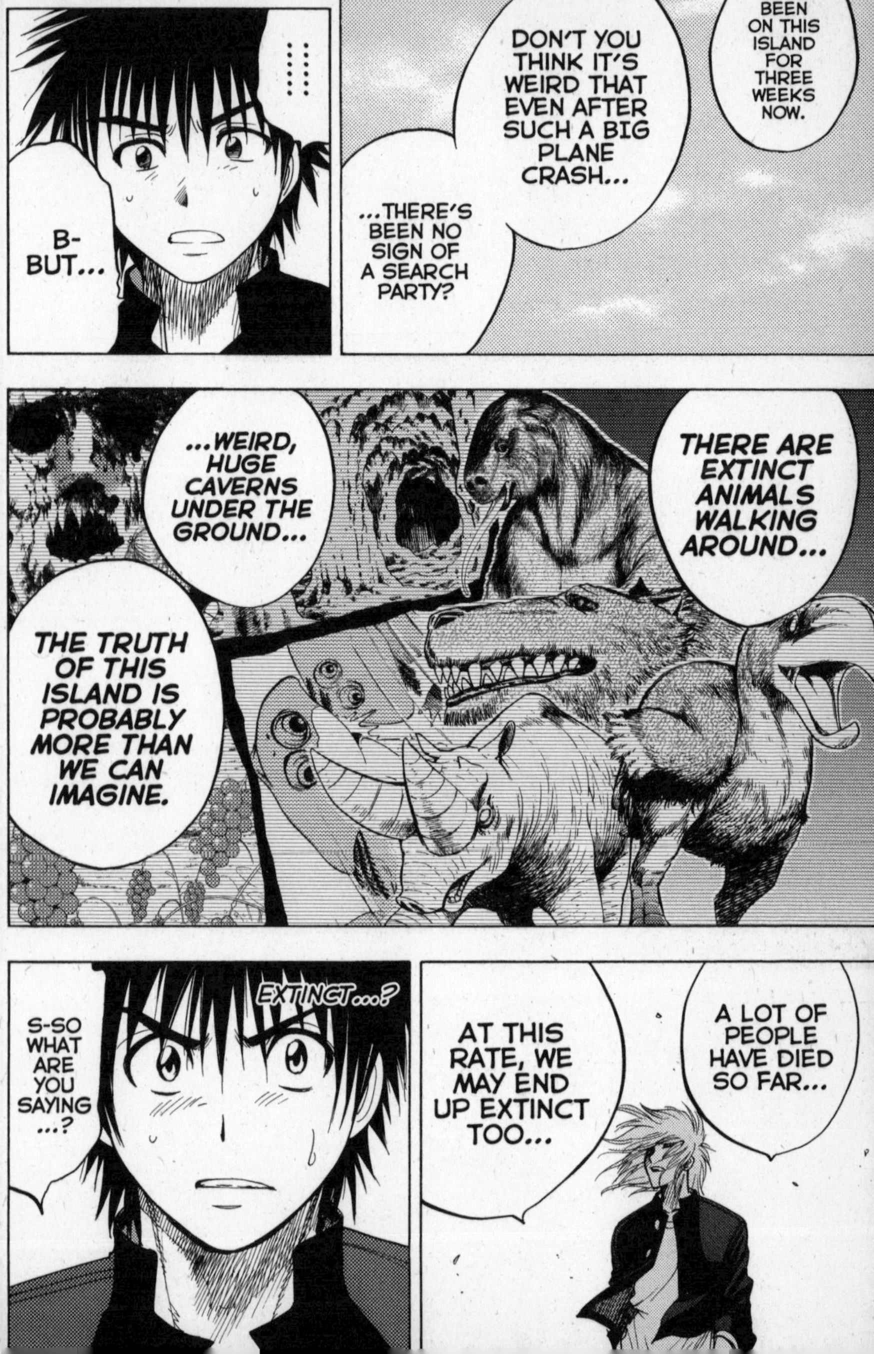
WE'VE BEEN ON THIS ISLAND FOR THREE WEEKS NOW.
DON'T YOU THINK IT'S WEIRD THAT EVEN AFTER SUCH A BIG PLANE CRASH...
...THERE'S BEEN NO SIGN OF A SEARCH PARTY?
......
B-BUT...
THERE ARE EXTINCT ANIMALS WALKING AROUND...
...WEIRD, HUGE CAVERNS UNDER THE GROUND...
THE TRUTH OF THIS ISLAND IS PROBABLY MORE THAN WE CAN IMAGINE.
A LOT OF PEOPLE HAVE DIED SO FAR...
AT THIS RATE, WE MAY END UP EXTINCT TOO...
EXTINCT...?
S-SO WHAT ARE YOU SAYING ...?

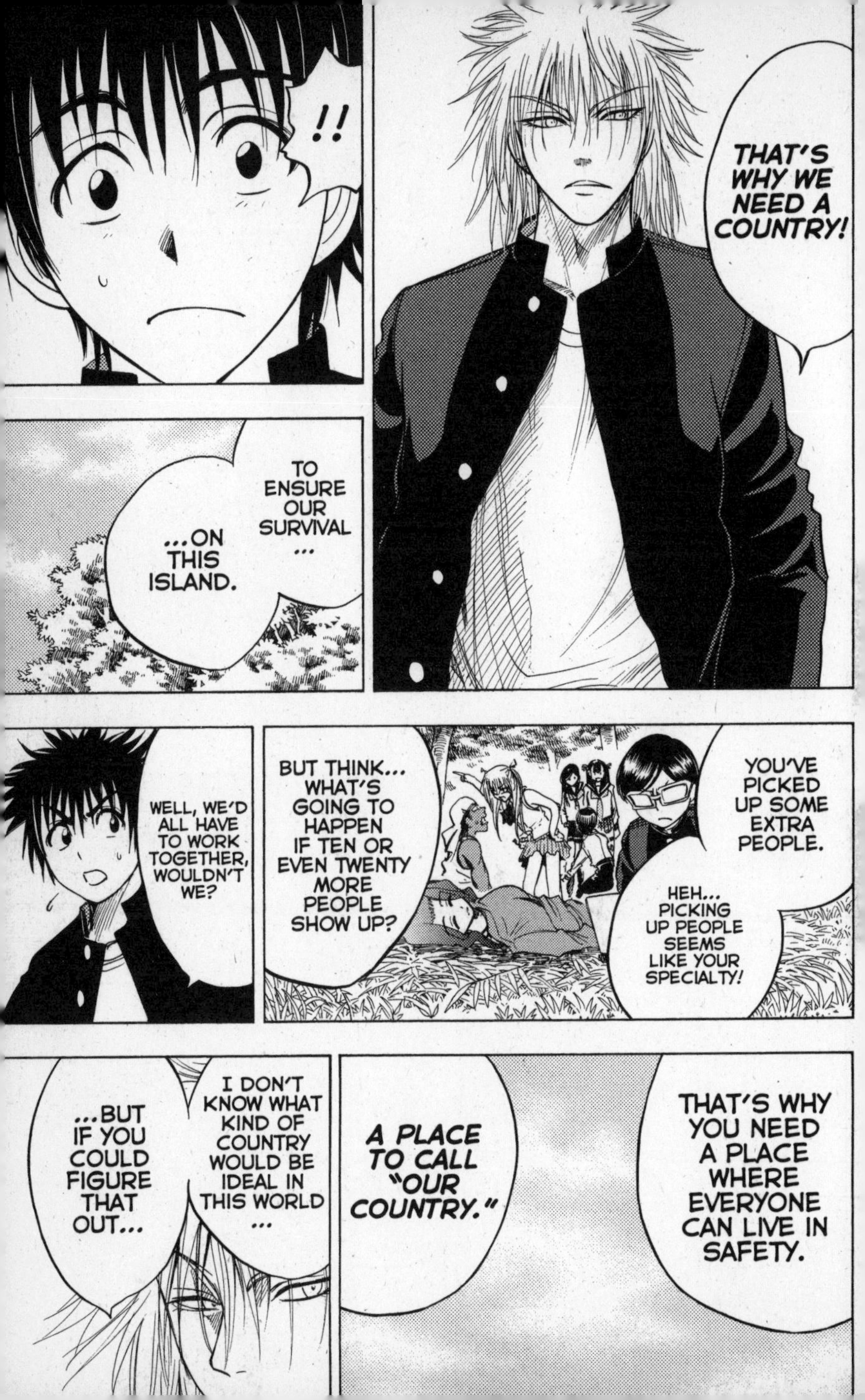

THAT'S WHY WE NEED A COUNTRY!
!!
TO ENSURE OUR SURVIVAL...
...ON THIS ISLAND.
YOU'VE PICKED UP SOME EXTRA PEOPLE.
HEH... PICKING UP PEOPLE SEEMS LIKE YOUR SPECIALTY!
BUT THINK... WHAT'S GOING TO HAPPEN IF TEN OR EVEN TWENTY MORE PEOPLE SHOW UP?
WELL, WE'D ALL HAVE TO WORK TOGETHER, WOULDN'T WE?
THAT'S WHY YOU NEED A PLACE WHERE EVERYONE CAN LIVE IN SAFETY.
A PLACE TO CALL "OUR COUNTRY."
I DON'T KNOW WHAT KIND OF COUNTRY WOULD BE IDEAL IN THIS WORLD...
...BUT IF YOU COULD FIGURE THAT OUT...

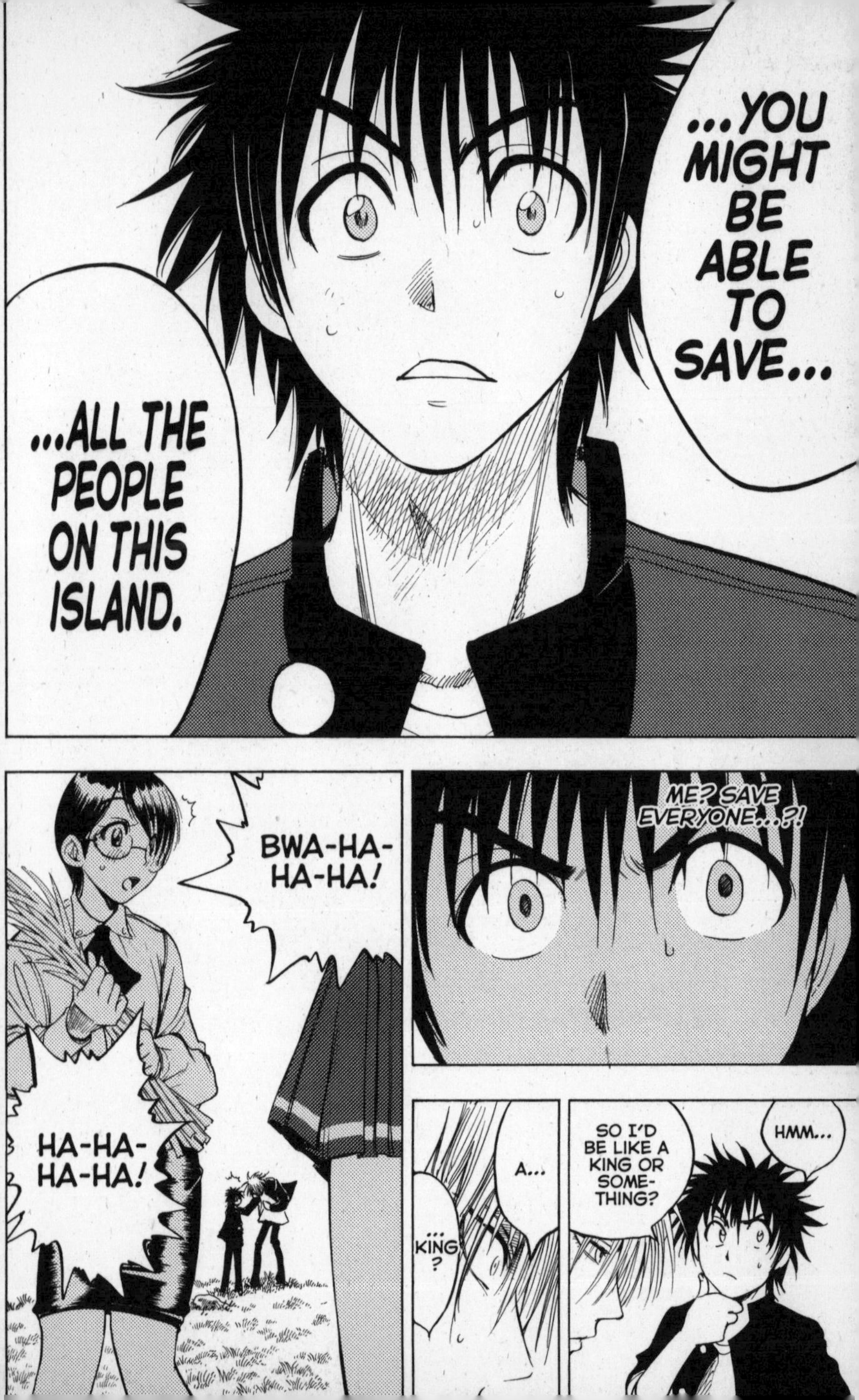
...YOU MIGHT BE ABLE TO SAVE...
...ALL THE PEOPLE ON THIS ISLAND.
ME? SAVE EVERYONE...?!
HMM...
SO I'D BE LIKE A KING OR SOME-THING?
A...
...KING?
BWA-HA-HA-HA!
HA-HA-HA-HA!

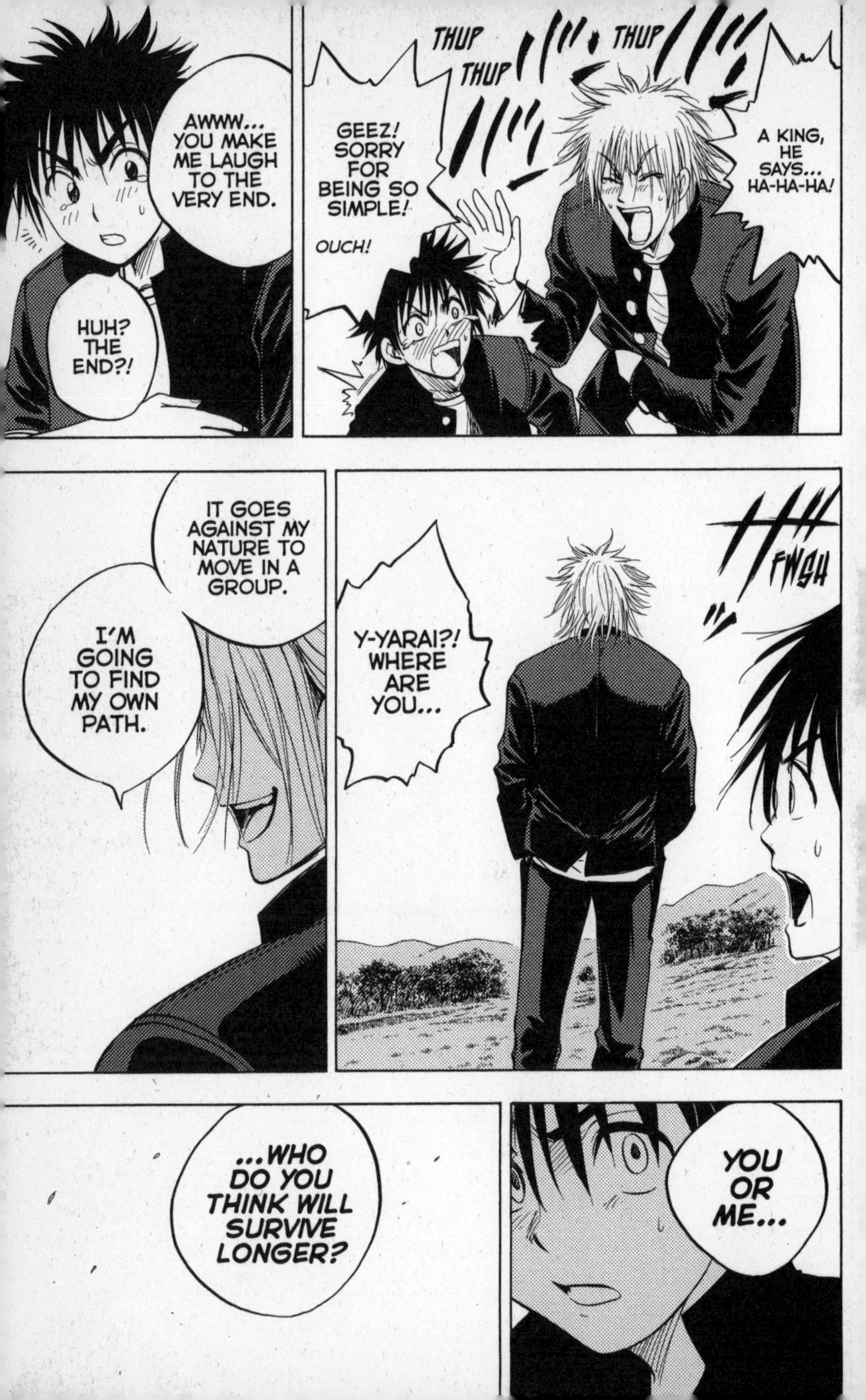
THUP
THUP
THUP
A KING, HE SAYS... HA-HA-HA!
GEEZ! SORRY FOR BEING SO SIMPLE!
OUCH!
AWWW... YOU MAKE ME LAUGH TO THE VERY END.
HUH? THE END?!
FWSH
Y-YARAI?! WHERE ARE YOU...
IT GOES AGAINST MY NATURE TO MOVE IN A GROUP.
I'M GOING TO FIND MY OWN PATH.
YOU OR ME...
...WHO DO YOU THINK WILL SURVIVE LONGER?

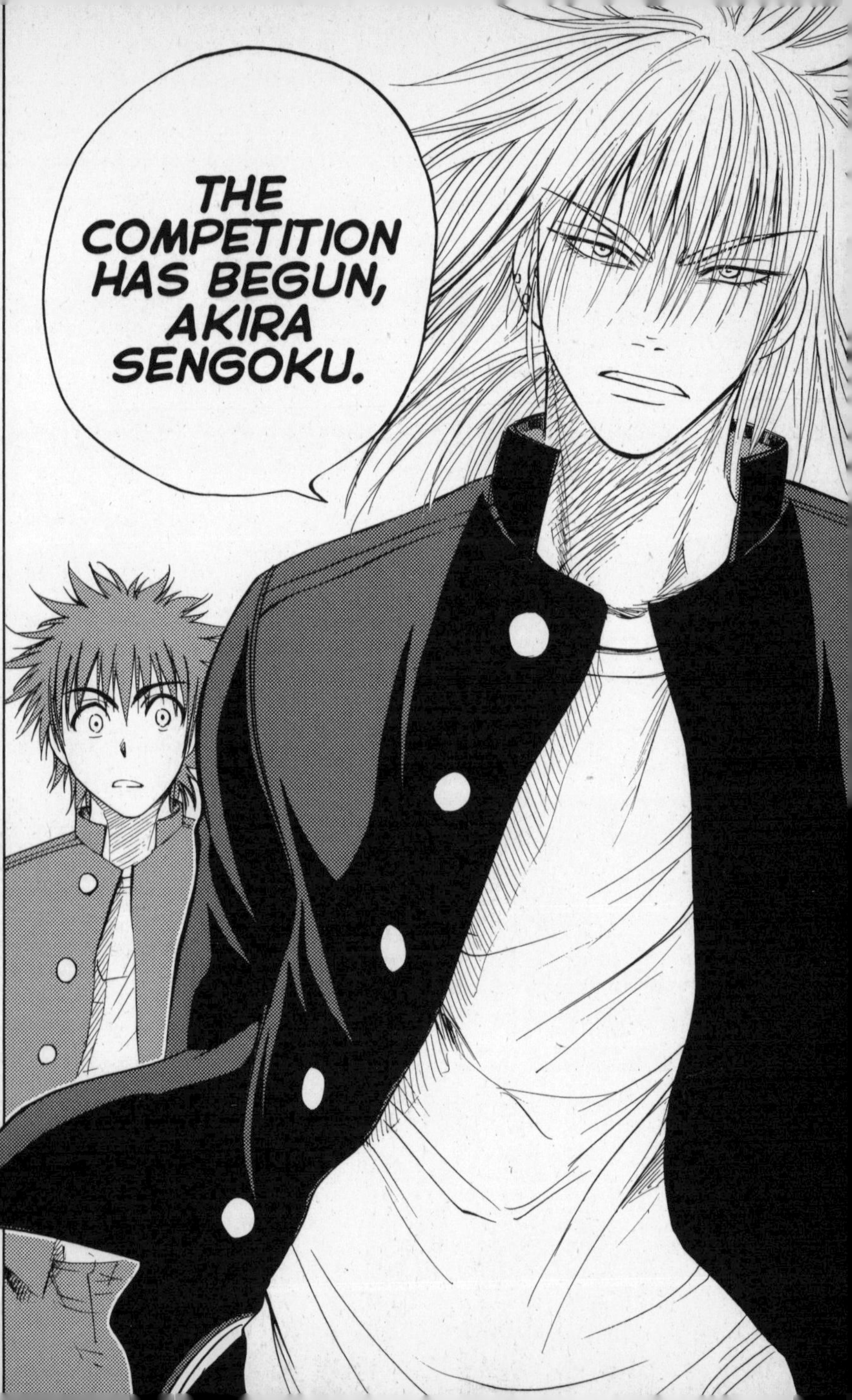
THE COMPETITION HAS BEGUN, AKIRA SENGOKU.

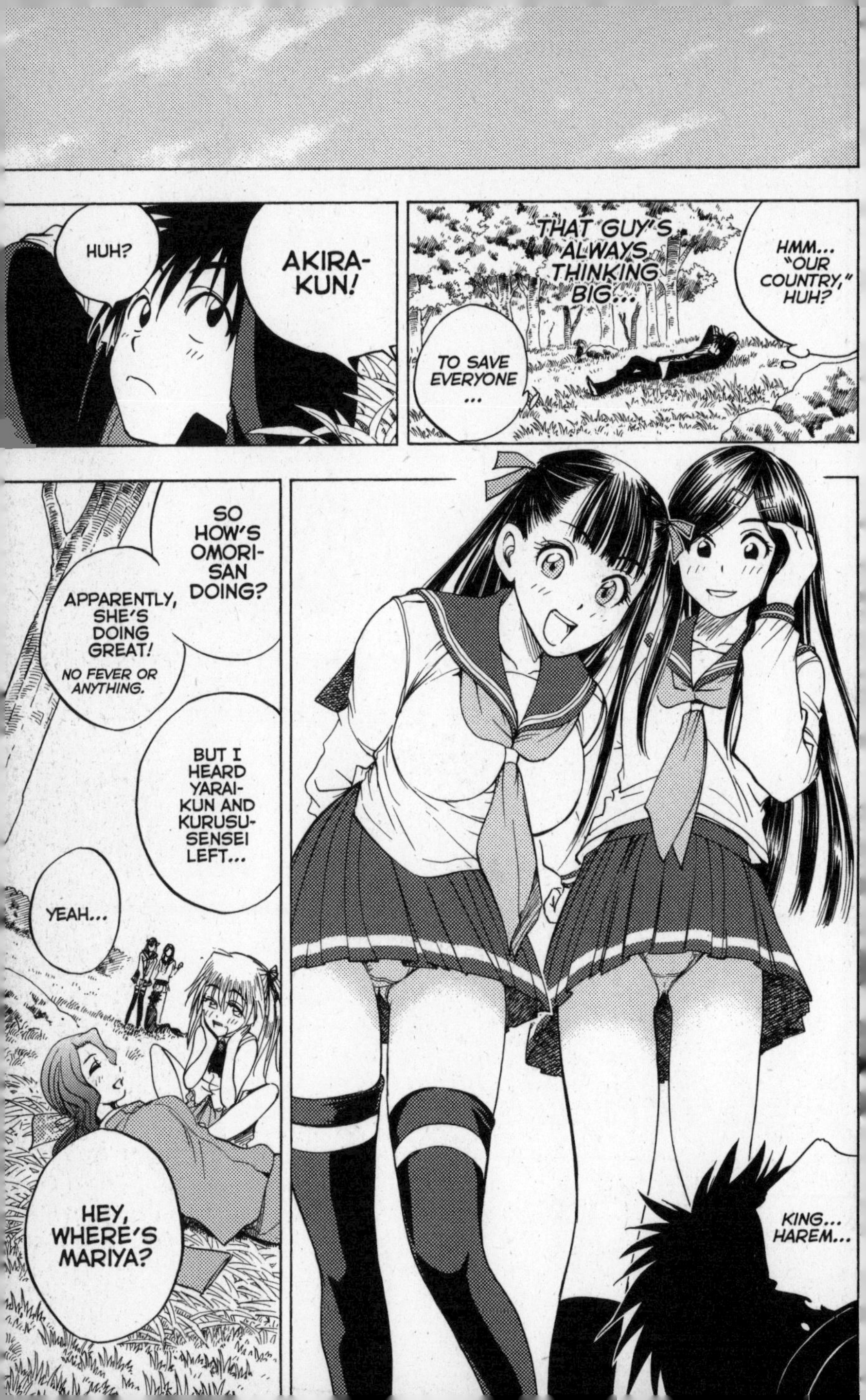
HMM... "OUR COUNTRY," HUH?
THAT GUY'S ALWAYS THINKING BIG...
TO SAVE EVERYONE ...
AKIRA-KUN!
HUH?
KING... HAREM...
SO HOW'S OMORI-SAN DOING?
APPARENTLY, SHE'S DOING GREAT!
NO FEVER OR ANYTHING.
BUT I HEARD YARAI-KUN AND KURUSU-SENSEI LEFT...
YEAH...
HEY, WHERE'S MARIYA?

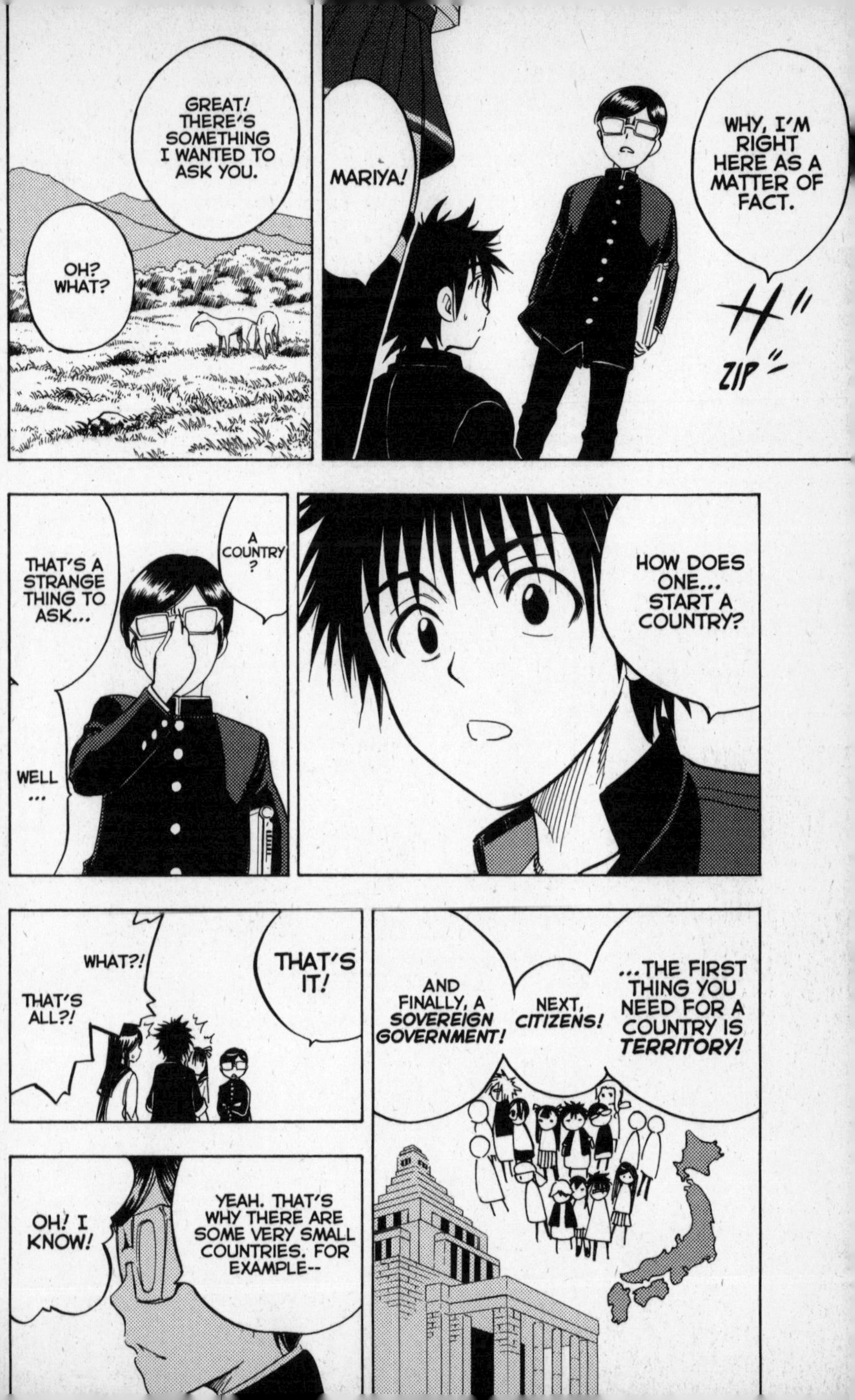

WHY, I'M RIGHT HERE AS A MATTER OF FACT.
ZIP
MARIYA!
GREAT! THERE'S SOMETHING I WANTED TO ASK YOU.
OH? WHAT?
HOW DOES ONE... START A COUNTRY?
A COUNTRY?
THAT'S A STRANGE THING TO ASK...
WELL...
...THE FIRST THING YOU NEED FOR A COUNTRY IS TERRITORY!
NEXT, CITIZENS!
AND FINALLY, A SOVEREIGN GOVERNMENT!
THAT'S IT!
WHAT?!
THAT'S ALL?!
YEAH. THAT'S WHY THERE ARE SOME VERY SMALL COUNTRIES. FOR EXAMPLE--
OH! I KNOW!

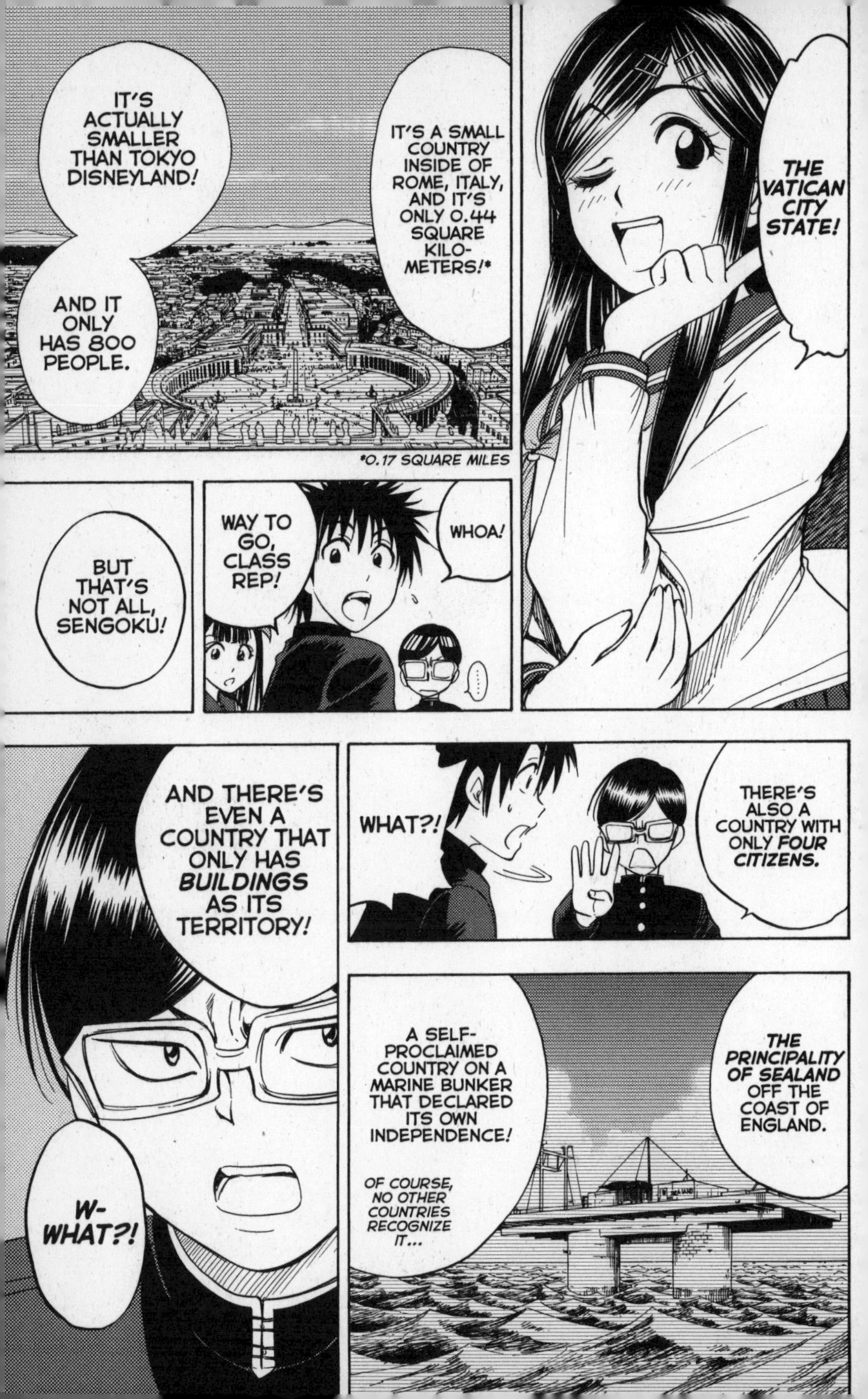
THE VATICAN CITY STATE!
IT'S A SMALL COUNTRY INSIDE OF ROME, ITALY, AND IT'S ONLY 0.44 SQUARE KILO-METERS!*
IT'S ACTUALLY SMALLER THAN TOKYO DISNEYLAND!
AND IT ONLY HAS 800 PEOPLE.
*0.17 SQUARE MILES
WHOA!
WAY TO GO, CLASS REP!
...
BUT THAT'S NOT ALL, SENGOKU!
THERE'S ALSO A COUNTRY WITH ONLY FOUR CITIZENS.
WHAT?!
THE PRINCIPALITY OF SEALAND OFF THE COAST OF ENGLAND.
A SELF-PROCLAIMED COUNTRY ON A MARINE BUNKER THAT DECLARED ITS OWN INDEPENDENCE!
OF COURSE, NO OTHER COUNTRIES RECOGNIZE IT...
AND THERE'S EVEN A COUNTRY THAT ONLY HAS BUILDINGS AS ITS TERRITORY!
W-WHAT?!

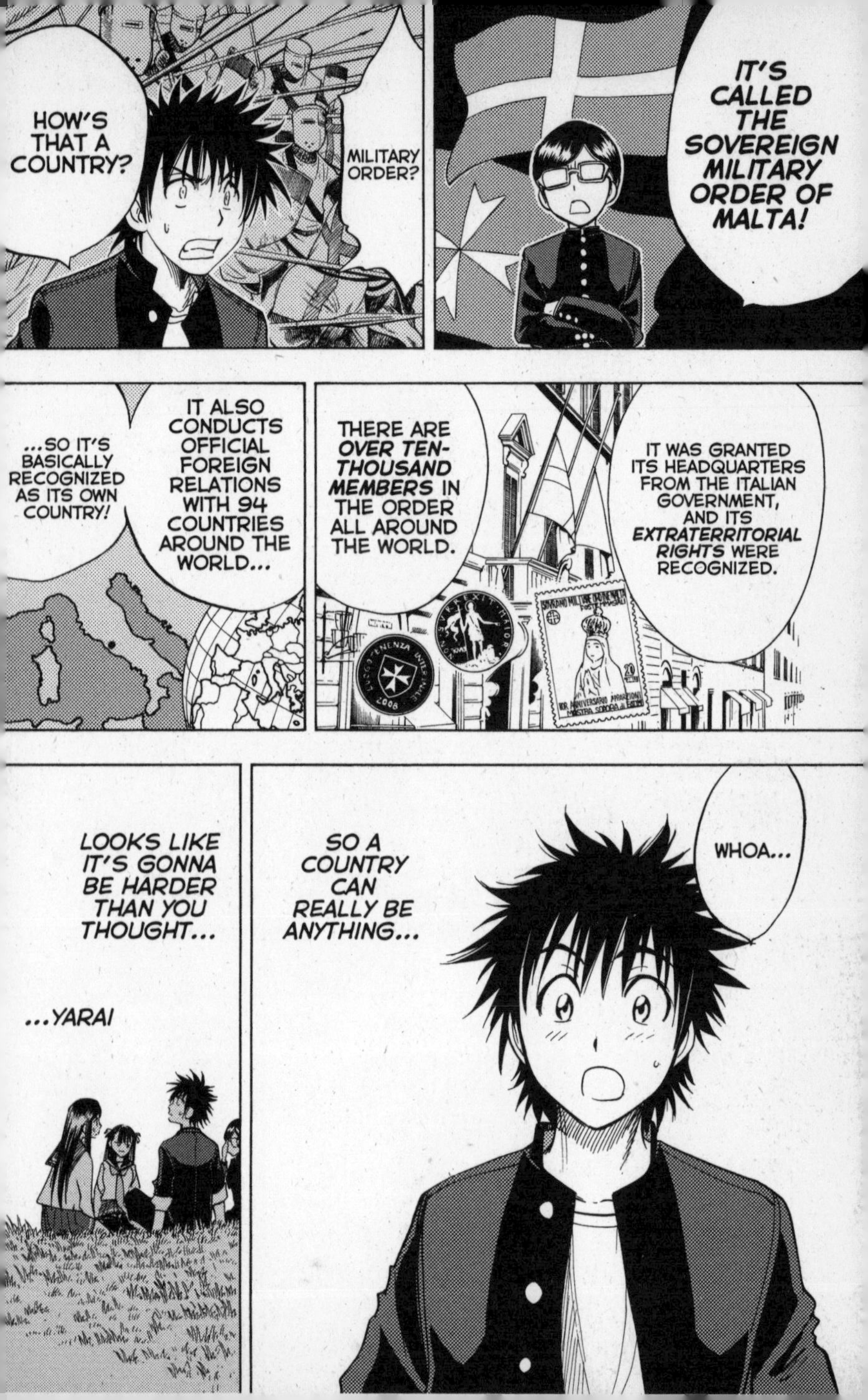
IT'S CALLED THE SOVEREIGN MILITARY ORDER OF MALTA!
MILITARY ORDER?
HOW'S THAT A COUNTRY?
IT WAS GRANTED ITS HEADQUARTERS FROM THE ITALIAN GOVERNMENT, AND ITS EXTRATERRITORIAL RIGHTS WERE RECOGNIZED.
THERE ARE OVER TEN-THOUSAND MEMBERS IN THE ORDER ALL AROUND THE WORLD.
IT ALSO CONDUCTS OFFICIAL FOREIGN RELATIONS WITH 94 COUNTRIES AROUND THE WORLD...
...SO IT'S BASICALLY RECOGNIZED AS ITS OWN COUNTRY!
WHOA...
SO A COUNTRY CAN REALLY BE ANYTHING...
LOOKS LIKE IT'S GONNA BE HARDER THAN YOU THOUGHT...
...YARAI

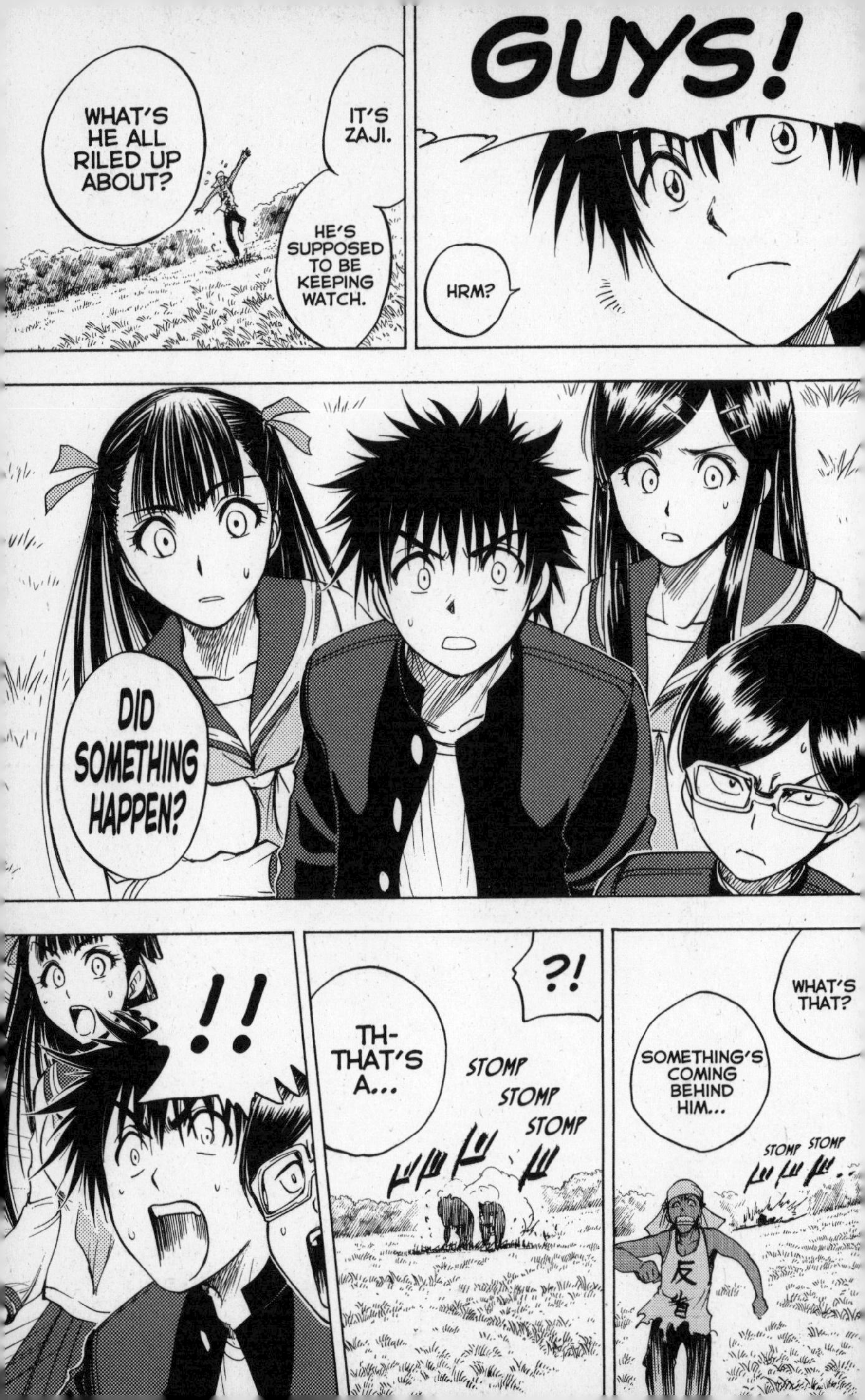
GUYS!
HRM?
IT'S ZAJI.
HE'S SUPPOSED TO BE KEEPING WATCH.
WHAT'S HE ALL RILED UP ABOUT?
DID SOMETHING HAPPEN?
WHAT'S THAT?
SOMETHING'S COMING BEHIND HIM...
STOMP STOMP
?!
TH-THAT'S A...
STOMP STOMP STOMP
!!

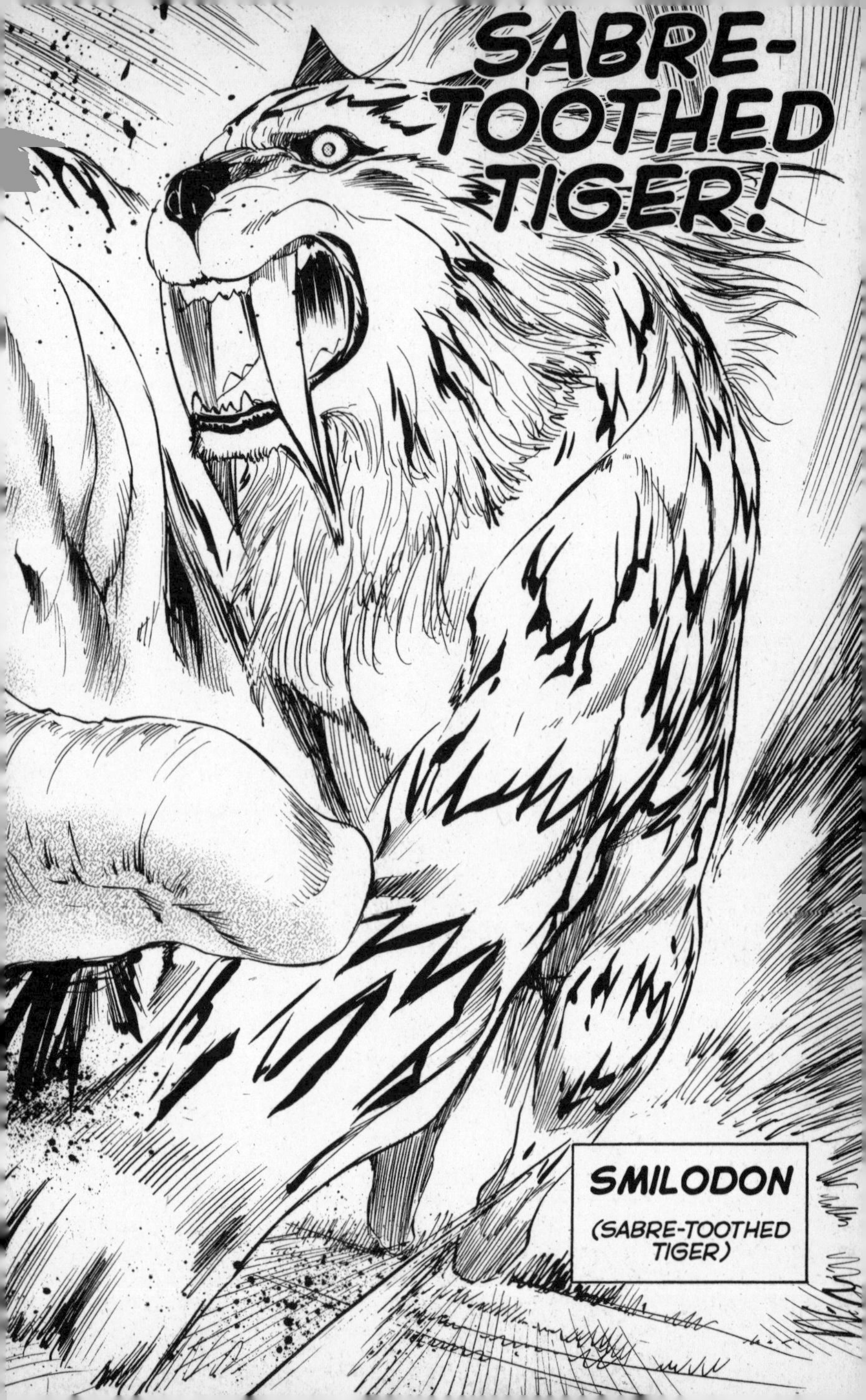
SABRE-TOOTHED TIGER!
SMILODON
(SABRE-TOOTHED TIGER)

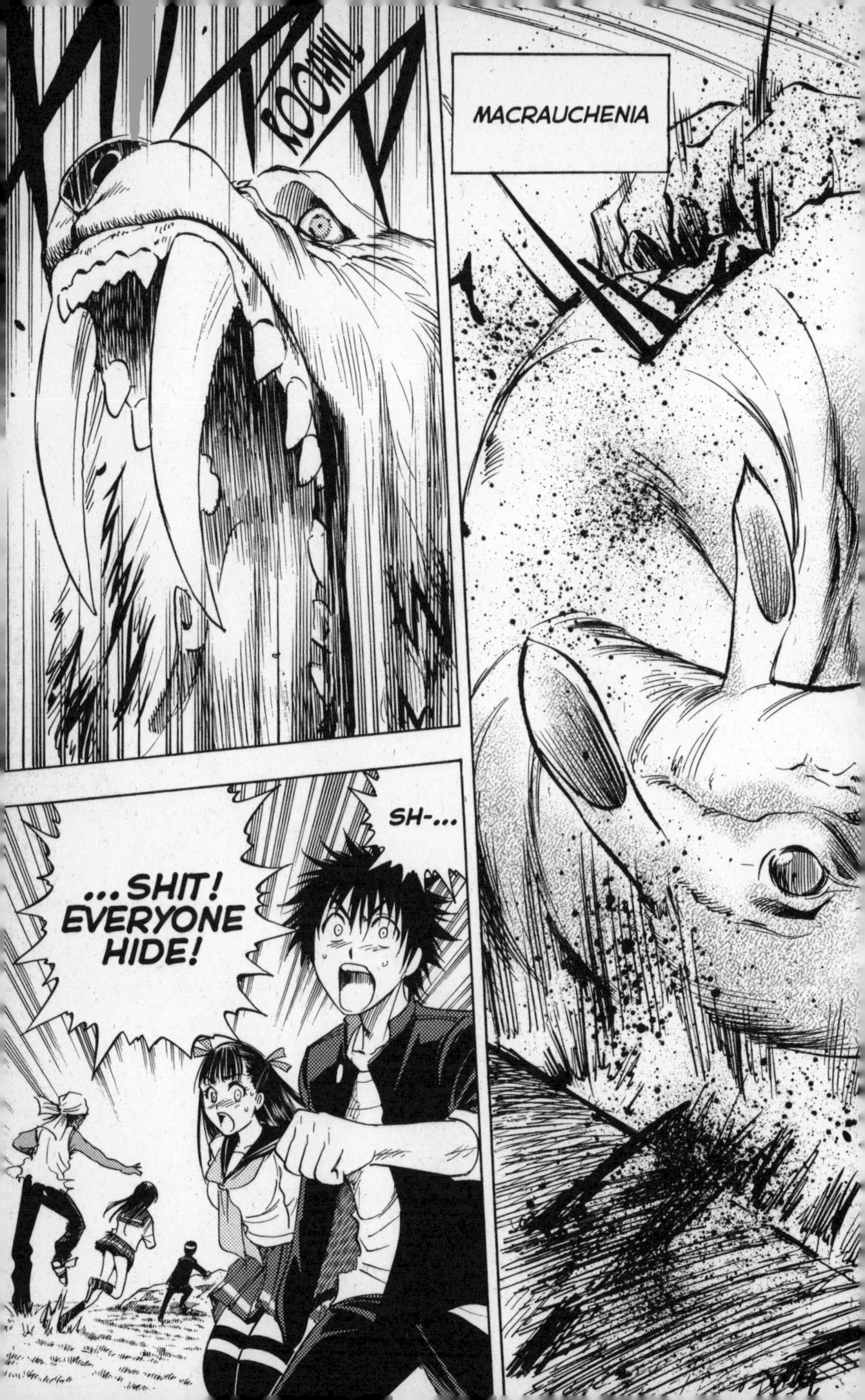
MACRAUCHENIA
ROOAW!!
SH-...
...SHIT! EVERYONE HIDE!

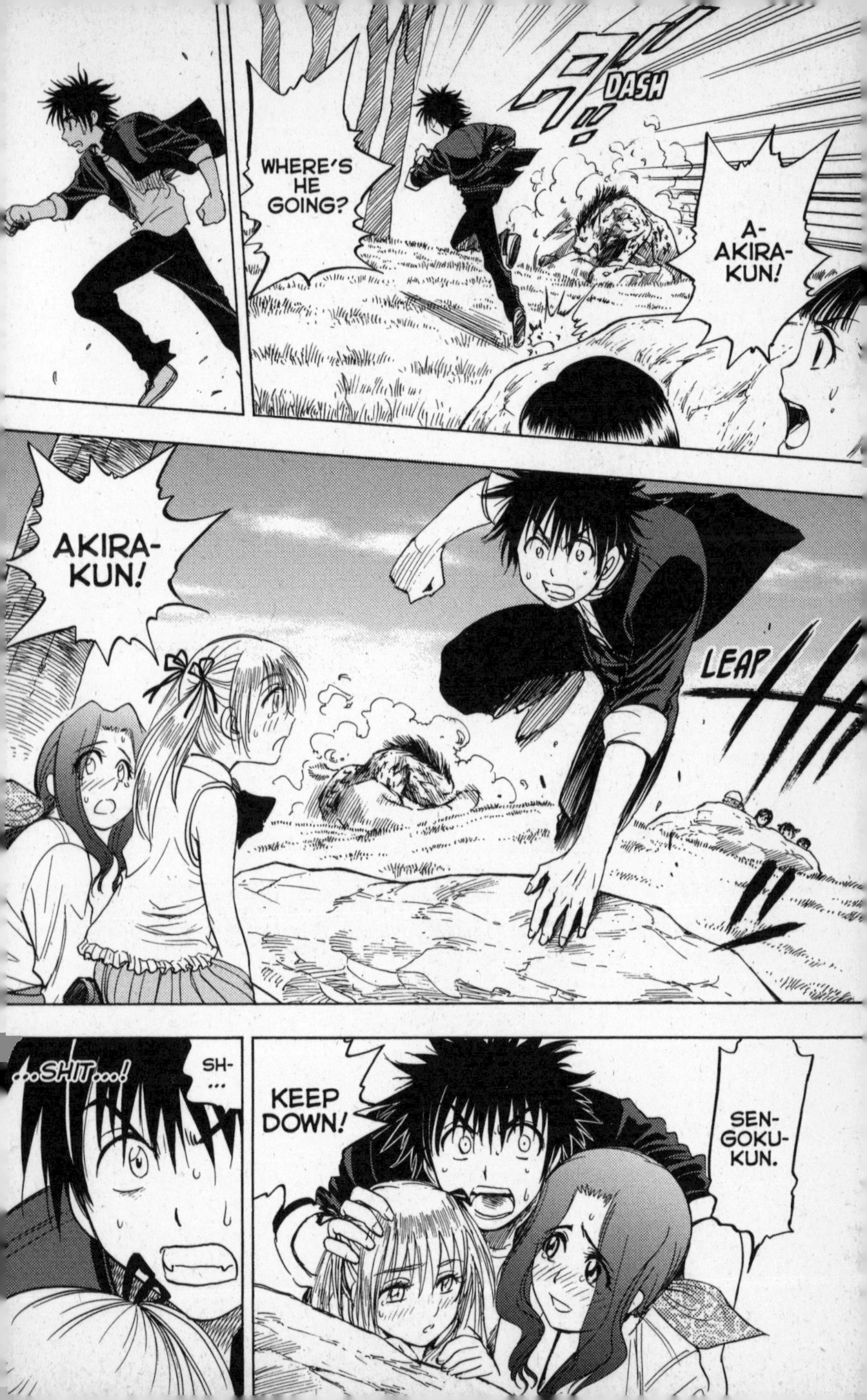
DASH
A-AKIRA-KUN!
WHERE'S HE GOING?
LEAP
AKIRA-KUN!
SEN-GOKU-KUN.
KEEP DOWN!
SH-...
...SHIT...!

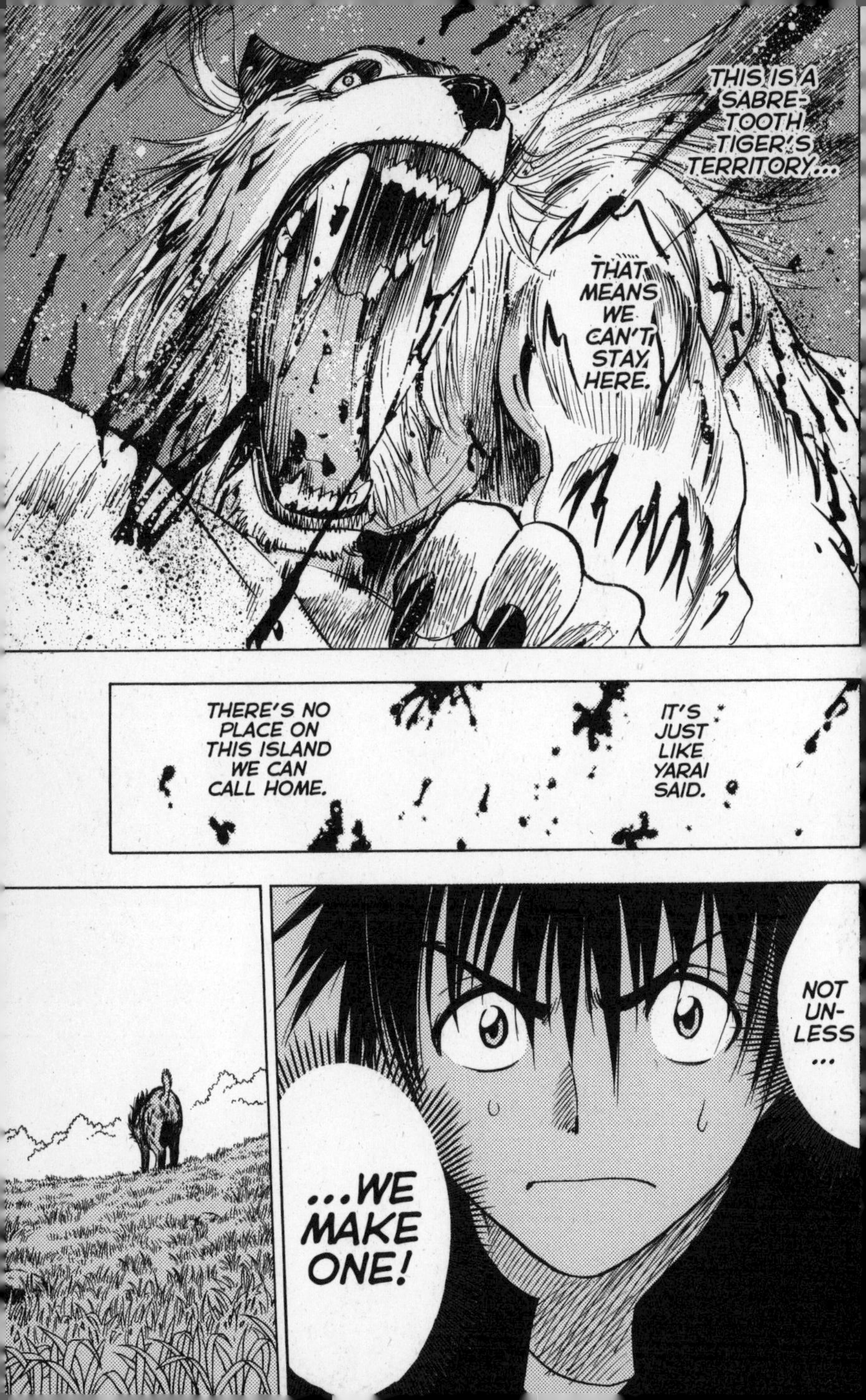
THIS IS A SABRE-TOOTH TIGER'S TERRITORY...
THAT MEANS WE CAN'T STAY HERE.
IT'S JUST LIKE YARAI SAID.
THERE'S NO PLACE ON THIS ISLAND WE CAN CALL HOME.
NOT UN-LESS ...
...WE MAKE ONE!

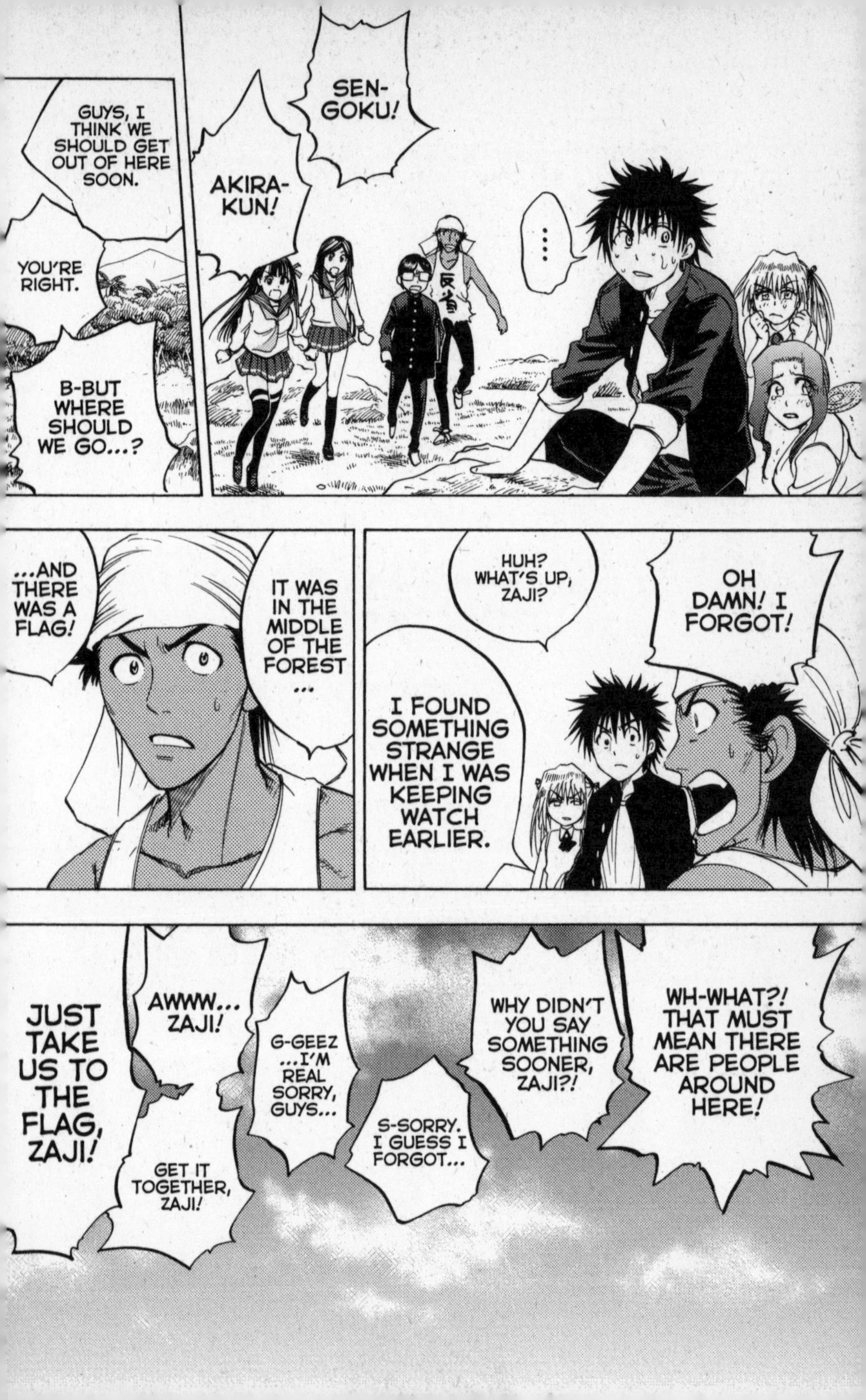
SEN-GOKU!
AKIRA-KUN!
.....
GUYS, I THINK WE SHOULD GET OUT OF HERE SOON.
YOU'RE RIGHT.
B-BUT WHERE SHOULD WE GO...?
OH DAMN! I FORGOT!
HUH? WHAT'S UP, ZAJI?
I FOUND SOMETHING STRANGE WHEN I WAS KEEPING WATCH EARLIER.
IT WAS IN THE MIDDLE OF THE FOREST...
...AND THERE WAS A FLAG!
WH-WHAT?! THAT MUST MEAN THERE ARE PEOPLE AROUND HERE!
WHY DIDN'T YOU SAY SOMETHING SOONER, ZAJI?!
S-SORRY. I GUESS I FORGOT...
G-GEEZ ...I'M REAL SORRY, GUYS...
AWWW... ZAJI!
GET IT TOGETHER, ZAJI!
JUST TAKE US TO THE FLAG, ZAJI!

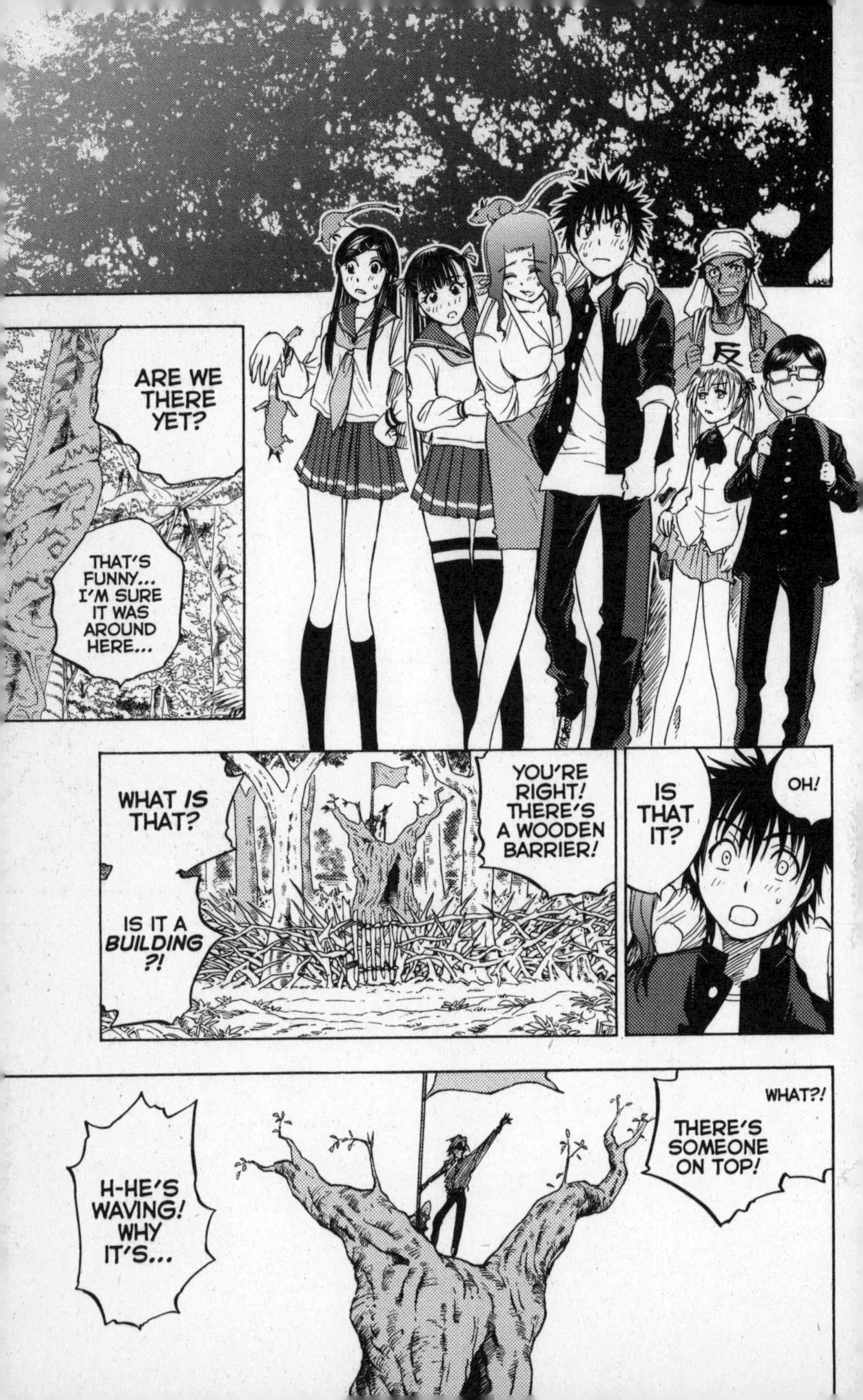
ARE WE THERE YET?
THAT'S FUNNY... I'M SURE IT WAS AROUND HERE...
OH!
IS THAT IT?
YOU'RE RIGHT! THERE'S A WOODEN BARRIER!
WHAT *IS* THAT?
IS IT A *BUILDING* ?!
WHAT?!
THERE'S SOMEONE ON TOP!
H-HE'S WAVING! WHY IT'S...

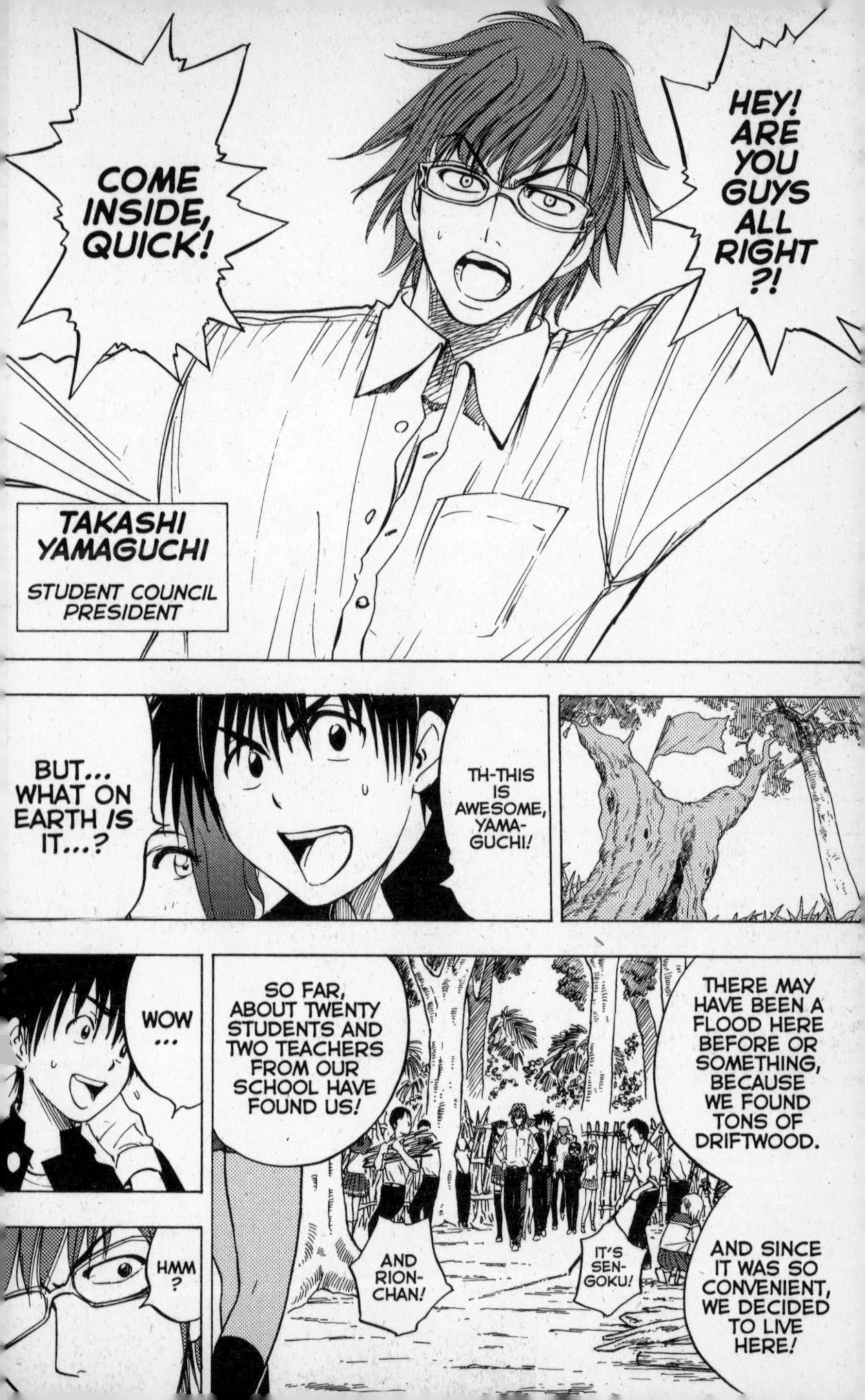
HEY! ARE YOU GUYS ALL RIGHT?!
COME INSIDE, QUICK!
TAKASHI YAMAGUCHI
STUDENT COUNCIL PRESIDENT
TH-THIS IS AWESOME, YAMA-GUCHI!
BUT... WHAT ON EARTH *IS* IT...?
THERE MAY HAVE BEEN A FLOOD HERE BEFORE OR SOMETHING, BECAUSE WE FOUND TONS OF DRIFTWOOD.
SO FAR, ABOUT TWENTY STUDENTS AND TWO TEACHERS FROM OUR SCHOOL HAVE FOUND US!
AND SINCE IT WAS SO CONVENIENT, WE DECIDED TO LIVE HERE!
IT'S SEN-GOKU!
AND RION-CHAN!
WOW ...
HMM ?

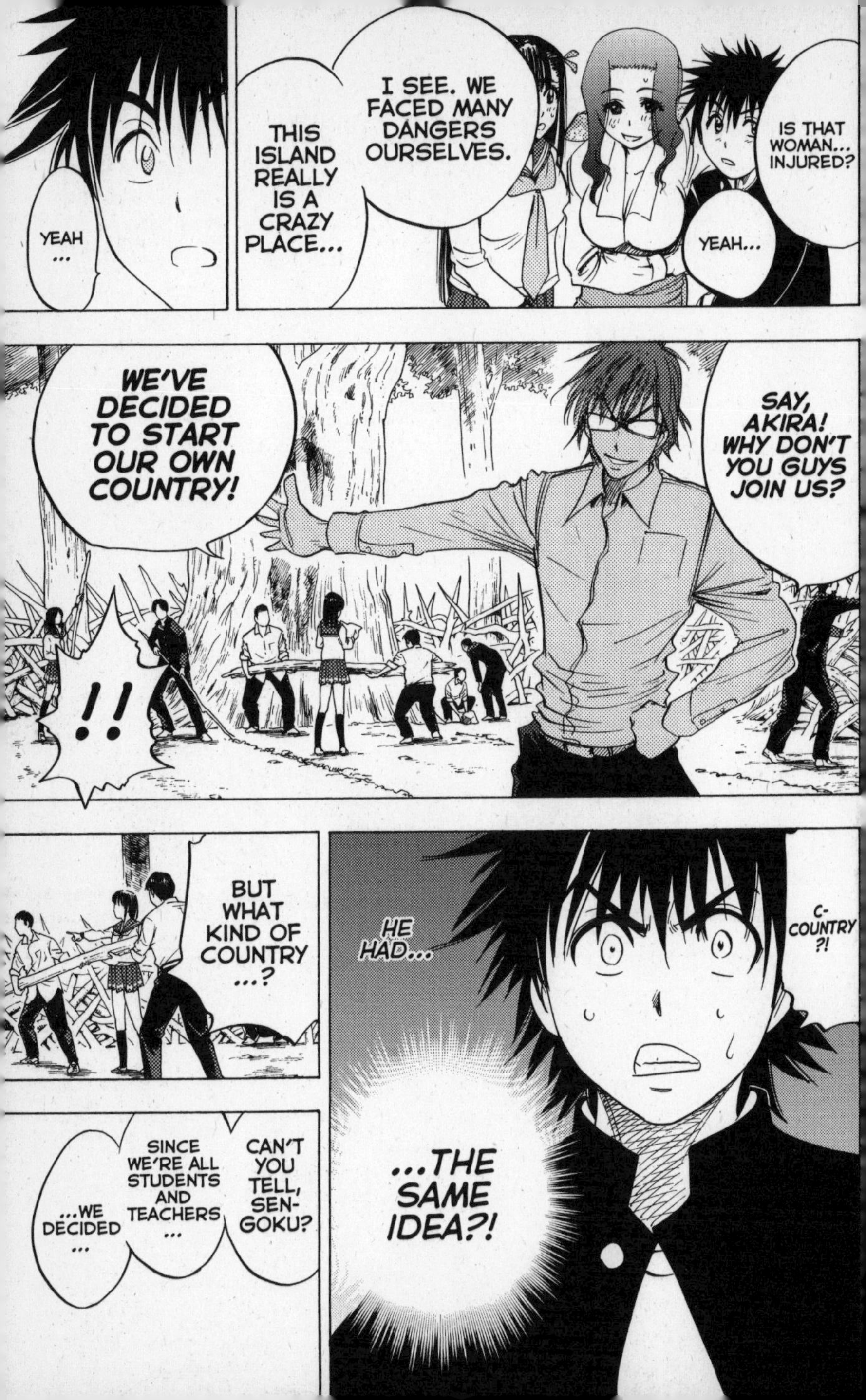
IS THAT WOMAN... INJURED?
YEAH...
I SEE. WE FACED MANY DANGERS OURSELVES.
THIS ISLAND REALLY IS A CRAZY PLACE...
YEAH ...
SAY, AKIRA! WHY DON'T YOU GUYS JOIN US?
WE'VE DECIDED TO START OUR OWN COUNTRY!
!!
C-COUNTRY?!
HE HAD...
...THE SAME IDEA?!
BUT WHAT KIND OF COUNTRY ...?
CAN'T YOU TELL, SEN-GOKU?
SINCE WE'RE ALL STUDENTS AND TEACHERS ...
...WE DECIDED ...

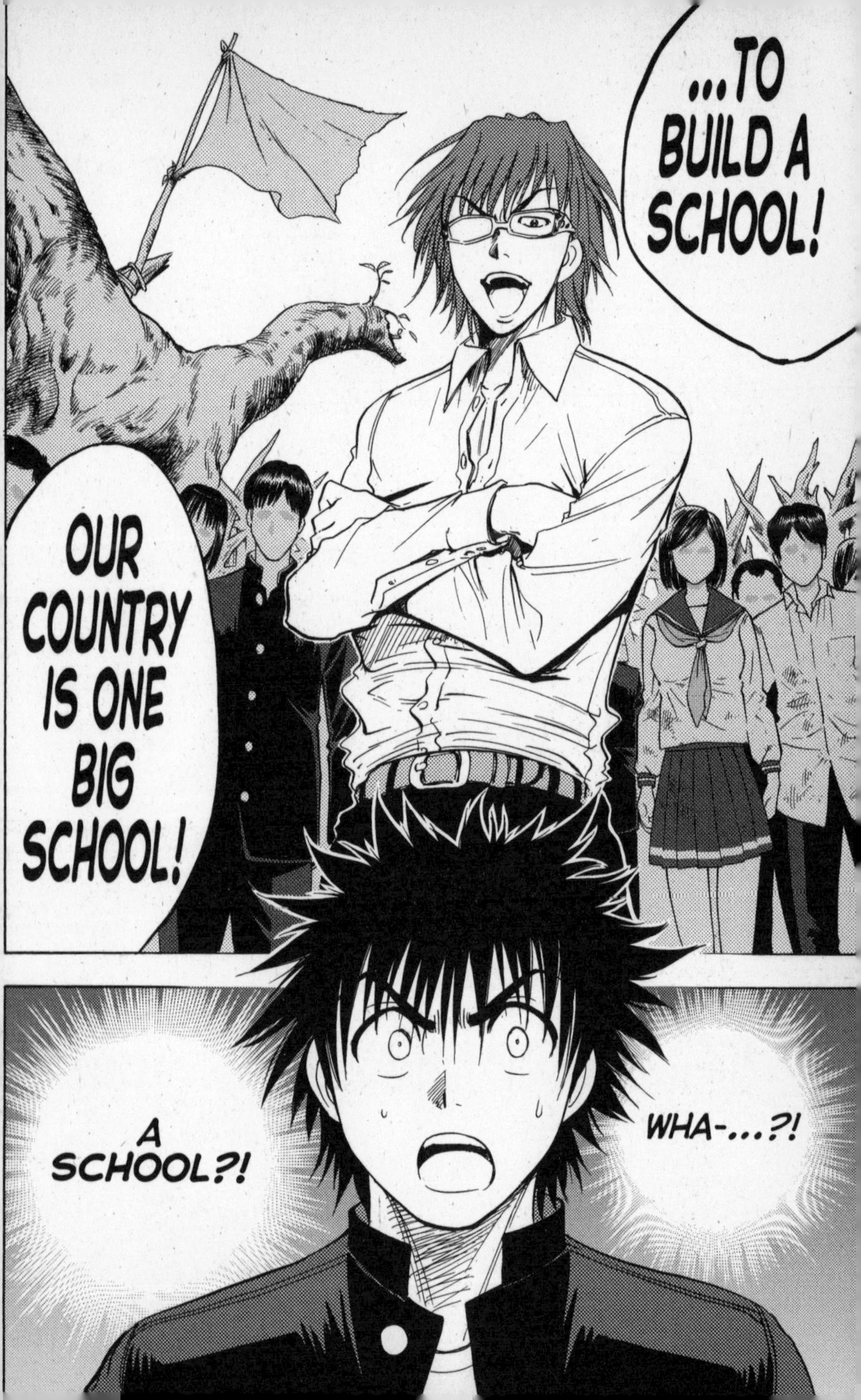
...TO BUILD A SCHOOL!
OUR COUNTRY IS ONE BIG SCHOOL!
WHA-...?!
A SCHOOL?!

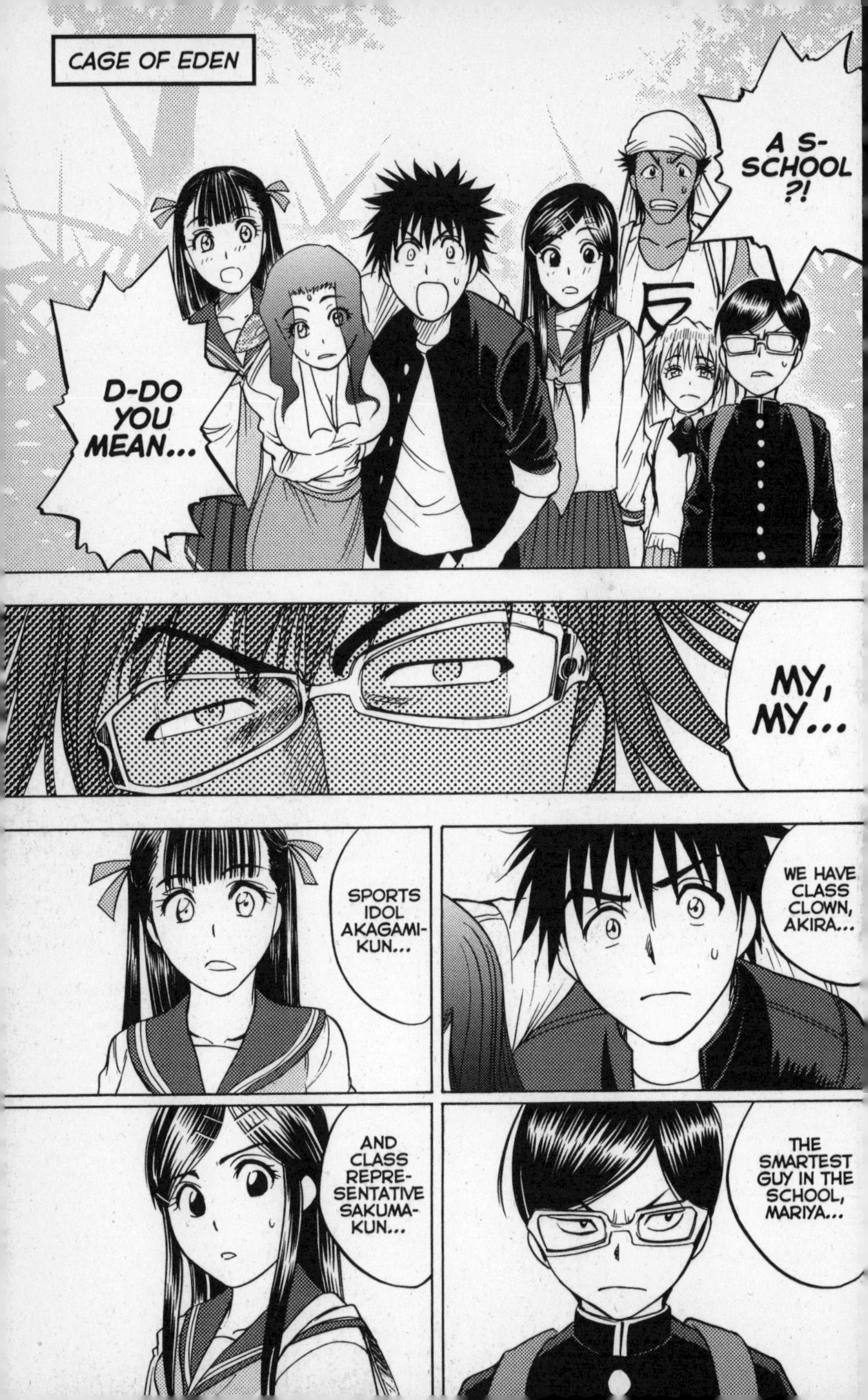
A S-SCHOOL ?!
D-DO YOU MEAN...
MY, MY...
WE HAVE CLASS CLOWN, AKIRA...
SPORTS IDOL AKAGAMI-KUN...
THE SMARTEST GUY IN THE SCHOOL, MARIYA...
AND CLASS REPRESENTATIVE SAKUMA-KUN...

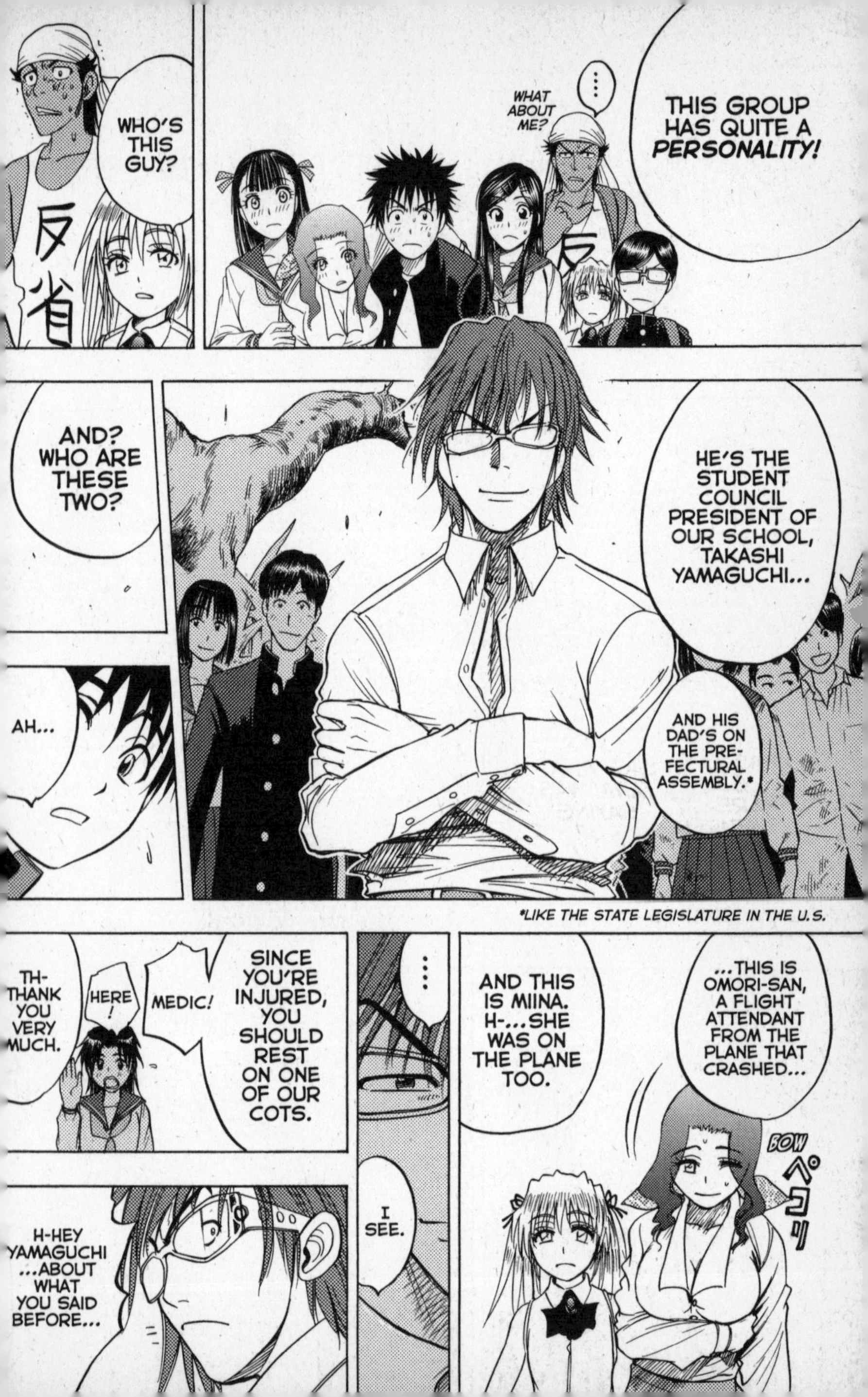
THIS GROUP HAS QUITE A PERSONALITY!
...
WHAT ABOUT ME?
WHO'S THIS GUY?
HE'S THE STUDENT COUNCIL PRESIDENT OF OUR SCHOOL, TAKASHI YAMAGUCHI...
AND HIS DAD'S ON THE PRE-FECTURAL ASSEMBLY.*
AND? WHO ARE THESE TWO?
AH...
...THIS IS OMORI-SAN, A FLIGHT ATTENDANT FROM THE PLANE THAT CRASHED...
BOW
ペコッ
AND THIS IS MIINA. H-...SHE WAS ON THE PLANE TOO.
....
I SEE.
SINCE YOU'RE INJURED, YOU SHOULD REST ON ONE OF OUR COTS.
MEDIC!
HERE!
TH-THANK YOU VERY MUCH.
H-HEY YAMAGUCHI ...ABOUT WHAT YOU SAID BEFORE...

*LIKE THE STATE LEGISLATURE IN THE U.S.

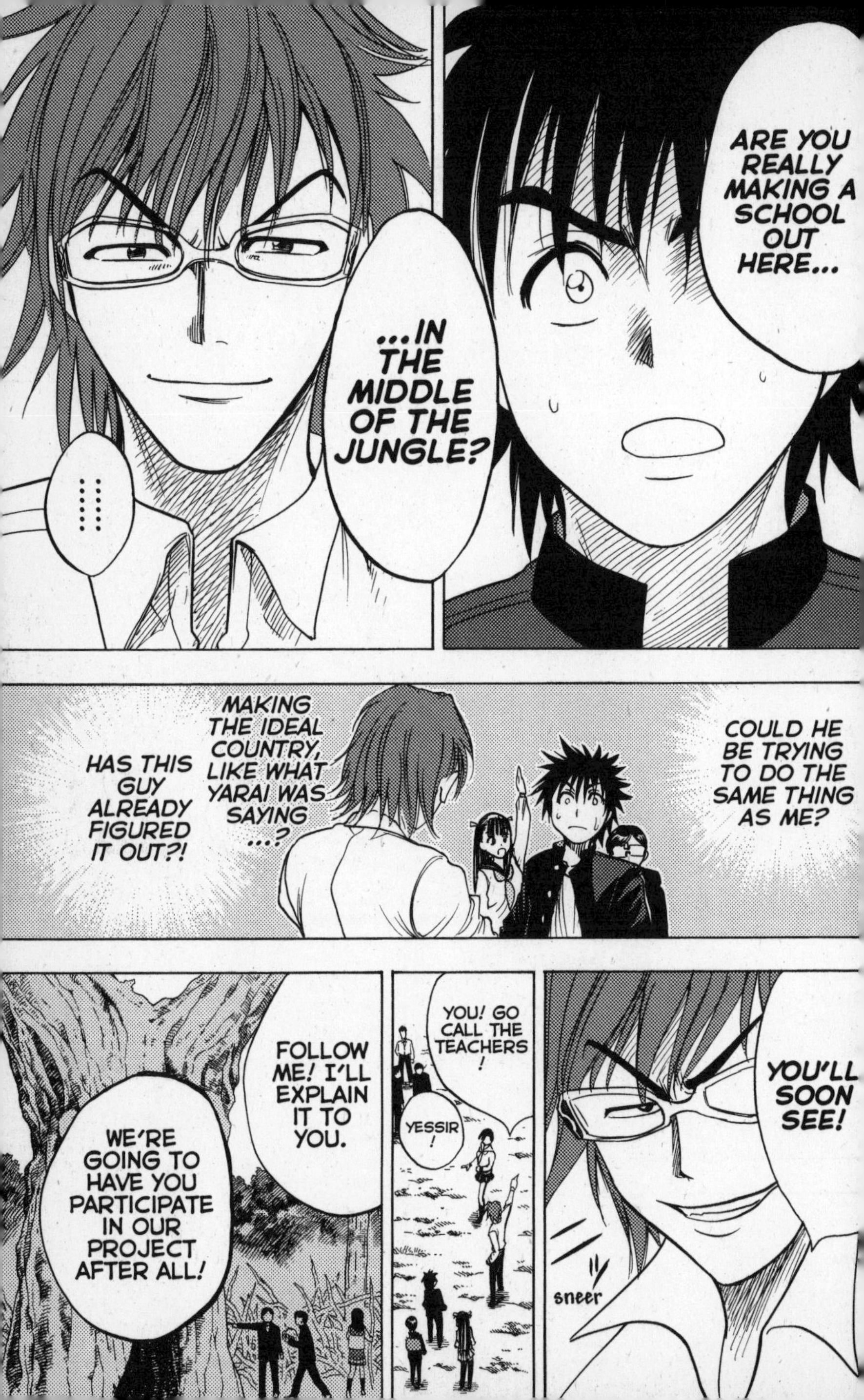
ARE YOU REALLY MAKING A SCHOOL OUT HERE...
...IN THE MIDDLE OF THE JUNGLE?
......
COULD HE BE TRYING TO DO THE SAME THING AS ME?
MAKING THE IDEAL COUNTRY, LIKE WHAT YARAI WAS SAYING...?
HAS THIS GUY ALREADY FIGURED IT OUT?!
YOU'LL SOON SEE!
sneer
YOU! GO CALL THE TEACHERS!
YESSIR!
FOLLOW ME! I'LL EXPLAIN IT TO YOU.
WE'RE GOING TO HAVE YOU PARTICIPATE IN OUR PROJECT AFTER ALL!

Episode 38 The Dream Behind the Flag

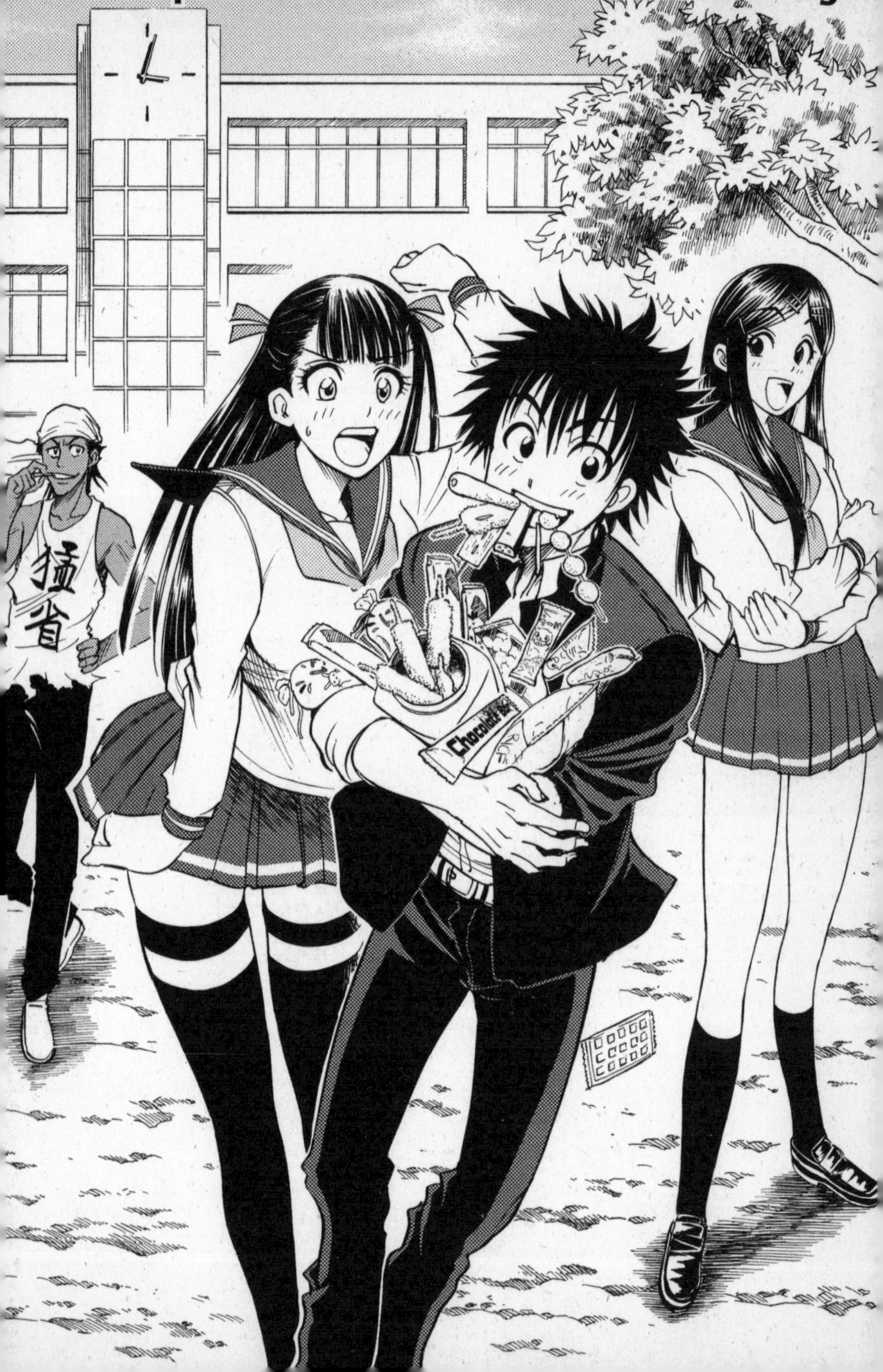
猛省

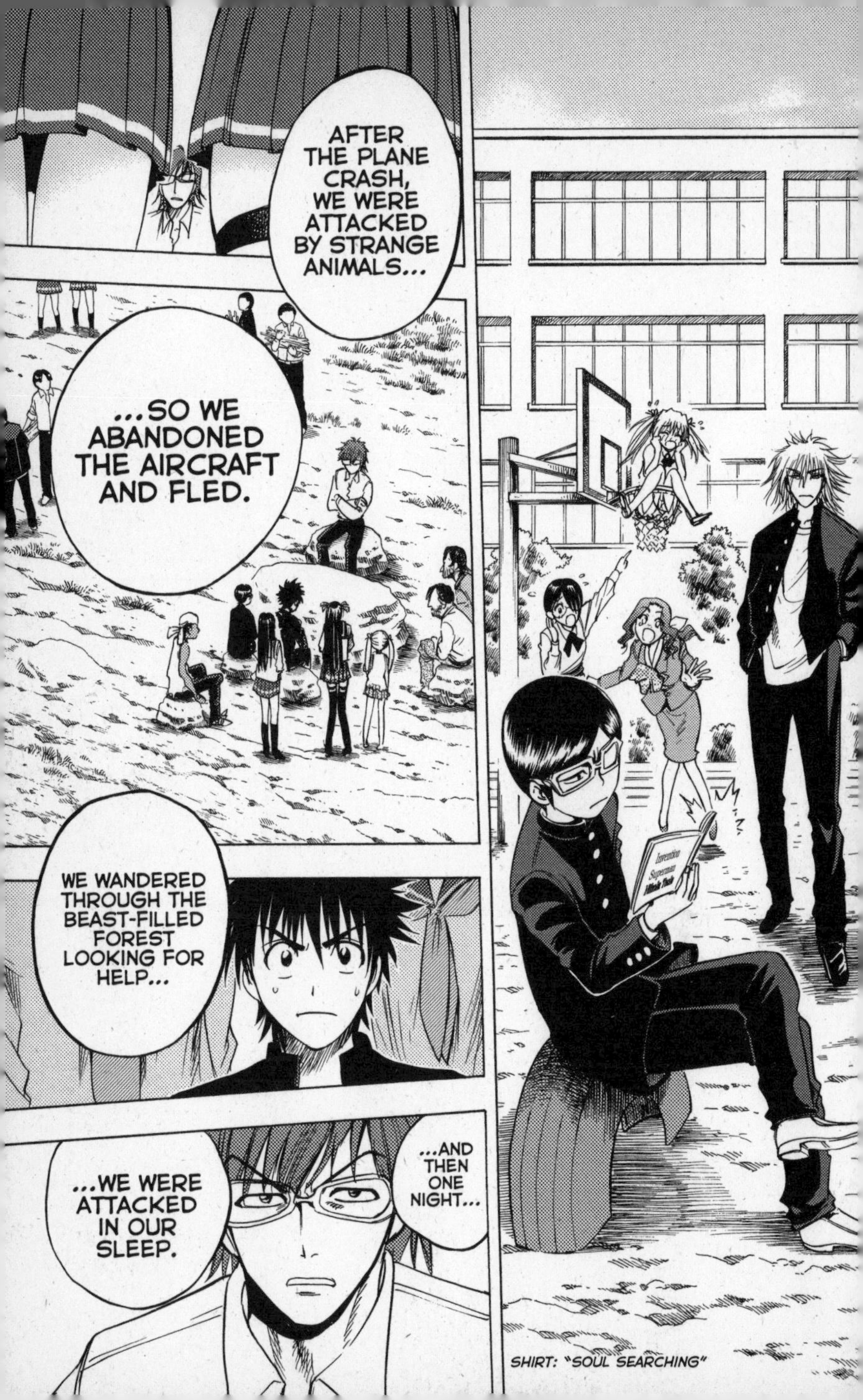
Invention
Superman
SHIRT: "SOUL SEARCHING"
AFTER THE PLANE CRASH, WE WERE ATTACKED BY STRANGE ANIMALS...
...SO WE ABANDONED THE AIRCRAFT AND FLED.
WE WANDERED THROUGH THE BEAST-FILLED FOREST LOOKING FOR HELP...
...AND THEN ONE NIGHT...
...WE WERE ATTACKED IN OUR SLEEP.

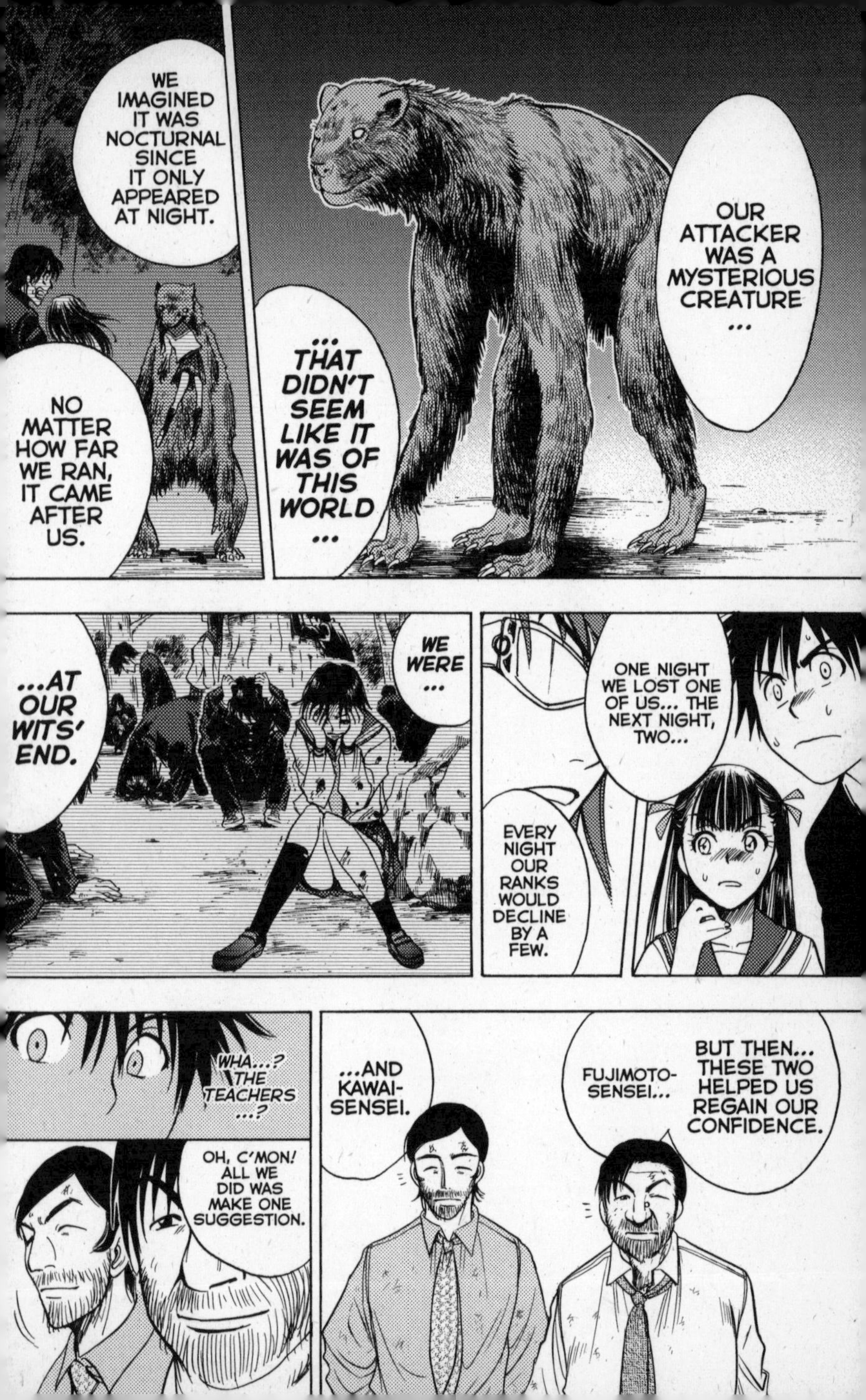
OUR ATTACKER WAS A MYSTERIOUS CREATURE ...
... THAT DIDN'T SEEM LIKE IT WAS OF THIS WORLD ...
WE IMAGINED IT WAS NOCTURNAL SINCE IT ONLY APPEARED AT NIGHT.
NO MATTER HOW FAR WE RAN, IT CAME AFTER US.
ONE NIGHT WE LOST ONE OF US... THE NEXT NIGHT, TWO...
EVERY NIGHT OUR RANKS WOULD DECLINE BY A FEW.
WE WERE ...
...AT OUR WITS' END.
BUT THEN... THESE TWO HELPED US REGAIN OUR CONFIDENCE.
FUJIMOTO-SENSEI...
...AND KAWAI-SENSEI.
WHA...? THE TEACHERS ...?
OH, C'MON! ALL WE DID WAS MAKE ONE SUGGESTION.

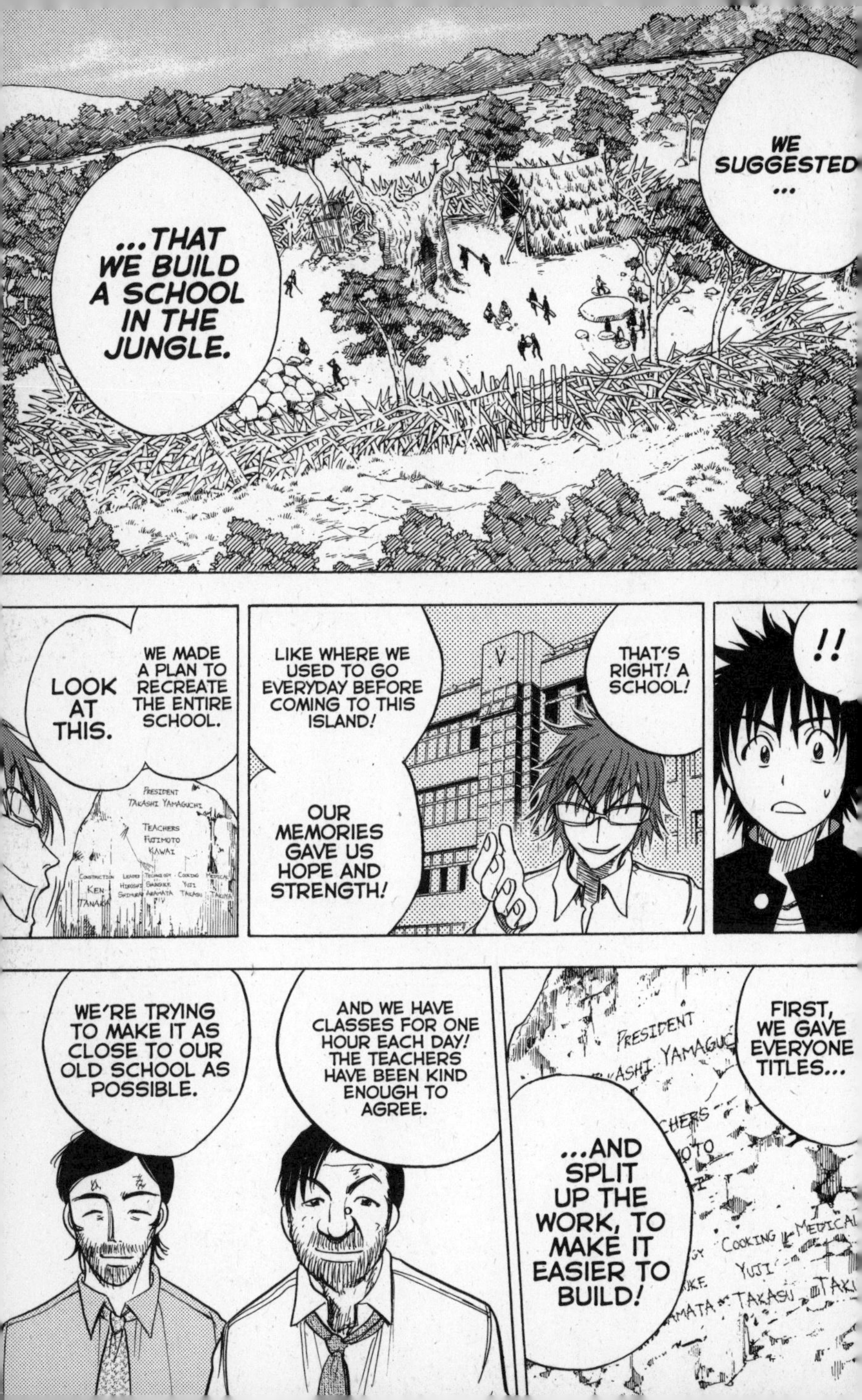

WE SUGGESTED...
...THAT WE BUILD A SCHOOL IN THE JUNGLE.
!!
THAT'S RIGHT! A SCHOOL!
LIKE WHERE WE USED TO GO EVERYDAY BEFORE COMING TO THIS ISLAND!
OUR MEMORIES GAVE US HOPE AND STRENGTH!
WE MADE A PLAN TO RECREATE THE ENTIRE SCHOOL.
LOOK AT THIS.
PRESIDENT
TAKASHI YAMAGUCHI
TEACHERS
FUJIMOTO
KAWAI
CONSTRUCTION
KEN TANAKA
FIRST, WE GAVE EVERYONE TITLES...
...AND SPLIT UP THE WORK, TO MAKE IT EASIER TO BUILD!
AND WE HAVE CLASSES FOR ONE HOUR EACH DAY! THE TEACHERS HAVE BEEN KIND ENOUGH TO AGREE.
WE'RE TRYING TO MAKE IT AS CLOSE TO OUR OLD SCHOOL AS POSSIBLE.

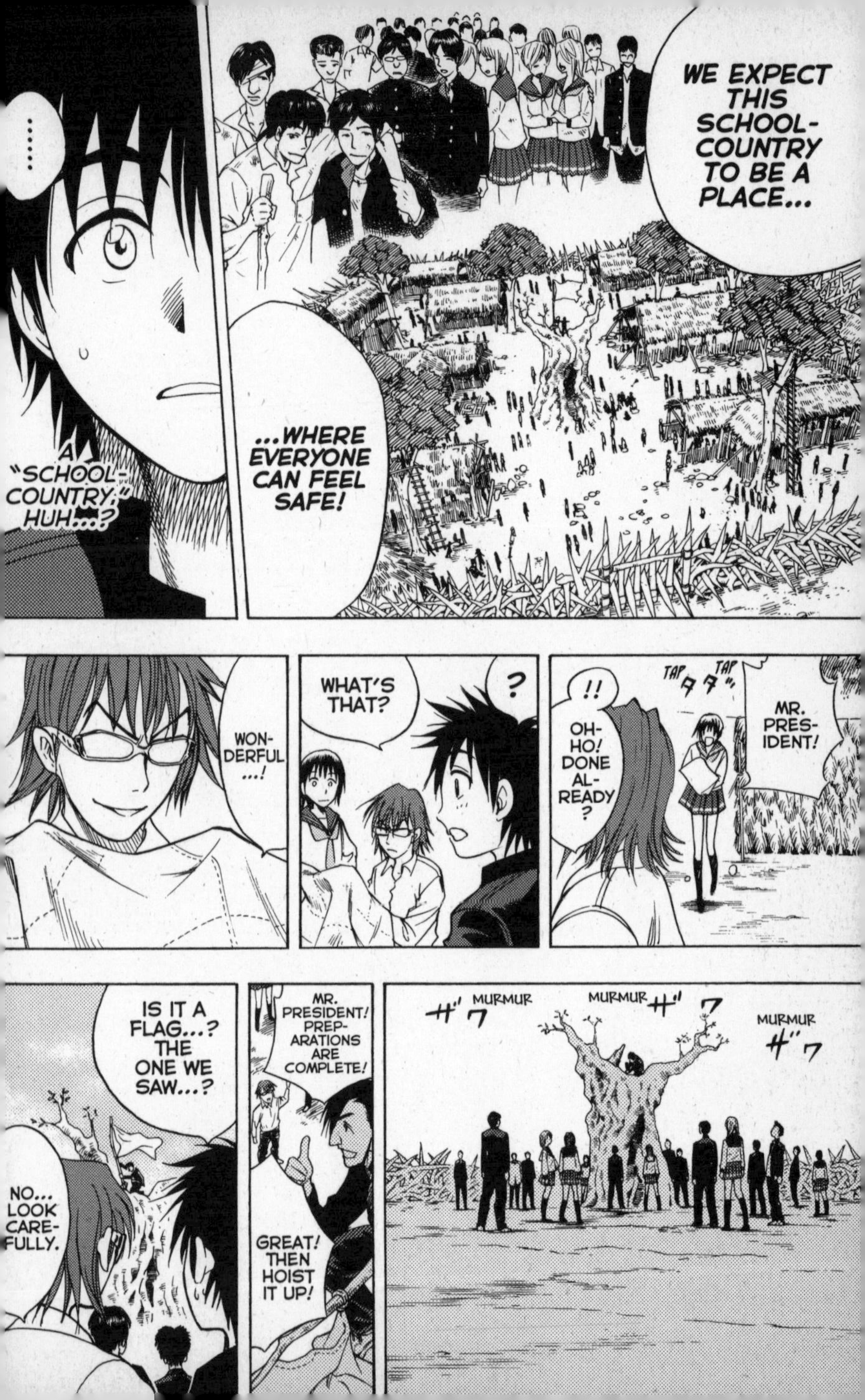
WE EXPECT THIS SCHOOL-COUNTRY TO BE A PLACE...
...WHERE EVERYONE CAN FEEL SAFE!
......
A "SCHOOL-COUNTRY," HUH...?
TAP タ TAP タ
MR. PRESIDENT!
!!
OH-HO! DONE ALREADY?
?
WHAT'S THAT?
WONDERFUL...!
ザワ MURMUR
MURMUR ザワ
MURMUR ザワ
MR. PRESIDENT! PREPARATIONS ARE COMPLETE!
GREAT! THEN HOIST IT UP!
IS IT A FLAG...? THE ONE WE SAW...?
NO... LOOK CAREFULLY.

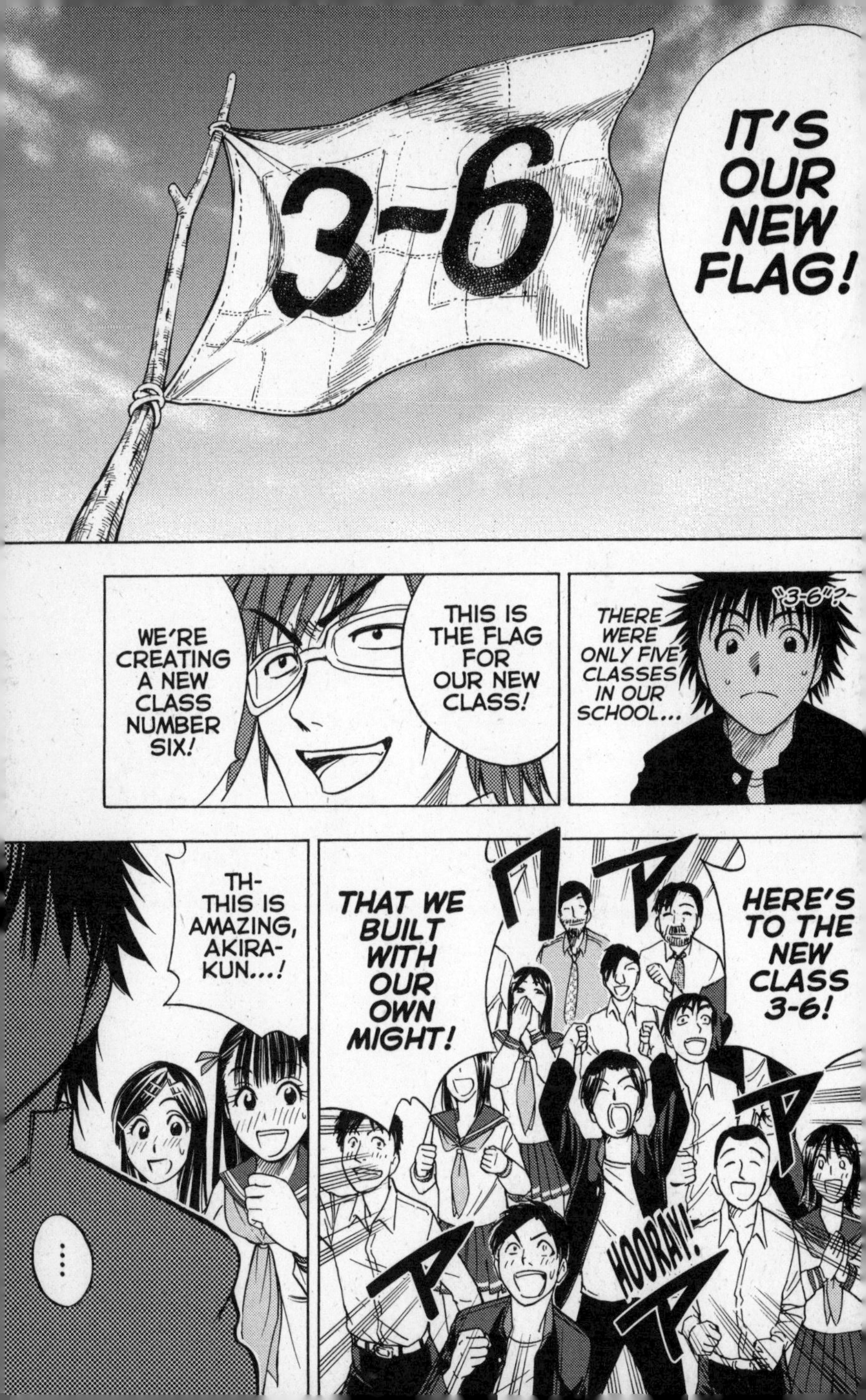
IT'S OUR NEW FLAG!
"3-6"?
THERE WERE ONLY FIVE CLASSES IN OUR SCHOOL...
THIS IS THE FLAG FOR OUR NEW CLASS!
WE'RE CREATING A NEW CLASS NUMBER SIX!
HERE'S TO THE NEW CLASS 3-6!
THAT WE BUILT WITH OUR OWN MIGHT!
HOORAY!
TH- THIS IS AMAZING, AKIRA-KUN...!
....

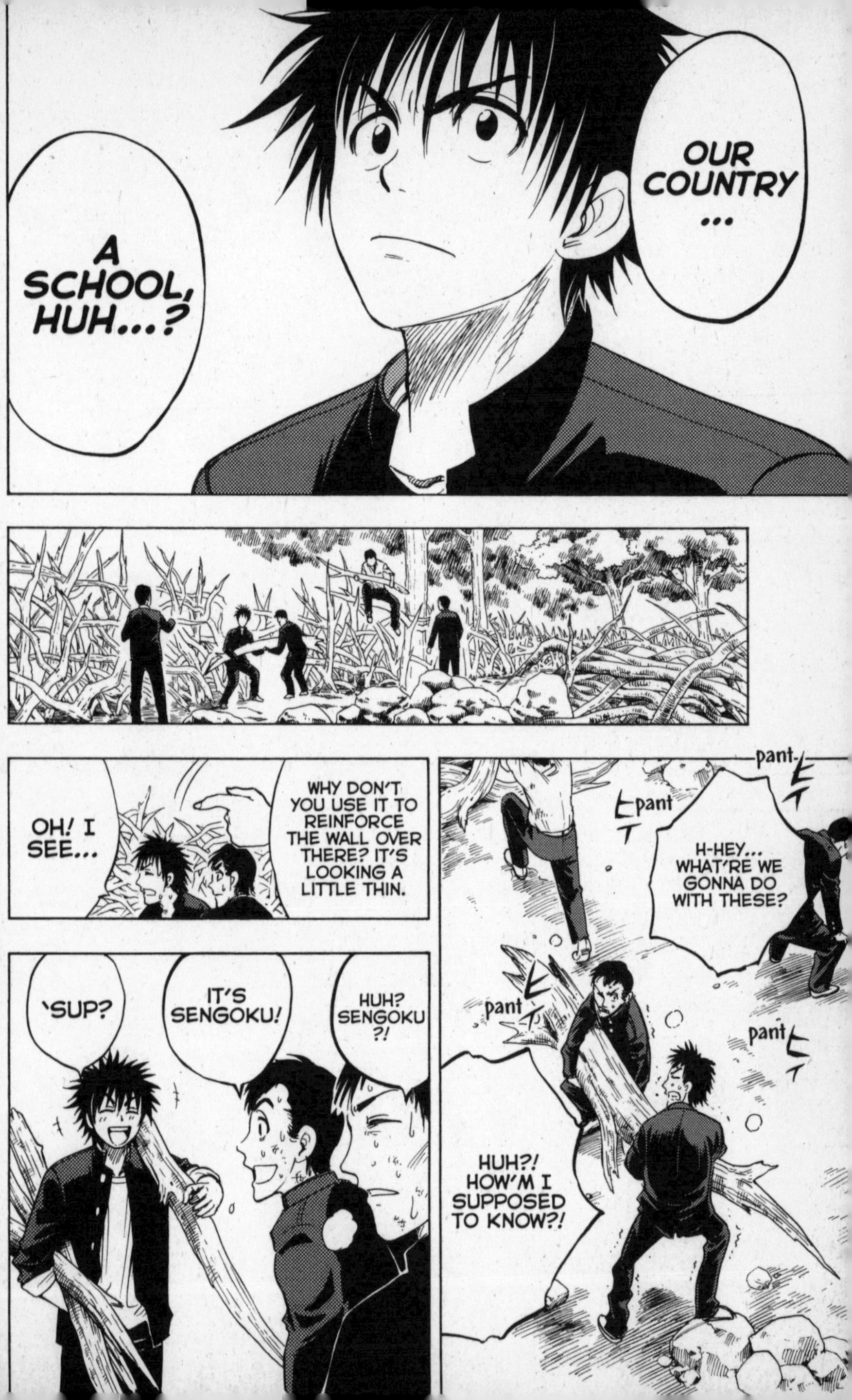
OUR COUNTRY ...
A SCHOOL, HUH...?
pant
pant
H-HEY... WHAT'RE WE GONNA DO WITH THESE?
pant
pant
HUH?! HOW'M I SUPPOSED TO KNOW?!
WHY DON'T YOU USE IT TO REINFORCE THE WALL OVER THERE? IT'S LOOKING A LITTLE THIN.
OH! I SEE...
HUH? SENGOKU ?!
IT'S SENGOKU!
'SUP?

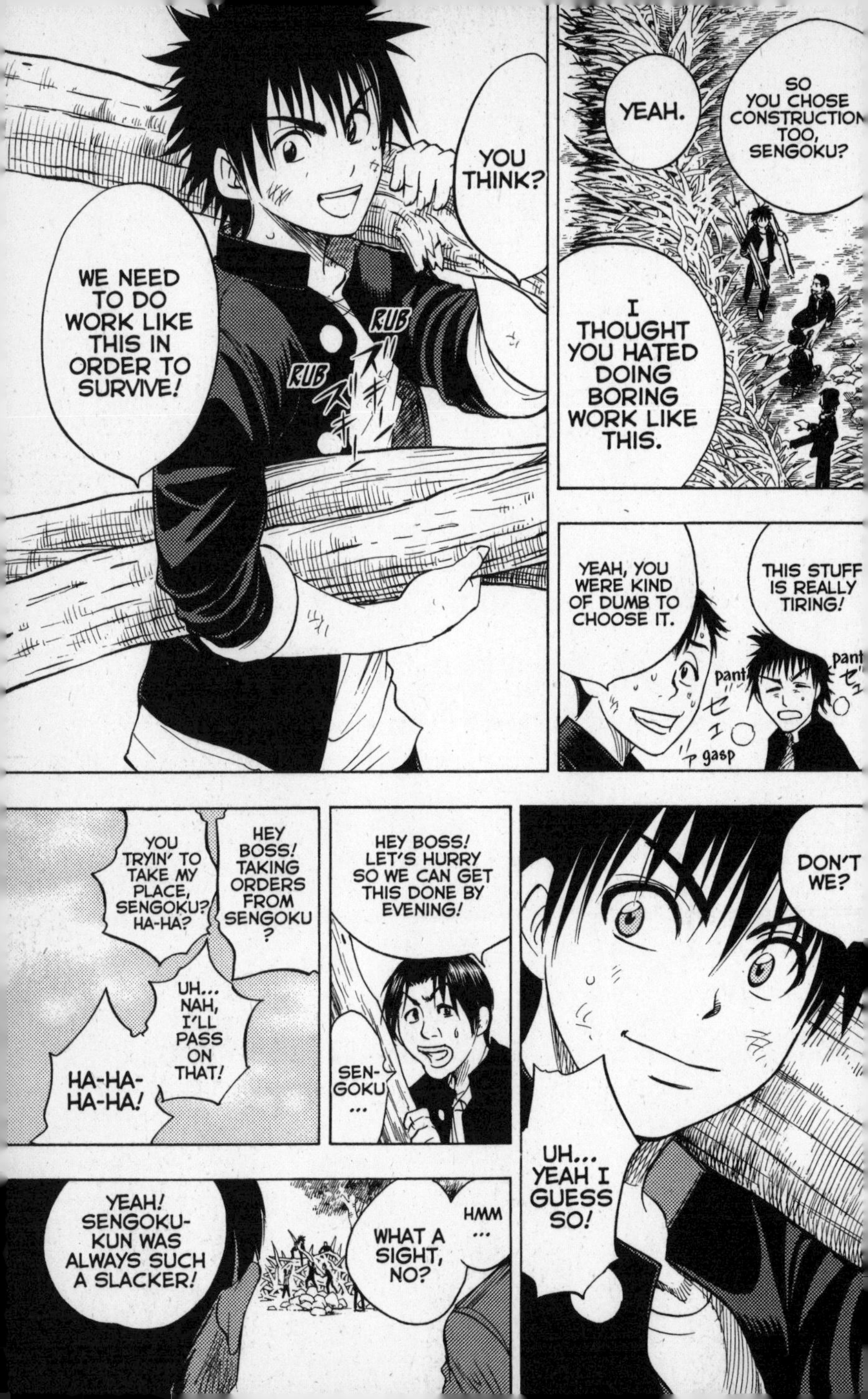
SO YOU CHOSE CONSTRUCTION TOO, SENGOKU?
YEAH.
I THOUGHT YOU HATED DOING BORING WORK LIKE THIS.
THIS STUFF IS REALLY TIRING!
YEAH, YOU WERE KIND OF DUMB TO CHOOSE IT.
pant
pant
gasp
YOU THINK?
RUB
RUB
WE NEED TO DO WORK LIKE THIS IN ORDER TO SURVIVE!
DON'T WE?
UH... YEAH I GUESS SO!
HEY BOSS! LET'S HURRY SO WE CAN GET THIS DONE BY EVENING!
SEN-GOKU...
HEY BOSS! TAKING ORDERS FROM SENGOKU?
YOU TRYIN' TO TAKE MY PLACE, SENGOKU? HA-HA?
UH... NAH, I'LL PASS ON THAT!
HA-HA-HA-HA!
HMM...
WHAT A SIGHT, NO?
YEAH! SENGOKU-KUN WAS ALWAYS SUCH A SLACKER!

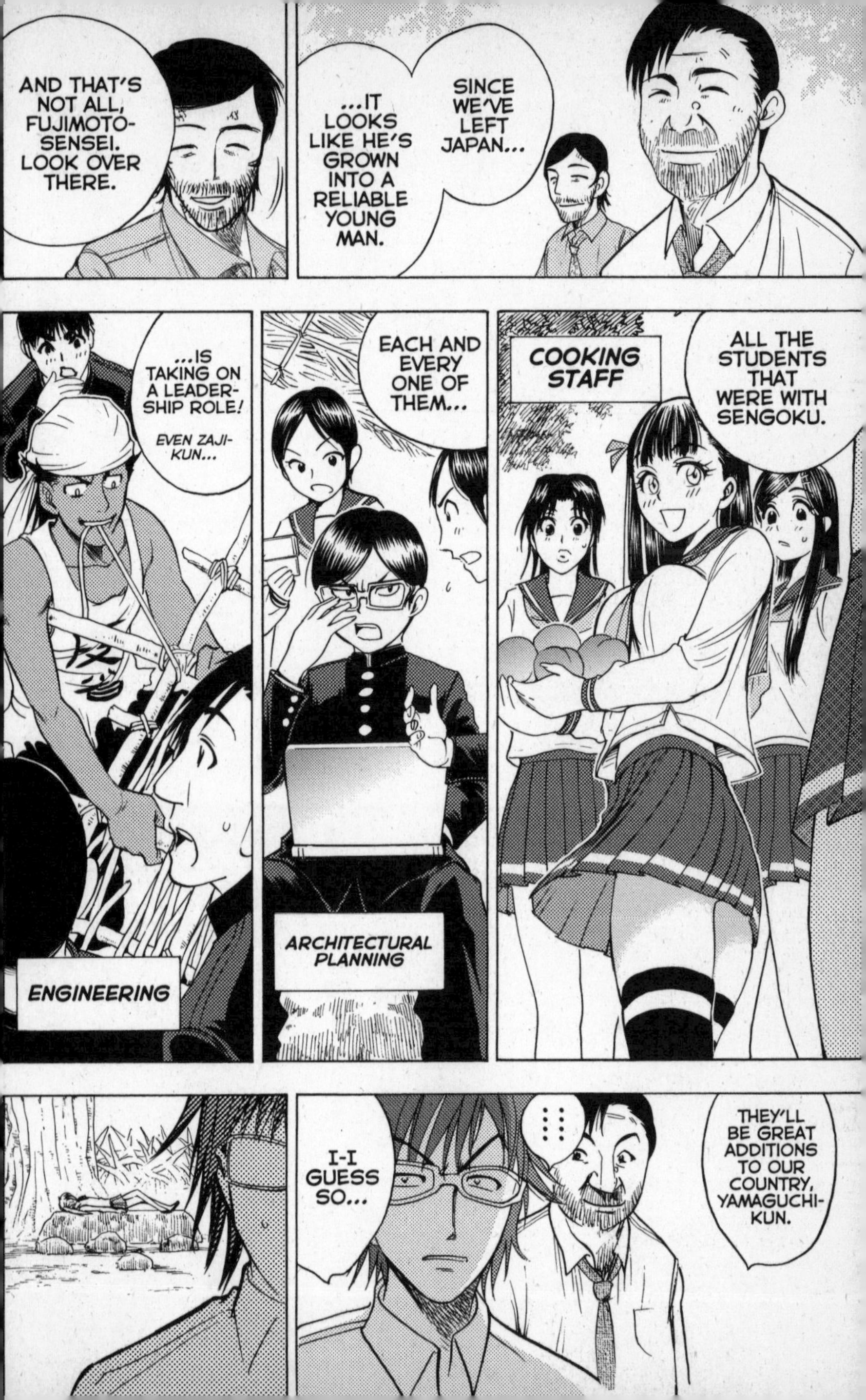
SINCE WE'VE LEFT JAPAN...
...IT LOOKS LIKE HE'S GROWN INTO A RELIABLE YOUNG MAN.
AND THAT'S NOT ALL, FUJIMOTO-SENSEI. LOOK OVER THERE.
ALL THE STUDENTS THAT WERE WITH SENGOKU.
COOKING STAFF
EACH AND EVERY ONE OF THEM...
ARCHITECTURAL PLANNING
EVEN ZAJI-KUN...
...IS TAKING ON A LEADERSHIP ROLE!
ENGINEERING
THEY'LL BE GREAT ADDITIONS TO OUR COUNTRY, YAMAGUCHI-KUN.
......
I-I GUESS SO...

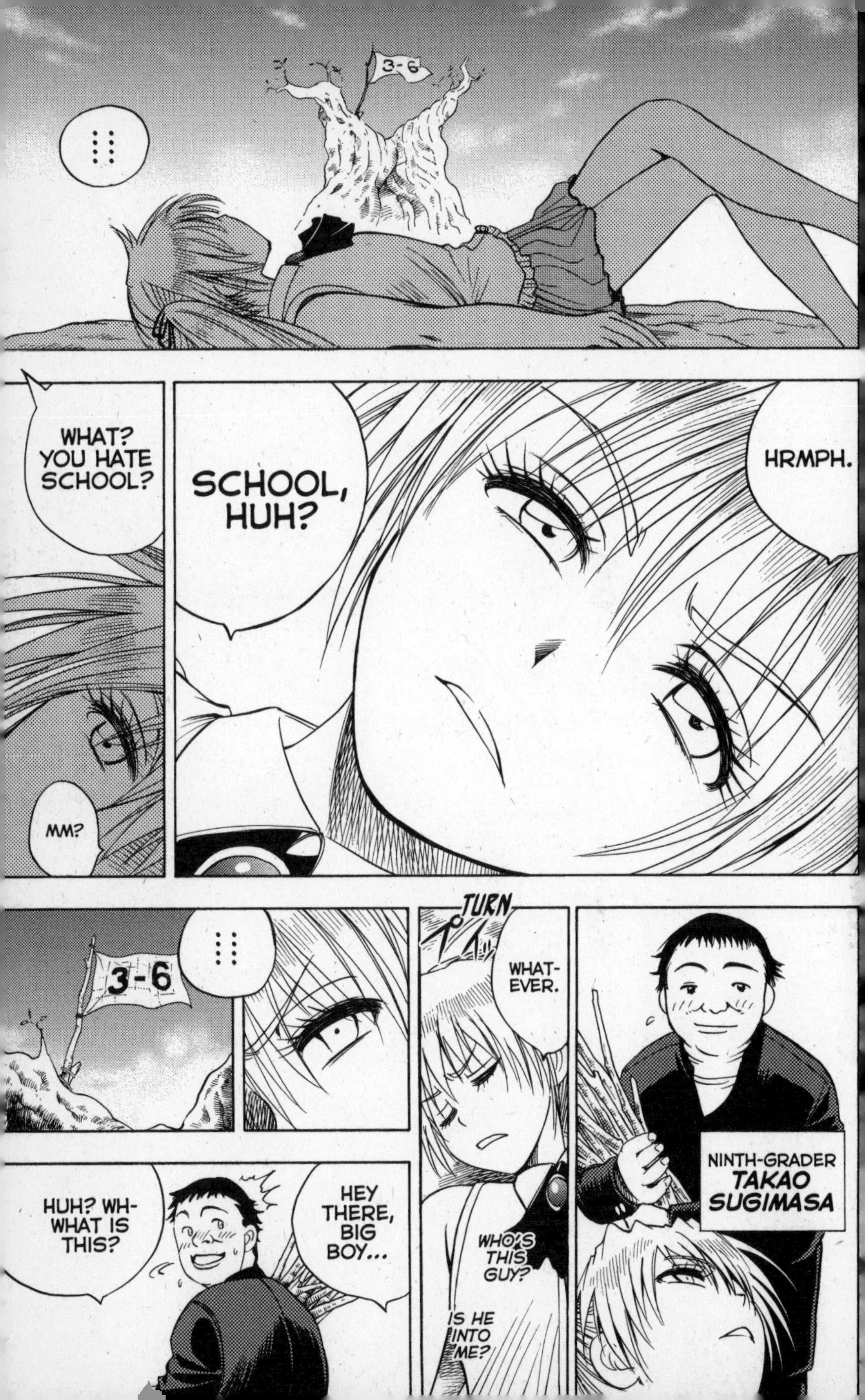
3-6
......
HRMPH.
SCHOOL, HUH?
WHAT? YOU HATE SCHOOL?
MM?
NINTH-GRADER TAKAO SUGIMASA
TURN
WHAT-EVER.
WHO'S THIS GUY?
IS HE INTO ME?
......
3-6
HEY THERE, BIG BOY...
HUH? WH-WHAT IS THIS?

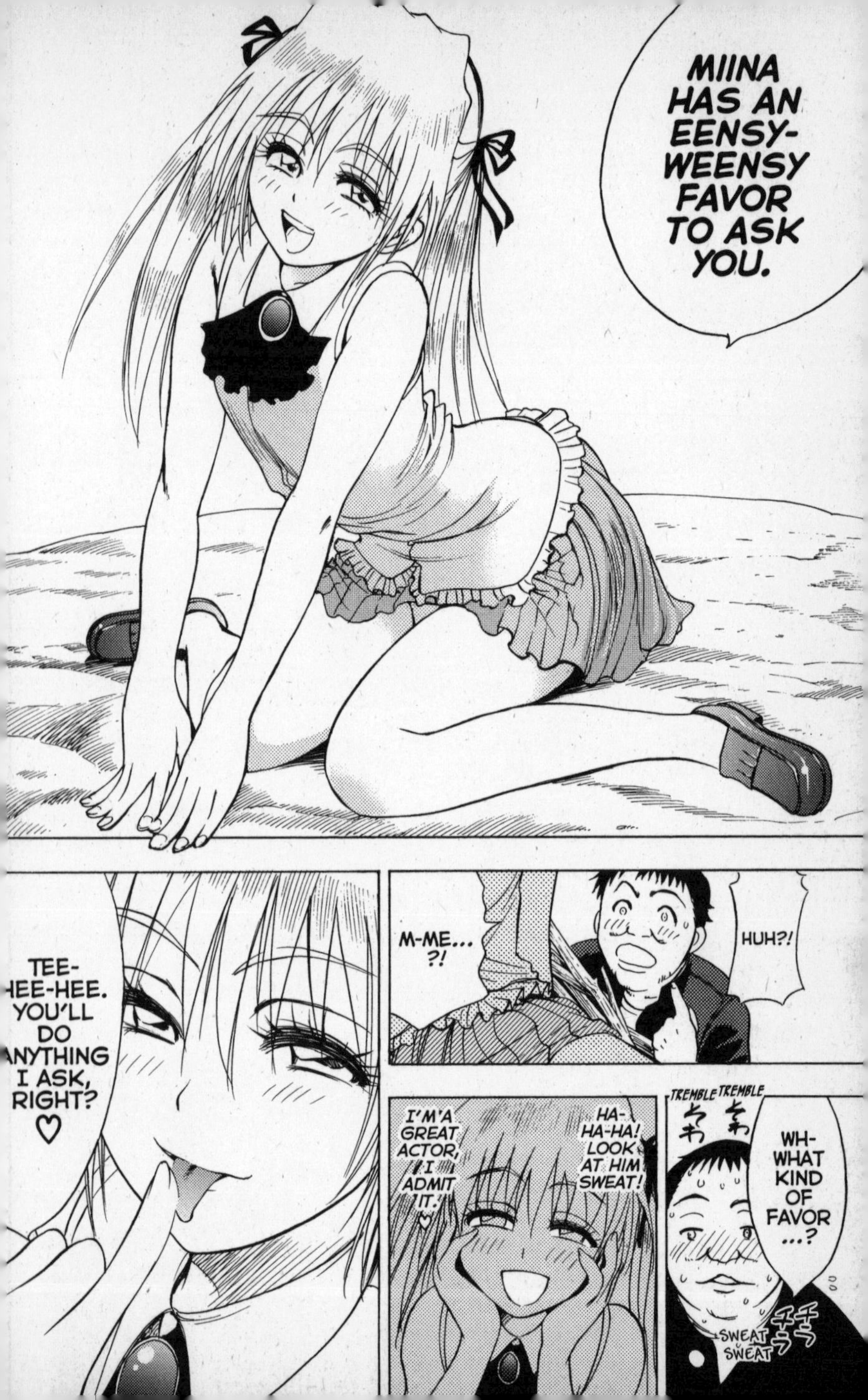
MIINA HAS AN EENSY-WEENSY FAVOR TO ASK YOU.
HUH?!
M-ME... ?!
TREMBLE TREMBLE
WH-WHAT KIND OF FAVOR ...?
SWEAT SWEAT
HA-HA-HA! LOOK AT HIM SWEAT!
I'M A GREAT ACTOR, I ADMIT IT. ♡
TEE-HEE-HEE. YOU'LL DO ANYTHING I ASK, RIGHT? ♡

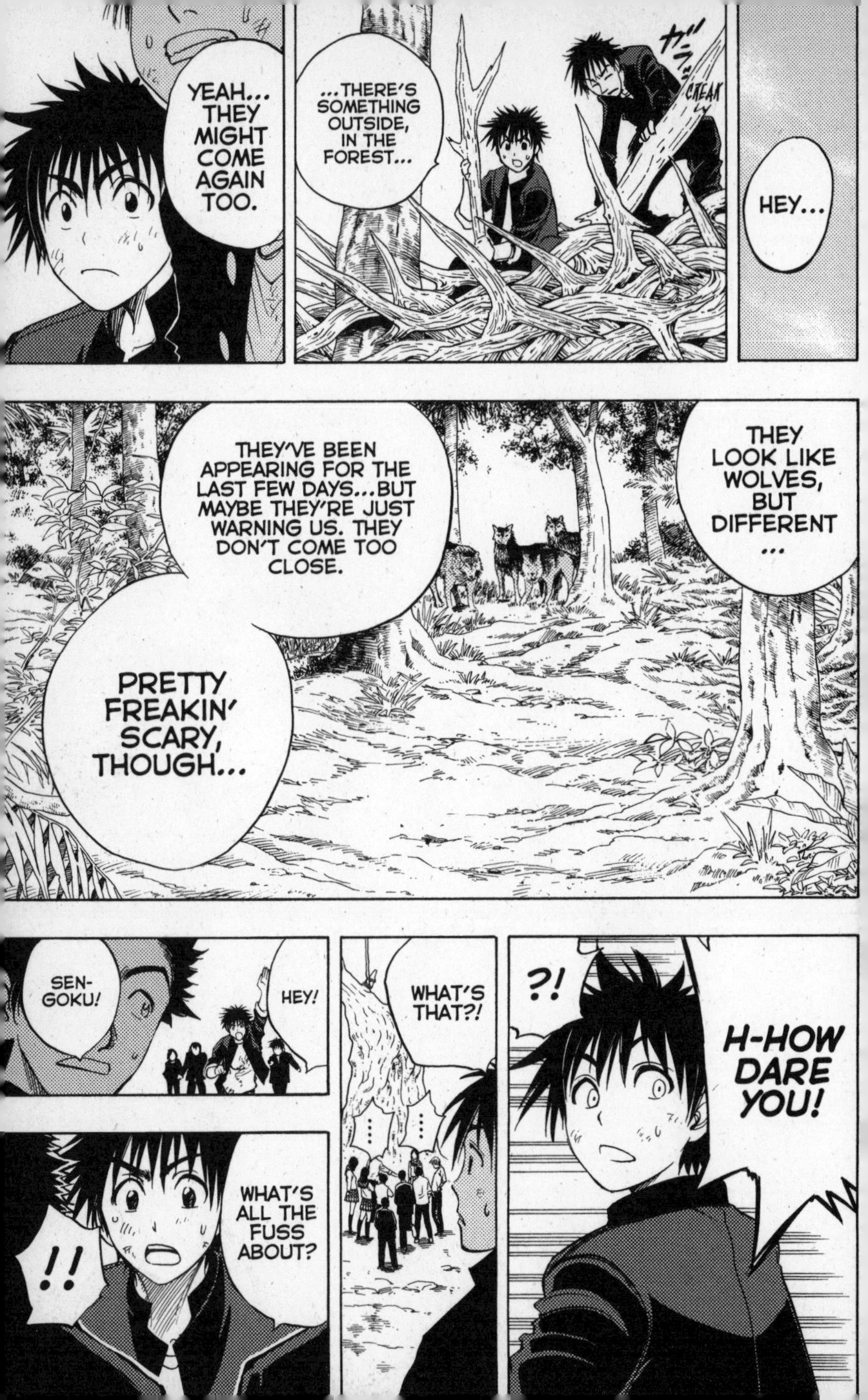
HEY...
CREAK
...THERE'S SOMETHING OUTSIDE, IN THE FOREST...
YEAH... THEY MIGHT COME AGAIN TOO.
THEY LOOK LIKE WOLVES, BUT DIFFERENT ...
THEY'VE BEEN APPEARING FOR THE LAST FEW DAYS...BUT MAYBE THEY'RE JUST WARNING US. THEY DON'T COME TOO CLOSE.
PRETTY FREAKIN' SCARY, THOUGH...
?!
H-HOW DARE YOU!
WHAT'S THAT?!
HEY!
SEN-GOKU!
WHAT'S ALL THE FUSS ABOUT?
!!

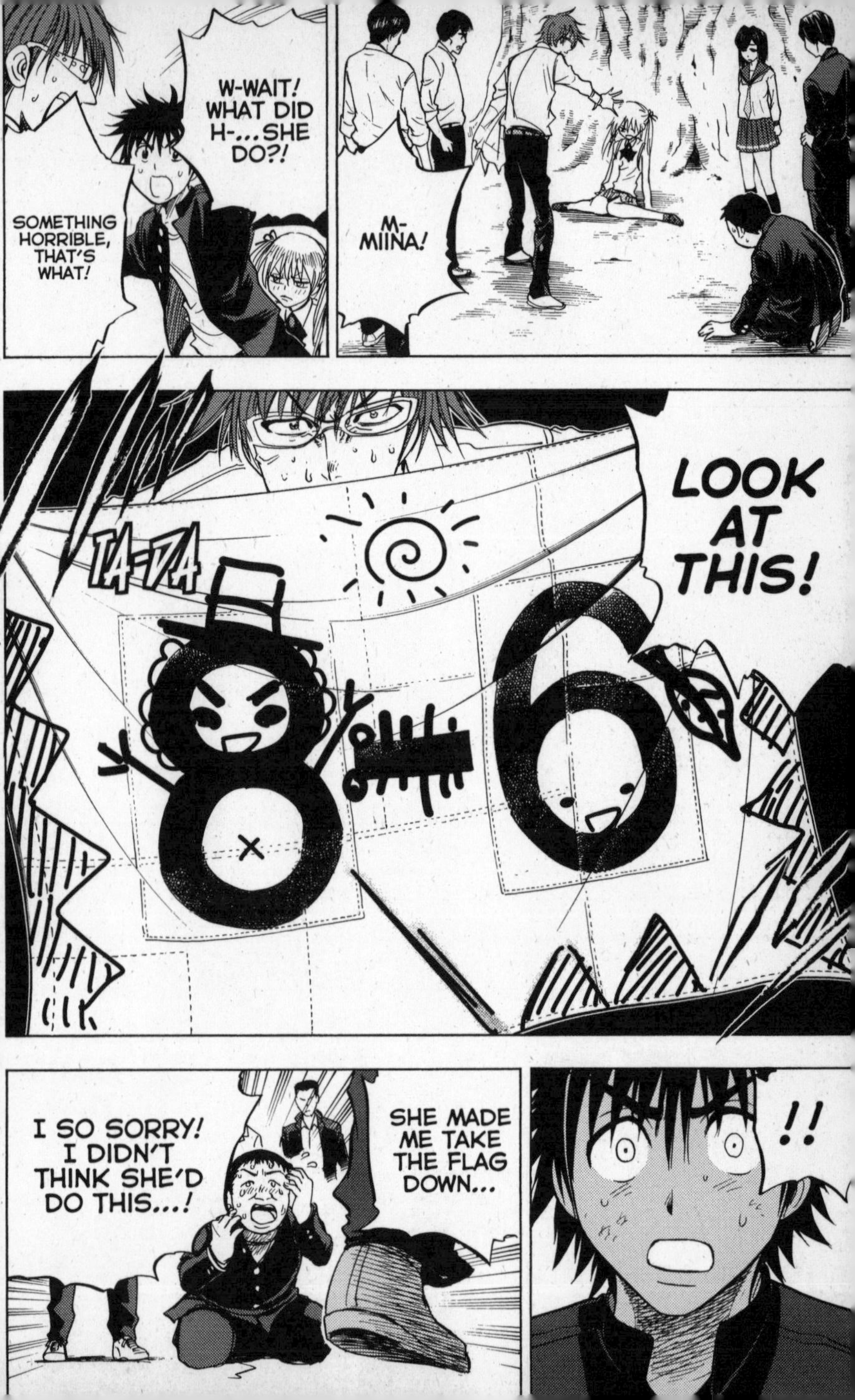
M-MIINA!
W-WAIT! WHAT DID H-...SHE DO?!
SOMETHING HORRIBLE, THAT'S WHAT!
LOOK AT THIS!
TA-DA
!!
SHE MADE ME TAKE THE FLAG DOWN...
I SO SORRY! I DIDN'T THINK SHE'D DO THIS...!

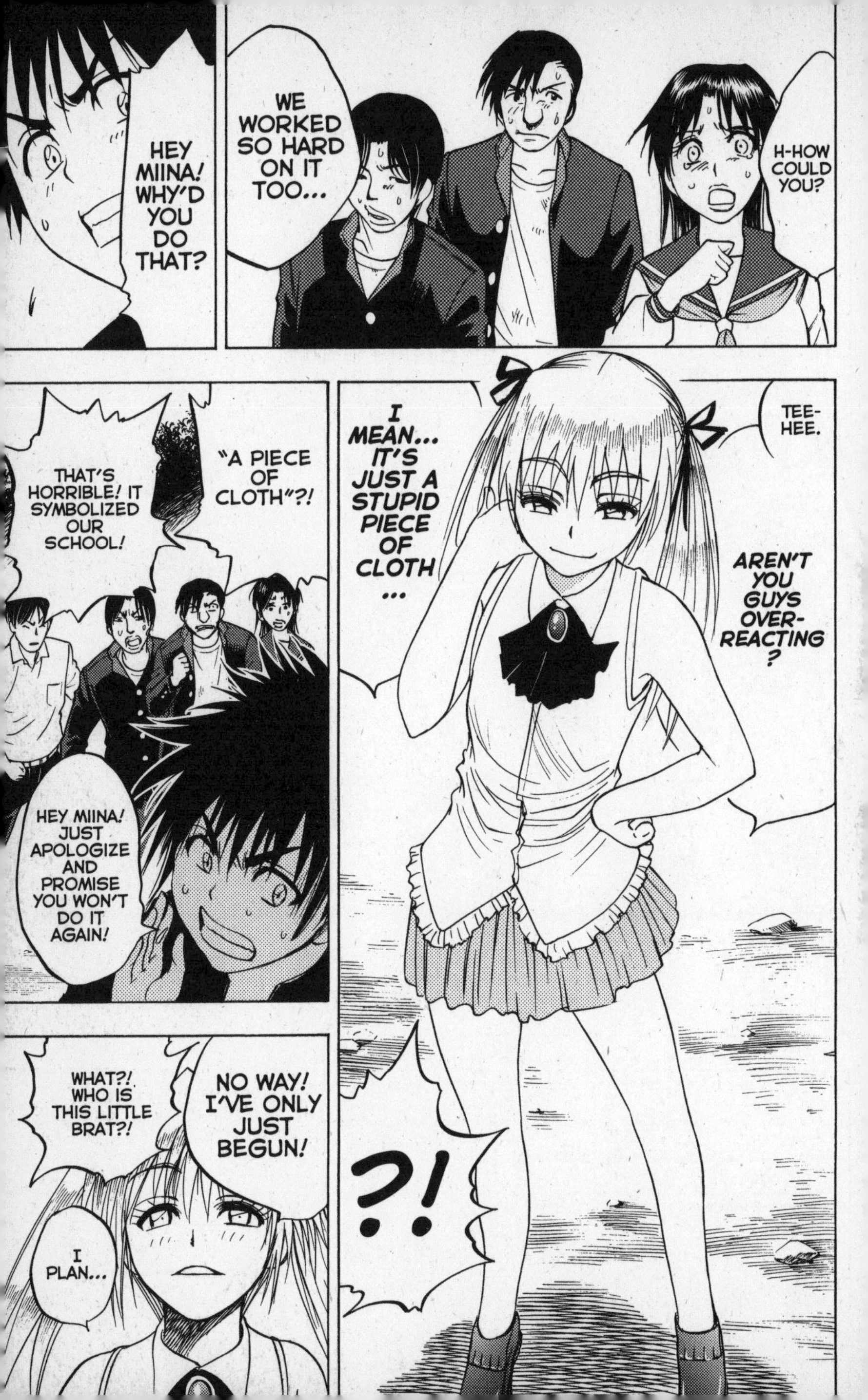
H-HOW COULD YOU?
WE WORKED SO HARD ON IT TOO...
HEY MIINA! WHY'D YOU DO THAT?
TEE-HEE.
AREN'T YOU GUYS OVER-REACTING?
I MEAN... IT'S JUST A STUPID PIECE OF CLOTH...
?!
"A PIECE OF CLOTH"?!
THAT'S HORRIBLE! IT SYMBOLIZED OUR SCHOOL!
HEY MIINA! JUST APOLOGIZE AND PROMISE YOU WON'T DO IT AGAIN!
NO WAY! I'VE ONLY JUST BEGUN!
WHAT?! WHO IS THIS LITTLE BRAT?!
I PLAN...

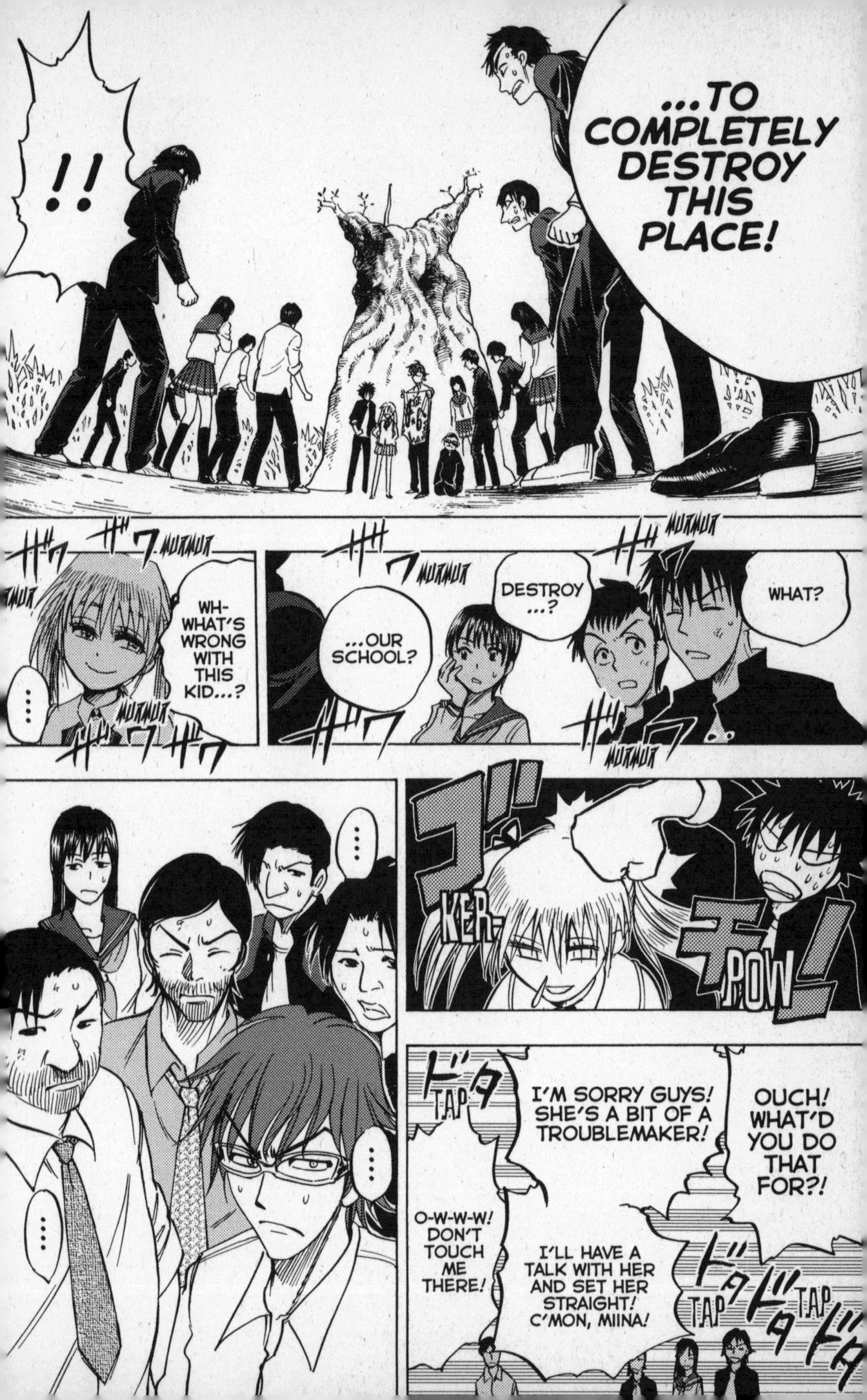
...TO COMPLETELY DESTROY THIS PLACE!
!!
MURMUR
WHAT?
DESTROY ...?
MURMUR
...OUR SCHOOL?
MURMUR
MURMUR
WH-WHAT'S WRONG WITH THIS KID...?
....
MURMUR
KER-POW
OUCH! WHAT'D YOU DO THAT FOR?!
I'M SORRY GUYS! SHE'S A BIT OF A TROUBLEMAKER!
TAP
I'LL HAVE A TALK WITH HER AND SET HER STRAIGHT! C'MON, MIINA!
O-W-W-W! DON'T TOUCH ME THERE!
TAP TAP
....
....
....

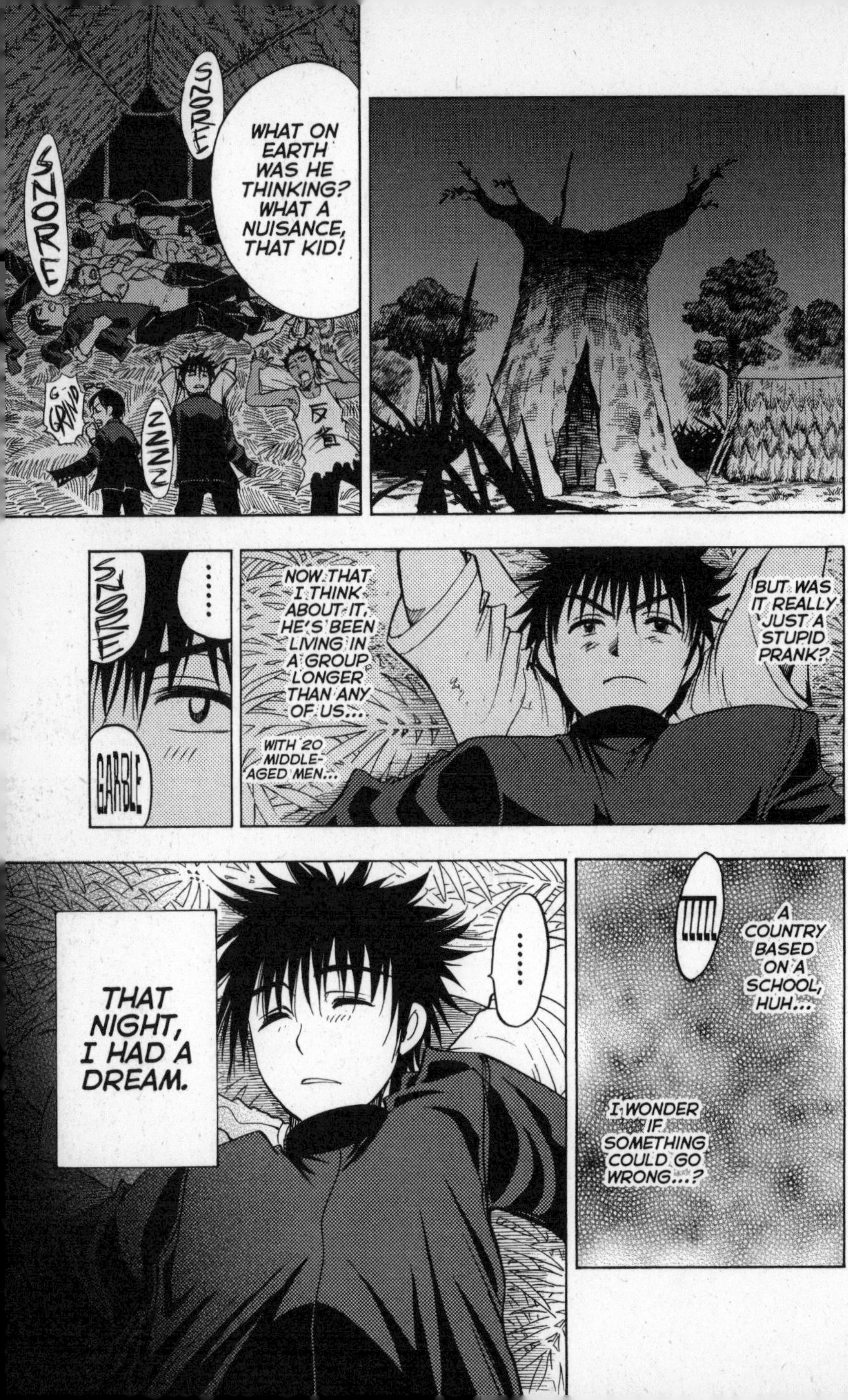
WHAT ON EARTH WAS HE THINKING? WHAT A NUISANCE, THAT KID!
SNORE
SNORE
反省
ZZZZ
G-GRIND
BUT WAS IT REALLY JUST A STUPID PRANK?
NOW THAT I THINK ABOUT IT, HE'S BEEN LIVING IN A GROUP LONGER THAN ANY OF US...
WITH 20 MIDDLE-AGED MEN...
......
SNORE
GARBLE
ZZZZZ
A COUNTRY BASED ON A SCHOOL, HUH...
I WONDER IF SOMETHING COULD GO WRONG...?
......
THAT NIGHT, I HAD A DREAM.

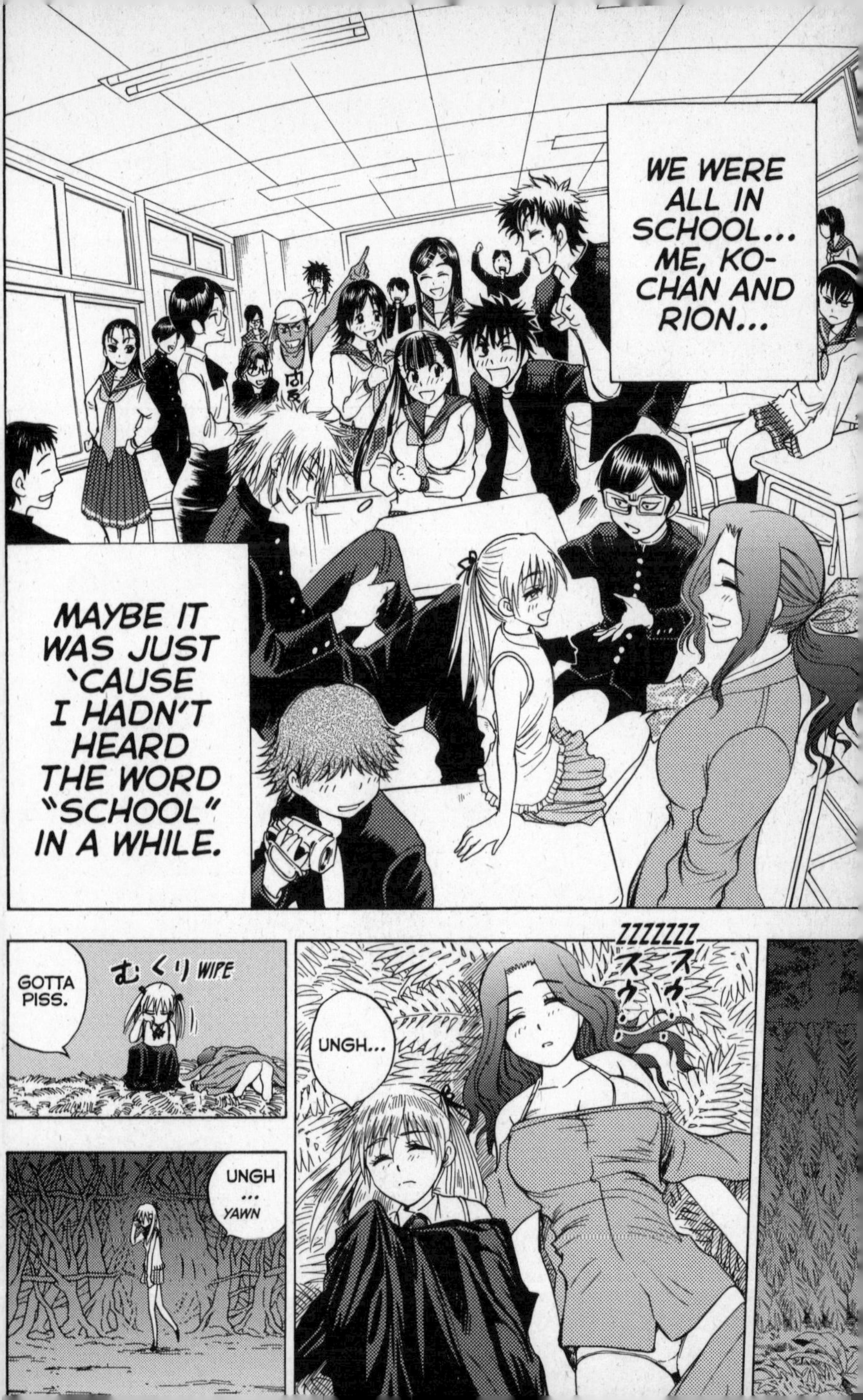
WE WERE ALL IN SCHOOL... ME, KO-CHAN AND RION...
MAYBE IT WAS JUST 'CAUSE I HADN'T HEARD THE WORD "SCHOOL" IN A WHILE.
ZZZZZZZ
スゥ スゥ
UNGH...
むくり WIPE
GOTTA PISS.
UNGH ... YAWN

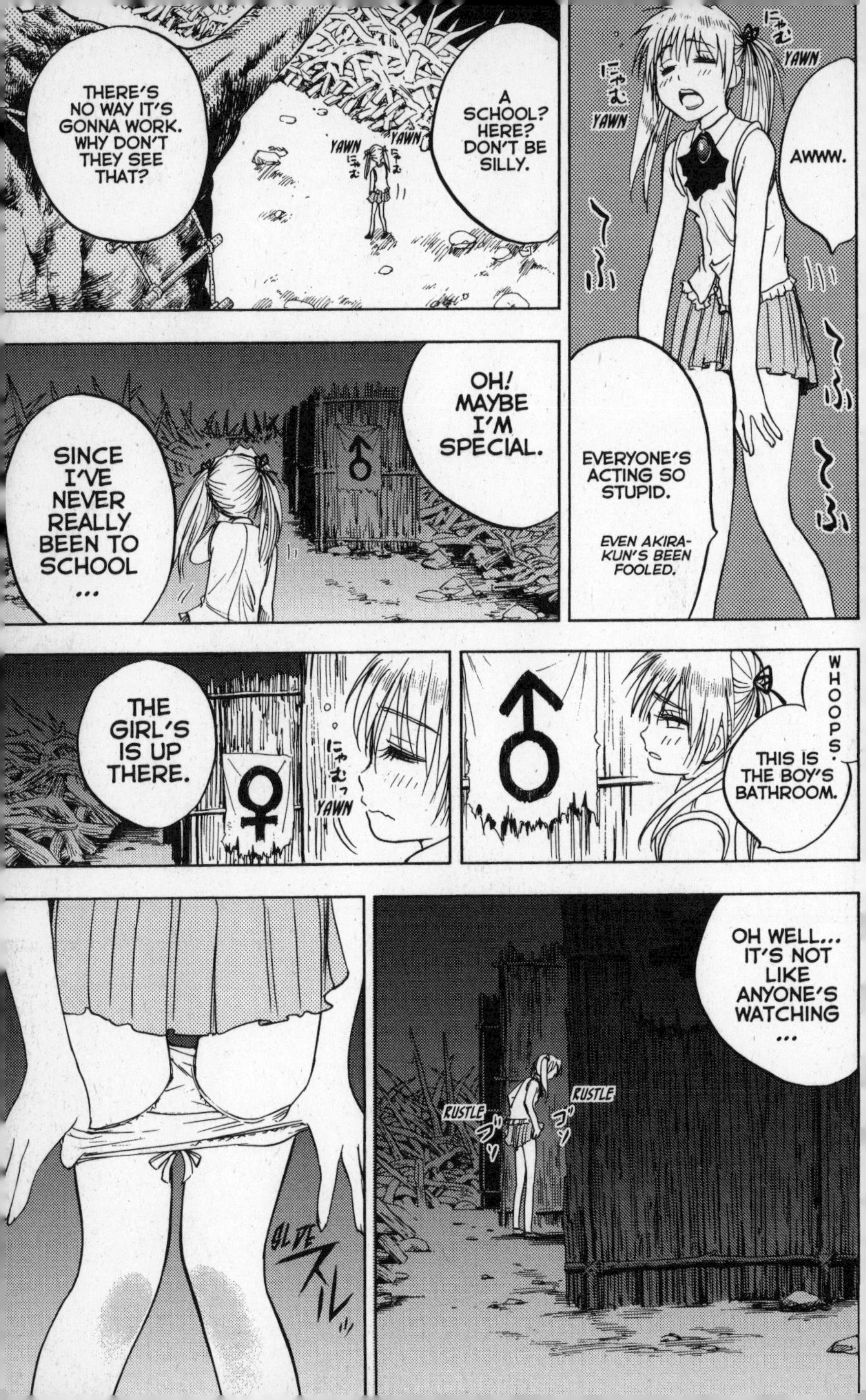
にゃむ
YAWN
にゃむ
YAWN
AWWW.
へーふ
へーふ
へーふ
EVERYONE'S ACTING SO STUPID.
EVEN AKIRA-KUN'S BEEN FOOLED.
A SCHOOL? HERE? DON'T BE SILLY.
YAWN にゃむ
YAWN にゃむ
THERE'S NO WAY IT'S GONNA WORK. WHY DON'T THEY SEE THAT?
OH! MAYBE I'M SPECIAL.
SINCE I'VE NEVER REALLY BEEN TO SCHOOL ...
WHOOPS.
THIS IS THE BOY'S BATHROOM.
にゃむっ
YAWN
THE GIRL'S IS UP THERE.
OH WELL... IT'S NOT LIKE ANYONE'S WATCHING ...
RUSTLE ゴソ
RUSTLE ゴソ
SLIDE スル

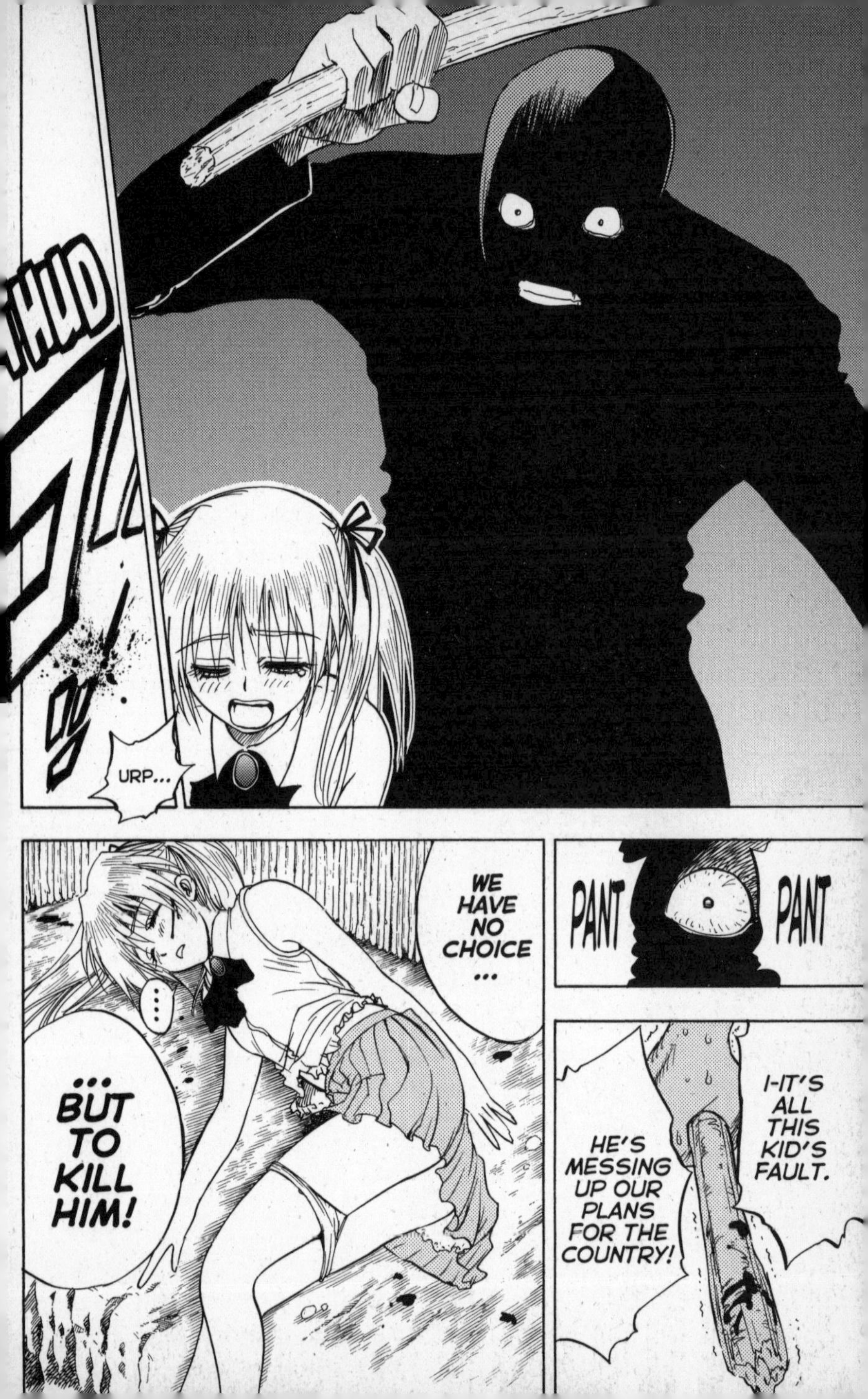
THUD
URP...
PANT PANT
I-IT'S ALL THIS KID'S FAULT.
HE'S MESSING UP OUR PLANS FOR THE COUNTRY!
WE HAVE NO CHOICE ...
...BUT TO KILL HIM!
...

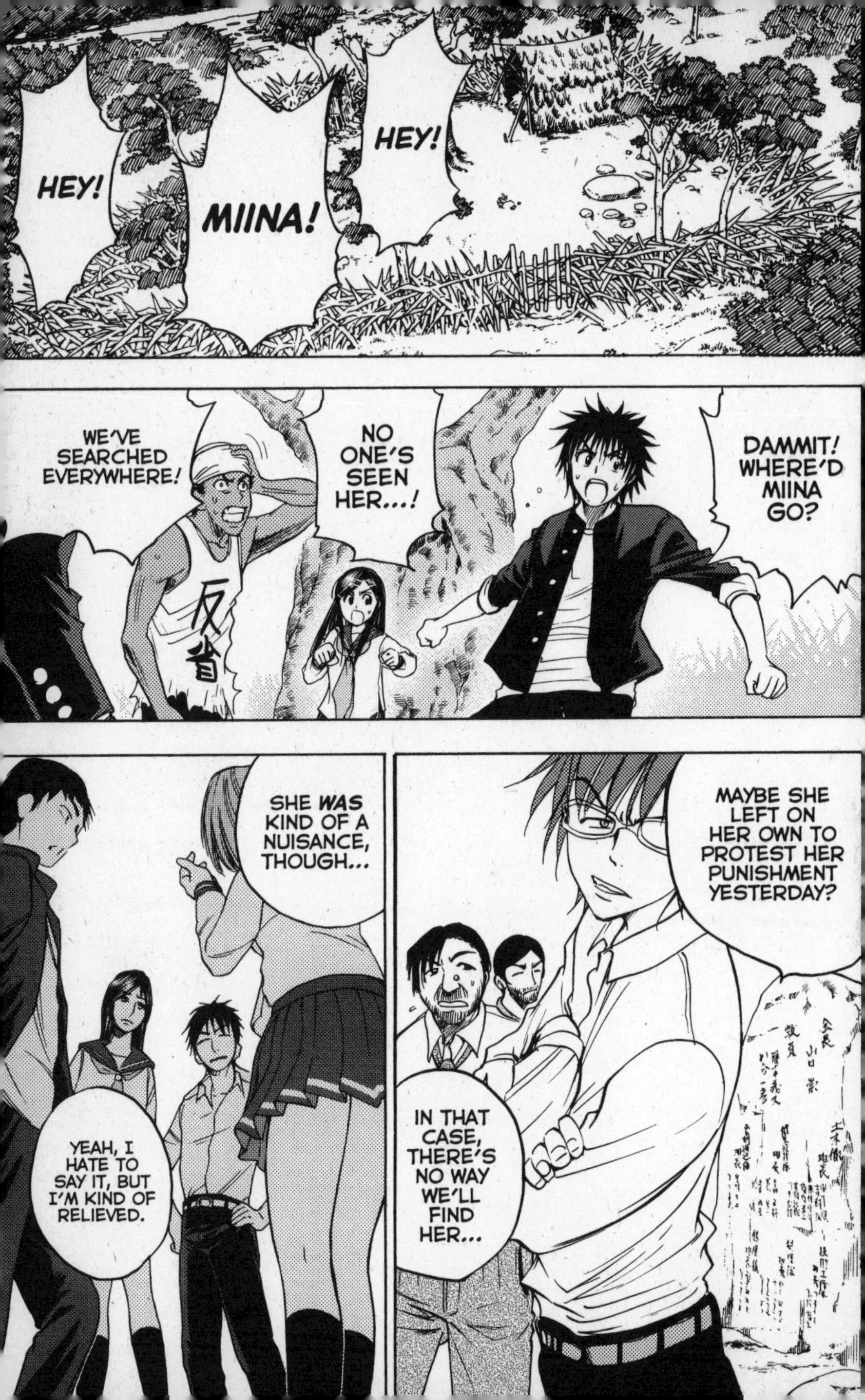
HEY!
MIINA!
HEY!
DAMMIT! WHERE'D MIINA GO?
NO ONE'S SEEN HER...!
WE'VE SEARCHED EVERYWHERE!
反省
MAYBE SHE LEFT ON HER OWN TO PROTEST HER PUNISHMENT YESTERDAY?
IN THAT CASE, THERE'S NO WAY WE'LL FIND HER...
SHE *WAS* KIND OF A NUISANCE, THOUGH...
YEAH, I HATE TO SAY IT, BUT I'M KIND OF RELIEVED.

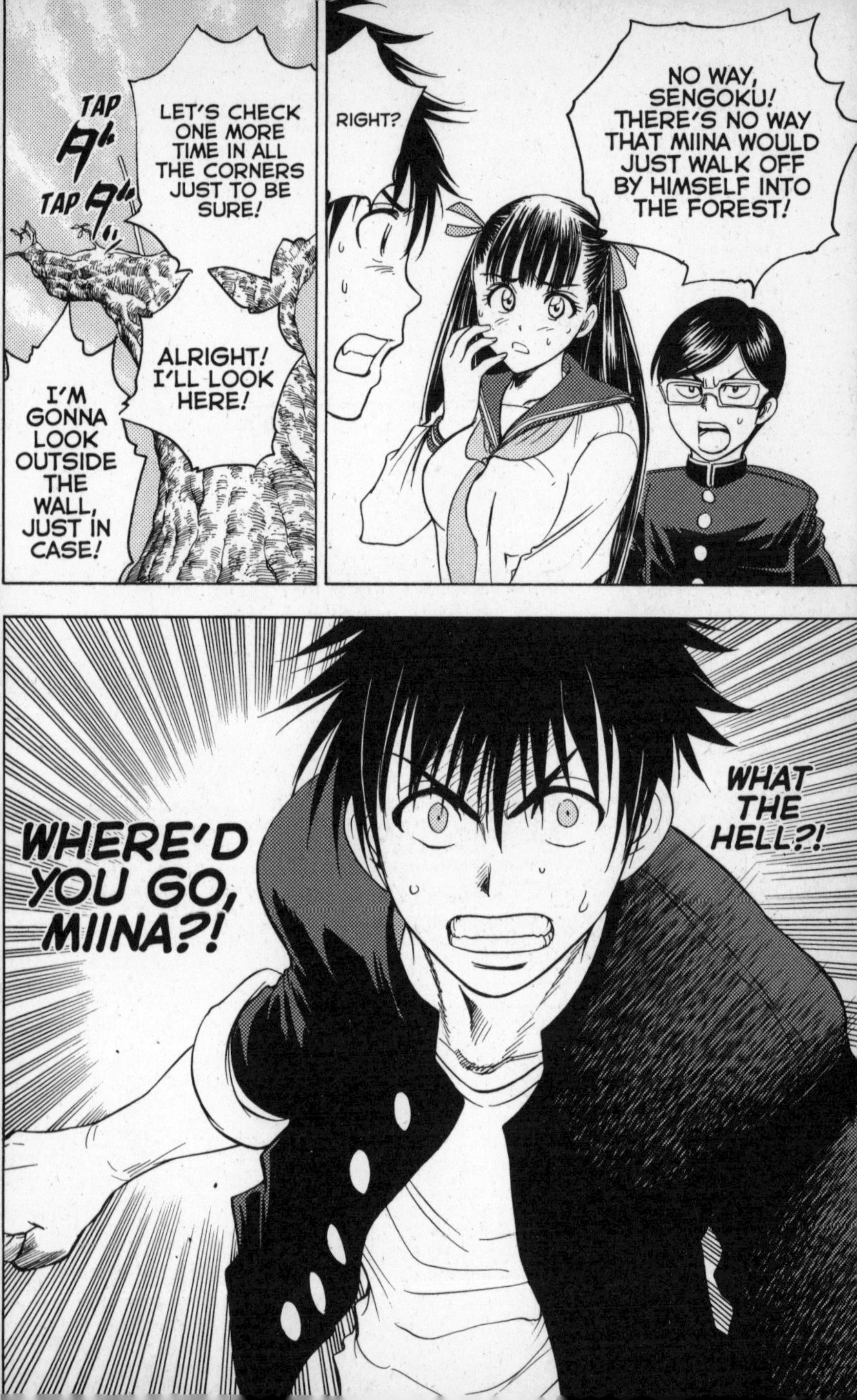
NO WAY, SENGOKU! THERE'S NO WAY THAT MIINA WOULD JUST WALK OFF BY HIMSELF INTO THE FOREST!
RIGHT?
LET'S CHECK ONE MORE TIME IN ALL THE CORNERS JUST TO BE SURE!
TAP
TAP
ALRIGHT! I'LL LOOK HERE!
I'M GONNA LOOK OUTSIDE THE WALL, JUST IN CASE!
WHAT THE HELL?!
WHERE'D YOU GO, MIINA?!

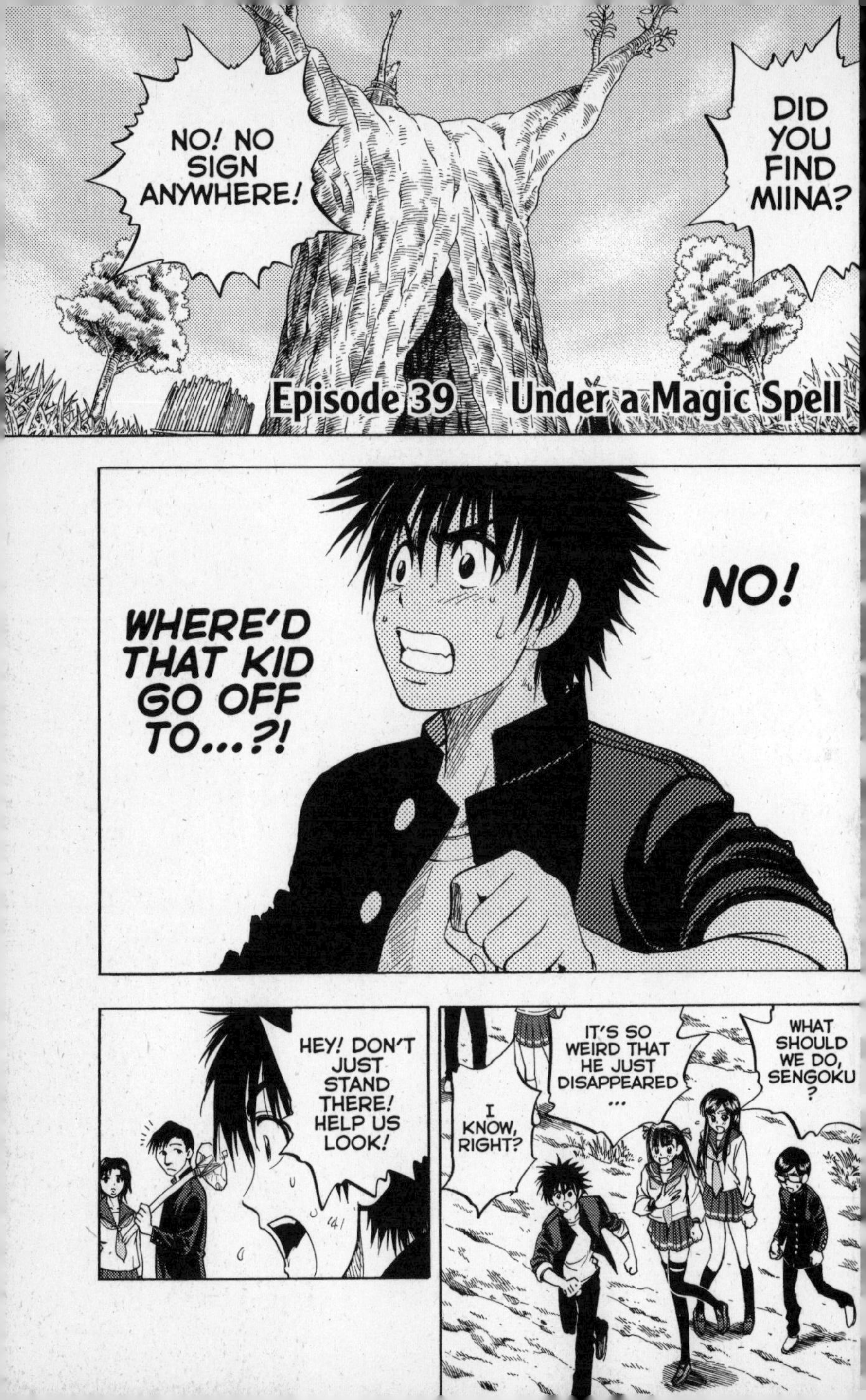
DID YOU FIND MIINA?
NO! NO SIGN ANYWHERE!
Episode 39 Under a Magic Spell
NO!
WHERE'D THAT KID GO OFF TO...?!
WHAT SHOULD WE DO, SENGOKU?
IT'S SO WEIRD THAT HE JUST DISAPPEARED...
I KNOW, RIGHT?
HEY! DON'T JUST STAND THERE! HELP US LOOK!

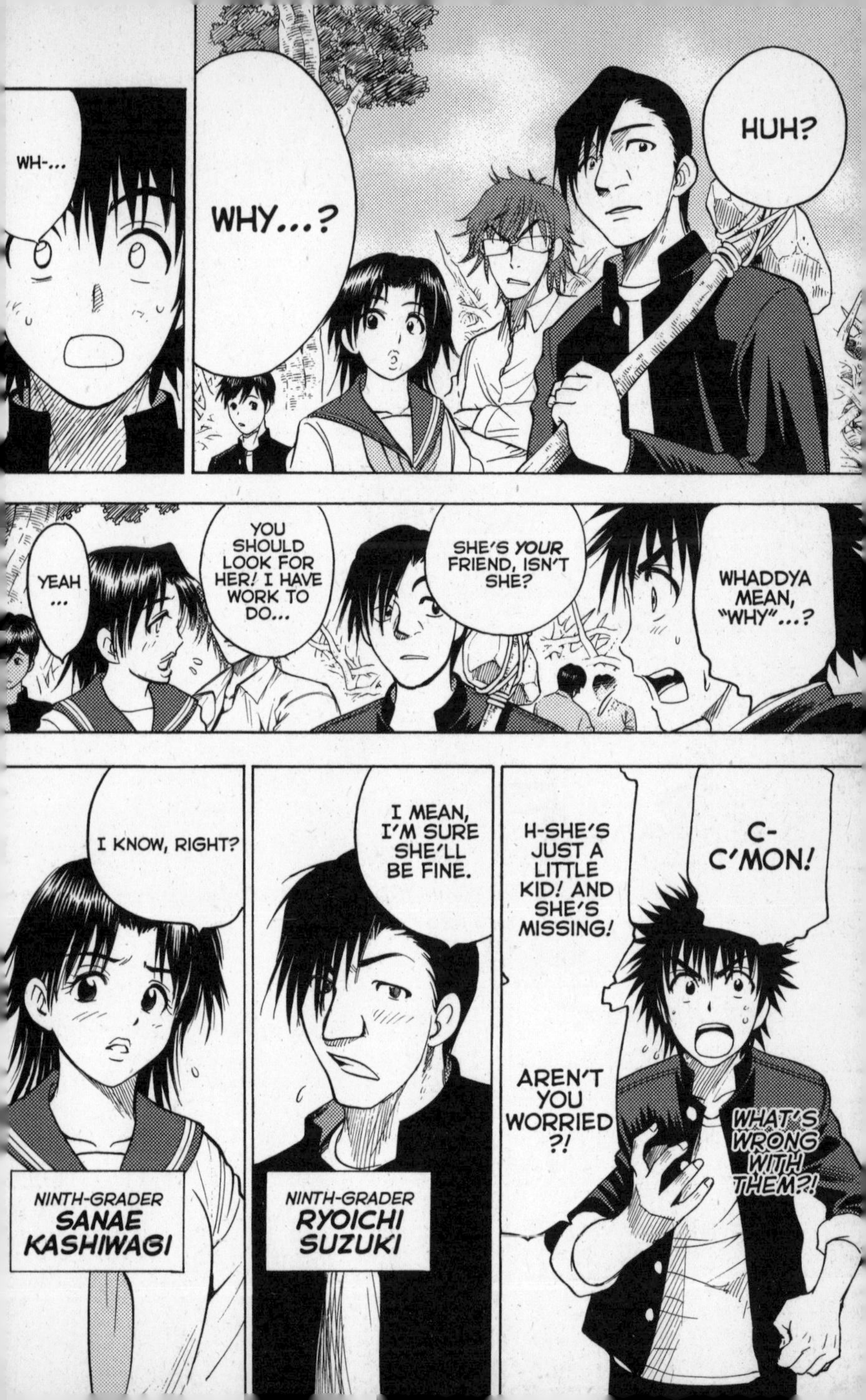
HUH?
WHY...?
WH-...
WHADDYA MEAN, "WHY"...?
SHE'S YOUR FRIEND, ISN'T SHE?
YOU SHOULD LOOK FOR HER! I HAVE WORK TO DO...
YEAH...
C-C'MON!
H-SHE'S JUST A LITTLE KID! AND SHE'S MISSING!
AREN'T YOU WORRIED?!
WHAT'S WRONG WITH THEM?!
I MEAN, I'M SURE SHE'LL BE FINE.
NINTH-GRADER RYOICHI SUZUKI
I KNOW, RIGHT?
NINTH-GRADER SANAE KASHIWAGI

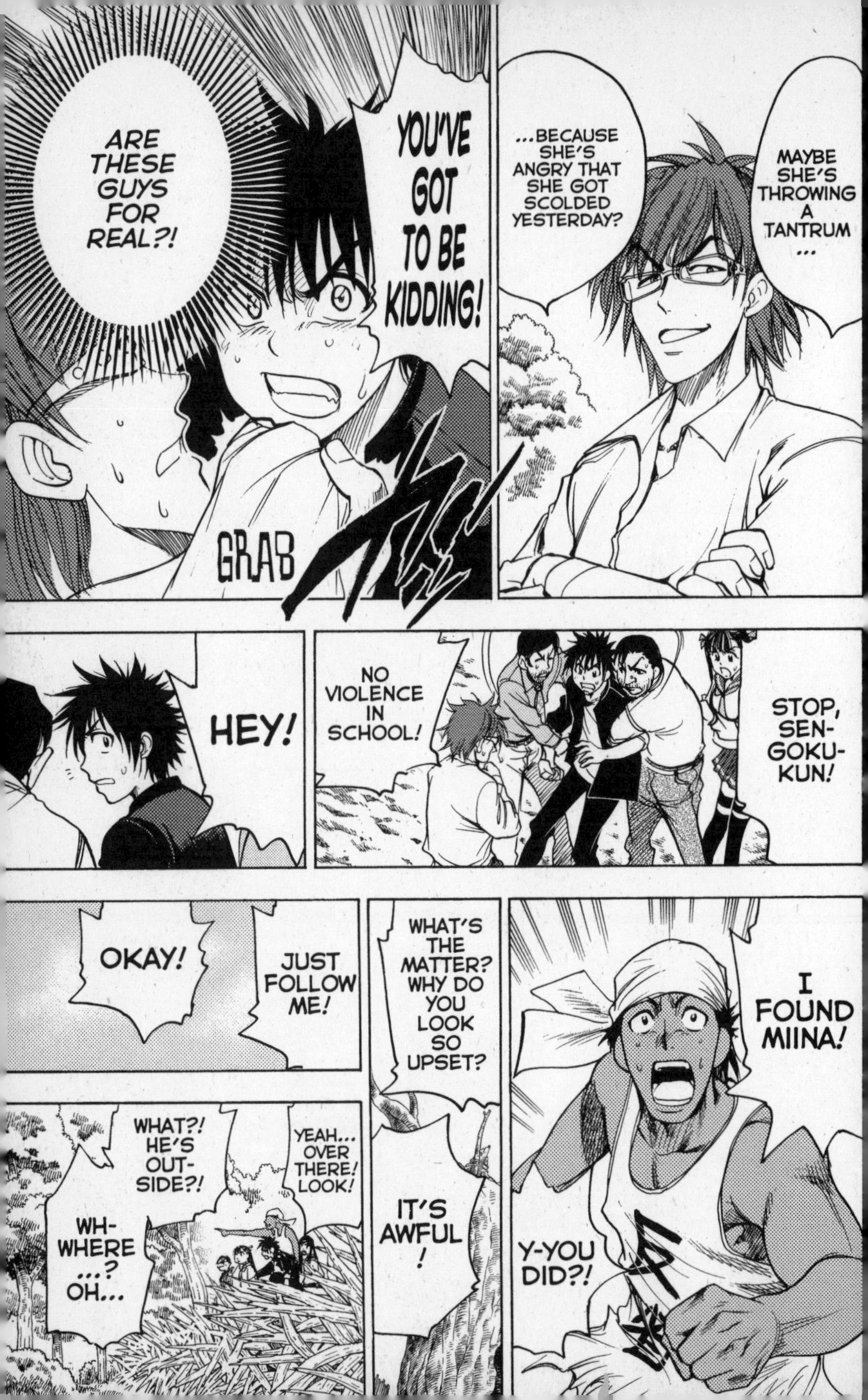
MAYBE SHE'S THROWING A TANTRUM...
...BECAUSE SHE'S ANGRY THAT SHE GOT SCOLDED YESTERDAY?
YOU'VE GOT TO BE KIDDING!
ARE THESE GUYS FOR REAL?!
GRAB
STOP, SEN-GOKU-KUN!
NO VIOLENCE IN SCHOOL!
HEY!
I FOUND MIINA!
Y-YOU DID?!
WHAT'S THE MATTER? WHY DO YOU LOOK SO UPSET?
IT'S AWFUL!
JUST FOLLOW ME!
OKAY!
YEAH... OVER THERE! LOOK!
WHAT?! HE'S OUT-SIDE?!
WH-WHERE...? OH...

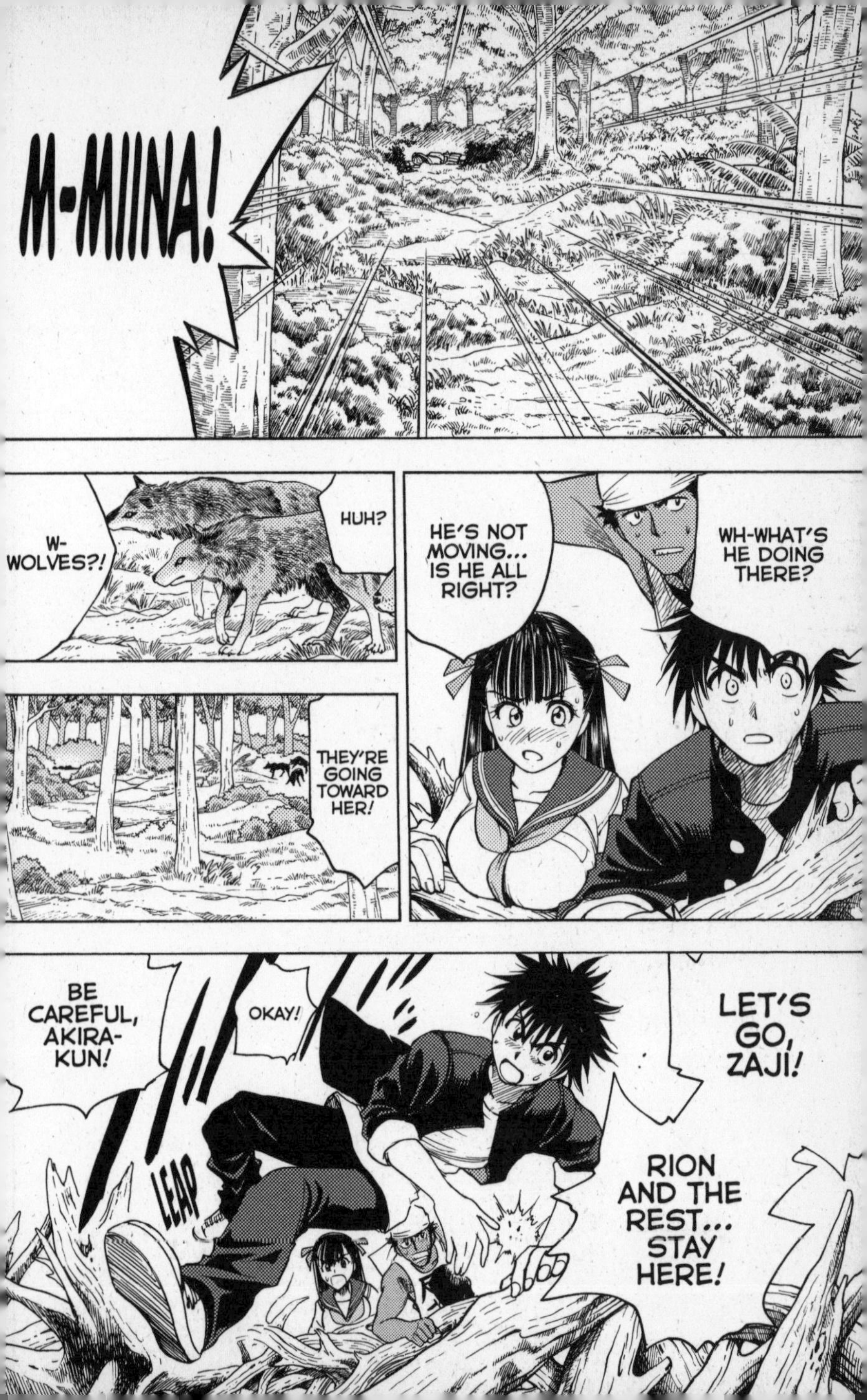
M-MIINA!
WH-WHAT'S HE DOING THERE?
HE'S NOT MOVING... IS HE ALL RIGHT?
HUH?
W- WOLVES?!
THEY'RE GOING TOWARD HER!
LET'S GO, ZAJI!
RION AND THE REST... STAY HERE!
OKAY!
BE CAREFUL, AKIRA-KUN!
LEAP

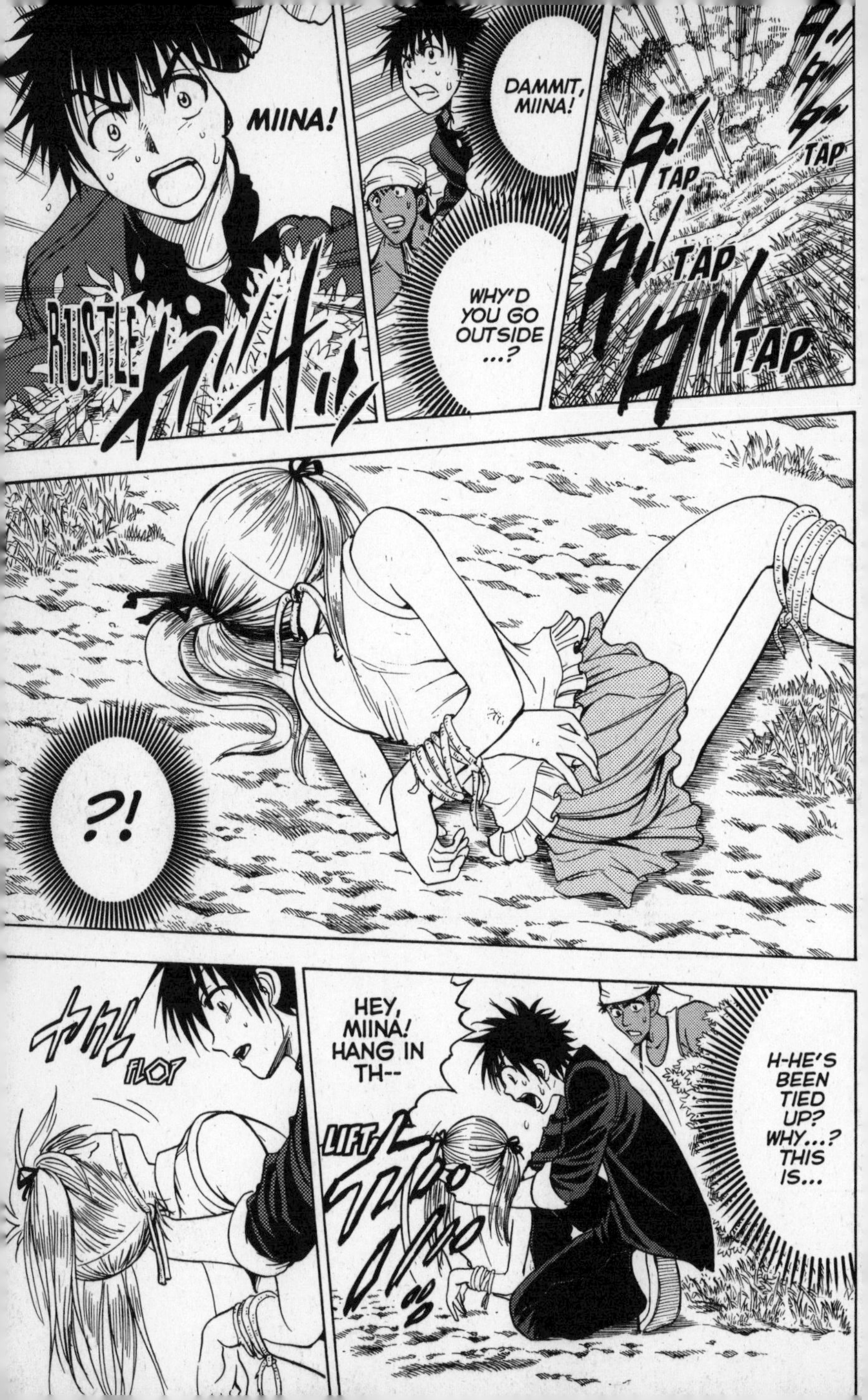
TAP
TAP
TAP
TAP
DAMMIT, MIINA!
WHY'D YOU GO OUTSIDE ...?
MIINA!
RUSTLE
?!
H-HE'S BEEN TIED UP? WHY...? THIS IS...
HEY, MIINA! HANG IN TH--
LIFT
FLOP

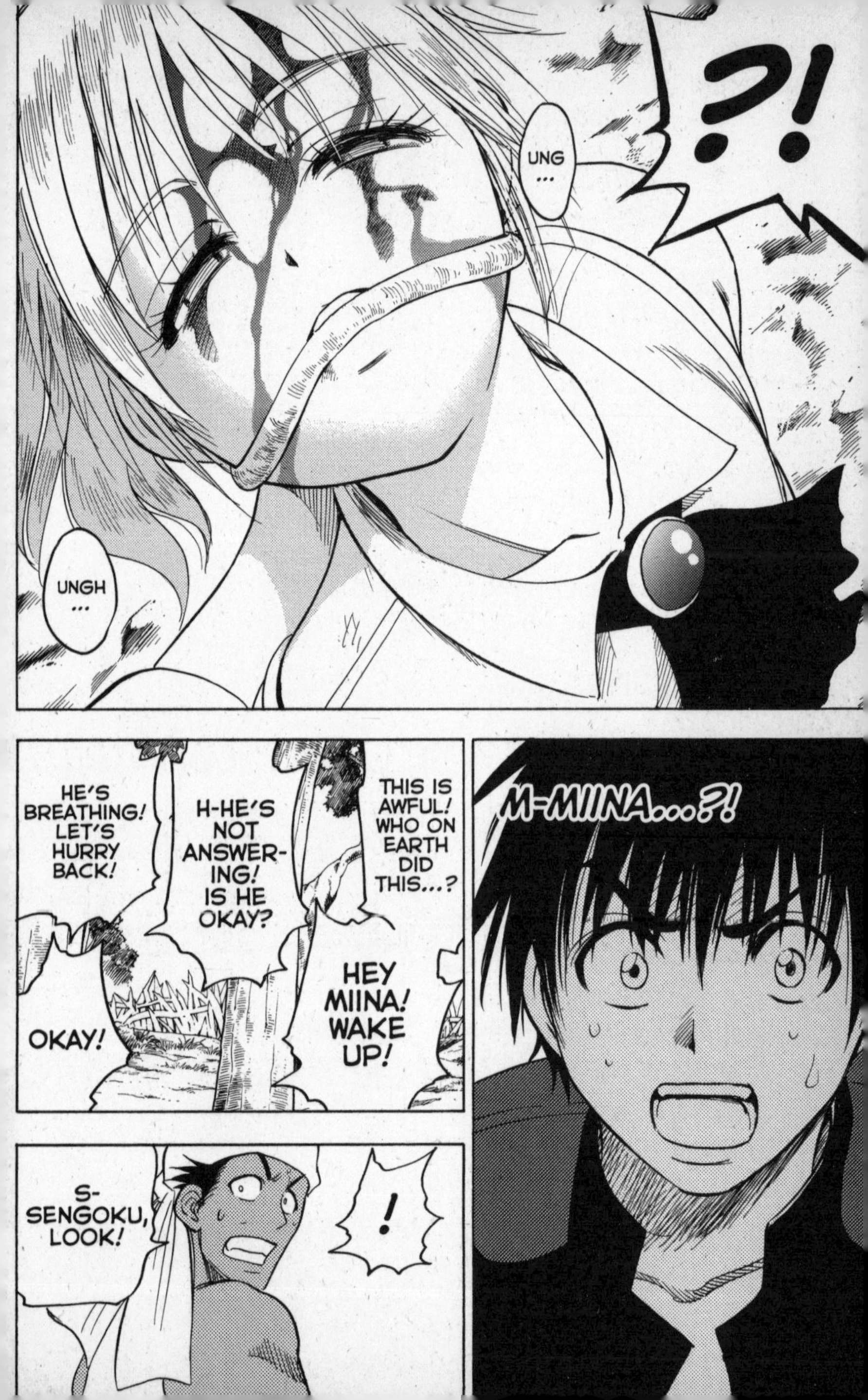
?!
UNG ...
UNGH ...
M-MIINA...?!
THIS IS AWFUL! WHO ON EARTH DID THIS...?
HEY MIINA! WAKE UP!
H-HE'S NOT ANSWERING! IS HE OKAY?
HE'S BREATHING! LET'S HURRY BACK!
OKAY!
!
S-SENGOKU, LOOK!

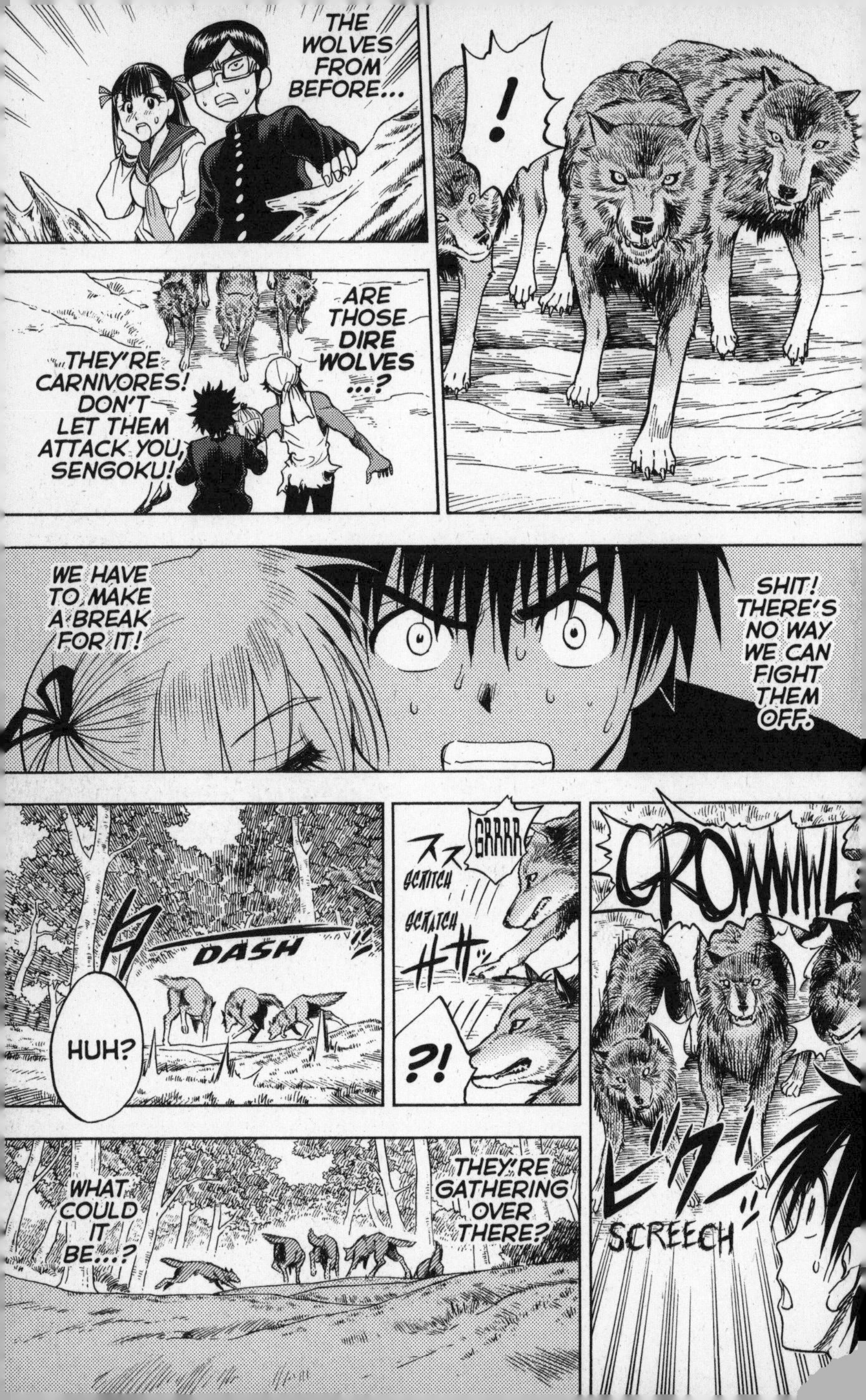
!
THE WOLVES FROM BEFORE...
ARE THOSE DIRE WOLVES ...?
THEY'RE CARNIVORES! DON'T LET THEM ATTACK YOU, SENGOKU!
SHIT! THERE'S NO WAY WE CAN FIGHT THEM OFF.
WE HAVE TO MAKE A BREAK FOR IT!
GROWWWL
SCREECH
GRRRR
SCRATCH
SCRATCH
?!
DASH
HUH?
THEY'RE GATHERING OVER THERE?
WHAT COULD IT BE...?

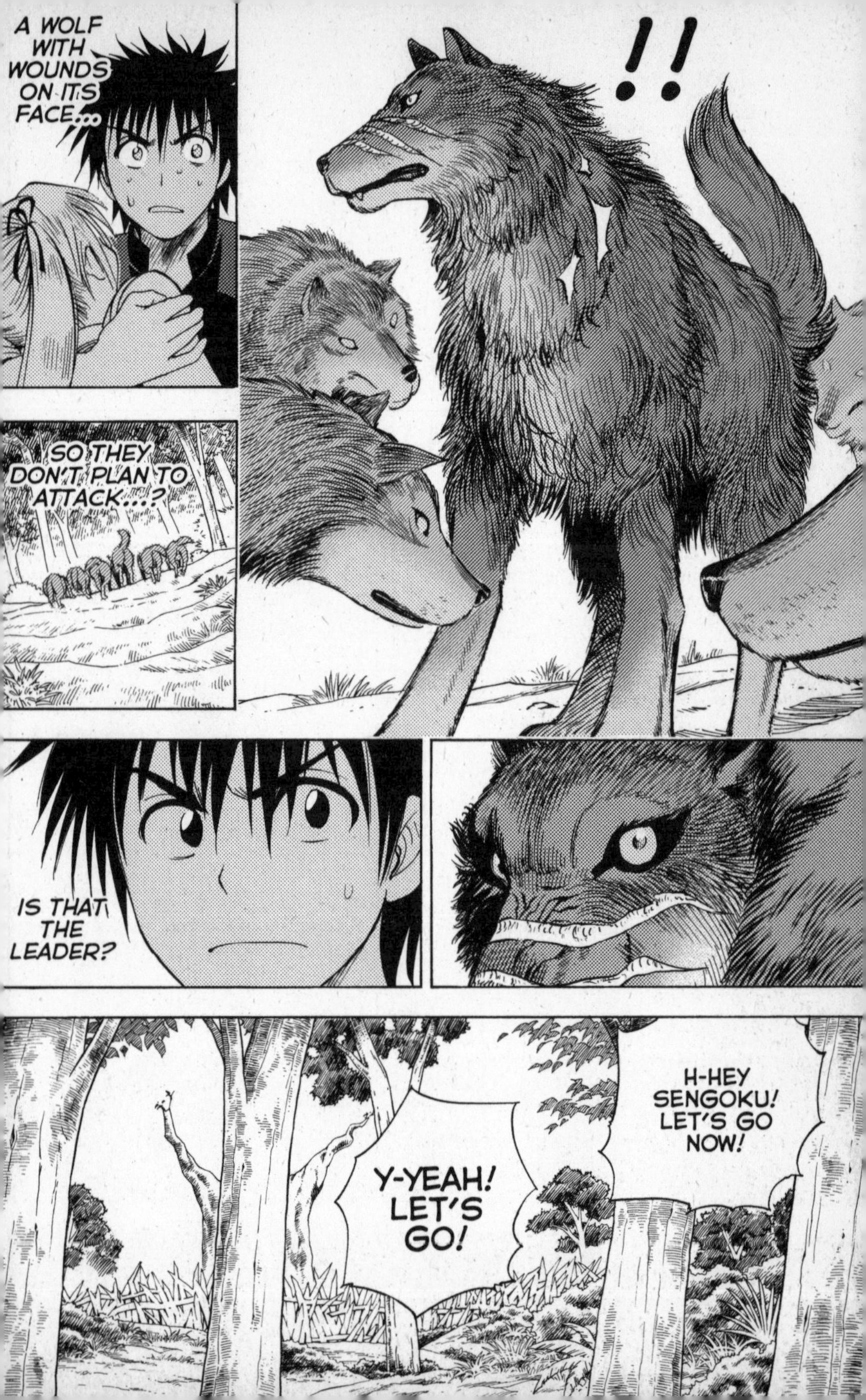
!!
A WOLF WITH WOUNDS ON ITS FACE...
SO THEY DON'T PLAN TO ATTACK...?
IS THAT THE LEADER?
H-HEY SENGOKU! LET'S GO NOW!
Y-YEAH! LET'S GO!

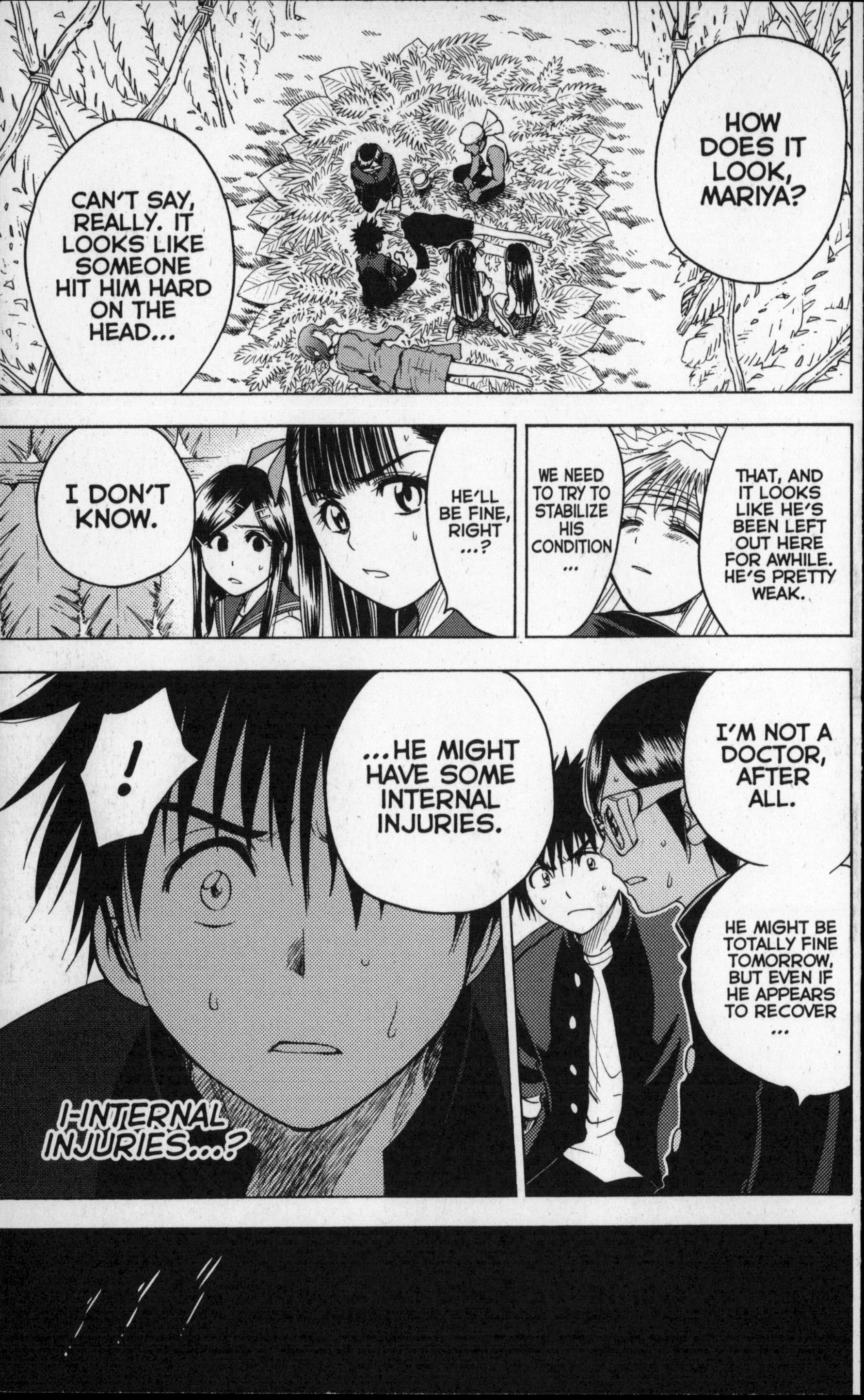
HOW DOES IT LOOK, MARIYA?
CAN'T SAY, REALLY. IT LOOKS LIKE SOMEONE HIT HIM HARD ON THE HEAD...
THAT, AND IT LOOKS LIKE HE'S BEEN LEFT OUT HERE FOR AWHILE. HE'S PRETTY WEAK.
WE NEED TO TRY TO STABILIZE HIS CONDITION ...
HE'LL BE FINE, RIGHT ...?
I DON'T KNOW.
I'M NOT A DOCTOR, AFTER ALL.
HE MIGHT BE TOTALLY FINE TOMORROW, BUT EVEN IF HE APPEARS TO RECOVER ...
...HE MIGHT HAVE SOME INTERNAL INJURIES.
!
I-INTERNAL INJURIES...?

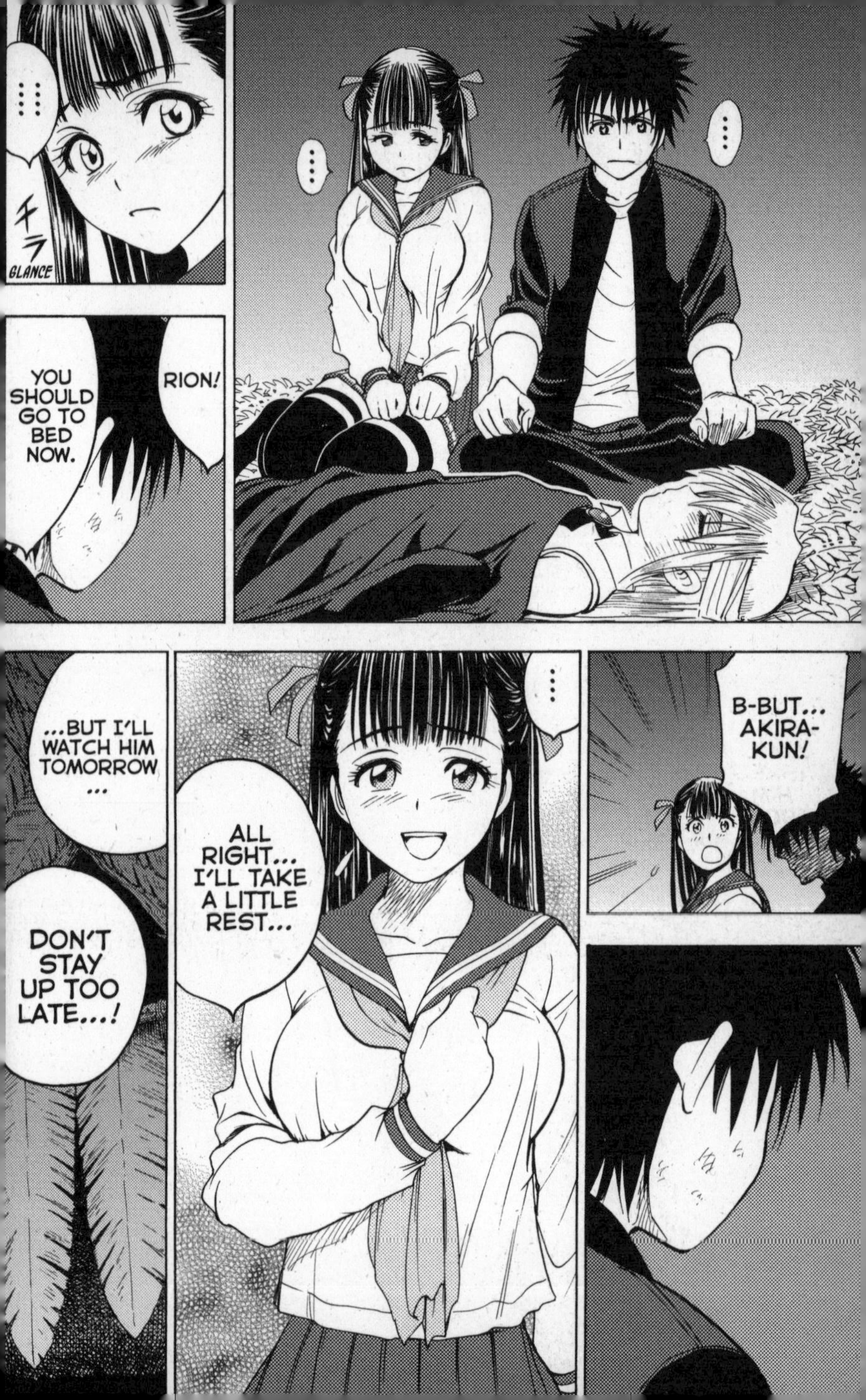
……
……
……
チラ
GLANCE
RION!
YOU SHOULD GO TO BED NOW.
B-BUT... AKIRA-KUN!
……
ALL RIGHT... I'LL TAKE A LITTLE REST...
...BUT I'LL WATCH HIM TOMORROW...
DON'T STAY UP TOO LATE...!

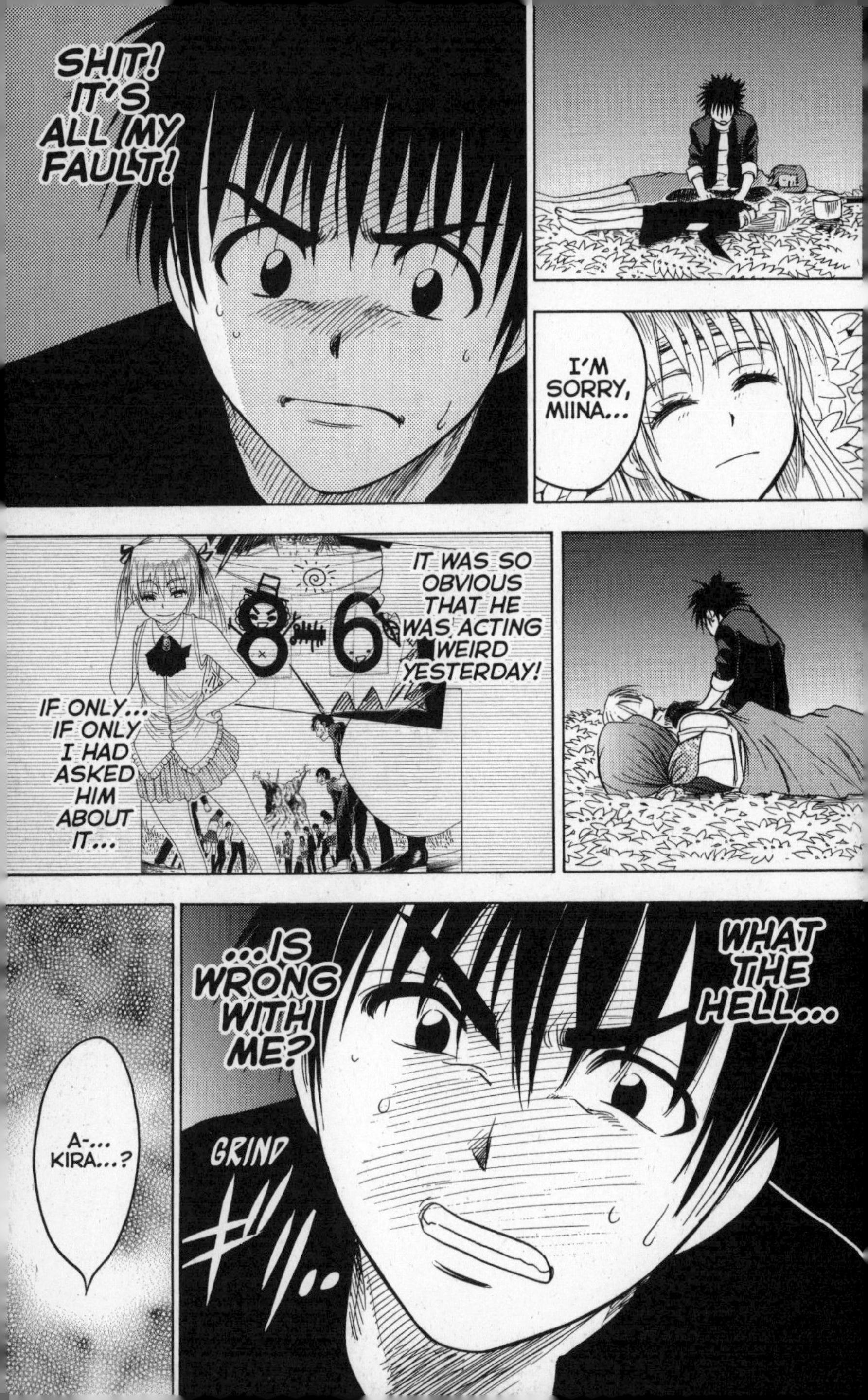
I'M SORRY, MIINA...
SHIT! IT'S ALL MY FAULT!
IT WAS SO OBVIOUS THAT HE WAS ACTING WEIRD YESTERDAY!
IF ONLY... IF ONLY I HAD ASKED HIM ABOUT IT...
WHAT THE HELL...
...IS WRONG WITH ME?
GRIND
A-... KIRA...?

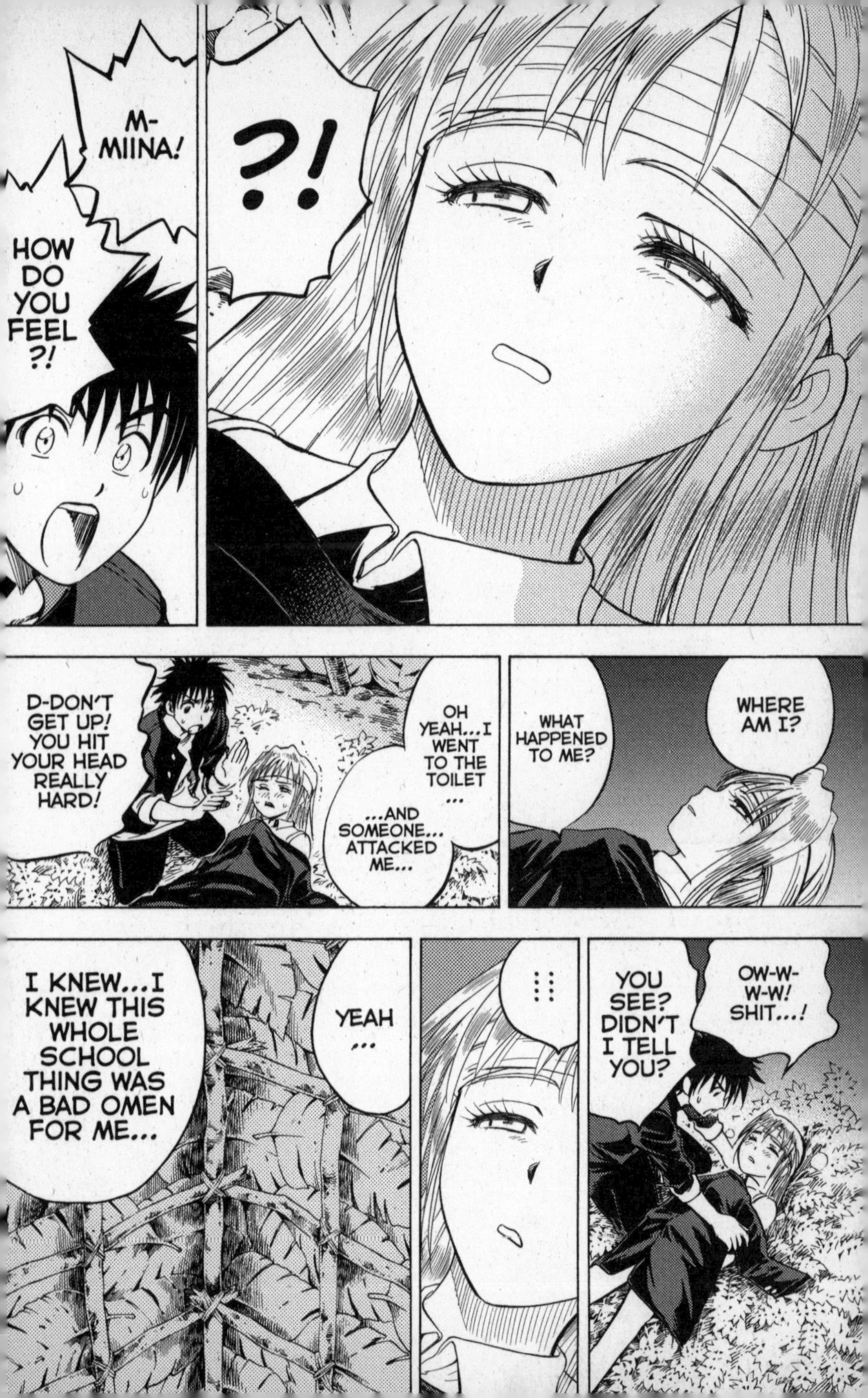
?!
M-MIINA!
HOW DO YOU FEEL ?!
WHERE AM I?
WHAT HAPPENED TO ME?
OH YEAH...I WENT TO THE TOILET ...
...AND SOMEONE... ATTACKED ME...
D-DON'T GET UP! YOU HIT YOUR HEAD REALLY HARD!
OW-W-W-W! SHIT...!
YOU SEE? DIDN'T I TELL YOU?
......
YEAH ...
I KNEW...I KNEW THIS WHOLE SCHOOL THING WAS A BAD OMEN FOR ME...

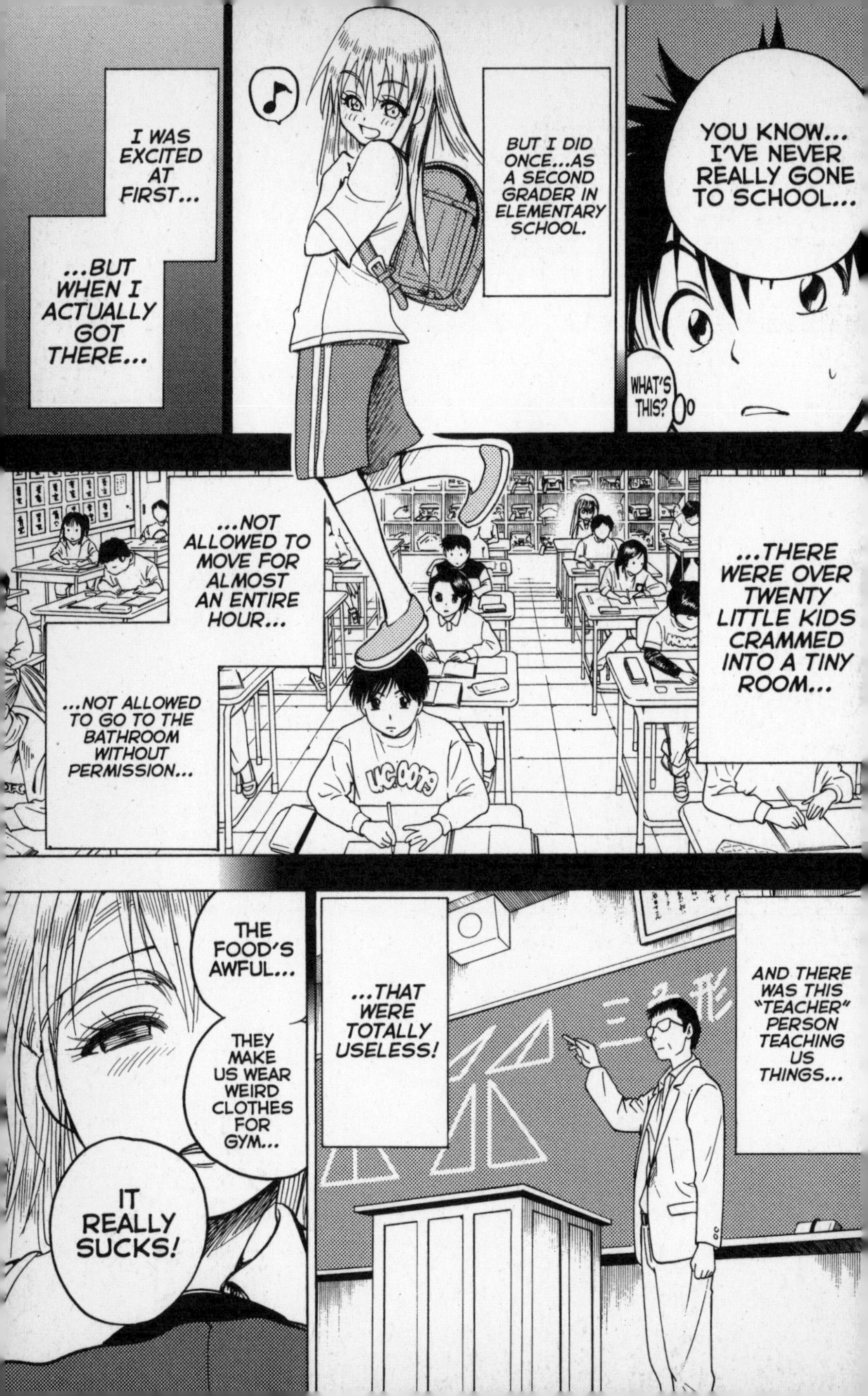
YOU KNOW... I'VE NEVER REALLY GONE TO SCHOOL...
WHAT'S THIS?
♪
BUT I DID ONCE...AS A SECOND GRADER IN ELEMENTARY SCHOOL.
I WAS EXCITED AT FIRST...
...BUT WHEN I ACTUALLY GOT THERE...
...THERE WERE OVER TWENTY LITTLE KIDS CRAMMED INTO A TINY ROOM...
...NOT ALLOWED TO MOVE FOR ALMOST AN ENTIRE HOUR...
...NOT ALLOWED TO GO TO THE BATHROOM WITHOUT PERMISSION...
AND THERE WAS THIS "TEACHER" PERSON TEACHING US THINGS...
...THAT WERE TOTALLY USELESS!
THE FOOD'S AWFUL...
THEY MAKE US WEAR WEIRD CLOTHES FOR GYM...
IT REALLY SUCKS!

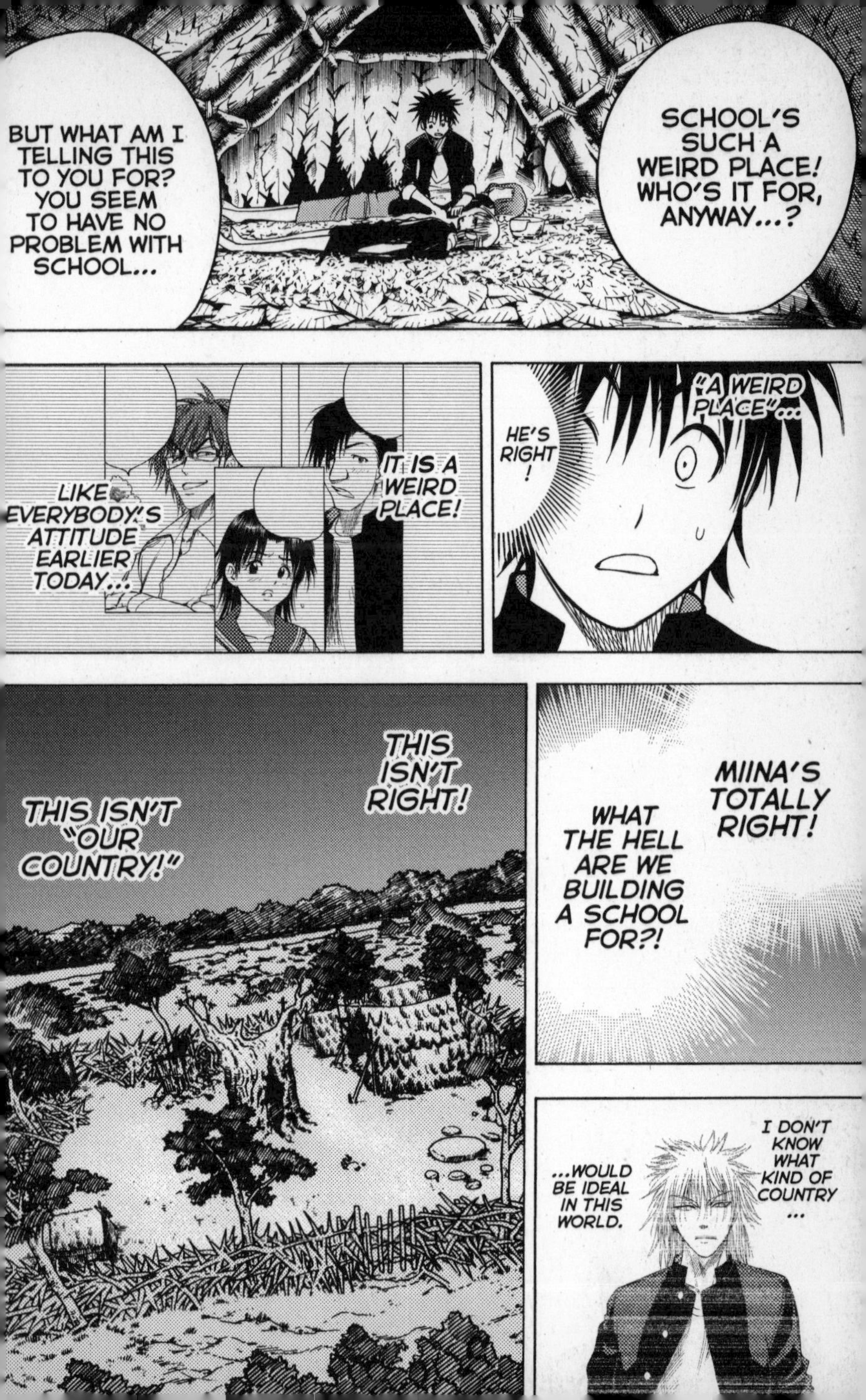
SCHOOL'S SUCH A WEIRD PLACE! WHO'S IT FOR, ANYWAY...?
BUT WHAT AM I TELLING THIS TO YOU FOR? YOU SEEM TO HAVE NO PROBLEM WITH SCHOOL...
"A WEIRD PLACE"...
HE'S RIGHT!
IT IS A WEIRD PLACE!
LIKE EVERYBODY'S ATTITUDE EARLIER TODAY...
MIINA'S TOTALLY RIGHT!
WHAT THE HELL ARE WE BUILDING A SCHOOL FOR?!
I DON'T KNOW WHAT KIND OF COUNTRY...
...WOULD BE IDEAL IN THIS WORLD.
THIS ISN'T RIGHT!
THIS ISN'T "OUR COUNTRY!"

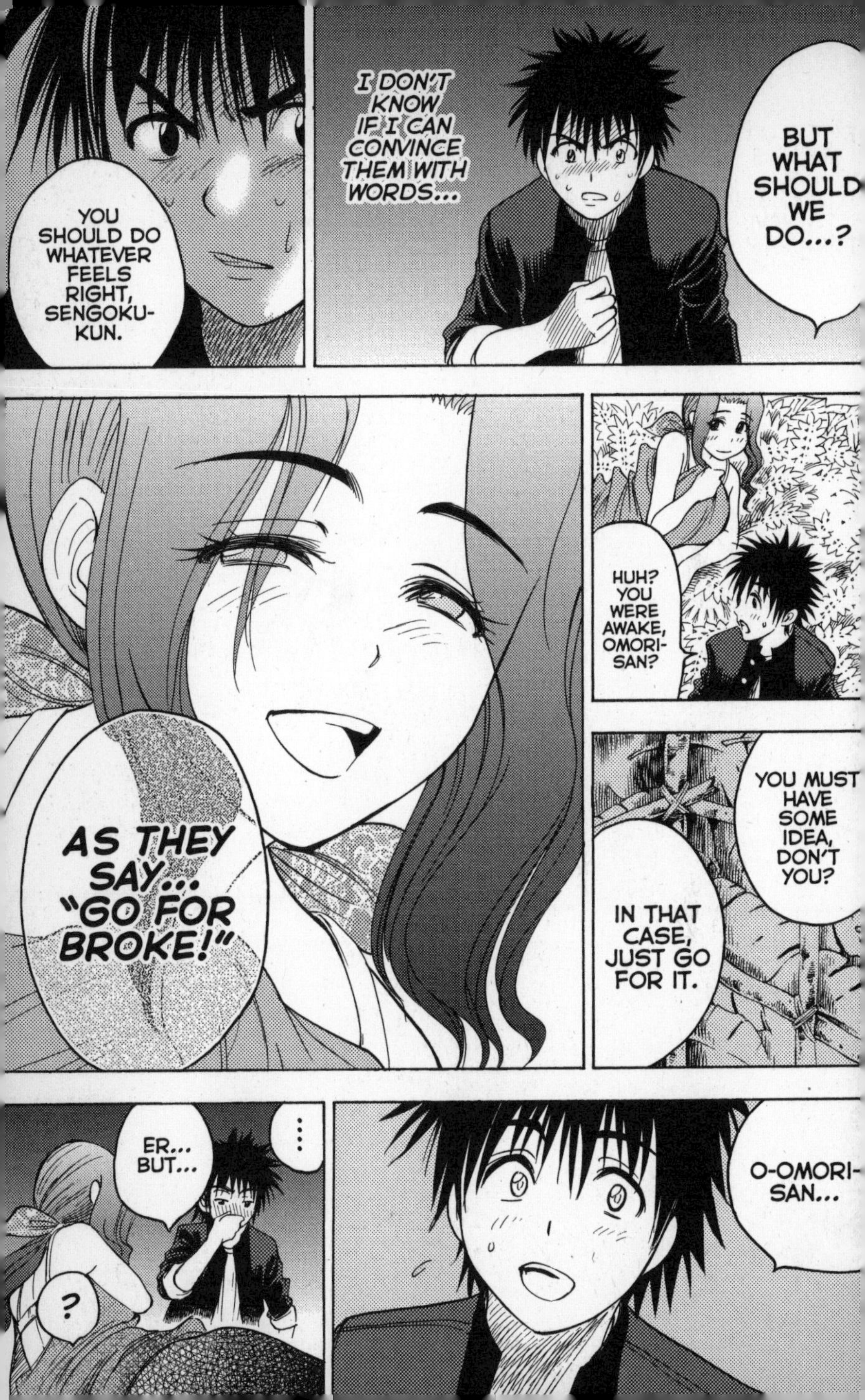
BUT WHAT SHOULD WE DO...?
I DON'T KNOW IF I CAN CONVINCE THEM WITH WORDS...
YOU SHOULD DO WHATEVER FEELS RIGHT, SENGOKU-KUN.
HUH? YOU WERE AWAKE, OMORI-SAN?
YOU MUST HAVE SOME IDEA, DON'T YOU?
IN THAT CASE, JUST GO FOR IT.
AS THEY SAY... "GO FOR BROKE!"
O-OMORI-SAN...
...
ER... BUT...
?

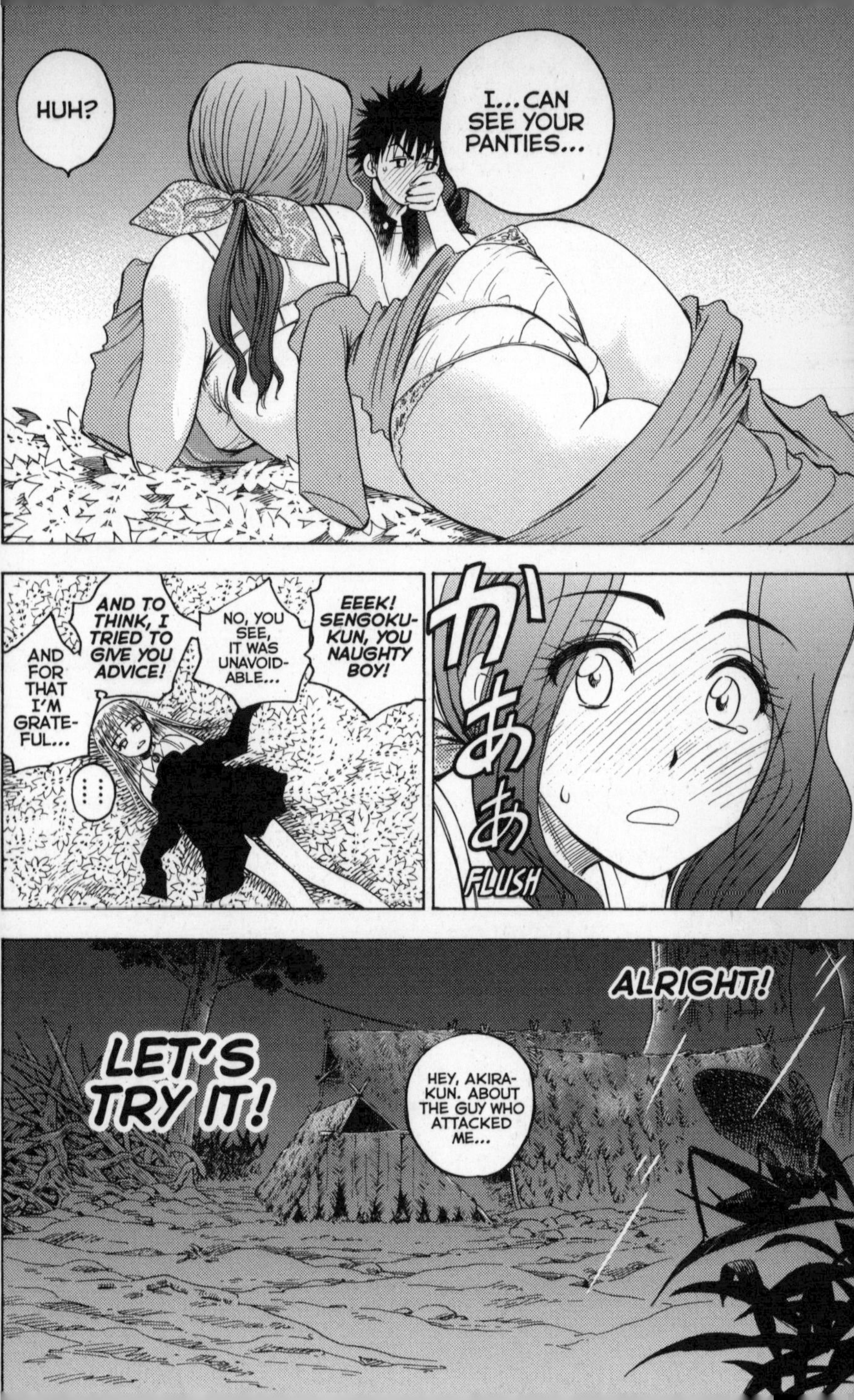
I... CAN SEE YOUR PANTIES...
HUH?
かあああ
FLUSH
EEEK! SENGOKU-KUN, YOU NAUGHTY BOY!
NO, YOU SEE, IT WAS UNAVOIDABLE...
AND TO THINK, I TRIED TO GIVE YOU ADVICE!
AND FOR THAT I'M GRATEFUL...
......
ALRIGHT!
HEY, AKIRA-KUN. ABOUT THE GUY WHO ATTACKED ME...
LET'S TRY IT!

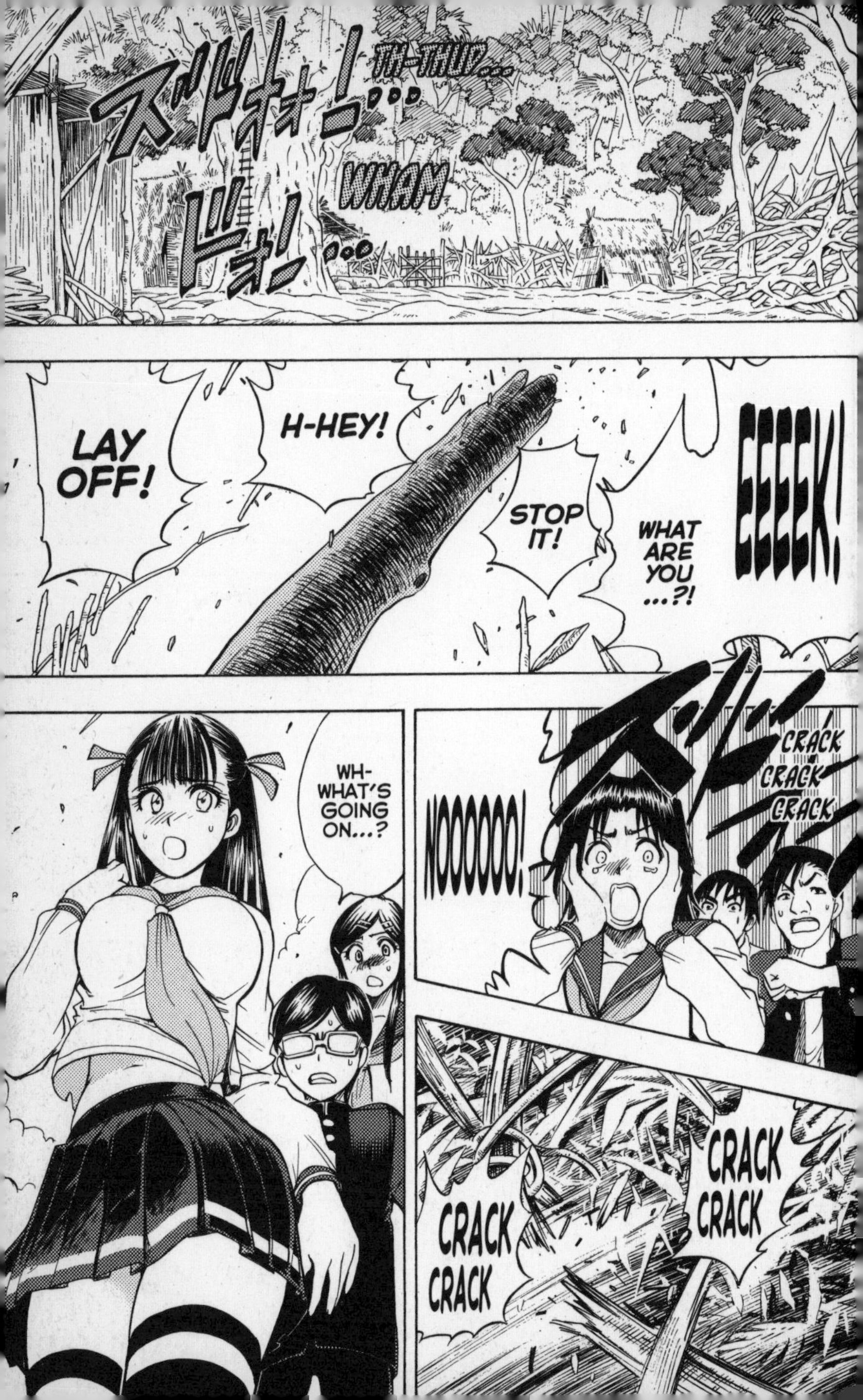
TH-THUD...
WHAM
EEEEK!
WHAT ARE YOU ...?!
STOP IT!
H-HEY!
LAY OFF!
CRACK CRACK CRACK
NOOOOOO!
CRACK CRACK
CRACK CRACK
WH-WHAT'S GOING ON...?

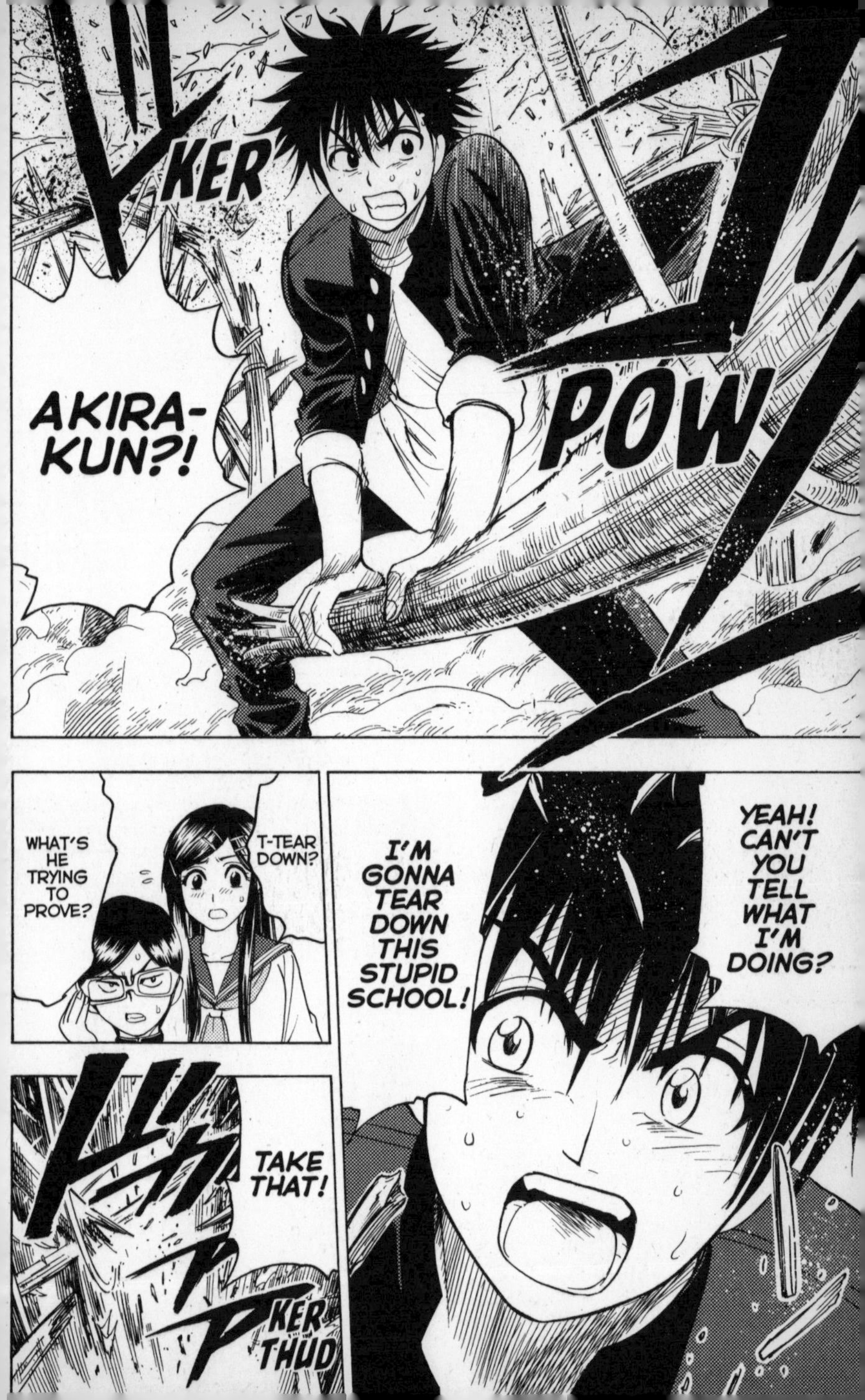
KER
POW
AKIRA-KUN?!
YEAH! CAN'T YOU TELL WHAT I'M DOING?
I'M GONNA TEAR DOWN THIS STUPID SCHOOL!
T-TEAR DOWN?
WHAT'S HE TRYING TO PROVE?
TAKE THAT!
KER THUD

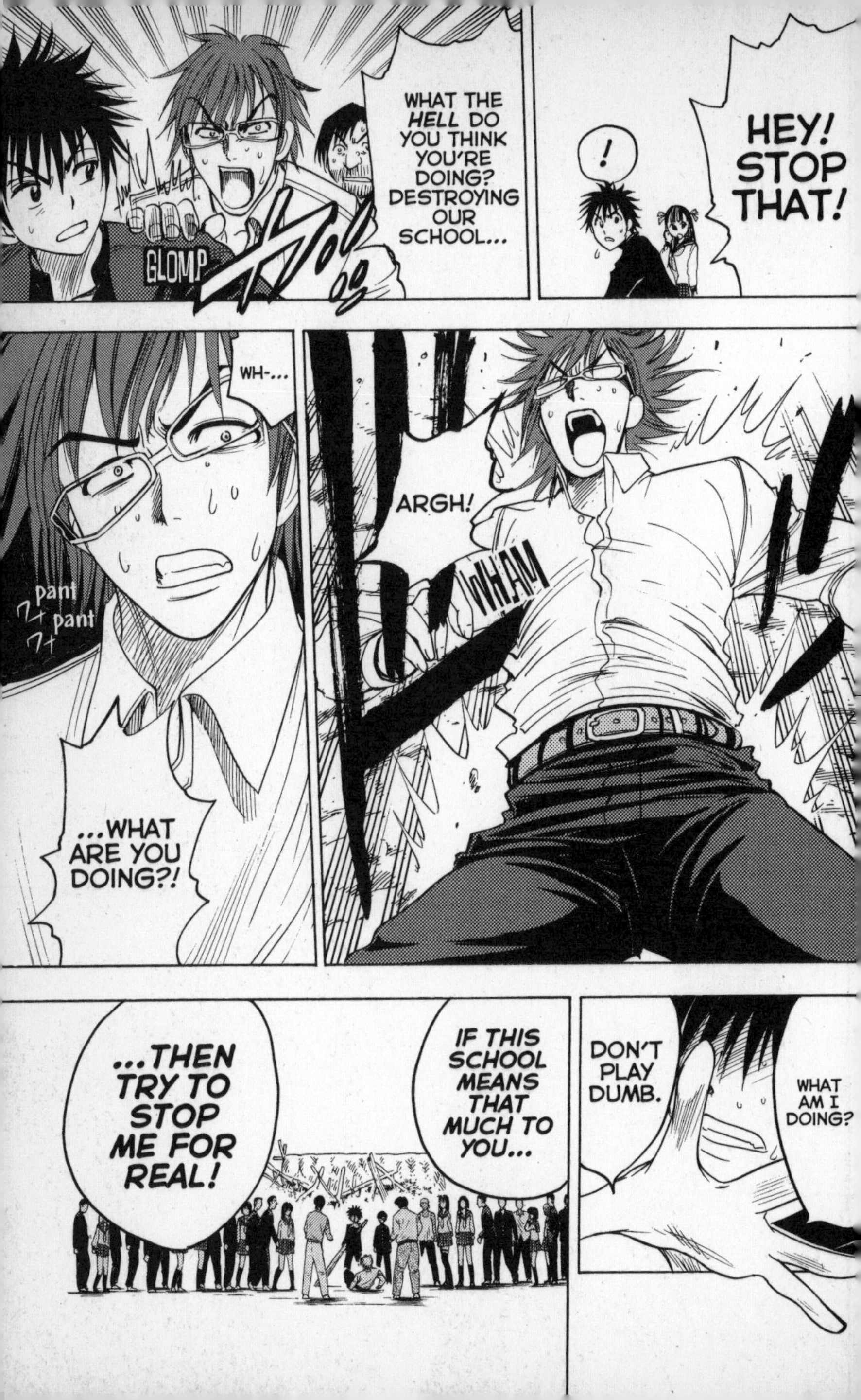
!
HEY! STOP THAT!
WHAT THE *HELL* DO YOU THINK YOU'RE DOING? DESTROYING OUR SCHOOL...
GLOMP
ARGH!
WHAM
WH-...
pant pant
...WHAT ARE YOU DOING?!
WHAT AM I DOING?
DON'T PLAY DUMB.
IF THIS SCHOOL MEANS THAT MUCH TO YOU...
...THEN TRY TO STOP ME FOR REAL!

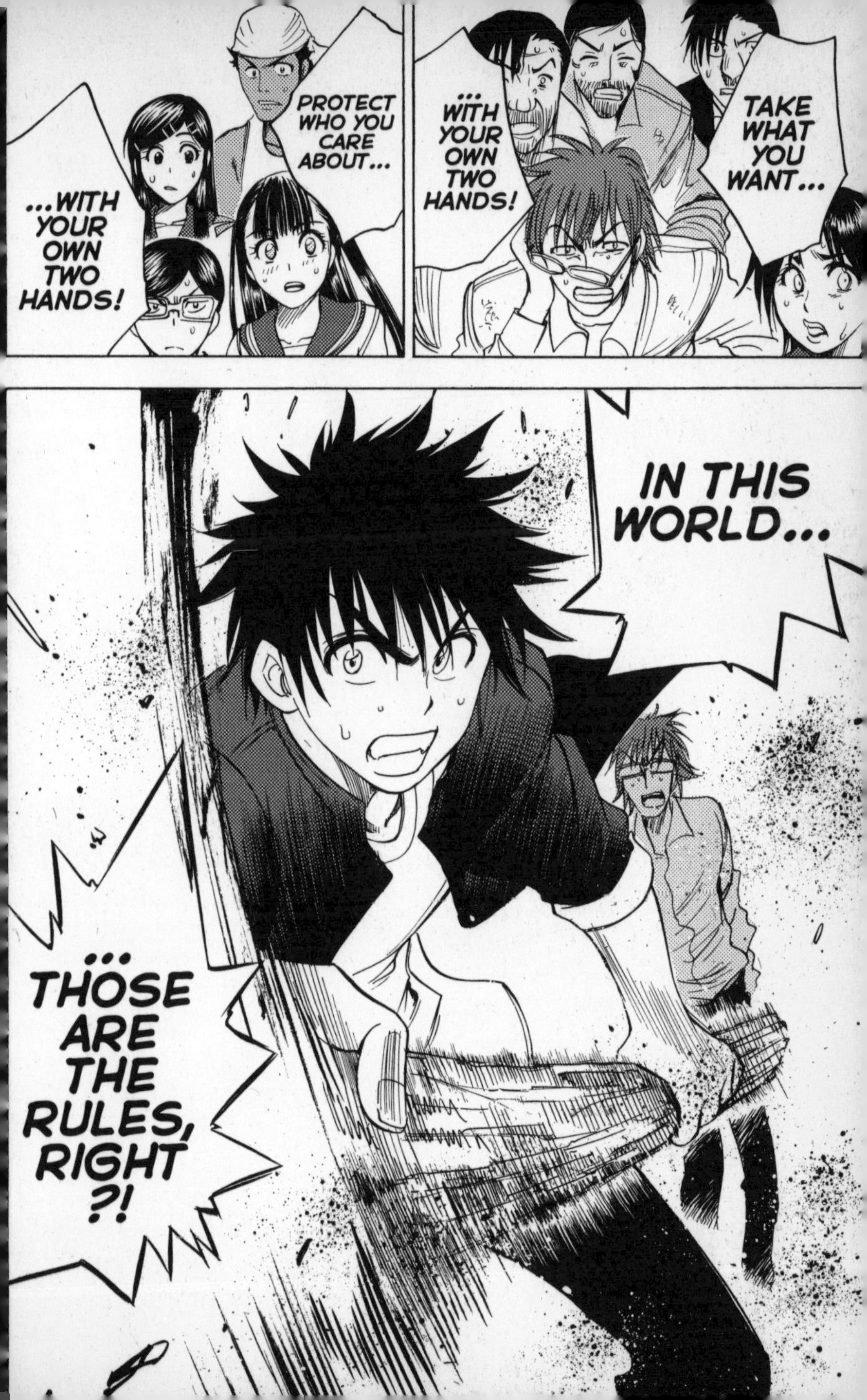
TAKE WHAT YOU WANT...
...WITH YOUR OWN TWO HANDS!
PROTECT WHO YOU CARE ABOUT...
...WITH YOUR OWN TWO HANDS!
IN THIS WORLD...
...THOSE ARE THE RULES, RIGHT?!

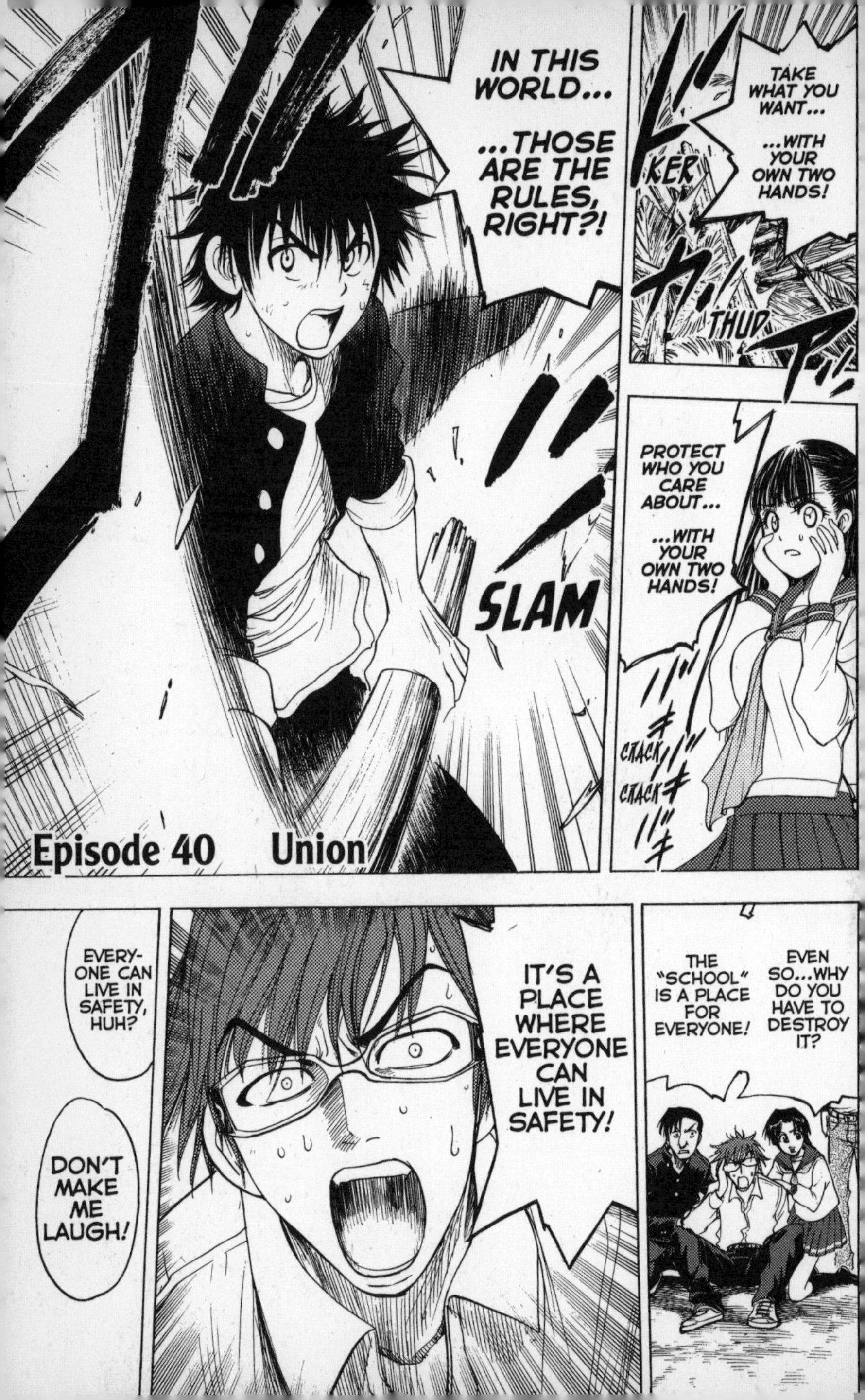
TAKE WHAT YOU WANT...
...WITH YOUR OWN TWO HANDS!
KER
THUD
PROTECT WHO YOU CARE ABOUT...
...WITH YOUR OWN TWO HANDS!
CRACK
CRACK
IN THIS WORLD...
...THOSE ARE THE RULES, RIGHT?!
SLAM
Episode 40 Union
EVEN SO...WHY DO YOU HAVE TO DESTROY IT?
THE "SCHOOL" IS A PLACE FOR EVERYONE!
IT'S A PLACE WHERE EVERYONE CAN LIVE IN SAFETY!
EVERYONE CAN LIVE IN SAFETY, HUH?
DON'T MAKE ME LAUGH!

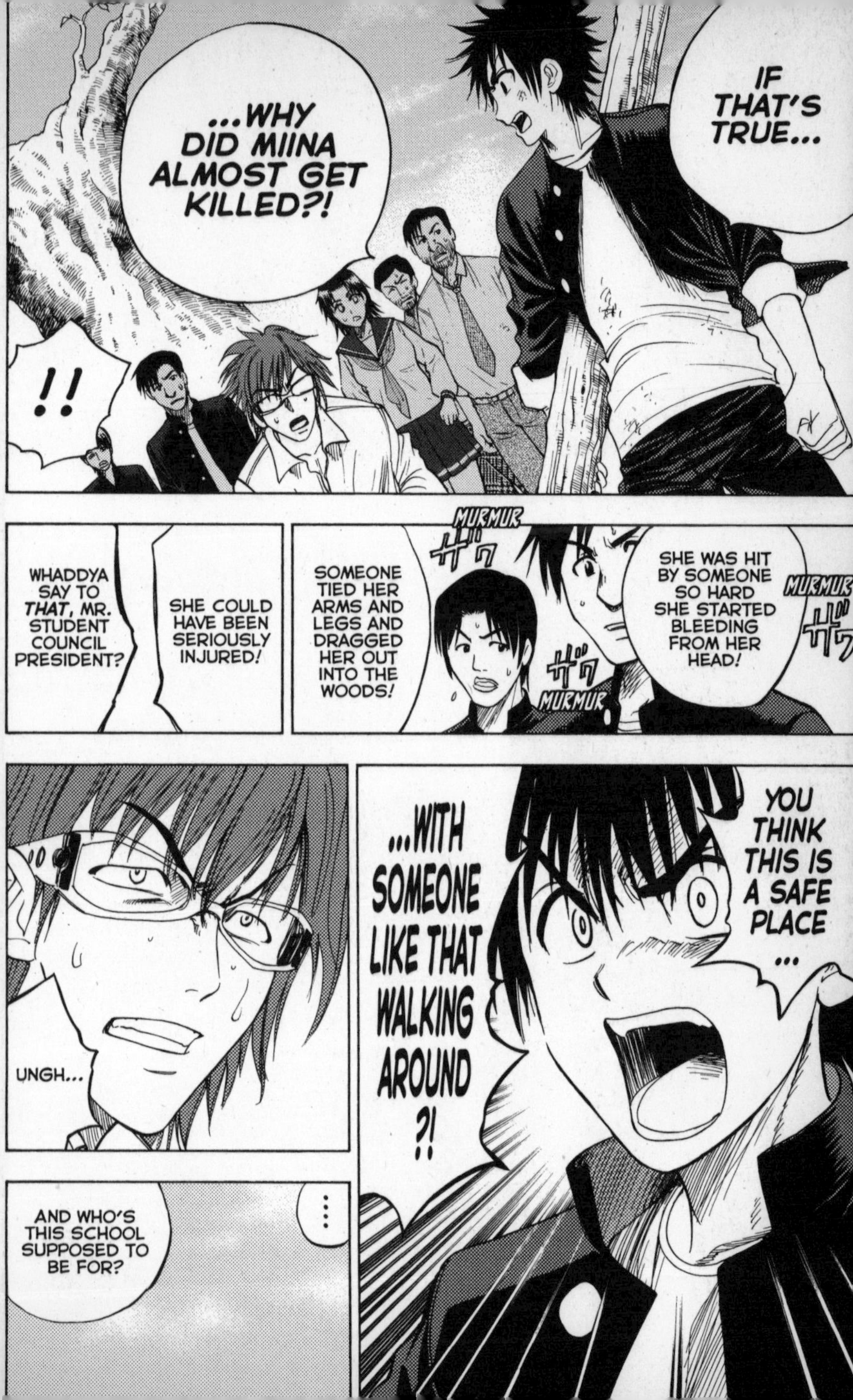
IF THAT'S TRUE...
...WHY DID MIINA ALMOST GET KILLED?!
!!
MURMUR
SHE WAS HIT BY SOMEONE SO HARD SHE STARTED BLEEDING FROM HER HEAD!
MURMUR
MURMUR
SOMEONE TIED HER ARMS AND LEGS AND DRAGGED HER OUT INTO THE WOODS!
SHE COULD HAVE BEEN SERIOUSLY INJURED!
WHADDYA SAY TO *THAT*, MR. STUDENT COUNCIL PRESIDENT?
YOU THINK THIS IS A SAFE PLACE ...
...WITH SOMEONE LIKE THAT WALKING AROUND ?!
UNGH...
....
AND WHO'S THIS SCHOOL SUPPOSED TO BE FOR?

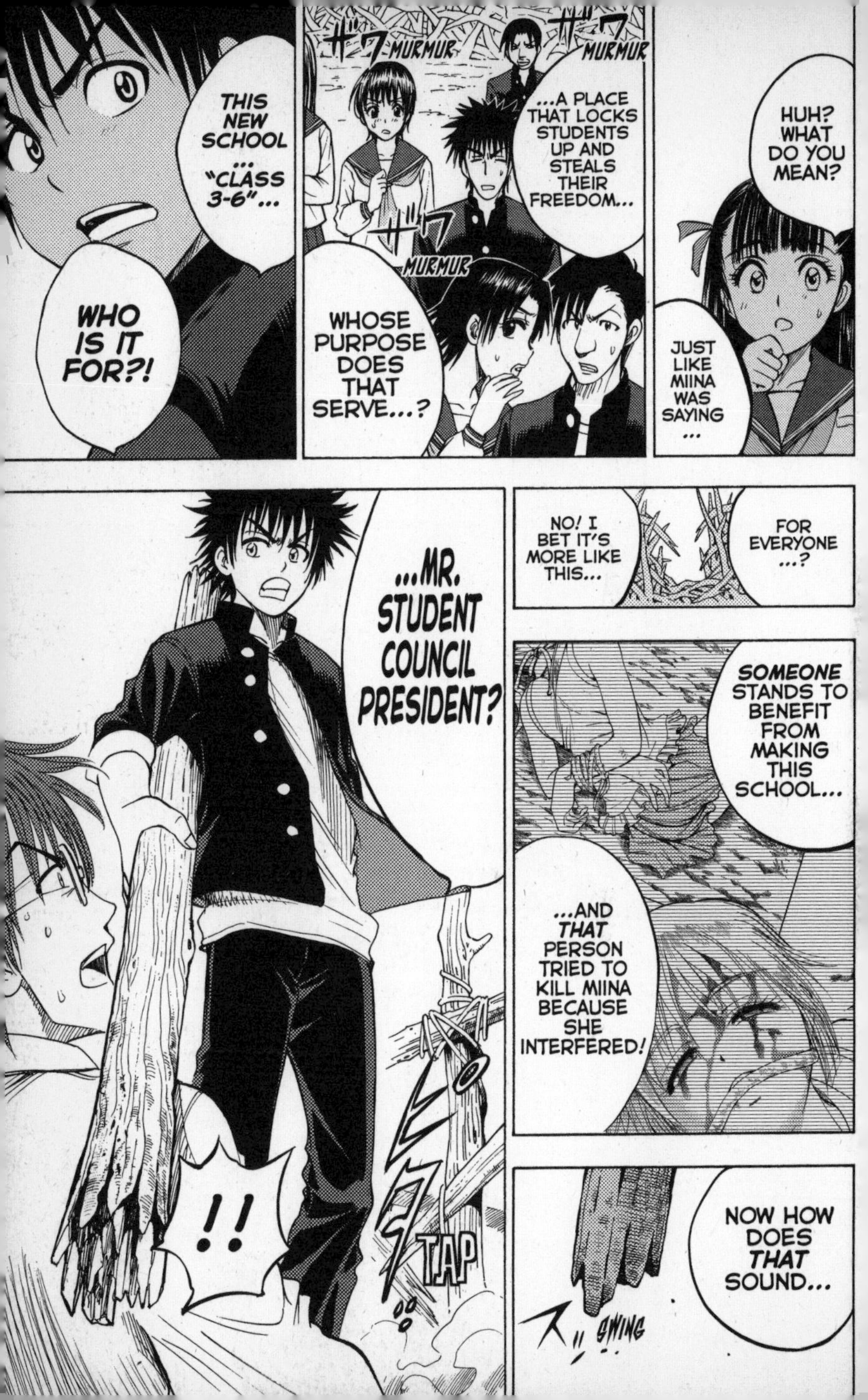
HUH? WHAT DO YOU MEAN?
JUST LIKE MIINA WAS SAYING...
ザワ MURMUR
...A PLACE THAT LOCKS STUDENTS UP AND STEALS THEIR FREEDOM...
ザワ MURMUR
ザワ MURMUR
WHOSE PURPOSE DOES THAT SERVE...?
THIS NEW SCHOOL ... "CLASS 3-6"...
WHO IS IT FOR?!
FOR EVERYONE...?
NO! I BET IT'S MORE LIKE THIS...
SOMEONE STANDS TO BENEFIT FROM MAKING THIS SCHOOL...
...AND *THAT* PERSON TRIED TO KILL MIINA BECAUSE SHE INTERFERED!
NOW HOW DOES *THAT* SOUND...
SWING
...MR. STUDENT COUNCIL PRESIDENT?
!!
TAP

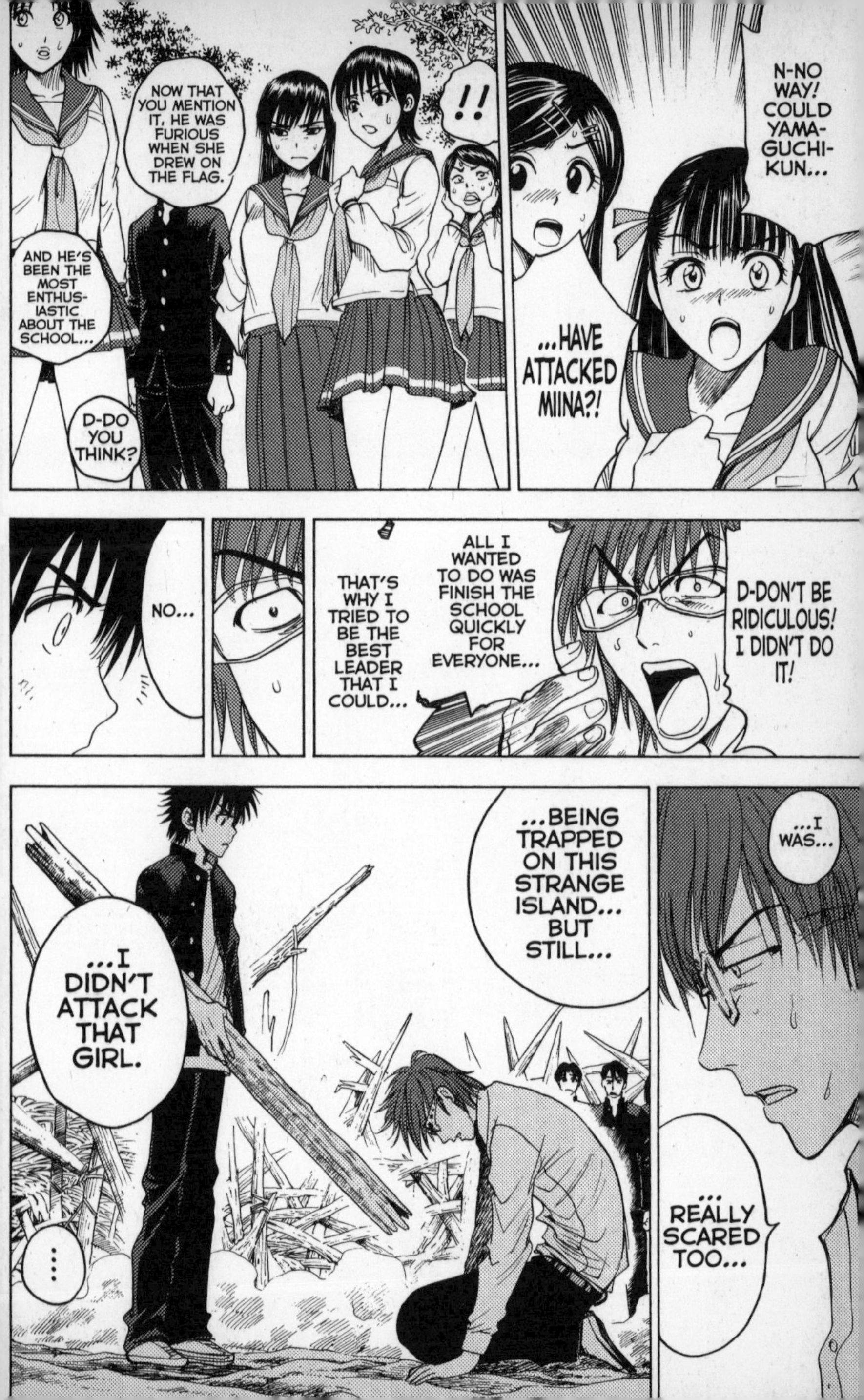
N-NO WAY! COULD YAMAGUCHI-KUN...
...HAVE ATTACKED MIINA?!
!!
NOW THAT YOU MENTION IT, HE WAS FURIOUS WHEN SHE DREW ON THE FLAG.
AND HE'S BEEN THE MOST ENTHUSIASTIC ABOUT THE SCHOOL...
D-DO YOU THINK?
D-DON'T BE RIDICULOUS! I DIDN'T DO IT!
ALL I WANTED TO DO WAS FINISH THE SCHOOL QUICKLY FOR EVERYONE...
THAT'S WHY I TRIED TO BE THE BEST LEADER THAT I COULD...
NO...
...I WAS...
...REALLY SCARED TOO...
...BEING TRAPPED ON THIS STRANGE ISLAND... BUT STILL...
...I DIDN'T ATTACK THAT GIRL.
....

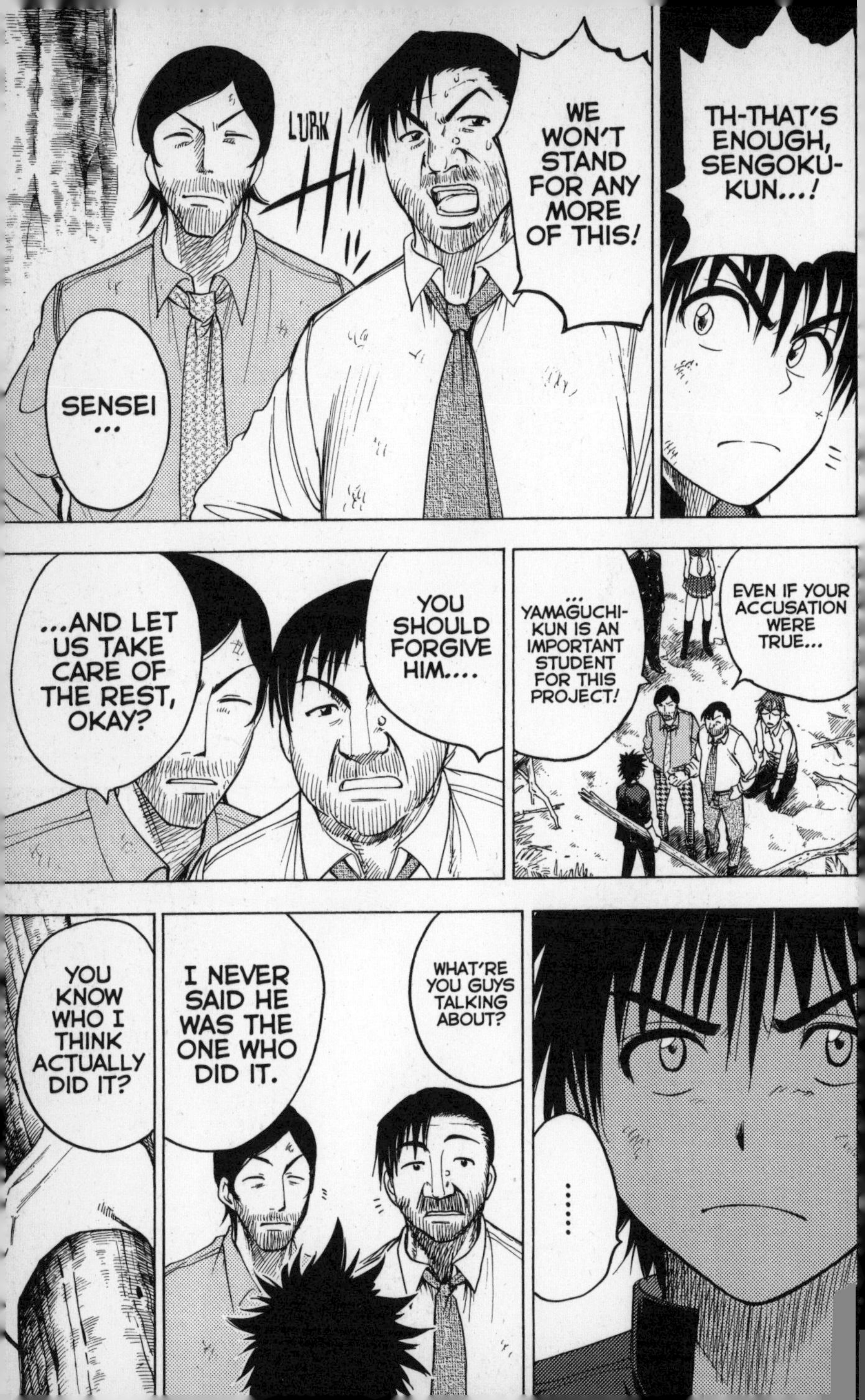
TH-THAT'S ENOUGH, SENGOKU-KUN...!
WE WON'T STAND FOR ANY MORE OF THIS!
LURK
SENSEI ...
EVEN IF YOUR ACCUSATION WERE TRUE...
...YAMAGUCHI-KUN IS AN IMPORTANT STUDENT FOR THIS PROJECT!
YOU SHOULD FORGIVE HIM....
...AND LET US TAKE CARE OF THE REST, OKAY?
......
WHAT'RE YOU GUYS TALKING ABOUT?
I NEVER SAID HE WAS THE ONE WHO DID IT.
YOU KNOW WHO I THINK ACTUALLY DID IT?

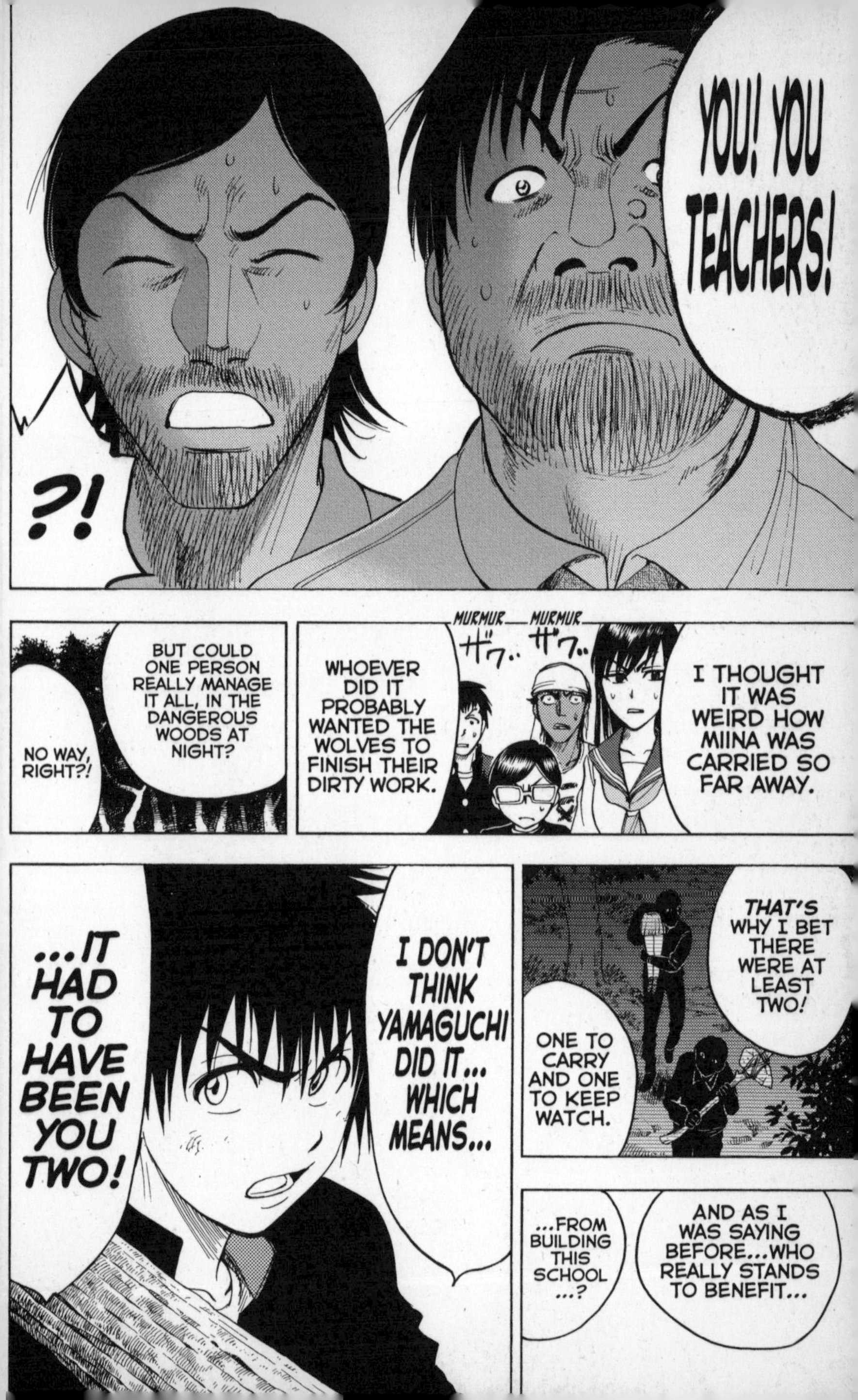
YOU! YOU TEACHERS!
?!
I THOUGHT IT WAS WEIRD HOW MIINA WAS CARRIED SO FAR AWAY.
MURMUR
ザワ..
MURMUR
ザワ..
WHOEVER DID IT PROBABLY WANTED THE WOLVES TO FINISH THEIR DIRTY WORK.
BUT COULD ONE PERSON REALLY MANAGE IT ALL, IN THE DANGEROUS WOODS AT NIGHT?
NO WAY, RIGHT?!
THAT'S WHY I BET THERE WERE AT LEAST TWO!
ONE TO CARRY AND ONE TO KEEP WATCH.
AND AS I WAS SAYING BEFORE...WHO REALLY STANDS TO BENEFIT...
...FROM BUILDING THIS SCHOOL ...?
I DON'T THINK YAMAGUCHI DID IT... WHICH MEANS...
...IT HAD TO HAVE BEEN YOU TWO!

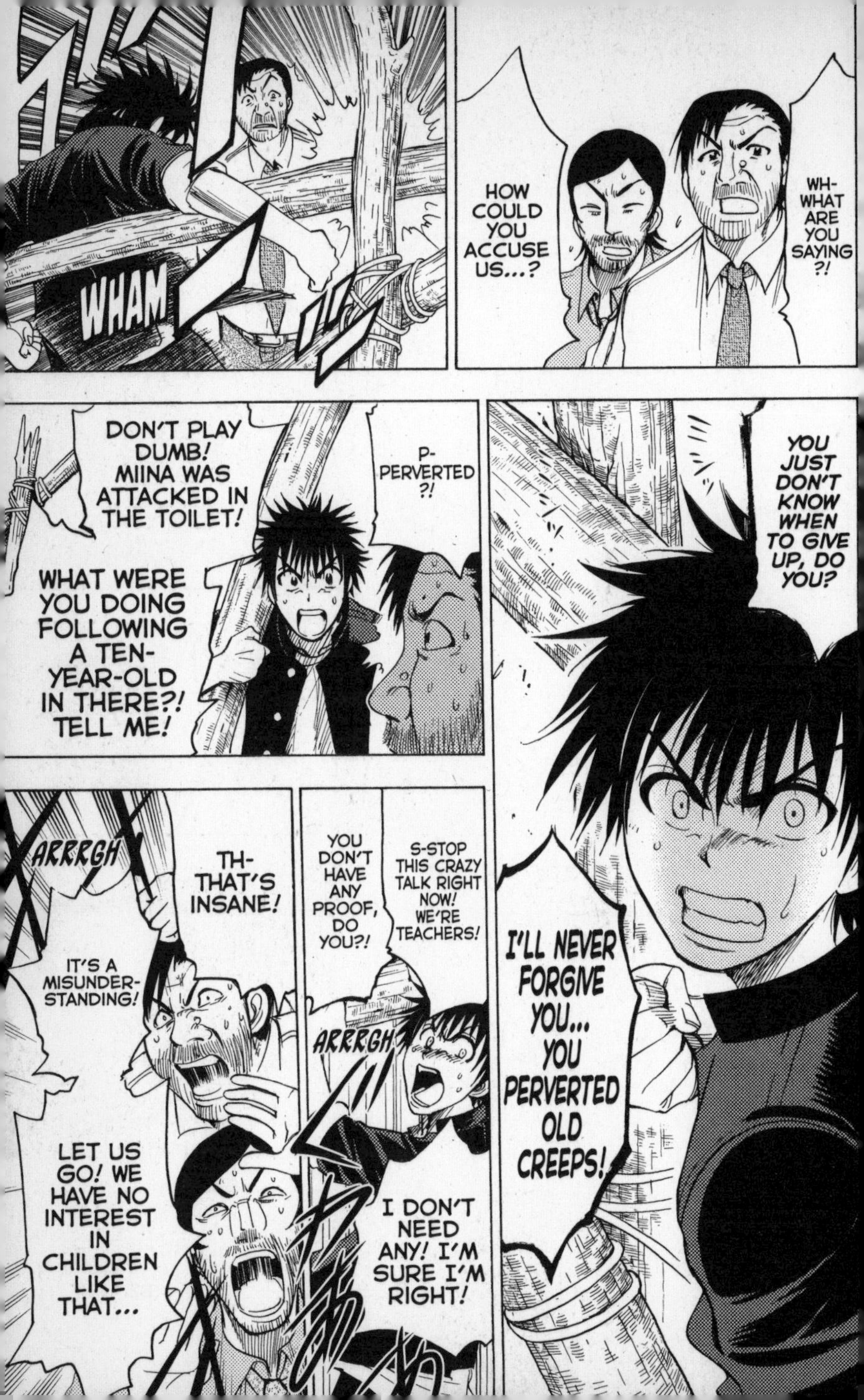
WH- WHAT ARE YOU SAYING ?!
HOW COULD YOU ACCUSE US...?
WHAM
YOU JUST DON'T KNOW WHEN TO GIVE UP, DO YOU?
I'LL NEVER FORGIVE YOU... YOU PERVERTED OLD CREEPS!
P- PERVERTED ?!
DON'T PLAY DUMB! MIINA WAS ATTACKED IN THE TOILET!
WHAT WERE YOU DOING FOLLOWING A TEN-YEAR-OLD IN THERE?! TELL ME!
S-STOP THIS CRAZY TALK RIGHT NOW! WE'RE TEACHERS!
YOU DON'T HAVE ANY PROOF, DO YOU?!
ARRRGH
I DON'T NEED ANY! I'M SURE I'M RIGHT!
TH- THAT'S INSANE!
ARRRGH
IT'S A MISUNDER-STANDING!
LET US GO! WE HAVE NO INTEREST IN CHILDREN LIKE THAT...

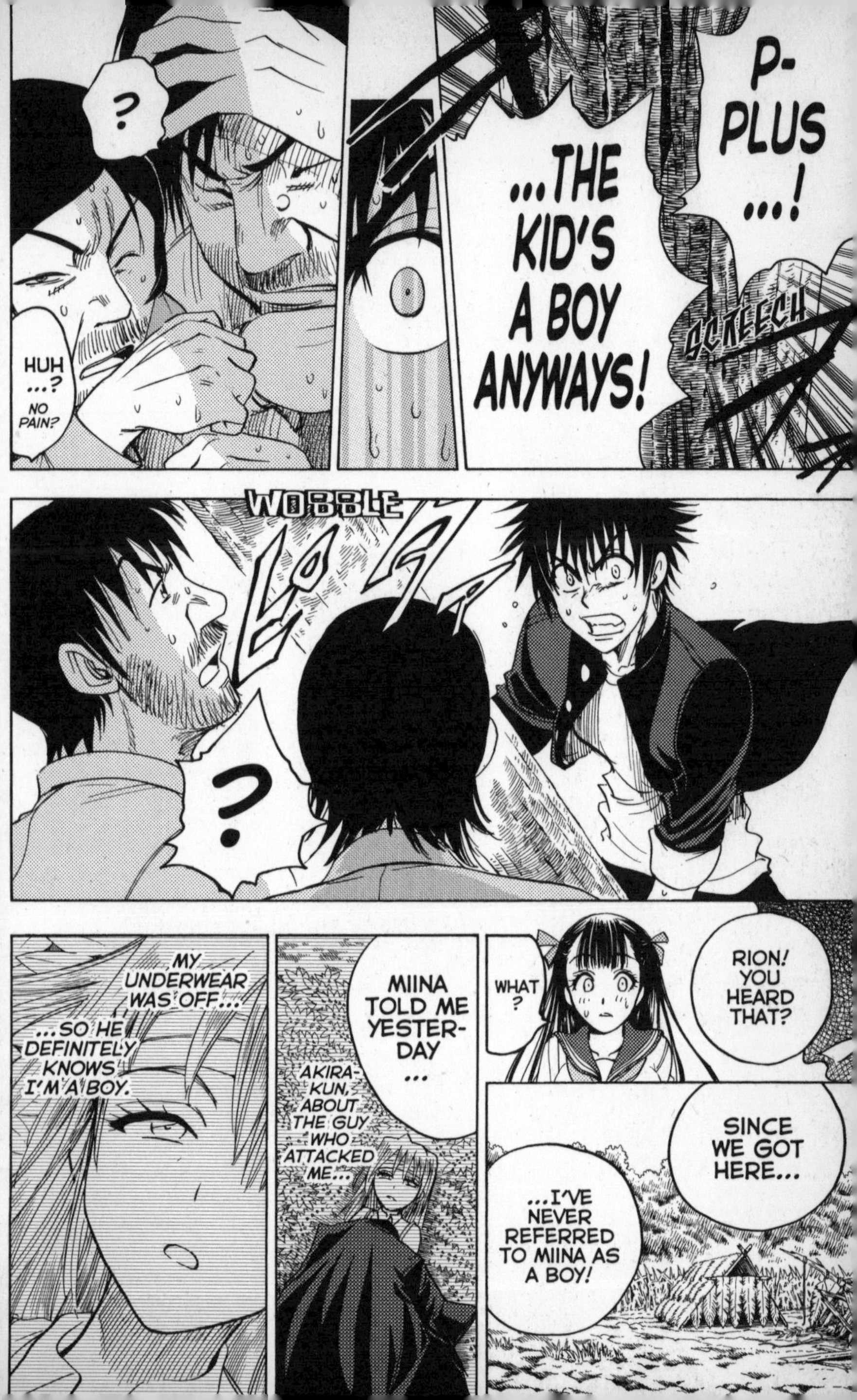
P-PLUS ...!
...THE KID'S A BOY ANYWAYS!
SCREECH
?
HUH ...?
NO PAIN?
WOBBLE
?
RION! YOU HEARD THAT?
WHAT?
SINCE WE GOT HERE...
...I'VE NEVER REFERRED TO MIINA AS A BOY!
MIINA TOLD ME YESTER-DAY ...
AKIRA-KUN, ABOUT THE GUY WHO ATTACKED ME...
MY UNDERWEAR WAS OFF...
...SO HE DEFINITELY KNOWS I'M A BOY.

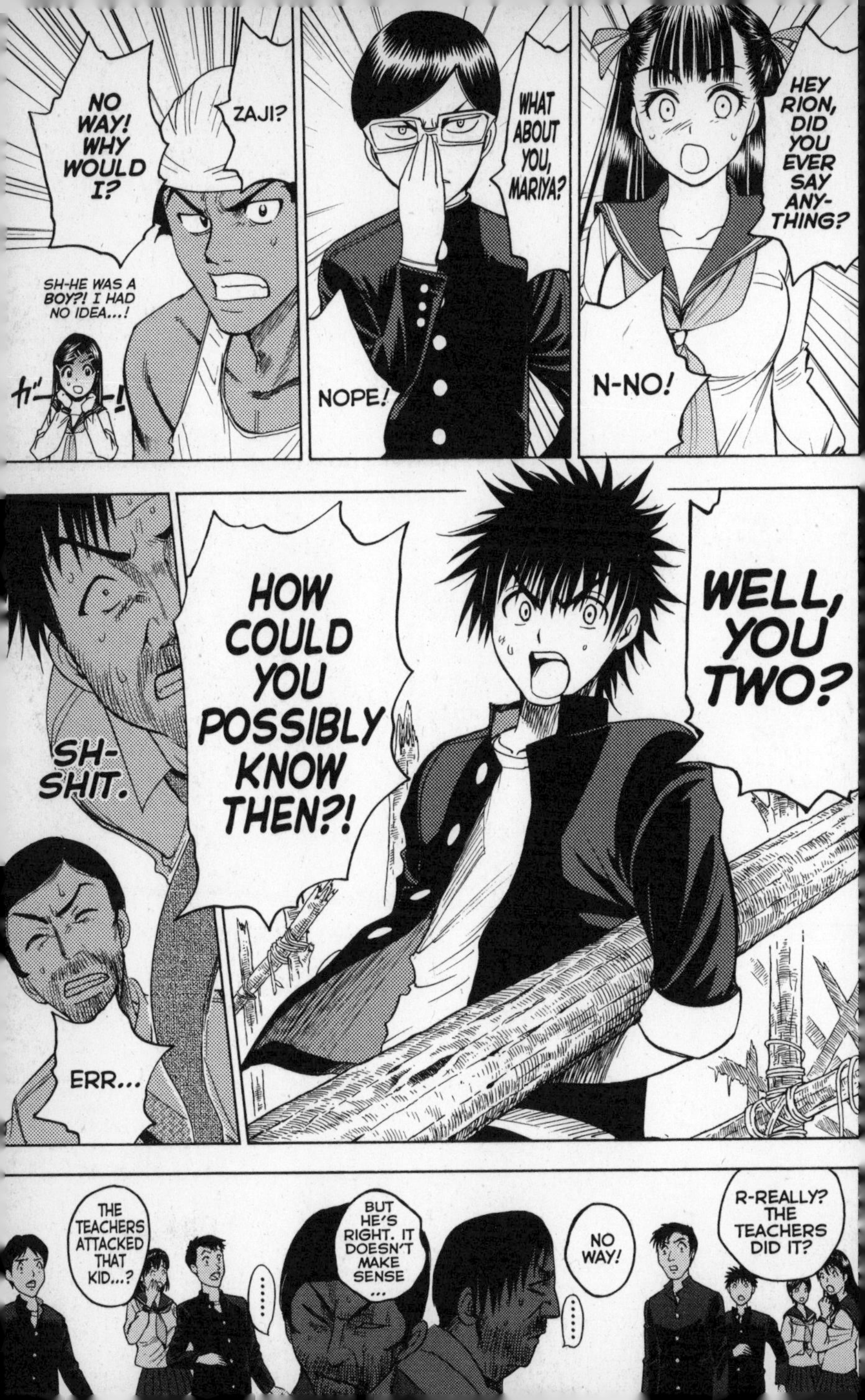
HEY RION, DID YOU EVER SAY ANYTHING?
N-NO!
WHAT ABOUT YOU, MARIYA?
NOPE!
ZAJI?
NO WAY! WHY WOULD I?
SH-HE WAS A BOY?! I HAD NO IDEA...!
ガー!
WELL, YOU TWO?
HOW COULD YOU POSSIBLY KNOW THEN?!
SH-SHIT.
ERR...
R-REALLY? THE TEACHERS DID IT?
NO WAY!
......
BUT HE'S RIGHT. IT DOESN'T MAKE SENSE...
......
THE TEACHERS ATTACKED THAT KID...?

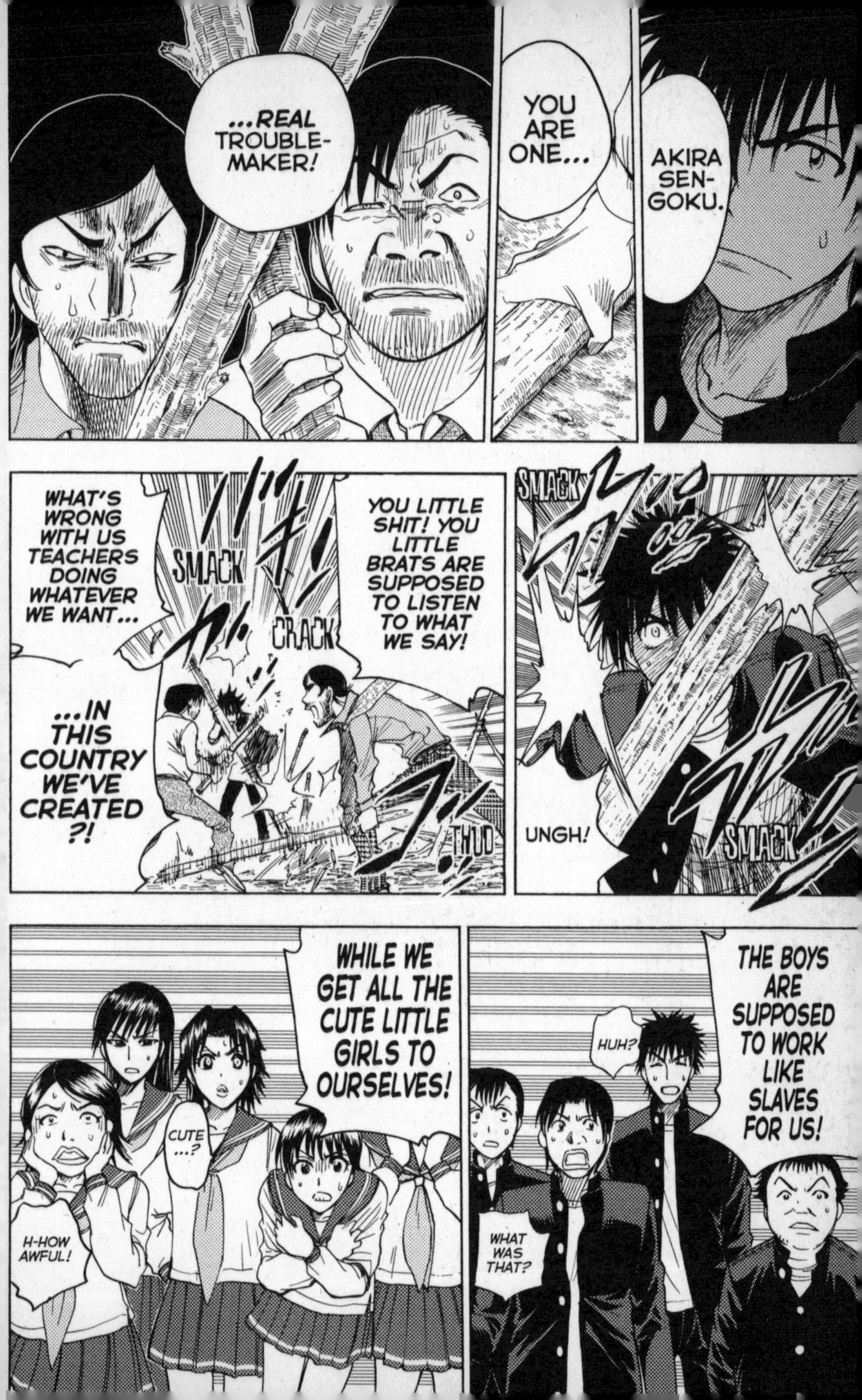
AKIRA SEN-GOKU.
YOU ARE ONE...
...REAL TROUBLE-MAKER!
SMACK
UNGH!
SMACK
YOU LITTLE SHIT! YOU LITTLE BRATS ARE SUPPOSED TO LISTEN TO WHAT WE SAY!
SMACK
CRACK
WHAT'S WRONG WITH US TEACHERS DOING WHATEVER WE WANT...
...IN THIS COUNTRY WE'VE CREATED?!
THUD
THE BOYS ARE SUPPOSED TO WORK LIKE SLAVES FOR US!
HUH?
WHAT WAS THAT?
WHILE WE GET ALL THE CUTE LITTLE GIRLS TO OURSELVES!
CUTE ...?
H-HOW AWFUL!

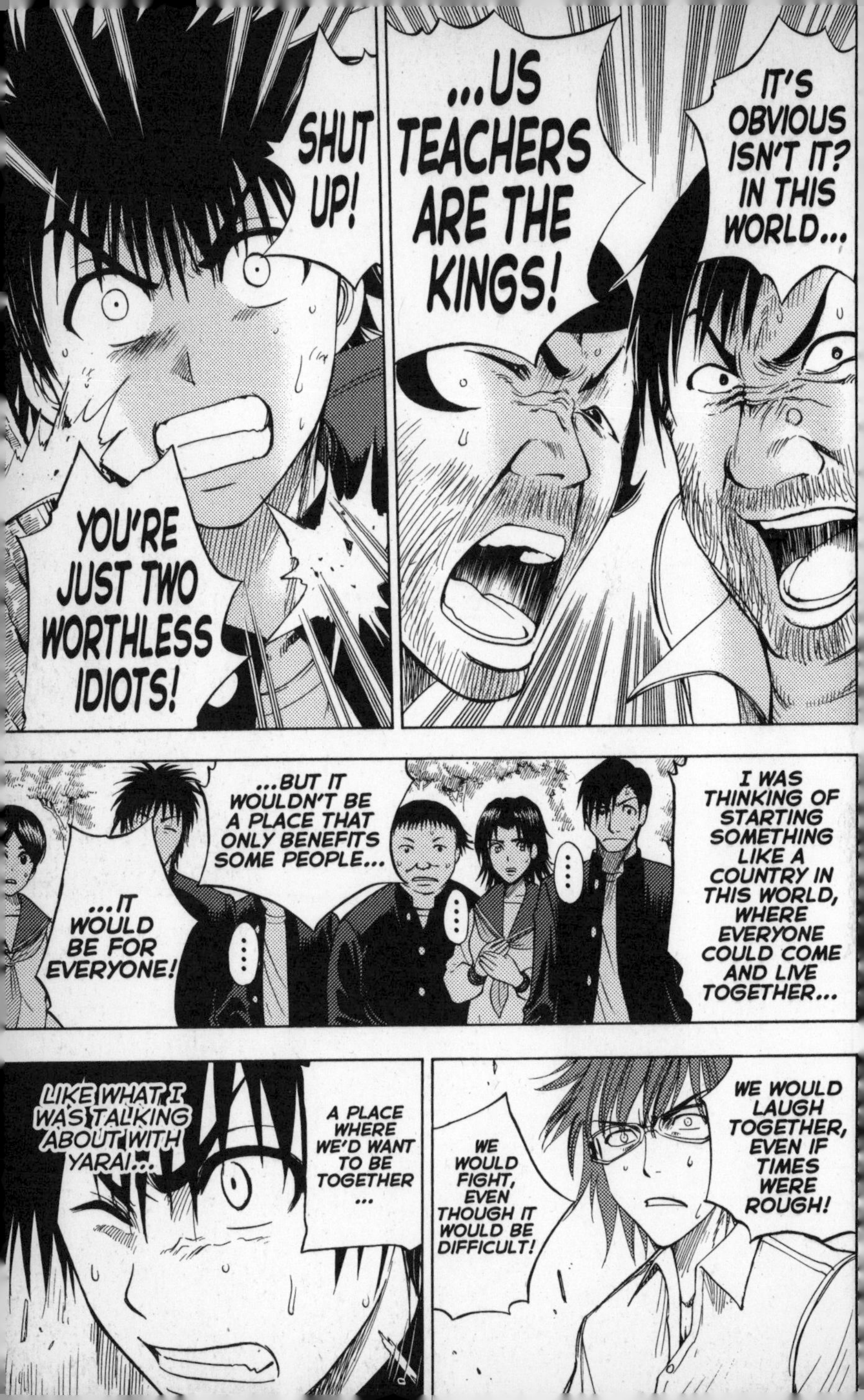
IT'S OBVIOUS ISN'T IT? IN THIS WORLD...
...US TEACHERS ARE THE KINGS!
SHUT UP!
YOU'RE JUST TWO WORTHLESS IDIOTS!
I WAS THINKING OF STARTING SOMETHING LIKE A COUNTRY IN THIS WORLD, WHERE EVERYONE COULD COME AND LIVE TOGETHER...
...BUT IT WOULDN'T BE A PLACE THAT ONLY BENEFITS SOME PEOPLE...
....
....
....
...IT WOULD BE FOR EVERYONE!
WE WOULD LAUGH TOGETHER, EVEN IF TIMES WERE ROUGH!
WE WOULD FIGHT, EVEN THOUGH IT WOULD BE DIFFICULT!
A PLACE WHERE WE'D WANT TO BE TOGETHER ...
LIKE WHAT I WAS TALKING ABOUT WITH YARAI...

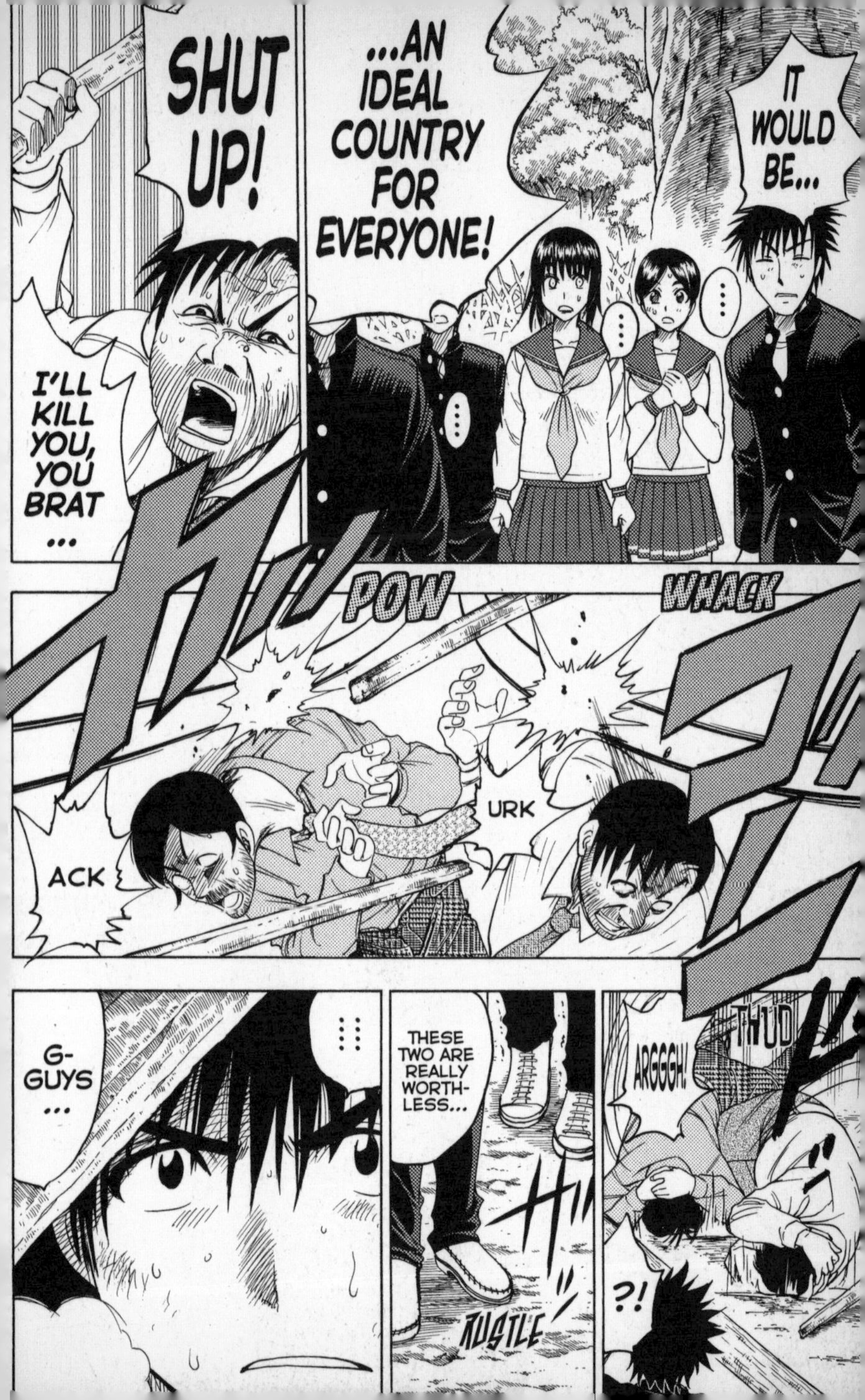
IT WOULD BE...
...AN IDEAL COUNTRY FOR EVERYONE!
...
...
...
SHUT UP!
I'LL KILL YOU, YOU BRAT...
WHACK
POW
URK
ACK
THUD
ARGGGH!
?!
THESE TWO ARE REALLY WORTHLESS...
RUSTLE
...
G-GUYS...

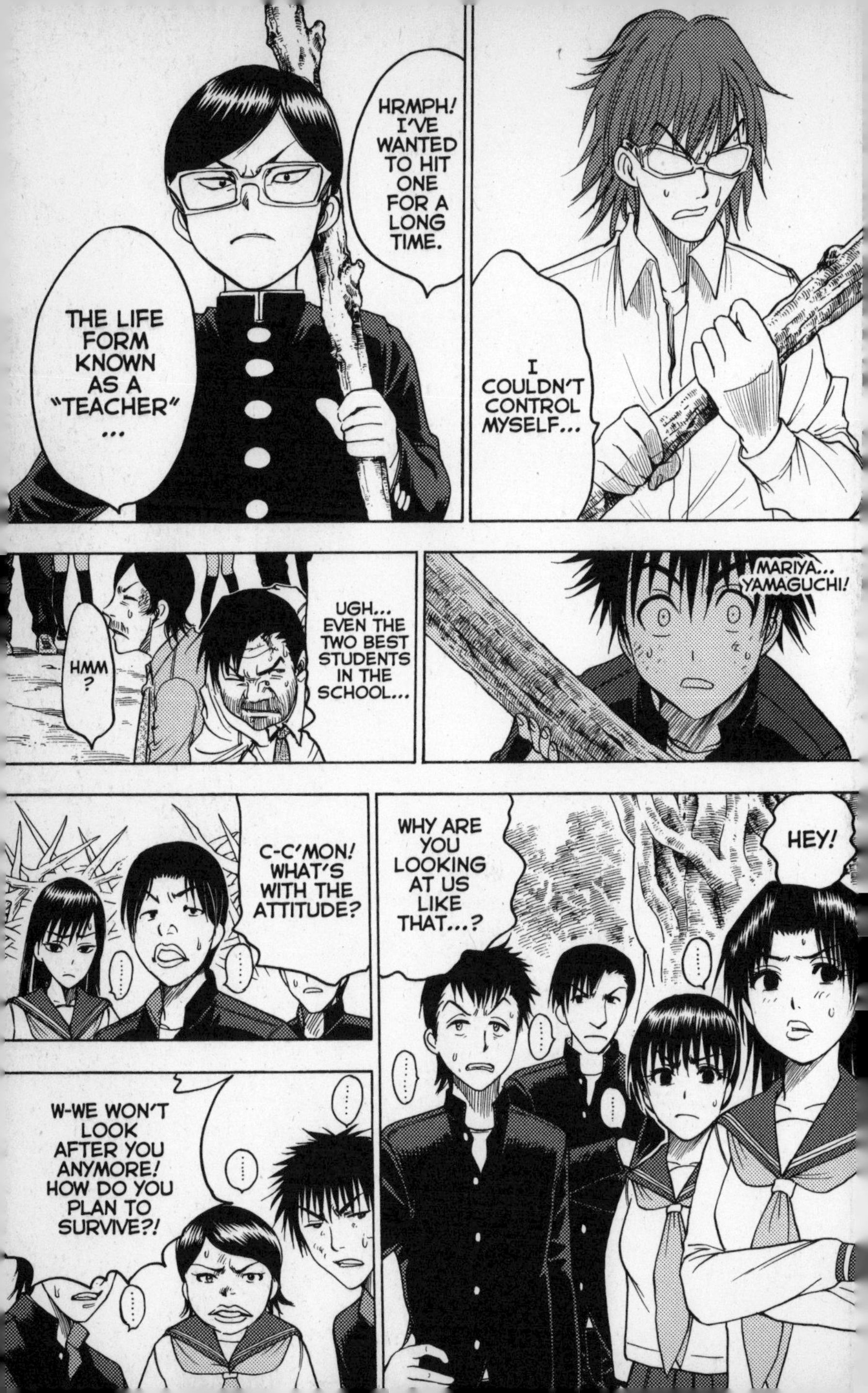
I COULDN'T CONTROL MYSELF...
HRMPH! I'VE WANTED TO HIT ONE FOR A LONG TIME.
THE LIFE FORM KNOWN AS A "TEACHER" ...
MARIYA... YAMAGUCHI!
UGH... EVEN THE TWO BEST STUDENTS IN THE SCHOOL...
HMM?
HEY!
WHY ARE YOU LOOKING AT US LIKE THAT...?
......
......
......
C-C'MON! WHAT'S WITH THE ATTITUDE?
......
......
W-WE WON'T LOOK AFTER YOU ANYMORE! HOW DO YOU PLAN TO SURVIVE?!
......
......
......

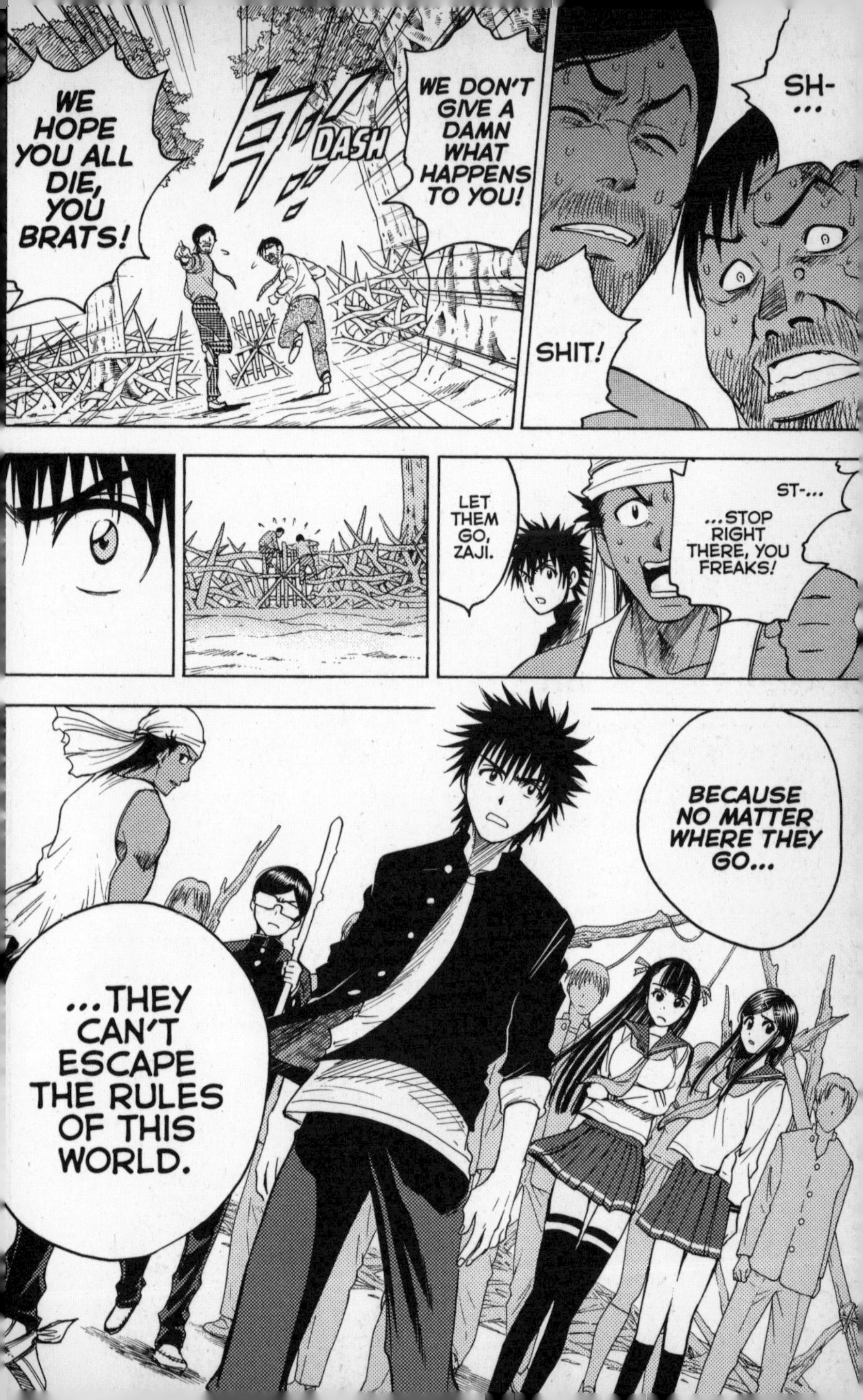
SH-...
SHIT!
WE DON'T GIVE A DAMN WHAT HAPPENS TO YOU!
DASH
WE HOPE YOU ALL DIE, YOU BRATS!
ST-...
...STOP RIGHT THERE, YOU FREAKS!
LET THEM GO, ZAJI.
BECAUSE NO MATTER WHERE THEY GO...
...THEY CAN'T ESCAPE THE RULES OF THIS WORLD.

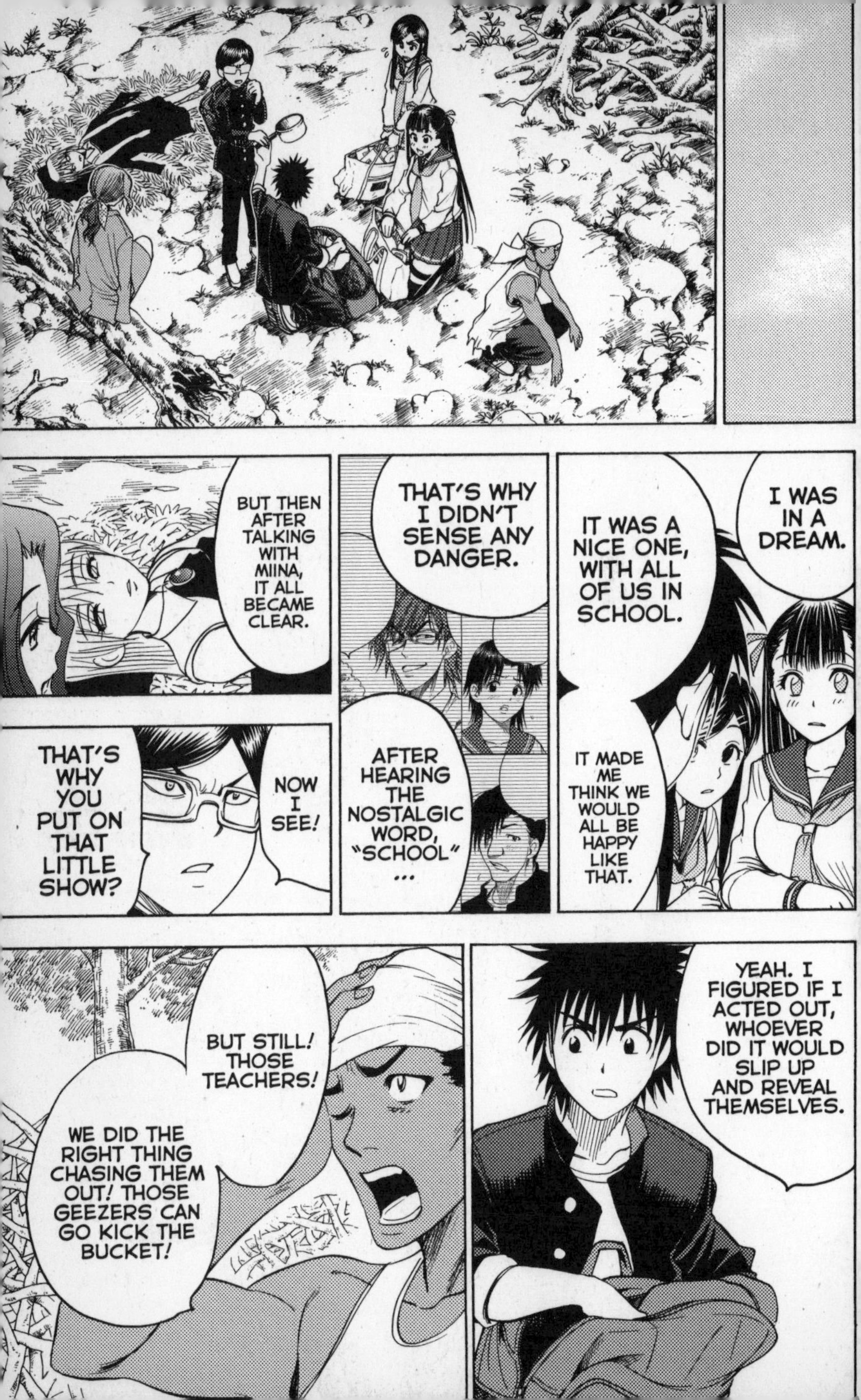
I WAS IN A DREAM.
IT WAS A NICE ONE, WITH ALL OF US IN SCHOOL.
IT MADE ME THINK WE WOULD ALL BE HAPPY LIKE THAT.
THAT'S WHY I DIDN'T SENSE ANY DANGER.
AFTER HEARING THE NOSTALGIC WORD, "SCHOOL"...
BUT THEN AFTER TALKING WITH MIINA, IT ALL BECAME CLEAR.
NOW I SEE!
THAT'S WHY YOU PUT ON THAT LITTLE SHOW?
YEAH. I FIGURED IF I ACTED OUT, WHOEVER DID IT WOULD SLIP UP AND REVEAL THEMSELVES.
BUT STILL! THOSE TEACHERS!
WE DID THE RIGHT THING CHASING THEM OUT! THOSE GEEZERS CAN GO KICK THE BUCKET!

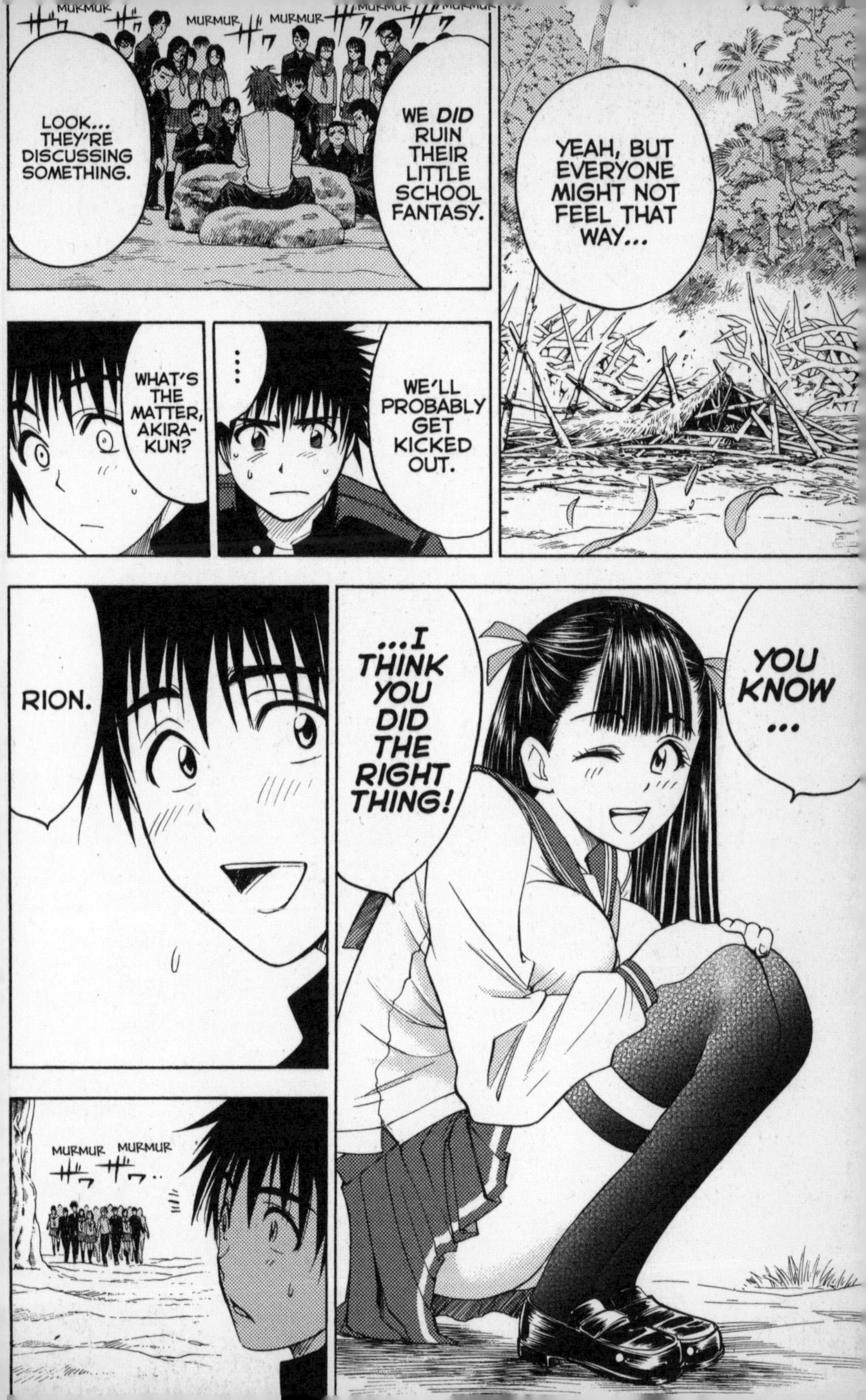
YEAH, BUT EVERYONE MIGHT NOT FEEL THAT WAY...
MURMUR MURMUR MURMUR MURMUR MURMUR
WE DID RUIN THEIR LITTLE SCHOOL FANTASY.
LOOK... THEY'RE DISCUSSING SOMETHING.
WE'LL PROBABLY GET KICKED OUT.
....
WHAT'S THE MATTER, AKIRA-KUN?
YOU KNOW...
...I THINK YOU DID THE RIGHT THING!
RION.
MURMUR MURMUR

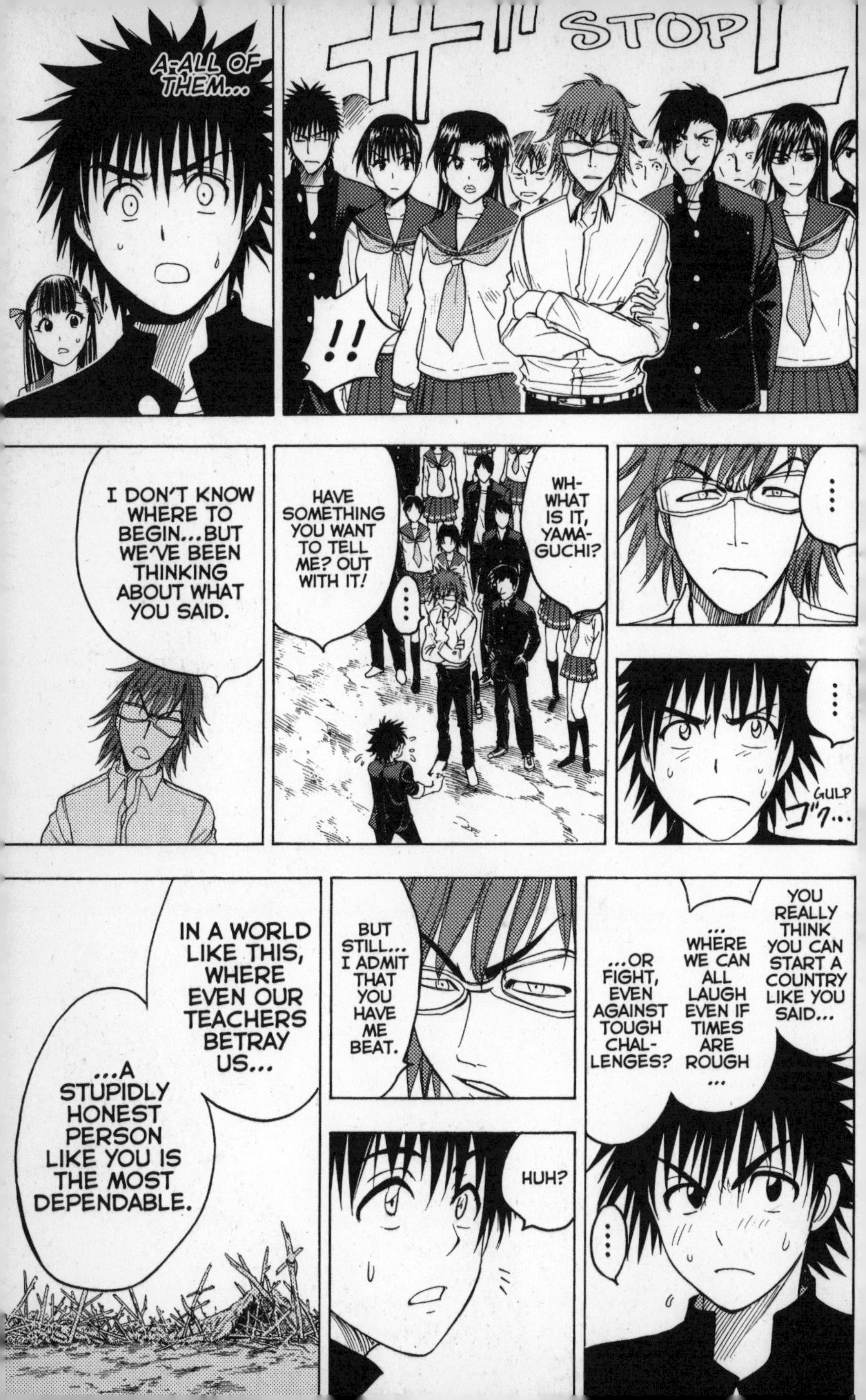
STOP
!!
A-ALL OF THEM...
....
....
GULP
WH-WHAT IS IT, YAMAGUCHI?
HAVE SOMETHING YOU WANT TO TELL ME? OUT WITH IT!
....
I DON'T KNOW WHERE TO BEGIN...BUT WE'VE BEEN THINKING ABOUT WHAT YOU SAID.
YOU REALLY THINK YOU CAN START A COUNTRY LIKE YOU SAID...
...WHERE WE CAN ALL LAUGH EVEN IF TIMES ARE ROUGH...
...OR FIGHT, EVEN AGAINST TOUGH CHALLENGES?
....
BUT STILL... I ADMIT THAT YOU HAVE ME BEAT.
HUH?
IN A WORLD LIKE THIS, WHERE EVEN OUR TEACHERS BETRAY US...
...A STUPIDLY HONEST PERSON LIKE YOU IS THE MOST DEPENDABLE.

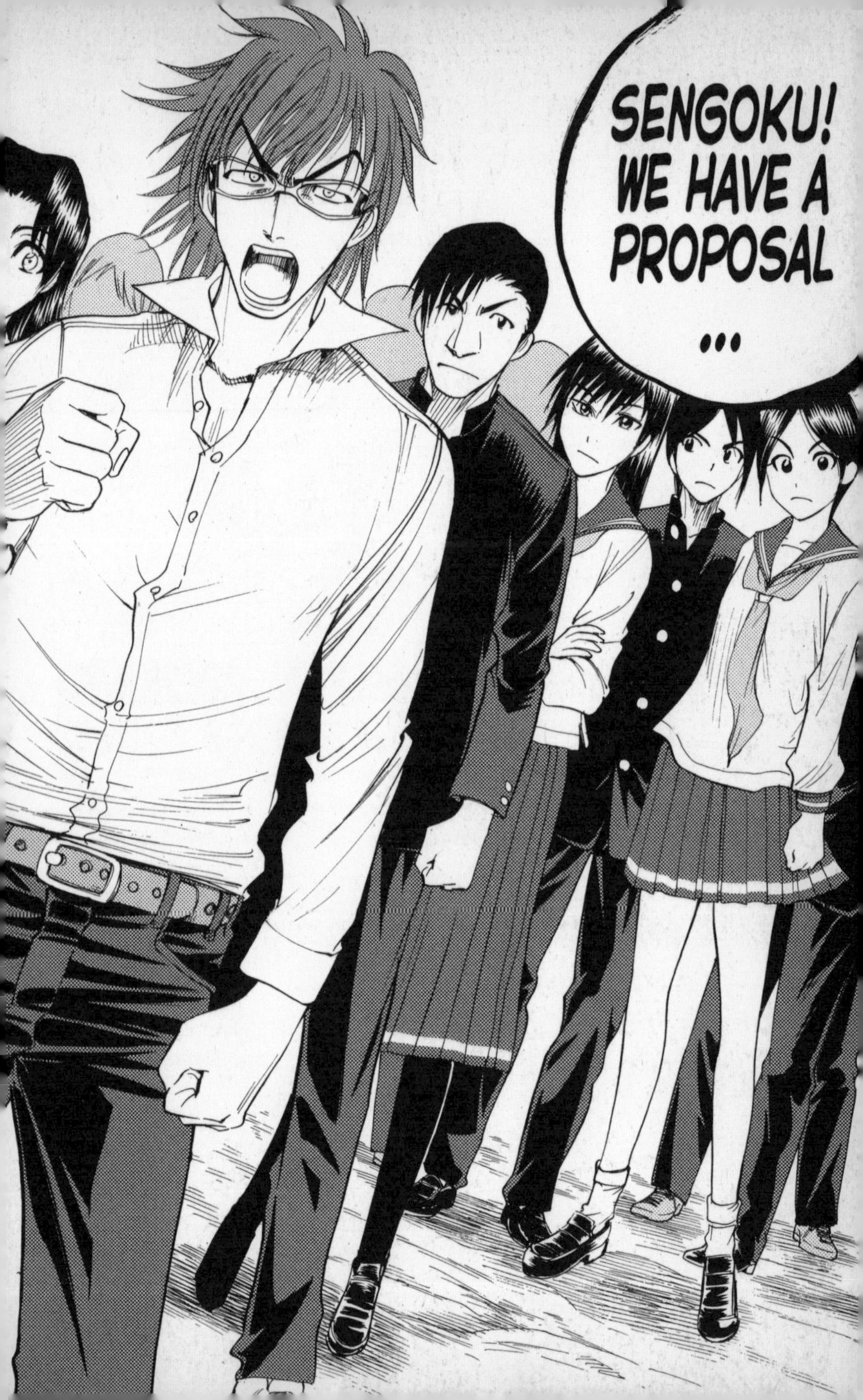
SENGOKU! WE HAVE A PROPOSAL ...

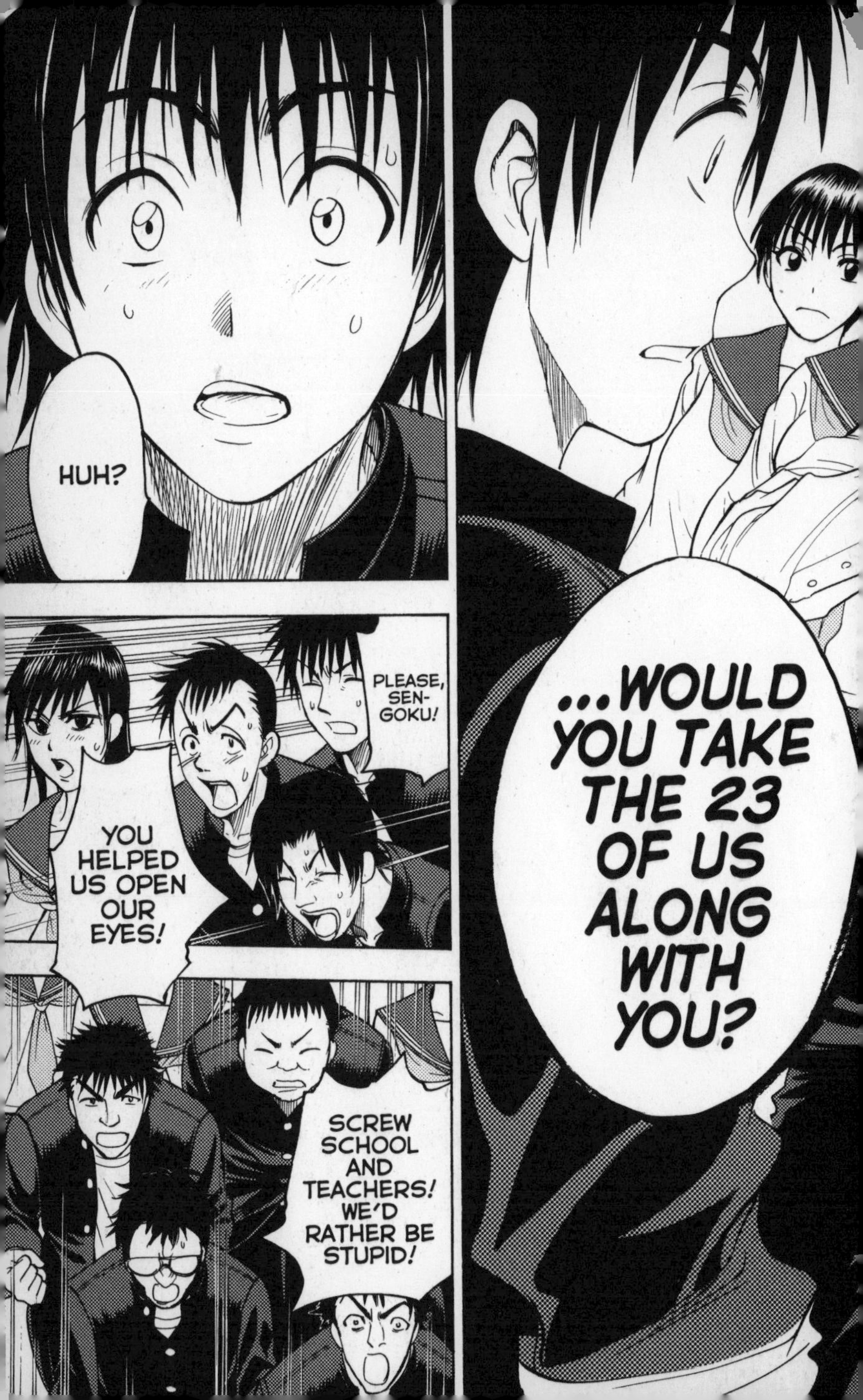
...WOULD YOU TAKE THE 23 OF US ALONG WITH YOU?
HUH?
PLEASE, SEN-GOKU!
YOU HELPED US OPEN OUR EYES!
SCREW SCHOOL AND TEACHERS! WE'D RATHER BE STUPID!

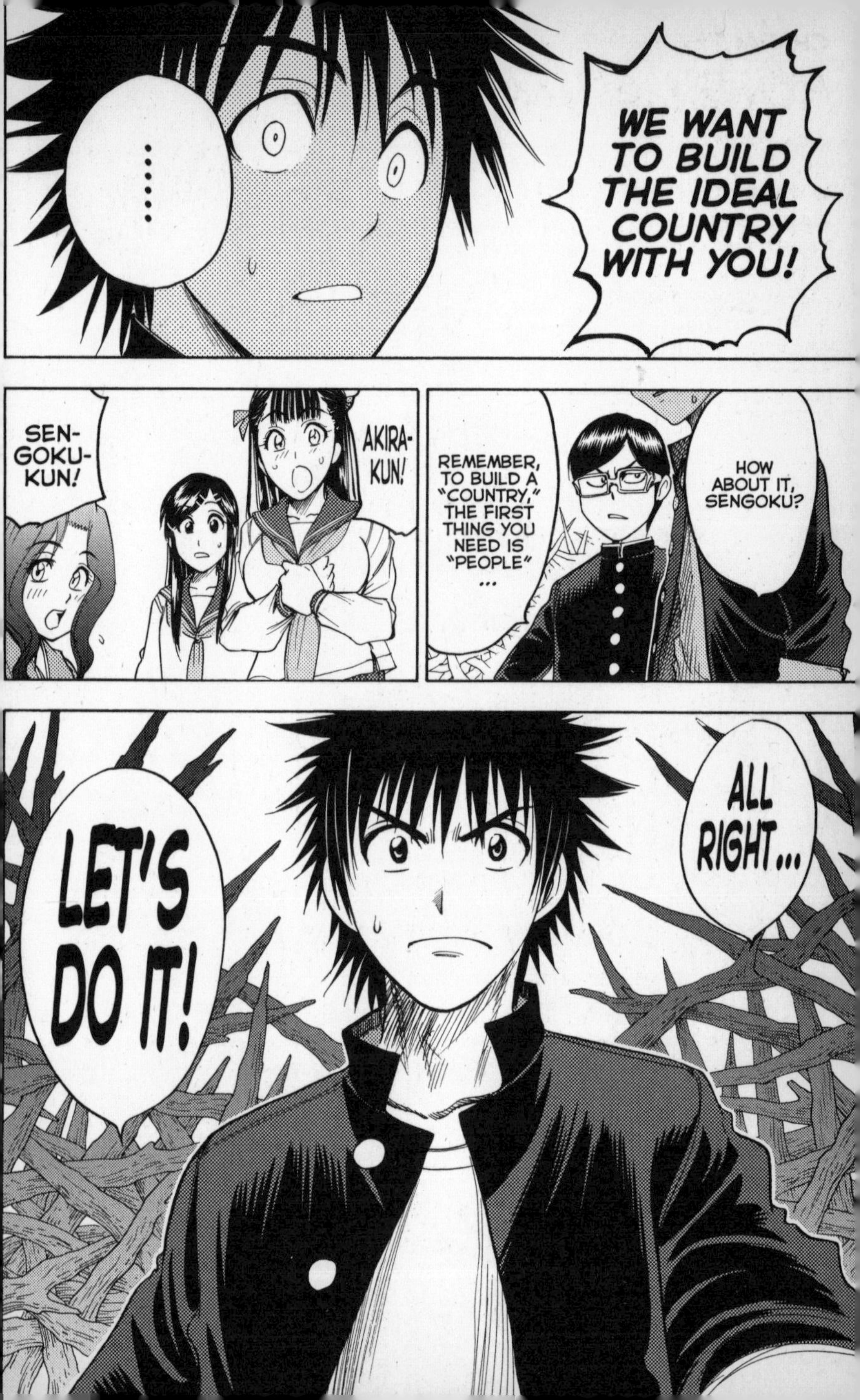
WE WANT TO BUILD THE IDEAL COUNTRY WITH YOU!
......
HOW ABOUT IT, SENGOKU?
REMEMBER, TO BUILD A "COUNTRY," THE FIRST THING YOU NEED IS "PEOPLE" ...
AKIRA-KUN!
SEN-GOKU-KUN!
ALL RIGHT...
LET'S DO IT!

CHARACTER PROFILE

KOHEI ARITA

BORN AUGUST 14TH

LEO

15 YEARS OLD

HEIGHT 184 CM (6 FT)

WEIGHT 70 KG (154 LBS)

BLOOD TYPE A

FAMILY: MOTHER, FATHER, LITTLE SISTER

FAVORITE THINGS: KARAOKE, COOKING

LEAST FAVORITE THINGS: BUTTERFLIES

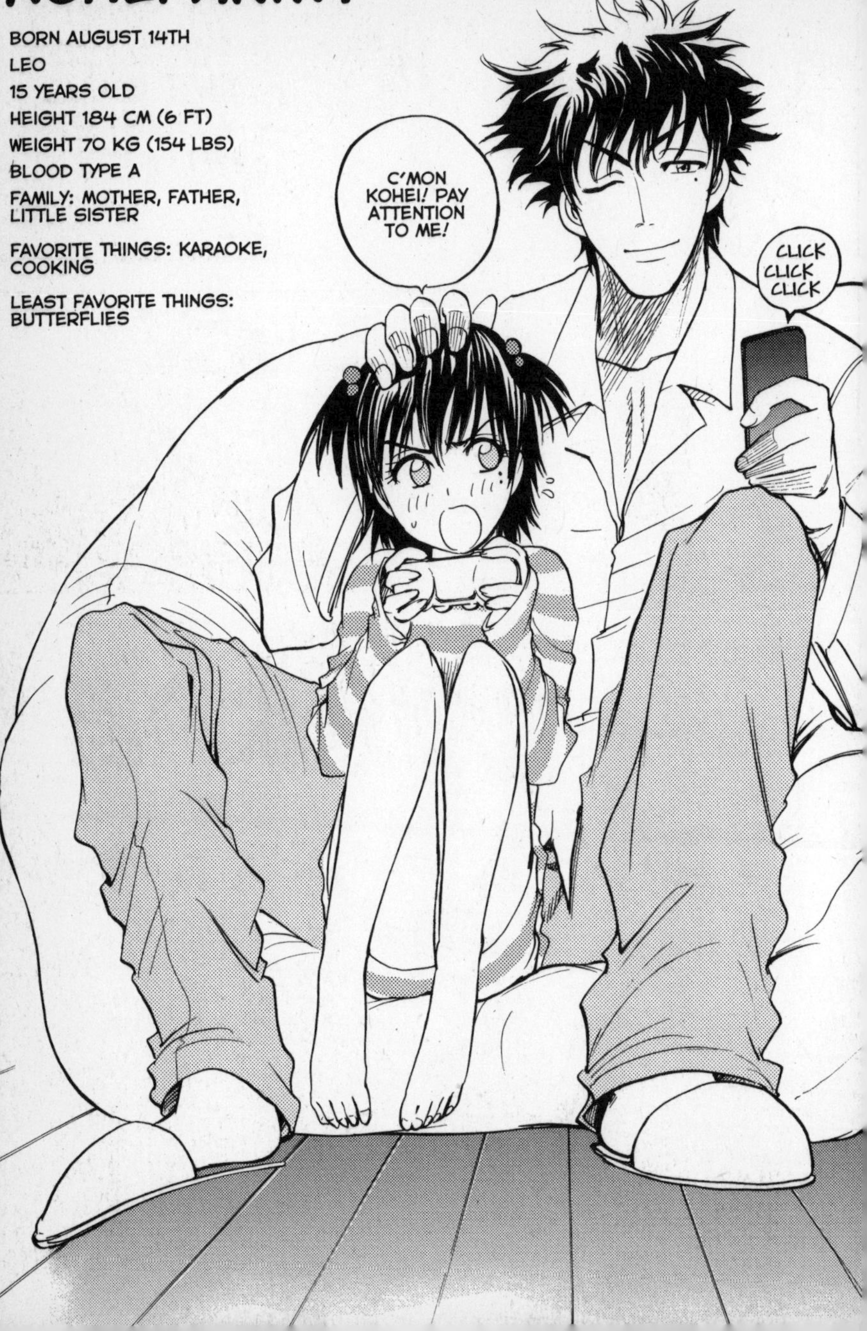
CLICK CLICK CLICK
C'MON KOHEI! PAY ATTENTION TO ME!

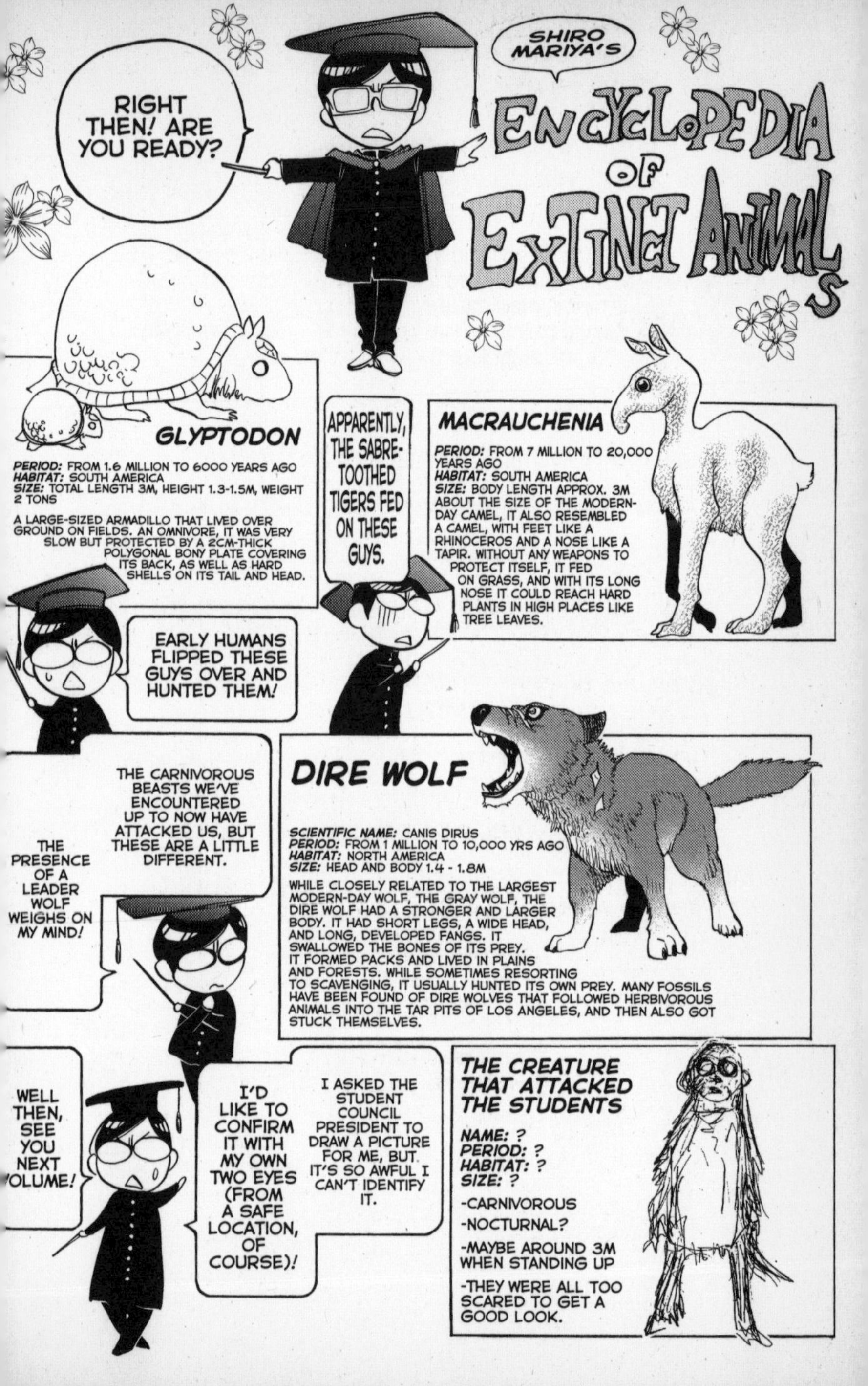

SHIRO MARIYA'S
ENCYCLOPEDIA OF EXTINCT ANIMALS
RIGHT THEN! ARE YOU READY?
MACRAUCHENIA
PERIOD: FROM 7 MILLION TO 20,000 YEARS AGO
HABITAT: SOUTH AMERICA
SIZE: BODY LENGTH APPROX. 3M
ABOUT THE SIZE OF THE MODERN-DAY CAMEL, IT ALSO RESEMBLED A CAMEL, WITH FEET LIKE A RHINOCEROS AND A NOSE LIKE A TAPIR. WITHOUT ANY WEAPONS TO PROTECT ITSELF, IT FED ON GRASS, AND WITH ITS LONG NOSE IT COULD REACH HARD PLANTS IN HIGH PLACES LIKE TREE LEAVES.
APPARENTLY, THE SABRE-TOOTHED TIGERS FED ON THESE GUYS.
GLYPTODON
PERIOD: FROM 1.6 MILLION TO 6000 YEARS AGO
HABITAT: SOUTH AMERICA
SIZE: TOTAL LENGTH 3M, HEIGHT 1.3-1.5M, WEIGHT 2 TONS
A LARGE-SIZED ARMADILLO THAT LIVED OVER GROUND ON FIELDS. AN OMNIVORE, IT WAS VERY SLOW BUT PROTECTED BY A 2CM-THICK POLYGONAL BONY PLATE COVERING ITS BACK, AS WELL AS HARD SHELLS ON ITS TAIL AND HEAD.
EARLY HUMANS FLIPPED THESE GUYS OVER AND HUNTED THEM!
DIRE WOLF
SCIENTIFIC NAME: CANIS DIRUS
PERIOD: FROM 1 MILLION TO 10,000 YRS AGO
HABITAT: NORTH AMERICA
SIZE: HEAD AND BODY 1.4 - 1.8M
WHILE CLOSELY RELATED TO THE LARGEST MODERN-DAY WOLF, THE GRAY WOLF, THE DIRE WOLF HAD A STRONGER AND LARGER BODY. IT HAD SHORT LEGS, A WIDE HEAD, AND LONG, DEVELOPED FANGS. IT SWALLOWED THE BONES OF ITS PREY. IT FORMED PACKS AND LIVED IN PLAINS AND FORESTS. WHILE SOMETIMES RESORTING TO SCAVENGING, IT USUALLY HUNTED ITS OWN PREY. MANY FOSSILS HAVE BEEN FOUND OF DIRE WOLVES THAT FOLLOWED HERBIVOROUS ANIMALS INTO THE TAR PITS OF LOS ANGELES, AND THEN ALSO GOT STUCK THEMSELVES.
THE CARNIVOROUS BEASTS WE'VE ENCOUNTERED UP TO NOW HAVE ATTACKED US, BUT THESE ARE A LITTLE DIFFERENT.
THE PRESENCE OF A LEADER WOLF WEIGHS ON MY MIND!
THE CREATURE THAT ATTACKED THE STUDENTS
NAME: ?
PERIOD: ?
HABITAT: ?
SIZE: ?
-CARNIVOROUS
-NOCTURNAL?
-MAYBE AROUND 3M WHEN STANDING UP
-THEY WERE ALL TOO SCARED TO GET A GOOD LOOK.
I ASKED THE STUDENT COUNCIL PRESIDENT TO DRAW A PICTURE FOR ME, BUT IT'S SO AWFUL I CAN'T IDENTIFY IT.
I'D LIKE TO CONFIRM IT WITH MY OWN TWO EYES (FROM A SAFE LOCATION, OF COURSE)!
WELL THEN, SEE YOU NEXT VOLUME!